European Telecommunications Liberalisation

Telecommunications is one of the most dynamic industries in the modern world, with new products and technologies appearing every week. As in many other industries, the last twenty years have brought extensive and far-reaching liberalisation, with more and more countries opening their markets. In the last decade all but five Member States of the European Union have legislated for full opening of all market segments. The remaining five look set for further liberalisation over the next five years.

This book examines the process and consequences of telecommunications liberalisation in the context of ever closer European union. The creation of a single market for telecommunications and of a wider European single market mirror one another. Telecommunications are also something of a test case for the privatisation process, as this sector has traditionally been a state monopoly.

The volume approaches the European experience from three angles:

- the politics of regulation and the process of liberalisation in the EU (including case-studies of the UK, France, and Germany)
- increasing global economic interdependence makes international comparisons essential, and the volume compares the EU experience with that of the Czech Republic, Israel and Thailand
- the consequences of technology and continuous innovation

The book includes contributions from scholars in ten countries.

Kjell A. Eliassen is Director of the Centre for European and Asian Studies at the Norwegian School of Management where he is also Professor of Public Administration. **Marit Sjøvaag** is a student at the London School of Economics and Project Manager at the Norwegian School of Management.

Routledge Studies in the European Economy

European
Telecommunications
Liberalisation

Edited by Kjell A. Eliassen
and Marit Sjøvaag

London and New York

First published 1999
by Routledge
11 New Fetter Lane, London EC4P 4EE

Simultaneously published in the USA and Canada
by Routledge
29 West 35th Street, New York, NY 10001

Typeset in Times by Kestrel Data, Exeter, Devon
Printed and bound in Great Britain by
Biddles Ltd, Guildford and King's Lynn

British Library Cataloguing in Publication Data
A catalogue record for this book is available from the British
Library

Library of Congress Cataloging in Publication Data
European telecommunications liberalisation/edited by Kjell A.
Eliassen and Marit Sjøvaag
    p. cm. – (Routledge studies in the European economy, 10)
    Includes bibliographical references.
1. Telecommunication–Deregulation–European Union countries.
2. Telecommunication policy–European Union countries.
I. Eliassen, Kjell A. II. Sjøvaag, Marit, 1967–   . III. Series.
HE8090.5.E87 1999
384'.094–dc21   98-31832
                                                                          CIP

ISBN 0–415–18781–8

Contents

Figures and tables

Figures

Tables

Contributors

Patrizia Cincera is a PhD student at the Université Libre de Bruxelles (ULB), working at the Institute of European Studies (IEE – Institut d'Etudes Européennes). Her thesis focuses mainly on the convergence phenomenon in the sectors of telecommunications, media and IT, particularly analysing EU involvement in the content aspects of the Information Society. She has a degree in Journalism and a Masters degree in Political Science and European Studies. Both degrees were obtained at the ULB.

Kjell A. Eliassen is Director of the Centre for European and Asian Studies at the Norwegian School of Management and Professor of Public Management. He is also a Professor at the Institute d'Etudes Européennes at Université Libre de Bruxelles. Professor Eliassen is former Vice-President at the Norwegian School of Management and has been Visiting Professor at several American and European universities. He has published twelve books and many articles on EC and European affairs, public management and political elites. Among his most recent publications are *Foreign and Security Policy in the European Union* (1998) and *The European Union: How Democratic is it?* (1996). He has considerable experience from consultant and management development programmes in public agencies and private companies both in the Nordic countries and Eastern Europe. He has been responsible for business school teacher-training programmes and management development programmes in both Eastern Europe and Pacific Asia. He is a graduate of the University of Bergen.

Christer Englund is Marketing Director at Mirasys Communications, Espoo, Finland. He is focuses on technologies for wireless voice telephony over IP and digital video surveillance applications. From 1970 until 1998 he was Research Scientist, Head of Section and Research Manager at VTT Information Technology, Espoo, Finland. Since 1997 he has been a PhD student at Helsinki University of Technology. His topic relates to telecommunications architecture and business administration.

Sebastian Eyre is a Research Fellow at the University of Exeter, specialising in UK and EU competition policy. He has published on utilities' adaptation to liberalisation and developments in competition policy.

Øystein D. Fjeldstad is Associate Professor in Strategy at the Norwegian School of Management. His current research is on models of value creation and competition, with emphasis on application to telecommunications, financial services, and up-stream oil. He holds a PhD from the University of Arizona in Business Administration. He recently published (with Charles B. Stabell) 'Configuring Value for Competitive Advantage: On Chains, Shops and Networks', in the *Strategic Management Journal* (vol. 19).

Zdenek Hruby is a Senior Fellow at the Institute of Economic Studies, Faculty of Social Sciences, Charles University, Prague. He is a researcher and teacher in the areas of regulation, network industries, and competition policies. He is a member and co-ordinator of international research projects, and a consultant to international agencies and to the Czech Republic's governmental bodies.

Ulf Körner holds a Chair in communication systems at Lund University, Sweden. His current research interests are focused on wide-band wireless systems and on high-speed network architectures. He is a member of the International Advisory Council for the International Teletraffic Congresses, and of the IFIP working group WG6.3. He is also a member of the ACM and the IEEE. He sits on the board of the Swedish post and telecommunications agency.

David Levi-Faur is Assistant Professor in the Political Science Department at the University of Haifa. He teaches comparative political economy and comparative public policy, and is currently doing research on telecommunications and electricity liberalisation in the EU, The Netherlands and Israel.

Martin Lodge is in the Department of Government at the London School of Economics. His main research interests include regulation, especially utility regulation, German politics, comparative public policy, EU public policy and public administration.

Toby Mason received his BSc in Government from the London School of Economics in June 1998, and is currently engaged on a Postgraduate Diploma in Journalism at Cardiff University. He hopes to become a political journalist.

Winston Maxwell is a partner in the US law firm Hughes Hubbard & Reed. He has been based in the firm's Paris office for thirteen years, where he specialises in telecommunications law. After graduating from Cornell Law School, Mr Maxwell worked on international telecommunications agreements for an incumbent operator. He now assists new operators regarding licensing and interconnection problems in France.

Prasit Prapinmongkolkarn holds a BEng degree in Electrical Engineering from Chulalongkorn University, Bangkok, Thailand, and a PhD from Osaka University, Japan. He is currently Professor in the Department of Electrical Engineering, Chulalongkorn University, and Director General of Chulalongkorn University Intellectual Property Institute. His areas of expertise are ATM switching and interconnectivity standard. He also specialises in the privatisation of the telecommunications industry.

Nick Sitter is Lecturer in European Politics at the American University, and a political consultant specialising in EU industrial policy. He is a PhD candidate at the London School of Economics and Political Science.

Marit Sjøvaag is a PhD student at the London School of Economics and Project Manager at the Norwegian School of Management. She has a Masters degree from the Norwegian School of Management and a BSc in Natural Sciences from the University of Oslo, Norway, and Université de Caen, France. Her main research interests include regulation, European telecommunications policy, comparative public policy, French and German politics, and security policy. Her latest publication is 'The Single European Act' in Kjell A. Eliassen (ed.) *Foreign and Security Policy in the European Union* (1998).

Mark Thatcher is Lecturer in Public Administration and Public Policy in the Department of Government at the London School of Economics, and ESRC Research Fellow. He has recently published 'Institutions, regulation and change' in *West European Politics* (vol. 21, no. 1, January 1998), and 'L'impact de la Communauté Européenne sur la réglementation nationale' in *Politique et Management Public* vol. 15, no. 3, September 1997.

Raymund Werle is a Principal Research Associate at the Max Planck Institute for the Study of Societies in Cologne, Germany. He has studied economics, sociology and political science. He is responsible for research in the areas of: development of large technical systems; governance of telecommunications, multimedia, and the Internet; technical standardisation. His latest publication (with Susanne K. Schmidt) *Coordinating Technology. Studies in the International Standardization of Telecommunications* (1998).

Foreword

January 1, 1998, was a watershed in the development of European tele-communications. By the end of February of that year more than 500 local loop licences had been allocated in the European Union. Very rapidly, the European Economic Area is turning into the largest liberalised tele-communications market in the world, with a new degree of freedom and a radically new orientation of the way its 380 million citizens use communications. And, more and more, we are witnessing the countries of Central and Eastern Europe opting to join this trend.

It is the right time to step back and to have a look at the fundamental forces of markets, technology, competition and regulation which have driven the process of Europe since its beginnings with the European Commision's 1987 Green Paper on telecommunications. This is one of the objectives of this book. All of us who have been in the midst of these breathtaking changes will see the last ten years of telecommunications as a unique period of development which we have experienced together.

Another aspect is to consider the current forces at work as we move into the future – and this is perhaps an even more ambitious aim of this book. The next major change is on the horizon. The changeover point in the use of mobile and fixed telephony will take place in the first half of the next decade, and even sooner in some of the Scandinavian countries that are leaders in this development. This will lead to another radical reshuffling and rethinking of the ways the telephone system should be managed, marketed and regulated. Also, the powerful combination of the Internet and broadband cable could lead to a multimedia revolution of convergence between telecommunications and the media, and a major debate on this has been launched at the European level. And, finally and perhaps most importantly, the massive emergence of e-commerce from the year 2000 onwards will lead to profound transformation of economic activities.

The explosive combination of the Internet, mobile and satellite is driving a globalisation which requires that analysis is undertaken from a global perspective, and this is testified by the contributions to this book. Globalisation will fundamentally change the world's economic patterns.

The World Trade Organisation agreement on telecommunications liberalisation is an obvious prelude to this. Globalisation of networks also takes us nearer to the realisation of the eternal human dream to transcend the limits imposed on the individual by distance and enable full access to knowledge and information. This is the true importance of the Internet which merges us into the global village and a world-wide pool of knowledge and experience.

Our citizens and our enterprises are taking up the new opportunities offered by liberalisation, deregulation and globalisation. But at the same time, some market actors may also try to resist the change of outdated structures because that change may be painful and often involves the loss of privileges which have come to be taken for granted. To tackle this challenge will become the major task for the new regulators and the competition authorities. They should not try to structure change, but they should step in where change may otherwise not happen and where citizens would be denied its benefits. This is the very essence of deregulation.

The future will decide if Europe will succeed in this task. This book makes a timely and welcome contribution to this debate.

Herbert Ungerer
Directorate General for Competition
European Commission

Preface

The volume of literature on telecommunications policy is exploding. The opening of the European market, which became a reality on 1 January 1998, initiated increased attention from social researchers all over Europe, indeed from all over the world. One should therefore have good reasons for contributing to the jungle of writings on a complex subject such as telecommunications policy.

We have reached a point in time where we are beginning to see the contour of the new market in the telecommunications sector, and we feel this is a good time to reflect on its present status and the process which has led up to this position. Telecommunications have, since the invention of the optical telegraph, dramatically transformed communications between people, but never before have we seen such drastic changes over so short a time span. New technologies challenge established beliefs about the possibilities for state intervention in economic sectors, and as a consequence the role of the state *vis-à-vis* its people. It is therefore time to sum up the changes so far and to attempt to identify crucial parameters which will determine future developments.

It is possible to identify similarities between the process of liberalisation in the telecommunications sector and the construction of the European Single Market. The concept of the Single Market was launched in the political environment of 1985, to become reality in 1992. Much opposition came from 'non-believers' who feared the free-market forces and saw their nation-states threatened. The industry, however, broadly embraced the new regime and acted accordingly. Before 1990 there had been hectic activity with mergers and acquisitions, building of alliances and restructuring of markets, so that when the Single Market was opened in 1992 the industry was prepared. These processes have their own dynamics, which are visible also in telecommunications policy: a sub-set of the internal market.

However, similar to the general situation in the internal market, the problem with European regulation of telecommunications is that the correct implementation of directives in national legislation is not sufficient. Use of the new regulatory framework relies upon the will and the capability of national regulators to execute unpopular decisions, and to be strict with national incumbent operators which in most cases have been symbols of national pride.

The telecommunications sector has traditionally been a state monopoly. Liberalisation is more difficult in sectors with strong monopolists, which is evident from the opening up of other sectors, such as air transport and energy. For liberalisation to become a reality, strong regulation of the incumbent operators is necessary in the initial phase, so that new entrants have a fair chance of entering the market.

In this volume we attempt to investigate the European experience from three angles. First, we look at the politics of regulation and the process of liberalisation in the EU and in some central EU countries, as well as presenting a theoretical framework within which to conduct the debate. Second, the international character of the sector, as well as the general increasing global economic interdependence, necessitates an international vantage point. Examples from the Czech Republic, Israel and Thailand highlight specificities in the European cases and provide comparison with other political systems. Third, technology is a central element in any debate on telecommunications.

This book is the result of an interesting and highly fruitful co-operation between sixteen scholars representing ten different countries in Europe and Asia. The study was conducted as part of a larger four-year project at the Centre for European Studies (CEAS) at the Norwegian School of Management – BI, sponsored by the Norwegian telecommunications operator Telenor.

We are indebted to a large number of people whose help and assistance has been crucial in preparing this book. We especially want to thank the president of Telenor, Tormod Hermansen, and Ole P. Håkonsen, Magnus Dokset and Sverre Holt for inspiration and economic assistance. Per Mognes, Anders Hellebust and Einar Utvik have generously shared their extensive knowledge with us. We also thank Alberta Sbragia and Marcel Haag for valuable comments both at our seminar in March 1998 and later. We have also greatly appreciated and benefited from comments and discussions with our fellow contributors to this volume throughout its development. The language has greatly profited from the valuable assistance of Verona Christmas, who has shown enormous enthusiasm in making the text accessible also to non-experts in the field. Our good friend and colleague, Catherine Børve Monsen at the CEAS, has contributed with inspiration, good ideas, enthusiasm and references. Thank you. Finally we express our heartfelt thanks to Grethe Haug, our Office Manager, for holding the organisation together.

Kjell A. Eliassen and Marit Sjøvaag
Sandvika, 1 August 1998

Abbreviations

AIS	Advance Information Service
AMPS	Advanced Mobile Phone System
ART	Authority for Regulation of Telecommunications – Autorité de Régulation des Télécommunications (France)
BAPT	Federal Office for Posts and Telecommunications – Bundesamt für Post und Telekommunikation (Germany)
BIBF	Bangkok International Banking Facilities
BKA	The Federal Cartel Office – Bundeskartellamt (Germany)
BMF	Bundesministerium der Finanzen (Federal Ministry of Finance)
BMPT	Federal Ministry of Posts and Telecommunications – Bundesministerium für Post und Telekommunikation (Germany)
BMWi	Federal Ministry of Economic Affairs – Bundesministerium für Wirtschaft (Germany)
BOT	Build-Operate-Transfer
BTO	Build-Transfer-Operate
CAT	Communications Authority of Thailand
CC	The Council for Competition (France)
CDMA	Code-division multiple access
CEC	Commission of the European Communities
CEE	Central and Eastern Europe
CPE	Customer Premises Equipment
CRa	Czech Radiocommunications
CT	Cordless telephone
CTIA	Cellular Telecommunications Industry Association
D-AMPS	Digital AMPS (a digital replacement of analog AMPS based on IS-54 Standard)
DCS	Digital Communication System
DECT	Digital European Cordless Telecommunications
DEL	Direct Exchange Line

DG III	The EU Commission's Directorate General for Industrial Policy
DG IV	The EU Commission's Directorate General for competition Policy
DG XIII	The EU Commission's Directorate General for Telecommunications, Information Technologies and Industries
DG	The EU Commission's Directorate General
DIN	Deutsches Institut für Normung
DON	Digital Overlay Network
DTAG	Deutsche Telekom AG
EC	European Commission
ECJ	The European Court of Justice
EIA	Electronic Industries Association
ETSI	European Telecommunication Standards Institute
EU	The European Union
EuroTel	Czech mobile operator
FCC	The Federal Commission of Communications (USA)
FDMA	Frequency division multiple access
FH	Frequency hopping
Fifteen	The fifteen Member States of the EU
FTC	The Federal Trade Commission (USA)
FWA	Fixed wireless access (also WLL)
GPRS	General Packet Radio Service (packet radio service in GSM)
GSM	Global System for Mobile Communications (originally Groupe Système Mobile)
HDTV	High Definition Television
HSCSD	High speed circuit switched data
HTTP	Hypertext Transfer Protocol
ICO	Intermediate circular orbit
IMT-2000	International Mobile Telecommunications year 2000
IP	Internet Protocol
IPO	Initial Public Offering
IS-136	EIA Interim Standard for USDC with Digital Control Channels
IS-54	EIA Interim Standard for US Digital Cellular (USDC) based on TDMA
IS-95	EIA Interim Standard for US CDMA
ISDN	Integrated Services Digital Network
ITU-R	Radio Communications Sector of International Telecommunication Union
ITU-T	Telecommunication Standards Sector of International Telecommunication Union
JDC	Japanese Digital Cellular (also PDC)

LAN	Local area network
LEO(S)	Low earth orbit (satellite)
MMC	The Monopolies and Mergers Commission (UK)
MOF	Ministry of Finance
MOTC	Ministry of Transport and Communications (Thailand)
MPEG-4	Moving Picture Expert Group 4 (ISO JTC1 SC29 WG11 initiative for low to medium bit-rate audio and video coding standard)
MSS	Mobile satellite services
NCC	National Communications Committee (Thailand)
NESDB	National Economic and Social Development Board (Thailand)
NMT	Nordic Mobile Telecommunications
NRA	National Regulatory Authority
NTC	National Telecommunications Committee (Thailand)
NTT	Nippon Telegraph and Telephone Corporation
OFT	The Office of Fair Trading (UK)
Oftel	The regulator for the UK telecommunications industry
ONP	Open Network Provision
OSI	Open System Interconnection
Paegas	Czech mobile network
PAT	Post Authority of Thailand
PBX	Private branch exchange
PC	Personal computer
PCS	Personal Communications Services (or System)
PDC	Personal (or Pacific) Digital Cellular (alternative for JDC)
PHS	Personal handy phone system
POTS	Plain old telephone service
PTD	Post and Telegraph Department
PTO	Public Telecommunications Operator
PTT	Postal, Telephone and Telegraph Administrations
QoS	Quality of service
Radiomobil	Czech mobile operator
Reg TP	The Regulatory Authority for Telecommunications and Post (Germany)
RF	Radio frequency
RPI	Retail Price Index (RPI–X represents a formula for profits that subtracts X from the RPI)
SCC	Shinawatra Computer and Communications plc
SEA	Single European Act
SIP	The Piedmont Hydroelectric Company (Italy)
SPT Telecom	Czech Telecom
STET	Italian Telecom
TA	TelecomAsia Plc.

TAC	Total Access Communications
TACS	Total Access Communication System
TAT	Telecommunications Authority of Thailand
TDD	Time division duplex
TDG	Teledienste-Gesetz (Teleservices Act) (Germany)
TDMA	Time division multiple access
TDRI	Thailand Development Research Institute
TKG	Telecommunications Act – Telekommunikationsgesetz (Germany)
TOT	Telephone Organization of Thailand
TT&T	Thai Telephone and Telecommunication Corporation
TWF	Directive on Television Without Frontiers
UCOM	United Communications Industry Plc.
UMTS	Universal mobile telecommunications system
USDC	US Digital Cellular (D-AMPS or North American TDMA are also used)
WAP	Wireless Application Protocol
WARC	World Administrative Radio Conference
WCDMA	Wideband CDMA
WLAN	Wireless LAN
WLL	Wireless local loop (the term FWA, fixed wireless access, is also commonly used)
WTO	World Trade Organization

1 Introduction

Kjell A. Eliassen and Marit Sjøvaag

A new paradigm is emerging for international trade in tele-communications. The old paradigm, which might be loosely described as 'inter-national' telecommunications, was based on bilateral relations between countries. The monopoly operators in those countries collaborated in the joint provision of international services. This model is now breaking down, not so much because the system is not working, but rather because it now fails to capture the full picture. A new pattern based on global competition is emerging. It recognizes that trade in tele-communication equipment and services now takes place in a multilateral environment in which the majority of trade relationships include multiple intermediaries between buyer and seller. We are moving from a world of one-to-one relations to a world of many-to-many. It is not nations that trade with other nations, but companies and individuals that conduct trade with each other.

(Report from the ITU)

Telecommunications is an area of explosive development. New products and new technologies appear almost every week. New companies, trying to fit into one of the new niches in the market, pop up faster than we can keep track of. Public authorities give their blessing to these developments through their new regulatory regimes, arguing that the consumer will benefit from the increased competition in the end, in the form of lower prices and more choice.

In this introduction we will set out a broad frame of reference for the discussion in the following chapters. We will sketch our interpretation of current developments, and raise some salient questions that will be revisited at the end of the book. We also pose the question: is the current liberalisation process with all its supporters, from all sides of the political spectrum, a real change in the thinking about public services, or are there signs that all we see is old politics and the protection of domestic industry in a new guise?

Introduction

There is little doubt that there is a radical liberalisation taking place in telecommunications sectors around the world. From the start of the process of privatisation and regulatory reform in the US and the UK in the late 1970s, countries all over the world have changed their regulatory regimes concerning telecommunications. Regulation of telecommunications in Europe has been transformed during the decade 1987–97. As a result, all but five Member States of the European Union (EU)[1] have legislated for the full opening up of all sectors from 1 January 1998, and most of the other five countries will open their markets well ahead of the year 2001. The real effect of this liberalisation process will, however, vary from country to country, depending upon local political and industrial culture and traditions, and the willingness and ability of the different governments to create a really competitive environment. Telecommunications are increasingly recognised as a key component in the infrastructure of economic development, yet telecommunications services in most developing countries continue to fall short of needs (Saunders, Warford and Wellenius 1994).

The Central and Eastern European Countries (CEECs) are going through a similar process, with privatisation of their telecommunications operators and openings for foreign companies. In addition to the wish for economic growth and technological development, a major reason for this development in the CEECs is the desire of these countries to adjust, as rapidly as possible, to the regulatory regime of the EU, in the telecommunications sector, as within other sectors of the economy. Moreover, all countries show a desire to privatise the former monopolist. The real implication of their attempts at liberalisation could, however, be questioned. The implementation of the new rules and regulations will take time, because of the lack of qualification and competence in industry and in the regulatory institutions (Kruse 1997), and also because of the difficulties for the ministries and the present monopolist to change their behaviour.

In contrast to European developments, telecommunications liberalisation, and in some instances privatisation, in Asia is not orchestrated by a common, general regulatory regime. The processes of regulatory reform in Asia will be based in the future on the new World Trade Organisation (WTO) agreement. It is, however, too early to see its full effect, and the question of the role that the WTO can play in opening up the markets of its members is still left unanswered (Kesavapany 1996). Today, the patterns of privatisation and liberalisation are mixed, but we find there is a uniform tendency in all countries towards liberalisation in the form of easier access to the market for new entrants, lowering of barriers for entry and exit, a plethora of new actors, and mainly private ownership of the companies. The methods used and the tempo of the process vary considerably, and the tendency towards privatisation of the former mono-polist is only present in some countries (Bruce and Cunard 1996).

In Latin America we find the same pattern of development, but the tempo in the liberalisation process seems to be higher. Indeed, some would claim that nowhere in the developing world has the movement toward restructuring the telecommunications sector been as rapid or as vigorous as in Latin America (Wellenius 1996). In addition, the desire for privatisation in Latin America seems to be higher than elsewhere, so that some of the biggest American and European operators are now positioning themselves for a stake in its telecommunications markets, which will further strengthen the liberalisation process.

Some of the legal changes necessary for these liberalisation and privatisation processes have happened strictly within a national framework, such as the splitting of AT&T in the US in 1982. However, more typically, these changes have taken place within the framework of international organisations, and certainly the European Union's impact on the liberalisation of the European telecommunications market cannot be ignored. Similarly, the International Telecommunication Union (ITU) and the WTO have been instrumental in preparing for the harmonisation of technology and the mutual opening up of markets, first with regard to customer premises equipment (CPE), and later in transmission technologies and services markets. The main aim of the two organisations are qualitatively different in that the ITU by principle does not interfere in telecommunications policy at the national level, nor does it promote specific policy solutions, except in technological fields, whereas the WTO presses more for liberal measures in politics. There is, however, little doubt that the two organisations together have contributed to making liberalisation feasible.

It is difficult, if not impossible, to discuss the development of regulatory structures in EU Member States without reference to the debate on European integration. The central role of the Commission in establishing a legislative framework, the increased importance of European competition rules for telecommunications companies, and the current restructuring of the market, are all factors that raise the question of whether there eventually will be one European market for tele-communications, with one regulatory regime and one 'watchdog', in the form of the EU Competition authority, DG IV. Even if the solution with one pan-European regulator has a certain elegance and is logically attractive, we believe that the issue is politically too controversial to be introduced now. In addition to legal barriers for the establishment of a European Regulatory Authority with powers to act as an independent body (Worthy and Kariyawasam 1998; Nera 1997), the legitimacy of the system at the European level is not great enough to support a pan-European regulator (Pelkmans and Young 1998: 171–95).

It is also important to bear in mind that the industry increasingly sees itself as global, and that regional regulators will have to relate to world-wide companies. We can therefore expect a need for even more far-reaching (in geographical terms) harmonisation of regulatory requirements. However, if international organisations are crucial in the liberalisation process, legislation still has to be implemented in national laws. Therefore, in order to understand the process of liberalisation and its outcomes, one must investigate the political process at state level.

A wider process of liberalisation

Telecommunications is not the only sector going through profound regulatory change. Similar developments take place in all public utilities, like electricity, gas, water and railways. The airline industry has likewise been opened up for more competition and private ownership. None of the former state monopolies seem to be exempt from the politicians' and bureaucrats' urge to open markets. On the surface, the different national processes seem to follow comparable paths, with a high degree of similarity in the new institutional structures, i.e. the use of an agency model regulator, and partly or complete privatisation of former state owned telecommunications operators (the mobile sector being the first one to open for new actors to deliver real-time voice transfer, and fixed line voice telephony being the last stronghold of the old monopoly). We believe, however, that different national traditions regarding institutions, ideas and actors involved in the policy-making in the sector have influenced the liberalisation process and induced important variations between different national regulatory practices.

It is striking to observe the extent to which politicians from a broad political spectrum have embraced the 'Friedmanesque' ideas of the benefits from competition and free-market structures. Under a banner of promoting national and European competitiveness, politicians from both the right- and left-wing political parties have legislated to remove the public utilities' protected positions, and to introduce new market and ownership structures in sectors that were traditionally organised as part of a ministerial administration. Will national governments implement these policies with all their consequences, or are they mainly paying lip service to the high principles of competition while finding new ways to protect their own national enterprises?

One of the aims of this volume is to scrutinise the liberalisation process in different countries, in order to compare the outcome of the process, to establish the extent to which national regulation of the telecommunications sector differ, and in what areas they experience problems with establishing a liberalised, free market. Moreover, we are looking for factors that will highlight the specific paths the countries presented in this book have chosen, and which may explain national differences in regulation.

The liberalisation and privatisation of the telecommunications sector have also taken place at a time of its rapid convergence with information technology and media services. This convergence process presents new and even more challenging tasks for regulation. For example, media content and ownership are much more difficult to regulate than market access and frequencies, and the combination of several of these elements complicates regulation even further (Blackman 1998; Clements 1998). At the same time, in many countries, like Germany and Belgium, media is governed at a regional level, whereas telecommunications are controlled at a national level in most countries. This adds another layer of complexity to institutional concerns.

National regulation and global competition

The concept of 'deregulation' of public services appeared in the mid-1980s. Anglo-Saxon academics, bureaucrats and right-wing politicians believed that by introducing competition to the sector, efficiency would increase, which would then lead to a broader choice for consumers, lower prices and a higher quality of existing and new services. If there were such a thing as a 'natural monopoly', this would at most be applicable to large infrastructures and, in the case of telecommunications, even this was questioned. The way to press through deregulation was to break up former public utility monopolies into segments of network operation, service provision, equipment and manufacturing, and regulation, although political and economic considerations complicated a direct splitting of the old monopolies. The privatisation of British Telecom, which was sold as a vertically integrated company, illustrates this.

Within the disciplines of today's business administration, it is possible for governments to correct a market failure, should it occur, and enhance an economy's efficiency (Stiglitz 1997). The everlasting question, however, is to what extent one should rely on the market and competition, or on government and regulation. The choice of one or the other will always affect some industry; i.e. any change towards more or less regulation from government will have implications on how the industry involved operates. Within the telecommunications sector, rather than direct state intervention, governments now liberalise the telecommunications market, but at the same time establish a new regulatory framework focusing on micro-economic management of the sector. The aim is for everyone to have the same possibilities of operating in the new open telecommunications market, but under specified rules set by the government in order to secure prices, standards etc. In fact, there is a need for regulations in order to prevent the market from destroying itself (Hernes 1978).

However, there were also practical difficulties attached to the opening up of the market. According to the new paradigm, prices of certain telecommunications services (especially those that could be exploited by a monopoly provider, such as interconnection into the fixed-line network) should be based on real costs. As long as the telecommunications operators were mainly ministerial offices of some kind, accounting systems were not adapted to reveal the real costs of providing specific services. The process of adapting the old dinosaurs to new management practices and a competitive environment was, therefore, to start with separate accounting for the different parts of the system, as well as introducing transparency to ensure equal treatment of former operators and new entrants (Walker 1996; WIK/EAC 1994; DPTE 1996). The open network provision, granting equal access to the network for all service providers, and interconnection between different network operators, was to instigate a system where deregulation would consist of ensuring freedom of trade (Stoffaës 1995). Within the changing global economy and policy environment, the information economy is emerging. Economies need to respond flexibly to what global economic forces are telling them if they are to maintain their competitive position. The increased application of information and communication technologies to all parts of the economy is symptomatic of such changes and is believed to deliver competitive 'flexible' enterprises into the new millennium (Turner 1997).

Questions have been raised, however, as to whether the sought-after effects result from competition itself or from the *threat* of competition. Evidence suggests that it is not the extent of real competition which is important, but how the market actors perceive the potential threat from competitors that induces the desired behaviour.

Contrary to popular belief, liberalisation is not synonymous with 'deregulation' in the sense that there will be less regulation. Fair competition requires tight regulation to prevent dominant players from abusing their position (Graham and Prosser 1987; Majone 1996). This is especially true in the telecommunications sector, where national companies have enjoyed a legal monopoly for a long period, and are still in a position to dominate the market and create barriers to entry that would distort fair competition. Authors have attempted to distinguish between the two concepts, by defining 'deregulation' as 'the loosening of restrictions on the entry or exit from a market and on the setting of prices', whereas 'liberalisation' would embrace both 'deregulation' and 'privatisation', i.e. 'the sale of the controlling public share in a firm or governmental body' (Rubsamen 1989: 105). This seems to us to be a workable definition.

However, in order to emphasise the fundamental change in thinking about the role of the state in public utilities sectors in general and telecommunications in particular, we suggest the term 'regulatory reform'. This term is used by the Organisation for Economic Co-operation and Development (OECD) in 'The OECD Report on Regulatory Reform' (1997). The report examines the 'significance, direction, and means of reform in regulatory regimes' (p. 3), and concludes that in order to be successful, regulatory reform needs high-level political support, but also openness and transparency in the process. This openness is, among others, expressed through the separation of regulatory and operational functions.

A typical first step towards liberalisation has been to separate regulatory from operational functions in the former telecommunications organisations, which for the EU Member States was a legally binding requirement from the EU (see, e.g., Directive 95/62/CE). In addition to separating regulation and operation, EU legislation demands that an *independent regulator* is established at national level. This regulator's tasks are to ensure fair and free competition and to implement a transparent decision-making process, especially with regard to interconnection agreements, which are at the heart of competition in telecommunications. Moreover, regulators typically are responsible for representing the country in international organisations, and for licensing requirements in areas involving scarce resources, such as frequencies in the mobile sector. In Israel no regulator is yet established; however, signs are that such an office will be created in the near future. In Thailand the National Communication Committee will be the regulatory authority.

It is intriguing that all countries seem to choose the agency model when establishing a new regulator, since the actual organisational model for such an office is left to the Member States. The EU directive states that the regulator has to be independent from *any operator,* which in theory enables the respective ministry to remain the regulating unit. With the exception of Italy, this possibility does not seem to have been discussed to any degree in any of the countries considered in this volume.

If a truly competitive market in telecommunications is the goal of the current liberalisation policies, the national regulatory agencies face the awkward situation that, if they are successful, they will be redundant. The function of regulation in sectors dominated by one or very few firms is primarily to act as a surrogate for market forces. In a competitive market, however, 'regulation must protect the process of competition, so that market competition can become reality' (Garfinkel 1994: 428). All market regulation could, in a fully competitive market, be handled by the general competition authorities. However, we do not believe that sector-specific regulation will disappear in the near future, even if several scholars have pointed out the benefits of having one central European regulator (Kramer 1992; NERA 1997). Experience with Oftel in the UK suggests that sector-specific regulation in the telecommunications sector persists long after the introduction of competitors to the incumbent operator. Social and political goals, especially universal service obligations, are used to argue for continued sector-specific regulation, instead of leaving it all to the competition authorities. Technological issues, such as licensing and the regulation of number series and frequencies, are also arguments in favour of a sector-specific authority. Moreover, for a European regulator to emerge, one would need both legal and political changes that at present do not seem likely to happen (see Lasserre 1992; Ungerer 1992; Arlandis 1993).

The significance of institutions

Fundamental regulatory reform is a political, and in most cases a heavily politicised, issue. Indeed, any political process involves some form of power struggle between actors and institutions, as can be seen from developments in the telecommunications sectors of countries in Europe. In many cases, the traditional public administration telecommunications providers had, by the mid-1970s, become enormous institutions with unmistakable dinosaur-like features,[2] and they met the increasingly diversified public demand with difficulty, if at all. Their employees' status, which in most cases was that of civil servants, functioned as an obstacle to reform (see Schmidt 1991, 1996; Duch 1991; Thatcher 1994). Tight policy networks with national industries benefiting from a protected status as suppliers to the domestic industry further reduced the chances of support for radical reform. In a European context, a visible change in policies emerged in the mid- to late-1980s. Since the publication of the European Commission's Green Paper on Telecommunications in 1987, the regulatory regimes have undergone significant changes in all EU member states.

The interesting question then becomes: how can we explain the emergence and the timing of new regulatory structures on a large scale? Institutionalists will point to the importance of supra-national institutions, both as legislator and as a vehicle for learning and exchange of ideas within national institutions. Sandholtz (1993) outlines two factors as having been necessary for regulatory reform in Europe. First, there was an adaptation at the national level, which led national governments to consider collective action as an alternative to unilateral approaches. Second, international leadership was provided (at least in the case of the European Union) in the shape of the European Commission.

The Single European Act of 1987 equipped the European Union with Art. 100a, which provides for the adoption of certain Council directives by qualified majority voting, namely those required to establish the Single European Market. Moreover, according to Art. 90 of the EC Treaty, the Commission can address directives or decisions to Member States 'in order to ensure that Member States neither enact nor keep in force any measure which is contrary to the Treaty rules with respect to their TOs [telecommunications operators] as holders of exclusive rights.' (Scherer and Bartsch 1998: 4). Two important directives were adopted with reference to Art. 90: the Terminal Equipment Directive (88/301/EEC); and the Services Directive (90/388/EEC). Both were challenged by Member States, which argued that the Commission was working outside its field of competence. Some Member States argued that the Commission's role should be limited to one of supervision, and that limitation of exclusive rights for the national operators was the task of the Council. The European Court of Justice, however, ruled in favour of the Commission (Scherer and Bartsch 1998: 19–24).

There is little doubt that the Commission has been an important driving force in the process of opening up the telecommunications markets in Europe. Even though our field of interest is not so much the impact of the Commission and its role in the policy-making process, as the differences among national regulatory structure, it is important to acknowledge that supra-national structures have had significant influence. Both European Union and WTO agreements have speeded up the process, and have also contributed to the relatively similar institutional bodies set-up in the different countries.

The EU has played a key role in the development of the European telecommunications sector since the late 1980s and a series of directives have been put into force in the member countries. The main liberalisation directives have been the Terminal directive (1988), the Service directive (1990), the Satellite directive (1994), the Voice Telephony directive (1995), the Mobil directive (1996), and the Full Competition directive (1996). As the list fully illustrates, 1998 is not the end of regulation of telecommunications in Europe, but rather part of a process of re-regulation, a regulatory reform.

EU legislation provides a framework for regulation of telecommunications, whose main aim is to secure fair and effective competition in all segments of the telecommunications sector. This framework is, however, wide and open to a substantial variation in the way it is implemented, and how the national regulatory authorities are structured. At the same time, it leaves a great deal of discretion to the national regulatory authorities. The EU has no say over the ownership of PTOs, but insists on a separation between regulation and supply of telecommunications networks and services. In crucial areas, such as licensing, interconnection and universal services, the European regulatory framework permits considerable scope for interpretation. In sum, the operation of the sector is harmonised across Europe, but the executive power still lies with the national institutions – and will continue to do so in the foreseeable future.

Rationale for liberalisation

The history of telecommunications policies in Europe coincides with the history of public administration. As a rule, telecommunications were under public monopoly until the 1980s. This trend started to change with the splitting of AT&T into one long-distance company and the five Baby Bells in 1982, and the beginning of British Telecom's privatisation in 1984. The evolution of the structure for the organisation and regulation of service providers is treated extensively in the literature, and an overview of the main events is also given in Chapter 2.

Explanations of the 'inevitability' of the liberalisation process have arisen from many different groups. Scientists focusing on technological development hold forth the impossibility of public authorities regulating the environment created by new technology. The growth of satellite communications, which opened up possibilities for American operators to bypass European national networks (Hills 1986), and the digitalisation of networks, which removed the principal difference between transfer of sound (for example voice telephony) and data (e.g. data transfer), made former legislation particularly muddy and unclear. Hence, technologists maintain that competitors to the 'plain old telephony service' (POTS) existed prior to regulatory reform, and hence spurred it on. There is, however, evidence that liberalisation was a political decision because, in order to make connections via satellites possible, companies needed national approval to erect earth stations.

Economists, on the other hand, would tend to stress the impact of globalisation of economies and increased world trade as an impetus for liberal measures. The growth of multinational and multi-domestic companies created users that demanded similar services in different countries, and at lower prices. Political economists might see this development as a victory of rationality over more 'irrational' arguments based on 'national sentiments', since competition in national markets is a way to meet the problem with regulatory capture of politicians from industry (Stigler 1971; Wilson 1984).

All these different explanations contain some truth. Telecommunications is a complex policy-making area, and all the above-mentioned factors are significant. However, the different views aim at different things in their account of reality. Some are more deterministic than others, some attempt to influence more than to explain. Our purpose in this work is to highlight similarities and differences of *experiences* in the development of regulatory regimes in various European countries.

The impact of technological development on regulation

One of the most challenging tasks for any student of regulatory reform in the telecommunications sector is to assess to what extent technology spurred on the process, and which decisions were purely political ones. Would liberalisation have happened had it not been for digitalisation and satellite communications? Is it possible to envisage regulatory reform without a shift in technology?

Telecommunications is a research and development (R&D) intensive sector. However, the lifespan of technology is decreasing and 'Moore's law', predicting in 1978 that the computing power of a single chip would double every 18 months, has had to be revised to take account of the increasing speed of technological development. The economic consequences of this rapid development are enormous, because as technology's lifespan drastically decreases, its investment needs are ever increasing.

These changes are important for the industry and for individual companies' chances of survival, especially because of the large investment needed. Although arrangements were made, in many cases, for public administrations to borrow directly in financial markets, the increasing costs were met with difficulty within a public-ownership model. During the 1970s and throughout the 1980s, national European governments realised that the current organisational models for their telecommunications sector were badly suited to cope with rapid development. The crucial role of the telecommunications industry as an infrastructure for other industries made it imperative to retain competitive telecommunications operators, both nationally and in the European context. For many countries, the answer lay in financial flexibility for the operator and more managerial discretion, often in the form of privatisation.

Furthermore, the increase of international and cross-border telecommunications services, of which call-back services are a good example, made it increasingly difficult to police the regulatory regimes. Unregulated competition undermined the position of the national operators and strengthened the need for change. The then Secretary General for Eutelsat, Caruso, said that: 'I do not remember any deregulatory tendency, at least in Europe, before the arrival of satellites' (quoted in Hills 1986). The new threats to the old monopoly PTOs that arose from technological developments were so ground-breaking that policy-makers were forced to review their policies. In a way, by supporting extensive R&D programmes, public authorities 'dug their own grave'.

The solution to the problem of the role of technology might be found if we look at the broader role of telecommunications in society. In addition to providing direct communication services to industry, the public sector, and private households, telecommunications is also an important part of the infrastructure of a country's industry. Countries with poor telecommunications infrastructure generally have a lower GDP per capita (Pelkmans and Young 1998: 14). As global competition increased, the threat from the US and Japan made it more important for national governments to strengthen their domestic industries than to hold on to traditional ways of organising the economy. Moreover, the telecommunications companies themselves increasingly understood that, in order to survive in the new technological environment, access to foreign markets was crucial. This spilled over to the policy-makers, which put international market access – 'the "bread and butter" of trade negotiators' work' (Broadman and Balassa 1993: 31) – at the focus of their attention.

This is not to say that anyone understood the full scope of the change induced by the new technologies from the beginning. Rather, once the process of global economies had gained momentum, certain consequences followed, among which was a need for new organisational and regulatory structures in parts of the economy (see, e.g., Bauer 1994). This does not explain why all countries seem to choose more or less similar models of regulation and control, but it points to the force of two concurrent events, i.e. increased economic interdependence, and new technologies which fall outside the scope of existing regulations.

Globalisation of economies and the WTO agreement

World trade is increasing. This is especially true in services industries such as telecommunications where, in terms of market capitalisation, the telecommunication industry now ranks third in the world behind health care and banking. Indeed, telecommunication and office equipment was the fastest growing sector of merchandise exports during 1995, and the global value of trading in telecommunications services has been evaluated at US$600bn, of which cross-border trade is estimated to amount to US$100bn (http://www.itu.org). The global nature of the telecommunications sector strengthens the need for a world-wide regulatory framework, and increasingly one which is not only bilateral in nature, but can reduce uncertainty for multinational and multi-domestic companies. The two main organisations for global co-ordination are the ITU and the WTO.

The International Telecommunications Union grew out of the need for an overarching framework for securing interconnection between different national telegraph and telephone networks. It became a specialised agency of the United Nations in 1947, and its main functions are to co-ordinate and regulate the use of the frequency spectrum, and to ensure the interoperability of telecommunications networks across national borders through standardisation of equipment and systems. Furthermore, the ITU is working to promote telecommunications in the less developed countries. However, the organisation does not possess direct sanctioning powers, except for the rules laid down in international law, of which the ITU constitution, its telecommunications regulation and its radio regulation are a part. It therefore works mainly as a forum for discussion and documentation, in conformity with its intentions, relying on the mutual benefit for its members to follow its recommendations.

The International Telecommunications Union states that:

> For many telecommunication users, the transition to a multilateral trading system will bring benefits in terms of greater choice and lower prices. For the majority of carriers, there will be significant benefits in terms of creating new market opportunities and a more level playing field. The goal is to extend the multilateral solution in which all

countries move forward together and in which all benefit, not just those carriers with market power. Only then will the benefits of global competition be extended to all the world's inhabitants.

Because of the lack of sanctioning powers, the ITU does not possess the necessary instruments to enforce global liberalisation. Of more immediate importance for trade agreements and the mutual opening of markets is the World Trade Organisation (WTO). This is the organisational framework embedding the General Agreement on Tariffs and Trade (GATT) and the General Agreement on Trade in Services (GATS). In 1997, the WTO telecommunication agreement opened the way for a multilateral framework for freer trade, market opening and competition. At the end of the negotiations on basic telecommunications, in February 1997, there were sixty-nine signatory governments to the Fourth Protocol, which sets out a global framework for mutual market opening in telecommunications. The sixty-nine countries constitute more than 90 per cent of the global market for telecommunications services.

Concerns related to establishing a regulatory environment to secure market access were at the centre of the negotiations on basic telecommunications. The parties agreed on a set of principles relating to competition safeguards, interconnection guarantees, transparent licensing processes, and the independence of regulators. There was also established a dispute settlement procedure, which is 'clearly structured, with flexible timetables set for completing a case' (http://www.wto.org). In the case of a dispute, first rulings are made by a panel, and final decisions are made by the WTO's full membership, ensuring that no single country can block such decisions. In addition to this innovation for international dispute settlement, the multilateral nature of the treaty means that the offers and commitments are binding on governments, and are practically irreversible. Thus a return to a system of national monopolies is excluded and the situation becomes one of increased international interdependence.

However, the effectiveness and efficiency of the WTO as a forum for international dispute settlement will obviously depend on the members realising the mutual benefit of co-operation. Since carriers operating in non-liberalised markets profit from the existing system, at least in the short term, they have few incentives to abandon it. The most important issue to promote a global industry is market access, which was at the top of the agenda of the Negotiating Group on Basic Telecommunications.

The latest developments in the ratification process of the WTO agreement indicates that the 'extension of the benefits of global competition to all the world's inhabitants' might still be some time away. Even though the participants managed to reach agreement on many important matters, full market liberalisation hinges on central principles (competition safeguards, interconnection guarantees etc.), being enforced by national legislators and policy-makers. By the February 1997 deadline, fifty-seven of the sixty-nine governments submitting schedules for the liberalisation of their telecommunications sector, had wholly, or with only minor modifications, committed themselves to the principles set out in the Reference Paper (http://www.wto.org). This agreement removed many of the previous weaknesses with the GATS agreement, but has been criticised especially because the accounting rate system (whereby international interconnection and termination tariffs are settled by bilateral agreements) is not being abolished. Moreover, the individual countries have considerable scope in which to interpret the framework. Thus, 'depending on how countries handle regulations, they can undermine the market access and national treatment commitments' (Fredebeul-Krein and Freytag 1997: 489).

Although the WTO agreement on telecommunications is a clear step towards greater market opening, as the ratification process has demonstrated, one should not believe that the process will be straight-forward, even if many countries have declared themselves in favour. Part of the problem is that national operators, as well as national governments, will hold on to their competitive advantages in the domestic market for as long as possible and hence will be reluctant to open up their home markets before they are sure of full access to those of other countries.

There is, however, little doubt that the WTO holds strong potential for establishing a new regime in the global telecommunications sector (Broadman and Balassa 1993). With a regulatory framework governed by a supra-national organisation, and member states that stick to its rulings, one can easily envisage a sector where the role of the nation-state is being reduced to the benefit of multinational and also multi-domestic firms, and – hopefully – to the benefit of the consumers.

Before 1998, however, most international agreements on trade in tele-communications services were done on a bilateral basis. It is therefore also interesting to investigate how liberalisation has occurred in countries outside the European Union, and for this reason we have chosen to include the cases of the Czech Republic, Israel and Thailand in this volume.

New services, new business opportunities, and new challenges for the regulators

Telecommunications is at the heart of the large and expanding industry of information and communication ('infocom') which, in 1995, was evaluated to be worth some US$1.370bn (http://www.itu.org). The convergence of the telecommunications sector with the computer and broadcasting worlds is creating new synergy, most evident in the growth of the Internet, which continues to double in size every year.[3] The significance of the Internet has an enormous potential for development and can be regarded as the prototype of a global information infrastructure that will provide the platform for the electronic commerce of the twenty-first century.

Technology has been an important driving force of the liberalisation process since digitalisation. Although the French had already adopted a law in 1837 which put *all* transmission of signals, by telegraph *or by any other means*, under state control, and in that way regulated with regard to service and not to technology, the traditional regulation of telecommunications has been with reference to some kind of specific technology.[4] A distinction between broadcasting and telecommunications services was typically drawn between one-to-one and one-to-many transmissions, and even though the ownership of transmission equipment for the broadcasting sector was under the telecommunications operator, its use was regulated through separate institutions (typically the Ministry for Culture).

With technological convergence, the clear division lines of responsibility were blurred. There is, in principle, no difference between transmission of digital signals that are converted into real-time speech (voice telephony) and signals converted into a picture (fax or videotext services). With the digitalisation of television, one set of equipment can integrate telephone, value-added services, computer services, and television services. This evidently prompts the question of division of responsibilities for regulation. Until now, institutional traditions and the heavy politicised issue of content regulation (and national culture politics) have impeded the emergence of new 'infocom regulators' both at the national and at supra-state level (Levy 1997).

The impact of the process of convergence for regulation is difficult to overestimate but, as no one at present can predict the evolution of the information society, the regulators have a hard time anticipating forthcoming events. Part of this problem is technological: in a world where technology is developing so rapidly that it is rare to have planning horizons of more than 18 months, it is difficult, even within the industry itself, to identify the core elements by which to regulate, rather than linking regulation to technologies. It is not surprising, therefore, that regulators' perception of the world, and its political challenges, whether related to allocation, competition or redistribution of welfare in a wider sense, is inevitably influenced by what is technologically feasible at the time.

Another part of the problem, however, concerns the division of power between institutions, and the role of the state. The heavy political character of media politics 'has led to a strong desire to control the policy process and outcomes in a way that has limited the scope for technocratic decision making' (Levy 1997: 38), and the convergent industries might possibly be the real test of the impact of technology in regulatory policies.

There is no doubt that the technology is global, but regulation continues to differ across national borders.

New business logic

The telecommunications industry structure has changed enormously over the last decade. Privatisation means that telecommunications operators and service providers gain a new set of stakeholders for their activities. It also means that the old structures with 'royal suppliers' of equipment manufacturers, like Siemens in Germany or Alcatel in France, have disappeared. Instead of hierarchical and, in many cases, legally determined relations between the different companies in the sector, liberalisation has enabled the industry to reorganise itself. This reorganisation, characterised by the cascade of joint ventures, mergers, alliance building and co-operation in various projects and markets, works on a set of motivations which are very different from that which the industry saw less than five years ago.

The concepts of 'competitor' and 'customer' are getting less stringent, because in a networking environment such as telecommunications, different actors take on different roles at different times. One's customer in one field can be one's competitor in another setting.

Public switched telephony is still the core business of most incumbent operators. At the moment, value-added services, of which the Internet is an example, are being provided over the telephone network. However, in the future we might see that voice telephony will be only one of several services provided over other networks.

The changing nature of business logic in the telecommunications sector can also be illustrated by the ways in which new entrants enter the segment of public switched telephony. As Figure 1.1 shows, new entrants come from other types of public utilities, as well as directly from fringe industries in the private sector. This mixture of actors will inevitably change the way in which the industry operates, and incumbent operators will also have to change their traditional ways of doing business. We have already seen signs of such fundamental changes, sometimes through divestitures, sometimes through privatisation, but we are also convinced that we have only seen the beginnings of this process.

The content of the book

This introduction to some of the most salient factors in the discussion on regulation of telecommunications today illustrates the vastness of the field, as well as the complexity of the issues involved. It is important, therefore, not to lose sight of our main aim. In this book we will attempt to highlight the development of regulatory reform in certain countries, from three different vantage points, in order to indicate some explana-

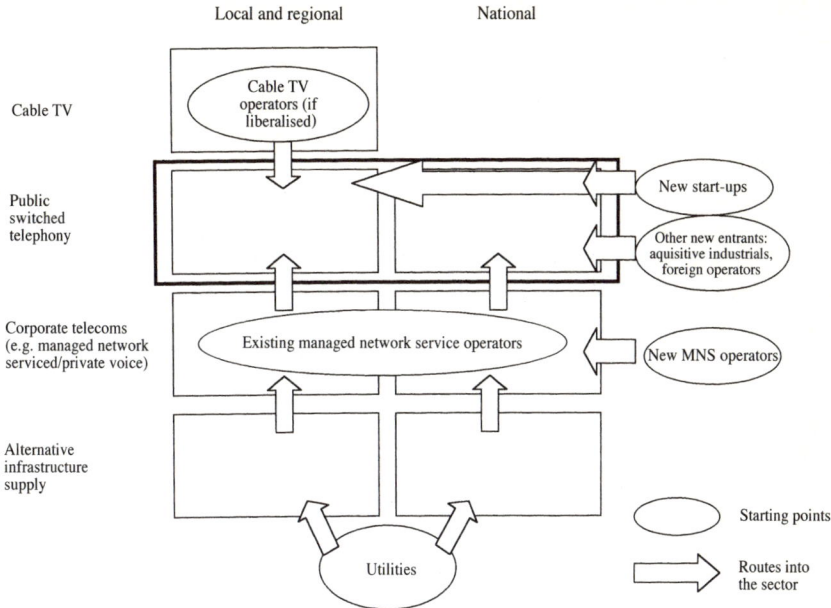

Local and regional   National

Cable TV

Cable TV operators (if liberalised)

Public switched telephony

New start-ups

Other new entrants: aquisitive industrials, foreign operators

Corporate telecoms (e.g. managed network serviced/private voice)

Existing managed network service operators

New MNS operators

Alternative infrastructure supply

Starting points

Routes into the sector

Utilities

Figure 1.1 Market entry routes into public switched telephony

tions for national differences in the current regulatory regime. The three vantage points (the European Union, the international arena, and the technological development) are treated in separate parts of the book.

The book has four parts. In Part I we present some trends from European integration in relation to regulation. The liberalisation process in the telecommunications sector within the European Union is presented to give a frame of reference to subsequent chapters (Chapter 2). The chapter shows the incremental nature of the regulatory reform, and discusses especially the role of the European Commission in the process. We have also included a chapter on theoretical approaches to regulation (Chapter 3), which both frames the discussion in the country chapters, as well as providing a basis for our concluding remarks. Our main focus is on the telecommunications sector, but we broaden the discussion by referring to other sectors and to the development of independent agencies in general. Chapter 4 introduces the concept of 'policy syncretism' to explain the growth of new regulatory institutions and models across the EU Member States. Furthermore, we found it important to open up for the debate on the regulation of content in the convergent sectors (Chapter 5). The regulation of multimedia poses huge difficulties for regulators in several sectors, and the chapter concludes that it is unlikely that an optimal model for regulation of convergent industries will emerge in the near future.

Part II is devoted to studies of some Member States of the European Union, covering the UK, Germany and France. These chapters highlight the national variations in the liberalisation process, even for countries where the European initiative is seen to be of great importance. The chapter on the UK (Chapter 6) demonstrates the futility of talking about 'deregulation', because public policy-makers remain vigorously active in the regulation of telecommunications in the UK almost two decades after the opening of the sector to multiple operators. The German case (Chapter 7) is another example of how a long and cumbersome reform process (covering eight years and three legislative reforms) has resulted in continued sector-specific regulation. There are signs, however, that the degree of liberalisation in the German market is significant. The chapter on France (Chapter 8) discusses the new regime and the possibilities for new entrants, in particular with regard to licensing rules and practices. Common to both France and Germany is the fact that it is too soon to make a full assessment of the liberalised environment, but there are signs which suggest that, in the not too distant future, we can expect more fully developed competition.

In Part III we look at countries outside the European Union, countries that to a large extent have managed their liberalisation within the framework of bilateral agreements, or with a perception of the competitive structures being formed within the WTO. The chapters on the Czech Republic, Israel and Thailand allow us to make important comparisons with regard to how much of the on-going process is specific to the European Union, and how much is part of a global phenomenon. As the chapter on the Czech Republic (Chapter 9) shows, we find the same issues and conflicts in the Czech situation as in various European countries. The question of ownership and control of operating companies ranks high on the list, and is difficult to solve because it lies at the heart of the role of the state and how it should create welfare for its citizens. Financial difficulties, however, are only part of the problem. As important is the need for the domestic industry to engage in global alliances.

The Israeli situation (Chapter 10) is in itself a very interesting case-study of how a traditionally 'etatist' governed sector has been liberalised 'from above', and reflects the importance of the national-level reform process wherein state officials were possibly *the* most important driving force for liberalisation. As global regimes develop, however, the need for co-ordination increases. Thailand (Chapter 11) is an example of how the need for new infrastructure has led the authorities to open up for new entrants. It also lays down some crucial factors for the future success of the regime, especially with regard to the nature of the new private-sector participating enterprises.

Part IV of the book covers some salient technological sectors, their impact on the industry, and a new way of thinking about the business consequences of this. The role of technology is, in our view, often overestimated, but if we believe that at least part of the liberalisation measures stem from practical difficulties of policing the new technological environment, then it becomes crucial to sketch some of the trends of future developments in this field. In addition, knowledge about the technological possibilities (as well as the developments to date) is crucial for the understanding of the regulatory challenges we are facing. We have chosen to focus on the mobile sector and the information-communication ('infocom') sector, as representatives of two market segments where technological development highlights the difficulties of regulating according to technology. The chapters on mobile technology (Chapter 12) and future infocom systems (Chapter 13) both stress the interdependence between new technological possibilities and new lifestyles, characterised by high mobility and demand for access of information independent of geographical position. Mobile communications and the Internet will be the two salient building-blocks for the future information society. This also has consequences for the industry (Chapter 14), where new models for value creation are needed to capture the functioning of the sector. Chapter 14 presents a model for thinking about how value is created in network systems, of which telecommunications is a prime example.

Notes

1 We will throughout this volume use the term 'European Union' for what has variously been known as the 'European Communities', the 'European Community' and the 'European Union', unless there are strong reasons for doing otherwise.

2 Deutsche Bundespost had 500,000 employees in 1982, of which about 216,000 were in telecommunications. This number did not significantly decrease over the following decade.

3 At the start of 1997, there were more than 16 million host computers connected to the Internet and more than 50 million users.

4 The use of the concept of 'regulation' is not very precise in this setting. The concept was not in common use in all countries until the 1980s, and signifies therefore a fundamental shift in thinking within state administrations. The concept in this context embraces administrative provision and control of telecommunications services also prior to the 1970s.

Part I

European integration

Part I of the book, on European integration, introduces the 'big picture' of the liberalisation process in the EU, as well as theoretical discussions of the evolving regulatory regime. Chapter 2 (Kjell A. Eliassen, Toby Mason and Marit Sjøvaag) tells the story of the incremental nature of the process at the EU level, setting it within a broader frame of international industrial trends, technological development and political debate in the EU Member States.

Martin Lodge (Chapter 3) discusses theoretical considerations of the problems of regulation, and points to the questions of distribution of social goods, legitimate state intervention, and design problems. The question of control, both by the state of the economic actors, and by the general public of the state officials, lies at the heart of this discussion.

Nick Sitter and Sebastian Eyre argue in Chapter 4 that EU Member States have adopted different approaches to regulatory reform at both domestic and EU level, resulting in a series of models of agency-based regulation. These Member State differences are explained in terms of their approaches to regulatory reform. The European regime (EU and Member States) is described as 'policy syncretism'.

Patrizia Cincera discusses in Chapter 5 the regulation of content. The chapter shows how it is important, in the view of the European Union, to harmonise legislation at EU level because, Cincera concludes, it seems unlikely that an 'optimal' regulatory framework of the global communication world will come into being in the near future.

2 European telecommunications policies – deregulation, re-regulation or real liberalisation?

Kjell A. Eliassen, Toby Mason and Marit Sjøvaag

Introduction

January 1, 1998, saw the final barriers to competition in the European telecommunications industry lifted. Aside from some brief derogations for countries with less developed telecommunications infrastructures (Greece, Italy, Ireland, Spain and Portugal), there now exists a Single Market for telecommunications of all types within the European Union. The last fifteen years have therefore seen a radical change in the way the telecommunications sector operates, and the regulatory regime within which it works. This chapter will trace this development, which is really a history of the European Union's gradual progression towards liberalising a sector which was based almost entirely on national monopolies of networks, infrastructure and equipment at the beginning of the 1980s. The contrast could not be starker with the current regulatory regime, which is designed to remove monopolies and ensure that telecommunications in Europe are administered in the spirit of the competition rules as laid down in the Treaty of Rome. The sector has also taken on a positively European character, as the EC has deliberately fostered a Europe-wide culture of both co-operation in development and infrastructure, and competition for contracts and customers. However, the EC, as in so many areas, has had to feel its way slowly towards this goal, as technology has developed at a dizzying pace and the regulatory regime has had to run to keep up. This is evidenced by the flood of Commission framework documents and proposals, as well as the myriad of technical groups and advisory panels involved in the process. It is, therefore, a story of incrementalism, but incrementalism towards a clearly defined goal of competition, which has now, to a large extent, been achieved. In a simplistic sense, the process has been to apply EC competition laws to the telecommunications sector, but as this chapter will show, the Commission has, in many ways, taken a far more radical, proactive course of action which has attempted to institute a dynamic and vibrant cross-European industry. The Full Competition Directive has now opened up the European market, and many companies are now offering competing services which are both cheaper and more advanced than before (see BT 1998).

Before liberalisation: the PTOs and the 'national champions'

In order to give some indication of the profound change which took place during the 1980s and 1990s, it is necessary to sketch the situation as it existed in Member States prior to any liberalisation. By sketching the broad picture of the factors that, taken together, led up to the implementation of the liberalisation, we provide the background against which the other discussions and analyses in this volume should be seen.

The telecommunications networks in virtually every European state – with the exception of Sweden – were operated as Post, Telegraph, and Telephone administrations (PTTs), which formed part of the governmental administration. They were usually integrated with postal services, many of them administered directly by ministries and staffed by civil servants. The PTTs held a de facto monopoly over the national telecommunications infrastructures, and had a double role as both regulators and suppliers (Dang-Nguyen, Schneider, and Werle 1993).

These monolithic creatures completely dominated the telecommunications industry, even extending to 'cosy' patent-sharing agreements with the manufacturers of customer premises equipment (CPE), the physical terminals necessary for the operation of the networks. Contracts were awarded in a political manner – i.e. there existed a deliberate policy of backing 'national champions' in each Member State. These were companies such as GEC/Plessey in Britain and Siemens in Germany. Each PTO had its own arrangement with the relevant company, and since the contracts were awarded by governments with the express intention of building up one company to the exclusion of others, it was hardly a case of 'open and fair competition'. The economic importance of the telecommunications equipment manufacturing sector, as well as its role in the research and development of a country's technological industry (including military industry), had, through the tacit definition of the telecommunications sector as belonging to the 'hard core' of national autonomy, ensured its exclusion from the competition rules in the Treaty of Rome from the beginning (Pelkmans and Young 1998: 26–7). Traditionally, the need for national security and complete national coverage at 'equal and affordable prices' (what was later to be called universal service) in communications was used as an additional political argument to keep both telecommunications and the postal monopolies well within the competencies of the nation-state.

Regulation of telecommunications in the context of the European Communities received little attention until the Green Paper of 1987. The speed with which this was done after 1987 provides an interesting study of the way the EU has extended its influence to a national sector where it previously would have been unable to act.

The system of 'national champions' was increasingly seen as restricting the European CPE manufacturers' ability to compete in design and innovation with the American and Japanese, and that some kind of co-ordination in research and development was necessary to avoid a European slump in the sector. The earlier system of national-level regulation was gradually replaced by a system in which the European Commission played a central role.

The first steps – harmonisation rather than legislation

The EC's initial strategy was not to use legislation to regulate the sector, since it lacked both the legitimacy and the resources to do this in the early 1980s. Instead, it chose to encourage harmonisation of networks and equipment. This was achieved by means of pan-European standardisation bodies, set up as a part of the EC strategy to harmonise technical standards throughout the region, in order to prepare for one single market in which goods could flow freely. This strategy was continued and integrated in the Trans-European Networks programmes (Turner 1997). In the Commission, a Special Task Force was set up within DG III to advise Commissioner Davignon about the prospects for reform. At this stage, the Commission laid the seeds of a genuinely European system, and its efforts were successful with many of the actors involved in the process. Commissioner Davignon played an important role during the early years of the process, to the extent that he could be called a 'visionary' of a Europe with a truly harmonised telecommunications sector. He was instrumental in gaining the crucial support of industry for the principle of EC-defined standards, and it was this, coupled with the zeal shown in persuading national governments of the benefits of collective action, that enabled many of the advances to take place (see Sandholtz 1993).

The effect of telecommunications on 'numerous other branches of activity' was recognised from the late 1970s. Several bodies were set up during these early years, predominantly composed of both officials from the Commission and also representatives of the Member States, emphasising the Commission's need to work in close partnership with the national governments. The industry, too, co-operated in establishing these standards, since there was a widespread recognition of the benefits from a 'research and development' point of view. The Commission had in its Community Action Programme on Telecommunications in 1984 identified three directions for Community effort in the field of telecommunications. First, network development for advanced services; second, a Community-wide market for equipment; and third, emphasis on forefront research and development (Kramer 1992). The only genuinely cross-national body in existence prior to this was CEPT (the European

Conference of Postal and Telecommunications Administrations) which was effectively a lobby group for the European PTOs, and concerned with neither liberalisation nor European co-operation.

The Commission also sought to promote trans-European co-operation through the establishment and co-funding of ambitious R&D programmes. The most important and long-running example of this would be the ESPRIT and RACE programmes. (The 'European Strategic Programme for Research and Development in Information Technology' and 'Research and Development in Advanced Communications', respectively). These can be seen as Commission attempts to gain a central position in the development of technology, but also as a recognition by many Member States that their national markets individually were too small to sustain the investment needed to keep their 'national champions' at the forefront of technology. However, there is little doubt that the Commission played a significant role in mobilising co-operation in this field (Sandholtz 1993).

Davignon identified the problems of European R&D compared to the American and Japanese, and invited representatives of the industry to sit on a 'Roundtable' which led directly to a plan for collaborative R&D programmes. This plan became ESPRIT in 1983, which was a programme covering thirty-eight separate areas of technological research (chosen by the Commission from over two hundred proposals) and jointly funded by the Commission and industry to the tune of 1.5 billion ECU. The programme was a success, and whetted the industry's appetite for trans-European collaboration, which would be vital when the Single Market became a reality. The programme was extended for five years in 1987.

The RACE programme, commencing in 1985, fulfilled a similar role, with greater emphasis on standards-setting by all the actors involved in the process, but also concentrating specifically on telecommunications. ESPRIT was primarily about developing new information technology systems, so RACE was the closest thing to a true Europe-wide programme for telecommunications R&D (Sandholtz 1993). The relationship between the EC and the industry was characterised by collaboration rather than conflict, which made the introduction of a more liberalised regime for PTO procurement more harmonious, given that the previously dominant CPE manufacturers were the big losers in the liberalisation process in this area.

First legislative strategies

The first real Commission initiative came with the 'lines of action', which it proposed to the Council at the beginning of 1983. These lines of action formed the basis for a telecommunications action plan, approved by the Council in 1984. They were a continuation of the previous strategy, and laid great stress on the research and design aspects of the sector. The most telling part of the package, perhaps, was what was left out. The Commission made no attempt to change the status of the PTOs, showing that the Member States, at this point, were determined to keep the status quo intact. There was not yet sufficient momentum for the entrenched national systems to be reformed.

What the package did do was to lay down the basis for the liberalisation of the market for terminal equipment. EC standards were to become the norm for this equipment, a prerequisite for introducing Europe-wide offerings of contracts for telecommunications equipment. This 'functional' strategy is an example of the Commission's use of technological advance to secure a more 'political' end – a technique which it would use more often in the following years.

The Commission also practised breaking the sector down into segments and hence regulating slices of the industry separately and at different times, rather than attempting to legislate for the industry as a whole. They broadly distinguished between three components: the *network,* i.e. the physical cables and switches which enable the data or sounds to be transmitted, including satellites; the *services*, including voice telephony, value-added network services (banking services) and data transmission; and third, the manufacturing of *CPE,* i.e. the technological equipment such as telephones, modems, fax machines and switching equipment (see Thatcher 1994).

The external impetus

There were, however, direct political events occurring in the field of telecommunications at this time which were to have an equally profound and catalytic effect on the Commission's liberalisation agenda. In the United States, the New Right government had decided on a 'big bang' deregulation and privatisation programme for its telecommunications sector (see Hills 1986). The de facto monopolist, AT&T, was forced to divest its regional operators (the so-called Baby Bells), and its monopoly was removed, paving the way for a more meaningful competition in a way which was impossible in Europe at that time.

The US programme of deregulation affected the European situation in two main ways. First, it was an example of the way a liberalisation programme could succeed and bring with it real benefits, and second, reciprocal liberalisation in the European market was insisted upon by the US government. If European companies were to be allowed to compete freely in the American market, then American companies should have the right to establish themselves in the European market – a situation impossible under the regulated monopolies of the PTOs. It was not first and foremost the providers of the 'plain old telephony service' who wanted to access the European market. The real pressure came from the manufacturing and especially the computer industry, mainly in the form of the American computer manufacturer IBM.

In 1984, the first programme of privatisation took place in Britain, as the Thatcher government, operating under a similar New Right ideology as the American administration, began to sell off the telecommunications wing of the GPO as British Telecom. British Telecom was therefore the first European PTO to be privatised. The British experience clearly showed the need for sector-specific regulation in a liberalised market (see Chapter 6), a lesson which was not missed by the European Commission.

There were other impetuses for the Commission to intervene in Europe's telecommunications market, especially in the area of CPE. Despite Europe's relatively strong performance in innovation, American and Japanese companies were becoming increasingly, and ominously, competitive in the field of advanced technology. Two British writers were sufficiently moved at the time to paraphrase a philosopher not given to eulogising the free market when they described the American/Japanese threat as 'a spectre haunting Europe' (Dyson and Humphreys 1986).

The Commission saw that the only way the European companies could keep up would be by the twin means of co-operation across Europe, and a Single Market for CPE within it. Hence this external pressure contributed to the Commission's attempts to liberalise this sector, arguing that the industry had to rationalise in order to survive. The Single Market approach resulted in an increased trade in CPE Europe-wide, but attempts to build genuine cross-national alliances between companies in this area, despite the ESPRIT and RACE programmes, were less successful. The Commission was worried about the prospects for European technological companies, and its efforts were directed at preventing complete American/Japanese dominance of the sector.

The changing role of the telecommunications sector

In understanding the way in which the telecommunications sector changed during the 1980s, it is crucial to see the way that governments of all levels – national and EU – changed their perception of the tele-communications sector and its role within the national and European economy. During the years in which the PTOs operated a relatively simple voice telephony service under the auspices of their governments, telecommunications were mainly seen as a public service, but little more. The monopoly PTOs were widely perceived as inefficient organisations not attuned to the private sector doctrines of profit and performance. Moreover, as customer demand became more fragmented (Stoffaës 1995: 14; Broadman and Balassa 1993), old-style public administration organisations had a hard time meeting the demand for specialised services. However, as technology developed during the early 1980s and the business community began to demand more complex and innovative services, the role of telecommunications in the generation of wealth became more evident. As the technology for the fast transferral of large amounts of data became more widely used, it was seen that the quality of a national telecommunications infrastructure and technology were becoming vital to a nation's economic competitiveness.

The Commission later used this argument on a Europe-wide basis for the efficiency benefits of its liberalisation programme for the European economy. Hence, one has to understand the development of the telecommunications sector's role in the national economies to fully comprehend why it assumed a far more central role in public policy-making. It was driven by three formidable forces: business demand for more advanced services and global networks; national governments' growing awareness of its centrality to national competitiveness; and the massive technological advances eventually leading to 'The Information Society'. The liberalisation of the sector can be seen in part as a means of stimulating development of technology and services (for discussions on regulation and innovation, see Antonelli 1997; Borthwick and Stehmann 1994; Grupp and Schnöring 1992). As a corollary of the standardisation programme established earlier, it was widely perceived that greater competition, both in CPE and for telecommunications services would lead to a culture of innovation and therefore increased benefits for both consumers and the wider economy. Moreover, a liberalised telecommunications network would make the country an attractive hub for multinational companies' global telecommunications networks, and thereby attract investment.

Telecommunications reform – the member states' perspectives

During the 1980s, all European countries were forced to re-evaluate their policies towards telecommunications. While it was the Commission that attempted to meld the differing debates in each country into a set of concrete proposals and directions in the 1987 Green Paper, it would be instructive to look at a number of the strategies considered by individual Member States at this time.

The Witte Commission in Germany was a good example of a Member State seeking to reform its telecommunications system on its own terms (Witte 1988). Its rationale for action was the increasing fragmentation of demand for telecommunications services, the need for a rapid implementation of an innovative infrastructure, and the pressing necessity of delineating the role of state-owned entities in relation to the emerging competitive environment (Witte 1988: 22–3). In addition, it was clear that Deutsche Bundespost would have difficulties meeting the new demands without substantial change. 'As the present legal status of the Deutsche Bundespost would make it difficult to adopt [the necessary flexible] approach, the need for action aimed at removing the obstacles to an active market policy on the part of Deutsche Bundespost becomes evident' (Witte 1988: 27). The Witte Commission suggested that the telecommunications branch should be administratively separated from the postal service and set up as DBP Telekom, with greater autonomy from governmental control (see also Chapter 8). However, it would be allowed to retain its monopoly on the basic network and on voice telephony (which amounted to around 90 per cent of all business).

This approach was indicative of many of the European states' initial antipathy towards 'true' liberalisation, as they preferred to retain some degree of privilege for the national carrier. In France, the government opened up for limited competition in CPE in the mid-1980s (see Dang-Nguyen 1988), but the socialist government in power from 1981 to 1986 was reluctant to introduce competition in the sector. The operation of telecommunications was under the administration of a 'functional office within the state administration', in 1988 given the name France Télécom. As late as 1990, the French government was reaffirming the right of France Télécom to retain a monopoly over the basic telecommunications services.

The Benelux countries also undertook similar cautious programmes of reform, whilst leaving the significant services immune from competition (Verhoest 1995). Only in Britain did the government institute any degree of meaningful liberalisation of the core services during these years (see Chapter 6), but BT's status as a private company meant that there was far less political risk attached to this strategy. Besides, weak regulation and a long period of transition from monopoly to competition meant that BT was able to maintain its dominant status comfortably during these years.

The 1987 green paper on telecommunications

The 1987 Commission Green Paper on Telecommunications (COM(87)290 final 1987) was the bedrock on which all subsequent reforms were built, and marked the point of departure for the liberalisation of certain segments and for systematic EU legislation (Scherer 1998: 1). It was an ambitious document, emerging from a Commission that had finally begun to believe that it could legislate to achieve its desired ends. The Commission was now acting with a great deal more authority and autonomy, and the scope of the paper reflects this. It marked an important step in the Commission's drive to make Member States aware of the benefits of, and need for, liberalisation, and demonstrated their willingness to legislate actively to ensure that the process of liberalisation took place. It has to be remembered that there was a growing feeling in many Member States that liberalisation was 'a good idea', and that many of the Commission's proposals might have emanated directly from the national administrations. Expressed at EC level it reduced the possibility of controversy at the national level. The Paper was, therefore, both a crystallisation of many of the national positions in the debate at this time, and also reinforced and extended many of the Commission's previously stated aims and objectives.

The principles of the Paper are worth examining in some detail since they provide a full and clear explication of the Commission's objectives, and all future developments must be understood in this context. The main rationale for this document was the long-standing view that the competition provisions in the Treaty of Rome needed to be applied to the telecommunications sector. The industry as it stood was in breach of, or at least going against the spirit of, the competition clauses in the Treaty of Rome. The PTOs represented an unacceptable monopoly in their sector, whilst the 'cartel' system relating to the national champions was particularly restrictive. The 1987 Green Paper set out to remedy this. One should also note the consultative nature of this exercise – consensus was reached with the Member States on most, if not all of the Commission's proposals. However, the document should be seen as much as a strategy for advancing and improving the telecommunications sector as a doctrinaire application of the EC's competition policy.

It is important to bear in mind that the Green Paper did not require a fundamental change in the status of the PTOs – they could remain as public bodies and retain their monopoly on basic telephone networks and infrastructure. This was in accordance with the findings of almost all the policy review bodies in the Member States, such as the Witte Commission detailed above, and demonstrated that the Member States were not yet ready to surrender the monopolistic position on basic services, nor be bounced into the kind of privatisation measures introduced in Britain and the US. There was also concern that preserving a universal service would require cross-subsidisation between services, since the policy hitherto in most countries had been to substantially overprice long-distance calls to the benefit of access charges, as well as to use the telecommunications operators as 'cash cows' for the Treasury (Kramer 1992; EIU 1995). However, the Commission recognised the need at this point for investment in the telephone infrastructures, and saw that this could best be achieved with the PTOs in public ownership and receiving sufficient revenue to make this possible.

The most far-reaching and influential of the provisions in the Green Paper are related to Open Network Provision (ONP), laying down rules for access to the transmission network. Access to the means of transmission is crucial to the development of competition. This provision remains the bedrock for the liberalisation and diversification of the tele-communications industry. ONP was designed to ensure that the public network operators were inhibited from frustrating competition by limiting access to the networks, thereby retaining their dominant market position not by efficiency and innovation, but by uncompetitive practices. Under the new ONP regime, any service provider could connect to the network as long as its equipment met the ETSI-defined standards. This harmonisation of access conditions to the network had the twin benefit of allowing new, smaller companies the crucial foothold necessary to begin meaningful competition, and also allow the PTOs in each country to take advantage of the European market as a whole, thereby increasing their competitiveness. The ONP provisions were to be crucial as the European market liberalised fully in the 1990s, when all services were opened to competition.

The other crucial requirement for this new regime was that the roles of market regulation and service provision were split, to ensure transparency in the sector. The idea of separation of regulation and operation had been forwarded in several countries, and resulted in administrative changes in many Member States around the turn of the decade, whereby operators were either defined as separate units, or (later) corporatised. Later, the ONP directive demanded the establishment of a National Regulatory Authority independent from the industry, which in most cases (with the exception of Italy) has resulted in an independent agency (see Chapter 4).

Liberalisation of CPE, satellite and mobile

The Terminal Equipment Directive – the first use of Article 90 in the telecommunications sector

In 1988, the Commission turned its attention to the liberalisation of CPE, something that had been called for in previous years, but not fully implemented. The main objective of the 1988 Terminal Equipment Directive is to gradually open the market for terminal equipment.

The Terminal Equipment Directive was issued as a directive under the Treaty of Rome Article 90(3), which empowers the Commission to address directives to Member States in order to ensure that Member States neither enact nor keep in force any measure which is contrary to the Treaty rules with respect to their telecommunications operators as holders of exclusive rights (Scherer 1998: 4). The use of Article 90 forced the Council to progress in the liberalisation process, and was significant in its implications for the pace of setting up a Community-wide legislative framework for the sector. The Directive was immediately contested by some Member States, and was brought before the European Court of Justice. The main claim was that the Commission by applying Article 90 in this context had acted outside of its competencies.

The legal process took almost 30 months to complete, but in March 1991 the Court of Justice stated that the Terminal Equipment Directive was to be upheld, at least in its most central parts. In particular, the Court held that the Commission had within its competencies to specify the relevant obligations of the Member States under the Treaty including the specification and limitation of exclusive rights, and that the abolition of exclusive rights in this field also was justified with reference to the principle of free movement of goods. One should also note that the Court in the same ruling limited the use of Article 90 to issues concerning *state measures*, and as such cannot be used to regulate anti-competitive behaviour of the relevant undertakings themselves (Scherer 1998: 5–6).

The directive obliges the Member States to abolish all 'exclusive rights' of their telecommunications operators regarding use and marketing for terminal equipment ('terminal equipment' includes telephone sets, private automatic branch exchanges, data transmission terminals and mobile telephones); to ensure that private suppliers can participate in the terminal equipment market; and to ensure that users have access to new public network termination points. In order to ensure a European market in terminal equipment, directives have been issued that establish the principle of full mutual recognition of type-approval. Hence, equipment that is approved in one Member State can freely be sold throughout the European Community.

Satellite communications

In 1990, the Commission published its Green Paper on satellite communications ('Towards Europe-wide systems and services'), designed to establish a more flexible regulatory system and foster the growth of satellite services. The case of satellite communications offers a good example of the difficulties in separating between regulation and operation of services, notably because of the many levels of interested parties. Regarding distribution of televised programmes, the regulatory authority lies within the nation-states, whereas access to the means of satellite communications was organised through international organisations such as Eutelsat, Intelsat and Inmarsat.

The Commission proposed in its Green Paper to extend the principles of abolition of special rights, of free and unrestricted access, and of harmonisation, to the satellite segment. These measures were seen to be paramount if a European market in satellite services were to be achieved.

Mobile communications

The mobile communications market was regulated very early in its development by the EC, through the setting of a European technical standard, the GSM. Prior to 1987, five different systems for mobile phones had been developed in the EU Member States (Scherer 1998: 8). As a consequence, mobile phones had low penetration throughout Europe. The exception to this was the Scandinavian countries, where the

NMT (Nordic Mobile Telephones) standard had been in use since the early 1980s. In 1987, the Council of Ministers adopted a recommendation for the introduction of the GSM standard (see Chapter 13 for an extended history of mobile communications).

The Mobile Directive entered fully into force in November 1996, and abolished the remaining exclusive rights within this market segment. The Mobile Directive requires that mobile licences be put out to competitive tender. In 1997, eighteen DCS1800 licences were granted amidst fierce competition. This sector is widely predicted, along with Internet technology, to be one of the fastest-growing areas of telecommunications in the next decade, both in terms of technology and volume of subscribers.

How did full liberalisation come about?

The most significant measure to have influenced the hitherto last round of Commission directives was the EU Telecom Review's consensus in 1993 that full liberalisation could not be restricted to the areas of VANS and other more marginal services. It would have to extend throughout the entire sector – local, long-distance and international calls, and all services and infrastructure. This was, of course, the logical extension of the Commission's position since the 1987 Green Paper. Ever since the Paper had recommended partial liberalisation in certain areas, the then 'reserved services', namely voice telephony, were the obvious next port of call as circumstances allowed. This required a revision of the ONP provisions, since they were originally designed to ensure an open market for VANS rather than voice telephony. It remains, however, the natural framework for the interconnection and access to infrastructure under the new fully liberalised regime.

The new regime was laid down in the ONP Interconnection Directive, passed in 1997. This replaced the concept of the monopoly network operator with the idea of many public network operators acting in competition. The Commission reintroduced the idea of rights and duties for these operators, with the rights referring to unfettered market and network access, and the duties to the obligation to guarantee universal service. Those companies with 'significant market power', defined as over 25 per cent of the market share, have a 'general duty to supply'. Universal service means that every citizen has a right to access to a certain set of basic telecommunications services at 'affordable prices'. The exact content of the concept of 'basic services' is left to the Member States to decide upon. For the time being, only the incumbent operators have sufficient market share to fall under the obligations of universal service.

There is, however, considerable political leverage in this question, as the question of 'affordable prices' is seen to entail a need for subsidisation of certain users. The problem of settling the debates about who should pay is handled differently in different countries. In France, a universal service 'fund' is established, to which all dominant operators will contribute. In Germany, however, there are legal provisions in place for the establishment of such a fund, but this will come into power only when no operator volunteers to supply the services. Taking into account that the operators then will have to contribute a certain percentage of their turnover to this fund, it seems reasonable to predict that no such fund will exist in Germany for a long time yet.

It must be noted that despite its long gestation period, the Full Competition Directive was still ambitious in setting an absolute deadline for every Member State to liberalise their telecommunications completely. Many states sought derogations from the Commission, claiming that their industries were simply not ready to liberalise. Some of these were granted, as in the case of Ireland. The national carrier, Telecom Eireann, had carried out a massive development of its network, and the investment necessary had led it into debt. Thus the immediate effect of a fully competitive market would have been disastrous to the company, as it needed the revenues from its continuing monopoly to justify its investment in the network. Similar 'structural' issues were claimed by other states, notably Greece, which was granted an extra year to carry out the necessary reforms. So the European states varied in their ability to implement the directive.

For those Member States who did not comply with regulation within the time frame, the Commission took action, first in the form of informal talks, and in more severe cases by taking Member States to court. This illustrates the 'guiding principle' of the DG IV in this question, that is it better to start the process on time even if the result is not perfect, rather than to await completely harmonised implemented legislation in all Member States. The final deadline for full liberalisation is 1 January 2000, even with the derogations, but it is unclear whether all states will be able to implement it even within the extended time-period.

1998 and beyond – the 'brave new world'

Let us now examine the 'brave new world' of post-1998 liberalised telecommunications. Now that special and exclusive rights over networks and services have been removed, what does this mean for the industry? The most obvious effect of the liberalisation has been the proliferation of new actors in the market. Small firms have been freed to compete with the previously dominant operators, and many such companies are taking the opportunity to undercut the larger operators and offer new and innovative services such as combined entertainment–Internet–telephony applications. The mobile market in particular has seen an explosion in the number of companies bidding for licences and providing services. Moreover, operators previously restricted to operate within their national boundaries are now expanding their markets and form joint ventures and alliances with other companies.

While the newer companies are finding their feet and establishing niches in the market, it appears that life beyond the 1998 market will be equally challenging for the former incumbent operators and dominant players. Many are having to face the uncomfortable realities of declining market share as the corporate sector in particular begins to take advantage of the services and savings offered by liberalisation. British Telecom's market share is expected to drop to 'only' 62 per cent in the early years of the next decade, and other incumbent operators are suffering similar or worse falls as the competition bites into their domestic markets. Cable companies have proven keen to expand their communications activities into telecommunications areas, and are routinely offering prices 10–20 per cent lower than on the conventional networks. The German regulator set its interconnection rates a good deal lower than Deutsche Telekom had anticipated – a clear sign that the older companies, at least in some countries, cannot expect preferential treatment from the newly empowered regulators (*Financial Times*, November 1997).

Questions are nevertheless being asked about the regime as it exists, and the next few years will see a growing debate about the way the new order is regulated. The Commission has gone about the task of ensuring that new market players have the ability to compete by introducing sector-specific legislation, that is, by laying certain obligations on the dominant market players in areas such as interconnection fees and numbering as well as the universal service obligations. This is obviously to the benefit of the smaller companies, but many of the largest companies – those with the most to lose – are muttering about market distortions caused by over-zealous regulation. The Commission seems to believe that only by legislating can dominant players be forced to allow free and fair access to the networks. The trend seems to be that the new operators will be given a 'window' by the legislation in order to gain a foothold, but the Commission cannot intervene in the regulation of national markets, simply because of their lack of legitimacy.

One can speculate, however, as to whether competition policy is the best instrument for the regulation of a European telecommunications sector. The question is whether, and possibly when, such a change will take place, but there is a powerful and vocal body which contends that a free market in telecommunications should mean just that. There is also some debate over whether a European Regulatory Authority will be necessary to police the new European market, and the industry seems guardedly in favour. A body such as this would be in line with the more federal arrangements in other telecommunications markets such as the United States, but the prospects for such a body in Europe are slim.

It is clear that a new culture of innovation and flexibility is beginning to pervade the previously relatively static and complacent PTOs, and this is nowhere better seen that in their attitude towards developing global strategies, rather than relying solely on the European market. Liberalisation and privatisation have freed the PTOs to seek mergers and alliances throughout the world, designed to protect their position against the new competition. British Telecom, for example, is part of a global telecommunications network known as Concert, in partnership with American and European telecommunications firms, aiming to provide a globally comprehensive service to business customers. Similarly, Deutsche Telekom and France Télécom are involved in an alliance called Global One with the American firm Sprint. This kind of vision was completely lacking in the PTOs prior to liberalisation, and demonstrates the way that deregulation and autonomy from national administrations has freed them to compete in the global marketplace.

With the Full Competition Directive, the Commission has made the last of its major legislative interventions in the sector. Having established the conditions for free competition, its role now is likely to be confined to enforcing Community legislation and policing the market as it settles into the new circumstances. Moreover, new technologies provide new challenges for the regulators. The Commission considered the case of voice telephony over the Internet in 1997, and concluded that it should not be classed according to the conventional voice telephony rules, but that attention would need to be paid to this area in the future as technology made it of better quality. Convergence of technologies raises the question of regulation across sectors, in one way the age-old problem of regulating technologies instead of end-products, but now with a complicating layer of institutional competition and cultural traditions.

It has been a bumpy ride for all the actors involved in the process – in common with most other programmes of trans-European interaction and integration – but liberalisation does seem to have delivered a stronger, more vibrant and outward-looking telecommunications sector for Europe. Whether full competition can be sustained in a market where gigantic mergers are becoming more and more commonplace, and the EU will see many of its current regulatory powers dissipated, however, remains to be seen.

3   Competing approaches to regulation

Martin Lodge

Reforms in the regulation of telecommunications have been at the spear-head of national policy programmes. The rhetoric of privatisation, deregulation and liberalisation has spread across Europe and beyond. Nevertheless, the issues of regulation, the rules, standards and their enforcement remain crucial for the development of the emerging markets in telecommunications. Since the 1980s the control of economic activities are said to have undergone a fundamental transformation, not only in telecommunications, but also in key industrial sectors such as financial markets or transport. Multiple pressures, ranging from technical-economic to supra-national factors and to the 'fiscal crisis of the state' in the 1970s, are held responsible for a shift in the attention of policy-makers, particularly in Western Europe, from traditional issues of questions of ownership and welfare provision to the study of rule and incentive structures as a means of political control of economic activities. Regulation – 'the sustained and focused control exercised by a public agency over activities that are valued by a community' (Selznick 1985: 363) – has therefore become one of the most crucial aspects of policy-making. This chapter does not deal solely with issues of tele-communication regulation, but also draws on some key issues discussed in the general regulation literature in political science and on experiences in other regulated industries in order to provide an overall perspective on regulation.

Competition between approaches to regulation occurs on two levels. First, on the national level, competing approaches to regulation indicate diverse national preferences and institutional traditions. Second, on the analytical level, competition exists between those arguments, which regard regulation as a functional response to market failure, and those which regard regulation as a product of 'capture'. A third strand in the literature concerned with questions of institutional design has shown that these two analytical approaches are not mutually exclusive. The following provides an account of some of the issues raised in the literature. After a review of three analytical strands on regulation, four organisational modes of regulation are presented and discussed. Finally, the issue of the emergence of the regulatory state is elaborated. Only limited attention will be paid to issues such as explanations of regulatory change (see Hood 1994: 19–36), discussions on the multiplicity of regulatory instruments or explanations of persistent national variations in regulation (see Chapter 15).

Views on regulation

Without claiming to be jointly exhaustive or mutually exclusive, here are three imaginary statements which provide perspectives on how to view regulation:

View I: Regulation as an act of benevolence

'Of course, it is necessary to regulate. Think of the protection of customers. In an industry which has natural monopoly characteristics with falling long-run average costs, only one firm is needed to supply the socially desired output efficiently and effectively. Customers have to be protected from the potential exploitation of a monopolist and require certain guaranteed levels of services. The state has also to intervene and regulate in order to counter externalities and information asymmetries.'

This view provides the standard arguments of welfare economics, which claims that regulation overcomes market failures and is beneficial. It highlights the key areas where regulation is said to be important and reflects the most widely used arguments to advocate regulation.

View II: Regulation as a conspiracy

'Regulation is a pure waste of resources. It is merely in the interest of those who are supposed to be regulated and protects their market shares by restricting market entry. As is well known, a "public interest" does not exist. Politicians are self-interested and will therefore provide regulation to further their re-election chances or job opportunities for their post-political life in the regulated industry. Regulators are usually captured and protect their jobs or act in other unaccountable ways. Political control hardly exists as it is mainly exercised by those who are most interested in the well-being of the industry.'

This view highlights the potential downside of regulatory activities. Actors promote regulation to further their self-interests such as the protection of market share, re-election chances or bureaucratic inefficiencies, called 'slack'.

View III: Regulation as a question of design

'Of crucial importance are issues such as agency relations, repeated games and the minimisation of transaction costs between actors such as citizens, politicians, agencies and regulated industries. Politicians will, given certain circumstances, delegate regulatory supervision in order to shift responsibility for unpopular decisions to non-political, administrative bodies. Regulatory instruments will be selected in order to minimise transaction costs and to make the policy irreversible. At the heart of regulatory problems lies not so much the problem of collective action, but information asymmetries. By institutionalising the participation of interests other than those of the regulated industry in the regulatory process as well as political control mechanisms, the possibilities of capture can be reduced.'

While the benevolence and conspiracy views offer competing approaches to regulation, the 'design' perspective regards regulation as neither evil nor good. The literature stresses the importance of the calculations and choices of legislators in designing regulatory institutions, which do not necessarily have to reflect a functional response to perceived market failures or some form of 'capture'.

This categorisation of approaches to regulation following these three views, the benevolence, the conspiracy and the design perspective, does not claim to represent all strands of the literature or to be mutually exclusive. Nevertheless, particularly the benevolence and the conspiracy views are widely utilised in regulatory disputes, for example in food safety or advertisement regulation. The issues raised in the literature therefore provide valuable parameters for analysing regulatory developments.

The account of regulation as the product of a benevolent state has been the traditional standard explanation of regulation. The market failure argument 'consists of a litany of ways in which the conditions for competitive equilibrium may fail to be satisfied' (Noll 1989: 1255; see also Ogus 1994: 1–71). Regulated industries are regarded as a natural monopoly with falling long-run average costs. Although a single firm can supply the goods at minimal costs, regulation in the form of output or price controls is required to prevent exploitation by the monopolist supplier in order to maximise social welfare.

Regulation is also supposed to be required should the product exhibit public-good characteristics, thus making exclusion from the consumption of the good too costly. Negative externalities, such as pollution, are supposed to be best tackled by regulation in order to internalise social costs of production into the cost function of the polluter. In cases of information asymmetries, regulation is said to help consumers arrive at optimal choices in their selection of goods (see Akerlof 1974).

Despite the widespread use of the arguments of a costless and benevolent regulator (others speak of the normative theory of regulation), evidence, mainly from the US, has not confirmed these assumptions. Doron, for example, has shown that the ban on cigarette advertising supported rather than harmed the position of the cigarette industry which was locked into an oligopolistic market (Doron 1979). Neither does the world of regulation seem to be positively correlated with the presence of economies of scale, supposed market failures or monopolistic market structures (see Mueller 1989: 235–8). Theoretical arguments exploring ways in which natural monopolies might be controlled, such as by establishing 'contestable markets' (Baumol 1977) or by 'competition for the market' via franchising (Demsetz 1969)[1] have also challenged the theoretical case for the necessity of natural monopoly regulation. However, despite these powerful challenges to the benevolence view of regulation, attempts to explain recent regulatory changes have led to a re-emergence of a public interest view of regulation: regulatory reform is explained by the emergence of new ideas, a receptive political climate and heroic political entrepreneurs (see, for example Keeler 1984; Derthick and Quirk 1985).

The conspiracy view of regulation has been advanced by a multitude of schools of thought ranging from Marxists to free marketeers, usually claiming that the 'public interest' has been captured and perverted by private interests. Marver Bernstein argued that regulatory agencies follow a 'life-cycle' from initial regulatory enthusiasm to decay. The establishment of a regulatory agency tends to follow a major policy fiasco and is usually heavily contested, with a dispersed group strongly advocating the imposition of regulation on a particular issue on the one side, against the concentrated interest of the affected industry on the other (Bernstein 1955). As a result, the founding statute reflects a bland ensemble which provides the agency with little scope for effective regulatory action. Over time, the interest and attention paid to the regulatory issue dwindles among the pro-regulation coalition and the vote-seeking politicians. As a result, the agency, in the medium term, is left to deal with the continuing lobbying efforts of the affected industry on its own. Being politically isolated and becoming tired of continuous regulatory fights with the industry, regulators over time either leave or become disillusioned. To maximise regulatory 'good-life', a close relationship with the regulated industry emerges where the agency regards the maintenance of the status quo as its primary duty and becomes the core advocate for the industry. In this way, regulatory agencies follow a seemingly inevitable 'life-cycle' of regulatory decay.[2] Kolko (1965), in contrast, argued that the origins of (US railway) regulation rested in the self-interested demands of the industry seeking a stabilisation of markets by eliminating competition.

Using microeconomic assumptions, Stigler claimed that 'as a rule, regulation is acquired by the industry and is designed and operated primarily for its benefit' (Stigler 1971: 3). Every industry which can organise collective action effectively will attempt to make politicians restrict entry into its industry. Regulation, being inefficient in social terms, is an outcome of inefficiencies in the democratic marketplace due to asymmetrical costs in organising collective action. Politicians, solely interested in their re-election by securing votes or resources, will offer regulation to those who provide the highest pay-off. Thus, policy outputs will favour 'low cost' groups (groups which are able to deliver the promised 'goods' after regulatory action due to low information and organisation costs) rather than fragmented constituencies ('high cost groups'). As business groups are generally better organisable and organised than consumer or even taxpayers' groups, a utility-maximising politician-regulator will become an advocate of the regulated industry. If all interests affected by a regulatory decision faced equal transaction costs, efficient outcomes would occur (see Becker 1983).

Despite the rhetorical attractiveness of the concept of regulatory capture, Stigler's account cannot explain the growth and endurance of social and environmental regulation which has favoured dispersed constituencies rather than concentrated industry interests (for example, Posner 1974). Indeed, agencies have been set up with the explicit aim of preventing capture (G. Wilson 1984). Moreover, the assumption that regulated industries are monolithic and therefore can easily organise and maintain collective action seems questionable (Williams 1976).

'Capture', therefore, is rather a special case of interest-group explanations of the politics of regulation, which regards regulation as the outcome of coalitions of various interests built by utility-maximising regulator-politicians (Peltzman 1976, 1989). Peltzman's regulators will allocate benefits across groups to maximise their utility. As long as consumers can offer votes or material resources in exchange for a minor shift from a purely producer-dominated policy, the regulator will include some input from consumers. How the trade-off is calculated depends on the nature of costs and benefits of the losers and winners of the policy (J.Q. Wilson 1980). In cases of capture, costs will be widely dispersed while benefits are concentrated, whereas concentrated costs and benefits lead to interest group politics as witnessed in UK railway freight rates before 1921. Similarly, in cases of environmental regulation, coalitions between dedicated environmentalists, so-called 'baptists', on the one side, and 'bootleggers', producers who receive a competitive advantage from producing to higher standards, on the other side, will achieve higher rather than lower product-related standard regulations. Thus, (then West) Germany's strong emphasis on introducing the catalytic converter for cars in countries of the EC from the mid-1980s was a product of the demands of such a coalition between 'Baptists' and 'Bootleggers', the latter consisting of the car industry, which due to its strong US export markets in large cars was already producing cars fitted with US-standard catalytic converters (D. Vogel 1995).

In most of the 'conspiracy' literature the focus rests on interests, i.e. the actors in the marketplace, the agora, who pressure actors on the acropolis, i.e. those at the centre of political decision-making, to provide certain beneficial policies. However, as regulation is formally made on the 'acropolis', any analysis therefore has to include the incentives, motivations and orientation of the political and bureaucratic actors therein (see Barke and Riker 1982). For example, it has been argued that regulated industries are less responsible for problems of 'capture' than inadequate political provision of funding and organisational resources (Williams 1976). Furthermore, regulators are usually not politicians but bureaucratic actors and should therefore be regarded as an interest in their own right (Hirshleifer 1976). In sum, 'conspiracy' accounts need to include the incentives and actions of the decision-making political, bureaucratic and regulatory actors on the 'acropolis'.

Regulation is not only a struggle of actors from the agora to capture actors on the acropolis. Actors from the acropolis also descend to win over various constituencies in the agora. Moreover, the paths between agora and acropolis are not straightforward and obstacle-free and variations in regulatory outcomes can be accounted for by differences in these paths and by the institutional positions of the actors. Furthermore, regulatory action may not necessarily be the result of collective action. Actors may be 'lucky' in that they obtain a favourable policy outcome without having to organise collective action (see Barry 1995; Dowding 1991, 1996). Although these additional dimensions to the 'conspiracy' view of regulatory policy thwart the clarity and potential testability of the original accounts, they highlight the diversity of interests which may influence regulatory policy.

Whereas institutions play only a minor role in the 'benevolence' and 'conspiracy' views, they feature strongly in the 'design' literature. The key questions addressed there are why regulatory tasks are delegated and how principal-agent problems can be overcome. The potential consequences of the delegation of policy tasks represents a substantial part of the legislators' calculations (Fiorina 1982). The legislator's individual choice is a trade-off between the desire to shift responsibility and decision-making costs by delegating tasks to an administrative unit and the desire to claim credit for vote-gaining policy outcomes: 'legislators not only avoid the time and trouble of making specific decisions, they avoid or at least disguise their responsibilities for the consequence of the decisions ultimately made' (Fiorina 1982: 47). The extent of the trade-off depends on the interest group configuration in the policy sector and will not only involve legislator-agency relations but also overall legislators' decision-making and participation costs, policy commitment costs and agency costs (see also Horn 1995: 7–39, 46–7).[3] Further arguments explaining delegation have focused on the need to concentrate expertise in an autonomous body, or to provide for wider and flexible consultation procedures than are feasible under the rules guiding government departments. Other explanations of the growth of agencies rest on the need to show policy action or to hide the true size of government (Baldwin and McCrudden 1987: 3–12). The emergence of regulatory agencies has also been explained by the need to show policy commitment (Majone 1996: 40–5). By delegating policy implementation to agencies, governments are said to indicate their willingness to abdicate policy discretion and to ensure policy consistency over time.

The question 'quis custodiet ipsos custodes?'[4] lies at the heart of principal-agent problems. Control mechanisms are sought in order to prevent both 'bureaucratic drift' and 'coalitional drift' from the initial intended policy outcomes. Structural solutions involve the allocation of resources and decisional authority within a regulatory agency, whereas procedural control solutions rely on administrative procedures which set the rules and standards applying to the agencies' policy decisions (McCubbins, Noll and Weingast 1987). At the core of both rests the problem of information asymmetries, including the unequal distribution of information and expertise and the potential agenda-setting ability of the 'agent'.

Structural design issues concern the extent of monitoring and the agency's incentive structure to perform according to the preferences of the delegating coalition of legislators. Such political oversight mechanisms are costly to exercise, reactive and inexact in their rewards and sanctions. Furthermore, the threat of sanctions might divert the agency or the industry from focusing on the delivery of its services. In contrast, procedural requirements shape the policy environment of an agency and therefore constrain the amount of policy options. Procedural tools are less costly to exercise, restrict information asymmetries between agent and principal and commit the agency to the policy preferences of the enacting political coalition. Procedural rules settle appointment procedures, establish the relationship of the agency's staff resources to its domain of authority, allocate the amount of subsidy available to finance participation by under-represented interests and provide resources devoted to the participation by one agency in the processes of another (Noll 1987; cf. McCubbins, Noll and Weingast 1987: 261–2). Thus, administrative procedures reduce the information costs of monitoring the agency's activities while facilitating 'fire-alarm' monitoring by interested constituencies. By guiding actors via procedures to desired policy outcome, sanctions are said to be avoidable. Together with structural mechanisms, procedural rules channel an agency's decisions in favour of the initially intended policy outcome (on the importance of procedural regulation, see also Mayntz 1983). For example, Levine and Forrence argue that at the heart of the problem of regulatory discretion lies 'slack', i.e. inefficiencies. 'Slack' is reduced by policies that demand increased self-publicity, political competition, the inclusion of interest groups, the publication of academic research and media exposure. These policy instruments will reduce the discretion of regulators to be captured or to act in, what Levine and Forrence have termed, 'other-regarding' ways (Levine and Forrence 1990).

Solutions to problems of 'bureaucratic drift' require closer political supervision. Closer political oversight, however, might lead to the problem of 'coalitional drift', the risk incurred by constituents that the flow of benefits might be altered or even reversed by a future legislature with different policy preferences (Horn 1995, Shepsle 1992). The 'enacting coalition' will therefore not only search for procedures that force bureaux to reveal information, make its internal processes transparent and provide for external consultation. These coalitions also have future legislatures in mind and therefore will use structural devices to insulate their policy choices from future alterations. Thus, institutional forms will be sought which do not allow too much agency discretion, whilst also seeking to increase the commitment costs to the regulatory policy in order to keep certain pay-offs secure from any shifts in coalitional preferences. Many of these issues are said to be solvable at the initial 'hardwiring stage' (Macey 1992), where legislators will minimise their transactions costs in institutional design with respect to the extent of policy delegation, governance and funding structure, procedural rules and monitoring mechanisms (Horn 1995: 25–6).

While the 'design' literature offers theoretical models of great clarity by focusing on principal-agent problems arising from incomplete contracting between actors, problems remain. While rules are important and 'institutions matter', the extent to which institutions really matter remains a matter of empirical investigation. Moreover, any empirical investigation of these models based on transaction costs is difficult to derive without becoming tautological – any action might somehow be explained by a minimisation of transaction costs. These approaches, therefore, only allow for broad considerations and comparisons between similar processes while neglecting the large degree of empirical variations. Furthermore, the literature does not include analysis of various modes of regulation which go beyond principal-agent problems.

Modes of regulation

The regulation of economic activities looks back on a long tradition using various forms of organisation, such as boards, commissions, agencies or courts. Comparisons of various modes of regulation usually contrast the regulation of private enterprises with public ownership (see Majone 1994, 1996). Despite the rhetoric of 'deregulation' during the last two decades, regulation of economic activities has rather increased in formality, with greater emphasis on social and environmental rather than economic regulation. Whether, however, an industry is privately or publicly owned, does not affect the potential control problems, as has been discussed. Although it is argued that private enterprises are less prone to government interference, this seems to be just another episode in the search for Herbert Morrison's vision of an 'arm's length relationship' between controlling, politically (and thus supposedly publicly) accountable ministers and efficiently managing managers.[5] Both public ownership and agency types of regulation are hierarchical modes of control which are potentially open to capture. Whereas in the case of regulation of private industry, regulators might be captured by private industries or by politicians, in the case of public ownership, the enterprises might be captured by politicians for electoral purposes or may themselves 'capture' ministers or departments by exploiting their informational advantages (Tivey 1982, see also Majone 1996: 11–15). Thus, the causes for problems with public enterprises concerning their 'regulation' such as *ad hoc* decision-making, confusion of objectives, political manipulation, lack of co-operation between administrators, ministers and industries or ineffective performance indicators, can also be applied to the regulation of private enterprises. Rather than witnessing an end to control problems the main change seems to have been the increase in organisational distance between government and operator by the introduction of regulatory agencies.

It is often argued that public ownership was supposed to deliver wider social goals than economic efficiency, while economic efficiency is said to be the sole goal of regulatory control. However, the controversy surrounding the setting of universal services standards in regulatory statutes and licences at both EU and national levels, shows that social concerns are still on the political and regulatory agenda as private enterprises are instructed to provide certain, sometimes uneconomic, services in the 'public interest'. It is therefore possible to claim that governmental and agency types of regulation of business activities can be classified as a hierarchical organisation of regulation with similar potential defects.

Hierarchy is, nevertheless, not the sole organisational mode of regulation. Organisational modes of regulation may be classified according to two dimensions. The first relates to the degree of formalisation of regulation, i.e. the extent to which control is exercised via formal rules and standards, or rather via informal tools such as price or trust. The second dimension refers to the nature of the target group. Formulation, implementation and enforcement are affected by factors such as status, 'organisability' and the 'capture-ability' of the group. This leads to four ideal types of organisational modes of regulation which, again, should neither be regarded as jointly exhaustive or mutually exclusive. However, it provides a typology which is broadly comprehensive and includes the main organisational modes which have been previously identified in the literature (for a broader view on governance and control structures, see Mayntz and Scharpf 1995).

Extent of formalisation

		high	low
Target **population**	*concentrated*	delegation	self-regulation
	diffuse	hierarchy	market

Figure 3.1 Four modes of regulation

Delegation can be found in various fields, such as the setting of standards or health and safety. Standard-setting tasks are delegated to independent, specialist bodies which usually provide industrial expertise. By delegating these tasks, the state creates additional legitimacy for setting standards while also binding the industry to its own standards. The German standards-setting agency DIN or the European organisation ETSI (European Telecommunications Standards Institute) might be regarded as examples of such bodies. As regulators, these bodies aim to prevent negative externalities in the development and application of technology which might occur due to the inability of the industry to regulate itself due to a constant incentive to free-ride (see Werle 1995). Other bodies include health and safety regulators. Health and safety tasks are often undertaken either by industry associations or by independent agencies which are, in turn, controlled by both labour and business representatives (for example the UK Health and Safety Commission/ Executive; see Baldwin 1996: 83–105). The regulation by delegation mode includes specialised bodies that are created by private associations, bodies created by statutory powers and bodies promoted by professional organisations (see Baggott 1989:437; Birkinshaw, Harden and Lewis 1990). They usually centre on the regulation of a particular industry and deal with an identifiable set of actors according to formally and mainly collectively agreed rules and standards.

Self-regulation is developed, administered and enforced by those people whose behaviour is supposed to be regulated (see Black 1997; Ogus 1995; Graham 1994; Page 1986). Self-regulation is exercised by those organisations whose activities are seen to require some form of control by private associations. Self-regulatory activities can be exercised both on a continuous basis, such as, in the UK, advertising, the media, sport and, until recently, financial services,[6] or in an *ad hoc* manner. For example, the Greenbury Report of 1995 on boardroom pay was initiated within business to pre-empt political action after public disquiet over 'fat cats' salaries of executives of privatised utilities. Self-regulation can also involve standard setting.[7] Self-regulation, due to its reliance on informal or self-agreed rules and conventions, requires 'trust'. Such 'trust' between actors requires an identifiable set of actors whose behaviour can be observed and who are not outsiders to the regulatory norms and conventions.

While both delegation and self-regulation may require the 'hidden hand' of the state as a sanctioning device, the public sphere is directly involved in the hierarchical mode of regulation. Hierarchical control includes government control and control exercised by agencies, such as the British telecommunications watchdog 'Oftel' or the German Regulierungsbehörde für Post und Telekommunikationswesen. The functions and control procedures have been designed by and within the governmental machine and usually include economic and social regulation. Regulation is specified through rules in statutes, licences and performance indicators. This, however, does not necessitate a hierarchical form of implementation, nor does it indicate a mere reliance on legal rules to enforce compliance. Agencies may rely on the dissemination of information as a regulatory instrument to encourage compliance (Majone 1997a).

Control by markets is exercised by competition on price and quality within a universal set of rules (on the importance of the national institutional context of the market, see Hall 1986). Certain services in otherwise regulated industries fall into this category, such as, for example, so-called charge-call telephone services in the UK.[8] Beyond the general rules which regulate general business activities, market-based regulation will rely on competition on price and quality, and on consumer choice. Markets as main regulatory devices are pre-eminent in areas where regulation seems unenforceable, either due to the ease by which the regulated may 'exit' from the control of regulatory authority or by the impossibility of monitoring and enforcing regulation.

These four modes of regulation can be further analysed according to the three views of regulation elaborated above.

Benevolence views

Hierarchical control is regarded as the natural response to apparent market failures which are perceived as requiring authoritative action. Hierarchical solutions are supposed to provide Weber's bureaucratic advantages of, for example, precision, speed, clarity, neutrality and continuity (Weber 1972 (orig. pub. 1922): 561–2). The establishment of agencies can be regarded as devices for providing further flexibility, discretion and innovativeness and speed in decision-making, in contrast to the rigid rules controlling government departments.

Delegation modes of regulatory control involve the expertise of actors from within the industry rather than the involvement of civil servants, while the (residual) presence of the state and the latent threat of shifting to hierarchical, direct regulation will make industry actors prepared to compromise on substantive interests (Streeck and Schmitter 1985).

Moreover, substantial costs are taken on by the industry in the formulation, implementation and enforcement of rules and norms. Similar to self-regulation, delegation is supposed to provide for faster decision-making, flexibility and adaptability, as it avoids the political or bureaucratic decision-making processes. Consensus is regarded as leading to solutions which are better tailored to individual circumstances. In the case of standard setting, it provides customers with cheaper and a more wide-ranging supply of services, while suppliers benefit from bigger markets.

In contrast, market solutions, once an impartially applied uniform set of rules has been established, are supposed to allow consumers an unrestricted choice between competing goods and services. In this Hayekian world, the market offers the greatest flexibility at little organisational cost in that it provides a mechanism for the revelation of consumer preferences. Markets and competition are said to be effective in that they support 'discovery' processes for the 'best' products in contrast to a centrally controlled provision of goods.

Conspiracy views

Hierarchical solutions are exposed to the problem of capture by the industry which is supposed to be regulated and problems such as 'bureaucratic drift' or 'coalitional drift' occur. Rational bureaucrats create agencies to shift blame in a 'bureau-shaping' manner by delegating unpopular management and regulatory tasks to agencies and supposedly autonomous regulatory offices (see Dunleavy 1991).

Claims that the regulated industry dominates the regulatory process also apply to the cases of delegation and self-regulation where the regulated industries themselves participate in the regulatory process. These modes are regarded as being an example of capture by a cartel from the outset with the public having neither control nor participation nor even accountable decision-making. Industry actors are willing to co-operate in delegation and self-regulation to avert direct, potentially more heavy-handed action and to facilitate their own market position by developing standards. As regulation is seldom market-neutral, the regulating cartel will restrict new entries into the market and promote its own position. Moreover, the costs of regulation to actors outside the cartel will not be included in the calculations of the regulating actors.

The main proponents of 'conspiracy' views would hold that market-based regulation, or at least competition for the market mechanisms, leads to economically efficient outcomes (not only because of the assumption of constant cost functions). Leaving aside the 'market failure' arguments, it could be argued that market competition control is promoted by hegemonic actors who would benefit most from 'free' markets. Hills, for example, argues that much of the US 'deregulatory' drive in the telecommunications sector was to promote the international position of AT&T and IBM (Hills 1986).

Without guidance, market competition leads to complexity and opacity, as can be witnessed in the emerging tariff structures in telecommunications. Markets lack a long-term orientation and democratic accountability in the form of participation in decision-making. Furthermore, regulatory competition might lead to a 'race to the bottom', known as the 'Delaware effect'. Following the US practice of mutual recognition in corporate chartering, which falls under the authority of the individual states, inter-state competition for the most business-friendly environment emerged. The least regulatory cost to business was provided initially by Delaware, which led to convergence of other states to the same (low) levels. Whereas this tendency has been witnessed in labour regulation (or process regulation), in the context of product regulation, i.e. standards, in some areas of environmental, social and financial regulation there has been a 'race to the top' towards stricter regulatory standards, which has been termed the 'California effect' (see D. Vogel 1995; Scharpf 1996; Lütz 1996; Genschel and Plümper 1997).

Design questions

In the cases of hierarchical, delegation and self-regulatory modes, the design of control mechanisms follow similar lines in stressing structural and procedural methods to achieve the desired policy outcome. To overcome information asymmetries, clear standards and performance measurements are required and interests other than those of the regulated industry have to be incorporated into the process to act as 'fire alarm' in cases of perceived misconduct. Others argue that the introduction of competition between agencies, departments and other bodies for competencies, budgets and public and political prominence will prevent the occurrence of principal-agent problems.

A balance between political and regulatory oversight and regulatory and regulatee discretion has to be found. Sufficient flexibility and autonomy are needed without leading to 'juridification', i.e. the elimination of flexibility by legal gridlock (see Teubner 1987). 'Juridification' is said to be avoidable by a greater reliance on procedural aspects, that is by attempting to set up a procedural framework which aims to guide actors to unspecified but politically desirable policy outcomes, while also increasing regulatory accountability (Mayntz 1983; Black 1997; McCubbins, Noll and Weingast 1987). Others argue that regulatory failure has to do with 'style'; thus an adversarial relationship will be less conducive to regulatory compliance and acceptance than a co-operative relationship (Kelman 1992; Scholz 1991; G. Wilson 1989). Decision-making styles are therefore a further important factor in addition to the institutional structure of the regulatory relationship (see Scharpf 1989). Thus, a self-regulatory style requires structures which reinforce trust and 'mutuality' by facilitating discussion and consensual decision-making via the establishment of committees, collegiate boards and the like (see Hood 1996).

These various modes of regulatory organisation can only indicate some ideal types. Their implementation will therefore vary widely. In fact, regulatory regimes consist of elements of all these organisational modes according to specific function and problem. Furthermore, all modes have their own peculiar strengths, weaknesses and issues of design, all of which have been identified in the literature on regulation.

The emergence of the regulatory state?

Although the developments in telecommunications at the European and national levels show that regulatory reforms take various paths and methods and that, whereas 'nations may be engaged in a single game, the players have different ideas of what the game is and how to win' (S. Vogel 1997: 181), recent changes are said to have led to a shift from the 'welfare' or 'positive' state towards a 'regulatory state' (Majone 1994, 1996: 56, 1997b). The emergence of a 'regulatory state' describes a shift from policies of public ownership, redistribution and economic stabilisation towards more indirect regulative, market-correcting measures. Examples of this shift are the end to direct service delivery by the state through homogeneously organised public bureaucracies, the creation of free-standing regulatory bodies and the increased formality of regulatory relationships (Loughlin and Scott 1997).

The emergence of the 'regulatory state' is regarded as an outcome of the interests of rational bureaucrats who, in the context of tight budgets, reshape and reorganise their office duties according to their interest and convenience, such as distancing and delegating 'costly' (in time or resources) activities. Others would argue that the emergence of the regulatory state has to be seen in the context of a cultural shift in trust which has led to an 'audit explosion' (Power 1994). It is nevertheless debatable whether the supposed emergence of the 'regulatory state' represents a *new* phenomenon.

Arguments that recent changes have led to a 'rolling back of the state' and 'deregulation' do not consider that there has mainly been a mere shift in 'visibility' of the state's involvement in economic affairs. Although recent regulatory reform is said to have increased the controlling capacities of the state, an emphasis on rules and incentives is nevertheless exposed to several theoretical and practical problems. Regulatory issues such as the relationship between political actors, regulators and operators; the regulatory objectives; the organisation of the regulatory body, whether personalised or collective, in a board-like arrangement; whether regulation should be industry or sector-based; and the definition and scope of regulatory independence, remain highly contested. Similarly, the definition and provision of so-called public services, the extent of competition, the structure of the industry, the accountability and transparency of the regulatory process, the regulation of price or rate of return, the danger of 'regulatory creep', and the relation between retrospective and prospective regulation remain politicised and controversial issues (see for example, Helm 1995; Foster 1992; Thatcher 1998).

At the same time, the action of the regulated industry attracts similar public exposure and controversy as under public ownership. For example, Deutsche Telekom's public announcement of price cuts at the end of 1997 (applicable as of 1 March 1998) and the later announcement of handling charges for customers transferring to other operators' services were little else than symbolic acts to create uncertainty among potential 'switchers' in order to deter interest in changing to new telecommunication service providers. Similarly, the new regulatory regimes are subject to changes at the political level. For example, the UK Labour government announced its intentions, following public excitement about perceived excessive profits of privatised utilities and excessive pay for their executives, to tighten political control over the regulators, demanding that greater regulatory priority being given to so-called 'consumer benefits' and wider access to decision-making to consumer groups. The scope and organisation of regulatory authorities are also under discussion. At the same time, UK regulators have led highly personalised bodies and have shown remarkable adaptability in their regulatory interventions according the changing attitudes of the public and the government. These examples of 'regulatee drift', 'coalitional drift', following a change in government, and 'regulatory drift' suggest that regulation is hardly a 'de-politicised' process, nor has it solved any of the control problems which have troubled publicly owned enterprises. The nature of the liberalised markets and the behaviour of the market participants, in particular that of the former public monopolies, seems more dependent on the market structure than on the regulatory regime. Thus, any analysis of a regulatory regime has to include the whole 'regulatory space' of the industry (see Hancher and Moran 1989; Scott, Hall and Hood 1997: 231–53).

Despite the perceived end to demand management and the claim of the disappearance of the 'welfare state', states have not withdrawn from policy areas such as welfare provision and industrial policy. This can be seen in the increasingly adversarial competition between sub-national governments to attract investment and the increased use of microeconomic forms of support for business. The regulatory regimes for utility industries also provide for several guarantees concerning so-called 'public services', ranging from the allowed extent of price increases to binding commitments to investment, often beyond those in the days of public ownership. Thus the regulatory state still maintains welfare functions, even if they are carried out by private rather than public actors.

Nor can the supposed emergence of the 'regulatory state' be regarded as a new phenomenon. The application of legal instruments has a long tradition in the control of economic activity, particularly in German public policy. Many of today's policy issues have been discussed and experienced in the past, with debates ranging from the extent of control, and the advantages and disadvantages of public ownership versus the regulation of private economic actors, to the setting of rates. Nevertheless, while the nature of the arguments on regulation has not changed, there has been a noticeable rebalancing between economic, social and environmental regulation as well as a shift towards procedural and performance-oriented regulation. These shifts in regulatory instruments arguably reflect deeper social, technological and economic changes. 'Informatisation' and 'contractualisation' result in better enforceable and transparent relationships between more diverse economic actors. The rise of health and safety regulation might also be associated with a general change in social attitudes towards risk and trust. Thus, while most of the arguments about the benefits and costs of regulation or its organisation are not new, and therefore do not support the claim of an 'emergence' of a regulatory state, there have been considerable changes in the instruments of regulation.

The creation and development of new regulatory regimes after periods of regulatory change have not led to a 'rolling back' but to a redefinition of state activities; nor has regulatory change been a mere 'one-way street'. Thus, despite a move towards 'de-bureaucratisation' in the delivery of public services, there has been, at least in the UK, a 'mirror-image' development towards an increased separation, formality and rule-boundedness in regulation within the public sector (Hood and Scott 1996; Hood *et al.* forthcoming).

In conclusion, this paper has attempted to provide a sketch of various aspects of regulation. The concept of regulation cannot be regarded as uncontested or incontestable. Competing approaches to regulation as presented in the categories of benevolence, conspiracy and design, highlight the key debates surrounding regulatory regimes. The focus on issues such as capture, bureaucratic drift and coalitional drift provides a sound basis for the analysis of the origins and practice of regulatory regimes. Beyond the rhetoric about the blessings and evils of 'privatisation' policies, the discussion of regulation directs attention to the nature of control relationships. Rather than following the oratory about paradigm changes due to changes in technology and globalised markets, the analysis of regulatory regimes reveals the continuing quest for a stable balance between managerial autonomy and public accountability, and between commercial and other, so-called 'public' interests.

Notes

1 Although Chadwick had already developed a similar argument in the mid-19th century in the context of the debate on regulating the emerging UK railway oligopoly.
2 The seeming inevitability of capture over time in Bernstein's account is hardly falsifiable as it is not indicated when 'capture' is bound to occur. Institutional design accounts provide ways and methods to overcome these problems.
3 The assumption that politicians can escape blame via delegation seems disputable, not the least because of the political capital any political opposition can potentially earn from pointing blame for policy failure at politicians.
4 'Who regulates the regulators?' (loose translation).
5 Herbert Morrison was primarily responsible for the blueprints for the nationalisation (then called socialisation) programmes of the Labour government in the UK after the Second World War. In broad terms, his concept of 'public corporation' was an attempt to separate between ministers who would protect the public interest and relatively autonomous managers who were supposed to guarantee the efficient and commercial running of the nationalised industries.
6 The establishment of the Financial Services Authority in the UK might be regarded as a shift to a delegated mode of regulation as a dispersed set of regulatory and self-regulatory mechanisms is brought together in a more high-profile body, dependent on government resources. A similar shift is reflected in the plans to establish a Food Standards Agency in the UK which is, according to the Labour government's original plans, supposed to be financed by the industry itself. Again, regulation is concentrated in one body, while the 'shadow of the state' is extended in the remaining self-regulatory areas.
7 The search for a universal standard for large-scale technological developments is often undertaken by producers in the pre-market stages, as co-operation at these early stages is beneficial to all producers as it allows for the development of compatible systems. Werle (1995) has termed these activities, which resemble the setting of a 'battle of the sexes' game, 'co-ordination' rather than 'regulation'.
8 These services charge users on their 'home' account and not at the place where the call is being made.

4 From PTT to NRA

Towards a new regulatory regime?[1]

Sebastian Eyre and Nick Sitter

Abstract

Since the 1970s the European Union (EU) and its Member States have seen a considerable shift from regulation by way of nationalised utilities and ministerial control to regulation through independent agencies; in the case of telecommunications, from Post, Telegraph and Telecommunication utilities (PTTs) to National (i.e. EU Member State) Regulatory Authority (NRAs). However, the Member States have adopted different approaches to regulatory reform at both domestic and EU level, resulting in a series of models of agency-based regulation. We suggest that although the EU may be moving toward a new regulatory regime, there is not yet a single new regime. Rather, the EU model permits a considerable degree of variation and discretion at Member State level, and is based on mutual adjustment and adaptation. These Member State differences are explained in terms of their approaches to regulatory reform, which warrant analysis of the rationale of regulation and reform, and in turn prompts our typology/taxonomy of telecommunications regulation in the EU. We approach the EU regime as one of many regulatory regimes, but one that is somewhat peculiar due to its supra-national nature. The European regime (EU and Member States) is therefore described as policy syncretism, the result of interaction between several systems rather than a teleological process of integration.

Issues in telecommunications regulation in the European Union

As the Fifteen signed the eponymous Treaty in Amsterdam on 17 June 1997, yet another battle in the struggle between advocates of industrial policy and competition policy was settled. True to form it reflected the preponderance of the forces of liberalisation. Efforts to rewrite Article 90, the Commission's powerful anti-monopoly weapon, came to little, though upon France's insistence a new Article 7 was written into the Treaty guaranteeing public-service provisions. Though this episode reflects an on-going contest between interventionist and free-market-oriented actors at EU level, and may provide for a degree of sanctuary for Electricité de France and Gaz de France, Article 7 came too late to save France Télécom from competition. As the previous chapter illustrated, telecommunications liberalisation has all but been achieved in the European Union, in no small part thanks to DG IV's repeated use of Article 90, where the Commission proved far less inhibited than it did in the energy sector.

The Commission's approach to the telecommunications sector reveals a preference for leaving the enforcement of EU policy up to the Member State's regulatory agencies (hereafter NRAs – National Regulatory Agencies). The regime is therefore far from harmonised, let alone uniform, though the Member States are moving in the same direction (Thatcher 1996). The EU regime relies on the principle of mutual recognition (and harmonisation only in terms of EU-level standards). This development raises a number of questions concerning the shift from nationalised utilities under departmental control to a Europe of privatised telecommunications operators regulated by NRAs and competition authorities. The most central question is whether there is one European model. In other words – is the EU moving toward a single new regulatory regime based on the agency approach? This in turn prompts a series of questions concerning the shift to regulatory agencies, the differences between Member States' telecommunications policies, and the driving forces behind regulatory reform.

The first question concerns the rationale for regulation, and the main answers usually relate to market failures, social goals and quality control. Regulation may also be desired by industry for its own protection. First, markets are imperfect. In the case of utilities, regulation is justified in terms of natural monopolies, an argument that applies more convincingly to networks than to service provision (though this distinction is not always made). The perceived need for a single national network was widely considered to justify single-service providers in post and telecommunications, rail transport, gas and electricity. The danger of 'natural monopolies' is, of course, abuse of a dominant position: a monopoly that prevents competition or extracts excessive profits. Yet the problem may be wider if we accept that markets are not necessarily natural and self-regulating, let alone in equilibrium. 'Markets are created by governments, ordered by institutions, and sustained by regulations' (Wilks 1996a: 538) In other words, all markets are regulated one way or another. This accounts for the paradox in the UK, where regulatory agencies such as Oftel were intended as temporary measures until free-market competition would reign supreme. They have proved persistent and necessary, both to promote and maintain competition. Second, public-service provisions have played a considerable role in West European regulation, and are integrated even into British regulatory regimes through obligations of service provision and quality of service (Prosser 1994). Distributive principles, such as equity of cost for consumers, have frequently been added to public-service provisions for telecommunications utilities, usually by way of tariff regulation. Finally, all regulatory regimes include an element of quality control through regulation of standards. These may operate to keep competitors out, raising the potential for 'agency capture'.

The second question concerns the goals and methods of utility regulation in general. The dominant West European approach was, until recently, one of national utilities that might or might not be owned by the state but which were regulated by government departments or ministers. For example, the UK's monopoly operator, the General Post Office, started life as a non-governmental department and was made into a statutory corporation in 1969, and became British Telecom in the 1981 demerger. However, Italy featured by far the most complex situation. The Piedmont Hydroelectric Company (SIP) emerged as the dominant tele-communications operator in the inter-war years, only to be rescued by the state-owned Institute for Reconstruction of Industry during the depression. It then survived fascism to see partial unification of tele-communications services in 1957. Full unification and privatisation followed in 1994. By contrast, the US approach featured private operators regulated by independent agencies that were subject to legislation and accountable before the judiciary. These elements of the US model, and deregulation in the US, had considerable influence on the process of regulatory reform in Europe, in terms of examples to be followed and dangers to be avoided.

But is the telecommunications sector peculiar? The answer to our third question is a guarded 'yes'. Like the energy and transport sectors, tele-communications presented problems for the Single Market programme because it featured national carriers or monopoly utilities. The gas, electricity, transport, and telecommunications sectors were dominated by publicly owned, national monopolies. They all faced the challenges inherent in the efforts to create a common market in Europe in general, and the Commission's anti-monopoly power in particular. Until the 1980s, however, the Commission was not willing to exercise its full powers, probably wisely in the light of Member State commitments to their monopoly utilities. However, in the last two decades, the telecommunica-tions sector has faced very specific technological challenges, e.g. digitalisation. To be sure, the telecommunications sector was not the only sector to face such sector-specific pressure for change, but in this case the changes undermined its 'natural monopoly' status and opened a window of opportunity for Commission initiative. In fact, something analogous happened in the gas industry, where the question of the EU's reliance on external supplies changed dramatically with the collapse of communism and the ensuing gas surplus (Stern 1995), a surplus that was increased by introduction of Middle Eastern gas, and expansion of Algerian and Norwegian supply capacities.

Recent developments in the West European politics of regulation prompt the fourth question. What forces have driven regulatory change in the telecommunications sector? Considering this, seven factors stand out:

- Sector-specific factors: the extent to which technological developments prompted questions about the industry's future, its 'natural monopoly' status and the potential for competition and profit.
- International competition: the concern that because of its importance in terms of infrastructure, an efficient competitive telecommunications sector confers competitive advantages on industry in general. Similar arguments apply in the case of most utilities, e.g. electricity, gas and transport. The US provided the competitive challenge.
- Disillusionment with Keynsianism: in terms of both ideology and actual results. Nationalised utilities came to be seen as a drain on West European economies and resources.
- Ideological pressure for deregulation: specifically New Right analyses of public and bureaucratic overspending due to lack of profit-oriented incentive structures (Niskanen 1973), and Olson's analysis of the rise and decline of nations (Olson 1982).
- Agency-driven reform: the extent to which institutions strengthen their own role in a polity, through adaptation, learning, problem-solving and exploiting alternatives (March and Olsen 1989). This is particularly relevant at EU-level, where the Competition Directorate General (DG IV) led its own metamorphosis into a 'federal agency' (Wilks 1992). A series of European Court of Justice decisions enhanced Commission's powers considerably during the two decades leading to the 1989 Merger Regulation (Schwartz 1993).
- Country-specific factors: this represents a necessary, albeit somewhat 'residual', category given the effect of factors such as Margaret Thatcher's quest for a 'shareholder democracy' and the 'Tangentopoli' scandals over corruption in Italy.
- The ultimate regime-specific factor is the EU's Single Market or '1992' programme, with the Single European Act (SEA) featuring a distinct (but ill-defined) free-market flavour.

Given the focus on a possible new European regulatory model, it is worth dwelling briefly on the question of the relationship between European integration and free-market-oriented restructuring. Though the SEA centred on the establishment of a single market, it avoided addressing the question of precisely what kind of free-market economy was to dominate the 1992 programme. This point has become increasingly clear after the collapse of communism, both as 'real existing socialism' and as a theoretical alternative to the free market (Wilks 1996a). The recent 'third way' debate has raised questions of the social and economic role of regulation and 'active government', even in Bill Clinton's US and Tony Blair's Britain, where the 'what works is what counts' philosophy reflects an approach hailed as pragmatic (Blair 1998). This is also reflected in the debate on the 1998 Competition Bill, and planned reform to bring regulation closer into line with the EU (*European Voice* 15–24 January 1998). Nevertheless, the EU's drive for liberalisation continues to reflect a clear shift from industrial policy to competition policy and away from acceptance of national monopolies (even the Swedish state alcohol monopoly has been modified through a European Court of Justice ruling (Case C-198/95, judgement 23 November 1997)). Given the nature of the EU, there are few alternatives to liberalisation, save a system of EU-level or EU-sanctioned monopolies. Because they are likely to distort free trade, regional or national monopolies are hardly compatible with free trade between Member States. Although in principle the EU should not distinguish between forms of ownership, the focus on competition means that in effect it does, the new Article 7 notwithstanding.

If the SEA both reflected and covered up the extent of competition between different models of the free-market economy, the Maastricht and Amsterdam Treaties provided little clarification. And, with several of the governments involved subject to re-election in any one year, the battle lines remained somewhat nebulous. In effect, the intergovernmental conferences reflected competition between 'negative' and 'positive' integration, where the former focuses on removal of barriers to trade and on liberalisation, and the latter is about establishing more interventionist EU-level policy initiatives. The 1992 programme was in many ways the ultimate in negative integration, as it was specifically oriented towards removal of all barriers to the free flow of goods, services, labour and capital. This was, of course, no accident, for it was precisely its free-market orientation that made the SEA acceptable to Thatcher (Taylor 1989). However, the integration process soon gave rise to demands for positive integration, such as EU-level intervention and action on, for example, social policy, regional policy and research and development. To the free marketers, these three sectors and the Structural Funds were the price to be paid for the abandonment of industrial policy. However, given the scope for differences in Member State economic policy and regulation, the EU can also be considered an arena for competition between different institutional models for the economy. This point was brought home by the Major governments through their focus on the UK's international competitiveness (credited to labour market and regulatory reform). Hence it is tempting to conclude that the result of the SEA has not been a drive toward convergence, but rather a process of accom-modating competing types of market economies, first by removing the barriers to trade (negative integration) and then by adopting EU-wide

regulatory and policy regimes (positive integration). In the telecommunications sector, regulation has largely taken the form of removal
of barriers to trade, by way of adapting an EU regulatory regime and
setting EU-level standards, the EU's pro-active R&D policy notwithstanding. We must therefore consider developments in theory and
ideology that underlie the triumph of the New Right and the shift from
industrial policy to competition policy in Europe, at Member State and
EU level.

These points lead directly to the main question of whether or not there
is a single new model for regulation – an agency model. The remainder of
this chapter will focus on the dynamics of integration in terms of the
development of an EU model of agency regulation, in the context of
different Member States' approaches. This analysis will suggest that, as
yet, there is no single unified model of a new regulatory regime. The next
section covers the pressure for change and the development from PTTs to
NRAs, discussing the agency mechanism and a taxonomy of agency
regulation, and comparing the agency mechanisms used in the Member
States and the EU. The third and final section considers the interaction
between the agencies and the development of the EU approach to telecommunications regulation, and sets out as the case for policy syncretism
by suggesting that telecommunications regulatory reform in the European
Union is based on mutual adjustment and adaptation.

From PTTs and industrial policy to NRAs and competition policy: telecommunications liberalisation in Europe

Until the early 1980s, the most striking feature of telecommunications
regulation outside the USA was stability and inertia. The general
assumptions were that problems of regulation, in this sector as in any
other, should be met with more regulation. The general West European
view of governments' role in management of the economy owed more to
Keynes than to Friedman and von Hayek. The results were opaque
systems of regulation with governments pursuing economic growth
through industrial policy. The nationalised utilities were used as instruments of industrial and economic policy, such as wage-price management
and employment reduction. The invisible hand was nowhere to be seen, at
least not as far as utilities were concerned. To be sure, much of Western
Europe's post-war economic policy reflected the need to re-build Europe
after the two world wars and the Depression. However, economic growth
in the 1960s continued to mask many of the potential problems associated
with public utilities. By the 1970s, when a combination of oil shocks,
recession and a weakened Breton-Woods system prompted some major
questions about industrial policy, the regimes were well established. 'New
institutionalist' analyses offer some clues to both inertia and the trajectory
of change. A prolonged period of state intervention in industry generates

a set of rules, norms and traditions that shapes industrial policy, a pattern which it might be difficult to change due to the power of entrenched groups. For example, Norwegian petroleum policy 'followed routines based on institutionalized norms and beliefs which can be traced back to economic problems of the 1920s and 1930s' (March and Olsen 1989: 36). 'Historical institutionalists' attempt to overcome the charge that 'institutionalism' explains principally resistance to change. They focus on how institutions shape the path of reform (Thelen and Steinmo 1992), e.g. the way country-specific factors such as the UK's centralised constitution affects the scope for policy change (Hall 1992). March and Olsen suggest that institutional change is particularly difficult to control precisely, and that '[it] rarely satisfies the prior intentions of those who initiate it' (March and Olsen 1989: 65). Gradually, however, the approach to industrial policy centred on public ownership and intervention gave way to a focus on pre-competitive research (R&D policy) and infrastructure support (regional policy, 'trans-European networks'), both at EU and Member State level (McGowan 1998). For the purpose of the current argument, suffice it to note that institutional arrangements played a considerable role in determining the trajectory of change. The challenges to the post-war industrial policy regime came on three levels:

- First, theoretical new right analyses, in the shape of attacks from the Austrian school and rational choice theorists, challenged state ownership *per se*. Public utilities and departments were seen prone to over-supply, due to a lack of market-based incentives. Both wings of this analysis contain not only a diagnosis of where the problem with public utilities lies, but also prescriptive elements. If the problems lie in the lack of profit motive, then the solution could lie in the introduction of a profit motive (Dunleavy and O'Leary 1987: 72–135), which is what the Thatcher government set out to provide by way of privatisation (Thatcher 1993: 676–85).
- Second, and more specifically, the West European utilities faced the problem of cost and efficiency across the board, including the channelling of profits from technological improvements into cross-subsidisation, rather than lower prices for consumers. The Conservative governments' disapproval of the public utilities was summed up in the observation that British Telecom 'had not the faintest idea which of its activities were profitable and which were not, let alone any finer points of management accounting' (Lawson 1992: 222).
- Third, at least in the UK, the Conservative governments set out to limit the role of the state in the economy, to create a large number of small shareholders and to raise revenue (Hay and Morris 1991; Thatcher 1993). Nigel Lawson[2] recalled the government's drive for wider share ownership: 'The general public are interested primarily in

holding shares in companies they know and of which they are regular customers. The ideal vehicle [for the breakthrough in the governments privatisation programme] was now at hand, in the shape of the telephone giant, British Telecom' (Lawson 1992: 221; Thatcher 1993: 676). At the time, Lawson observed: 'We are seeing the birth of people's capitalism', a term Thatcher amended to 'popular capitalism' (Lawson 1992: 224).

Thus, the challenge to interventionist industrial policy and public ownership owed more than a little to rational choice analysis of public policy. To this extent it represented, in part, an effort to establish a more rational model of utilities policy in general (Ogus 1994: 337–41). This debate is analysed in considerable detail in Chapter 2. As far as the telecommunications sector is concerned, the result was a new model of regulation centred on the independent agency and competition policy, involving privatisation of utilities (and demergers of PTTs where necessary). The public utility and regulatory agency models differ considerably in terms of ownership structure, the tasks assigned to the utility, the nature of the regulators and their links to competition policy (and the extent to which this covers utilities).

The diversity of telecommunications regulation in Europe derives from a combination of the institutional regimes, the drivers behind policy change and the dynamic of European integration. Traditionally, separate theories have been developed for analysis of the EU and Member State politics and policy. However, the last decade has seen increasing cross-fertilisation between the comparative politics and international relations disciplines. Prominent examples include Taylor's use of Lijphart's consociational theory of democracy in plural societies (Lijphart 1975;

Table 4.1 The key characteristics of public utility and agency models

	Operator (ownership)	*Primary tasks*	*Regulator*	*Competition policy*
Public utility model	Single vertically integrated monopoly utility (usually public)	Public service obligations (profit motiv)e	Utility/ Ministry	Limited or no impact, utilities may be exempt
Regulatory agency model	Multiple utilities with 'Chinese walls' (private)	Profit maximisation subject to regulation (including limited public service obligations)	Regulator (some ministerial control possible)	Shared competence utilities covered

1977) to account for the forces that limit European integration (Taylor 1991); the application of networks theory to the EU (Richardson 1996); and Hix's more general call for the use of comparative politics theories in the analysis of EU politics (Hix 1994; Hurrell and Menon 1996). In the telecommunications sector, the pressure for regulatory change has been similar at the Member State and EU level. However, regime-specific factors indicate a four-level pattern. First, some Member States have embarked on regulatory reform with little or no concerns for developments at the EU level. Taking the lead in liberalisation has permitted the UK to adopt an attitude of benign neglect toward EU telecommunications regulation in particular and competition policy in general, or at least not let it affect domestic developments (Bridgeman 1996; Wilks 1996b). One analysis of UK telecommunications regulation does not even consider the EU perspective (Burton 1997). Second, some Member States, with long-established competition policy regimes, have attempted to steer the direction of the development of the EU regime, particularly evident in Germany's quest for a European Cartel Office (Riley 1997). Third, the development of the EU regime reflects not only the different Member States' approaches to, and concern with, reform, but also the EU institutional set-up and its supra-national nature. Fourth and finally, some Member States only developed formal competition policy and/or telecommunications regulation as a result of the Single Market project, and have therefore been more heavily influenced by the EU regime. Needless to say, this also holds for prospective EU members, such as the Czech Republic.

Realist and rational choice analyses of European integration suggest that it (and hence regulatory reform too) is government-driven, which an authoritative study of the SEA appears to confirm (Moravcsik 1991). However, in the case of telecommunications, the realist approach is less persuasive, partly because Commission leadership was required to overcome 'logic of collective action' problems (Sandholz 1993; Olson 1965). In fact, despite being the leader in this case, Britain did little to project its own rules at the EU level, and EU reform was driven largely by the Commissioners for Industry (Davignon and Bangemann) and Competition (Sutherland, Brittan and van Miert). Neo-functionalists call this 'cultivated spillover' (Tranholm-Mikkelsen 1992; Haas 1958; Lindberg 1963). Add the pressure from national peak associations ('political spillover') and the push from the Single Market project ('functional spillover') and the neo-functionalist dynamic of integration is complete (Schneider 1992; Dang-Nguyen, Schneideer and Werle 1993). However, neo-functionalists have been taken to task for failing to consider international factors and domestic politics (George 1985). In the telecommunications debate, 'international factors' refers chiefly to deregulation in the US, which continues to influence regulatory reform at both EU and Member State level (Majone 1996a). And German and

French efforts to project their own regimes and institutions onto the EU level inevitably shaped the debate (Sandholz 1993; *Financial Times*, 28 November 1995 and 3 October 1995). Moreover, the focus on regime-specific factors draws attention to questions of resources and legitimacy. The EU has problems with both. Its limited resources and debatable legitimacy helps explain the EU's legalistic (rather than administrative) approach (Wilks 1996a). The reluctance of British courts to intervene, their recognition of Oftel's discretionary power, and the tendency for issues to be negotiated between firm and regulator, provide a stark contrast to the legalistic approach. It is based on a considerable degree of trust (Prosser 1994). International regulation also exacerbates credibility problems, multiplying questions about governments' short-term motives and therefore compliance. Hence the tendency to opt for agency-based regulation (which is supra-national), even though this may raise questions about accountability (Majone 1996b). This helps explain observations of EU telecommunications regulatory reform to the effect that 'it is striking that problems and solutions are presented in terms of trade barriers and free competition. The most sensitive distributive equity arguments have been evaded by leaving the Member States free to continue exclusive provision of network infrastructure and plain voice telephony' (Stevers 1989: 62). In fact, given the nature of the EU (and the free-market bias in the SEA), this is less than striking.

European regulatory reform in the telecommunications sector is therefore a pluralist project, the dynamics of which differs depending on the subject of analysis. Therefore, the six types of agency mechanisms set out in Table 4.2 represent a taxonomy (a classification based on systematic research of several cases) rather than a typology (classification by logical types). While the distinction between the departmental and the agency approach is based on logical antonyms, our six types reflect the recent history of telecommunications regulation in the EU and the US. The distinction between the six is drawn up around nine central questions about the philosophy behind regulation and its goals, the regime's institutional features and the nature of the reform process. In more or less chronological order, the six are: (1) the US model, based on a federal constitution that permits federal agencies considerable independence, featuring a legalistic approach that leaves little to discretion, and which leaves the agencies accountable primarily to the judiciary; (2) the British approach, which explicitly rejected US legalism in favour of a more administrative system of regulation based on negotiation, and where the agencies are, in effect, held accountable by the press and the financial markets in the City of London rather than the British executive or judiciary; (3) the federal German system, which, unlike the US or British approaches, is centred on both social and economic goals, but combines this with agency independence and legalism; (4) the public-service oriented French model, which has represented the main alternative to

German influence on the shape of the EU-level regime; (5) the EU regime, which is largely legalistic due not only to the Single Market programme but also to EU-specific factors such as lack of resources and problems of legitimacy and trust; and finally (6) the regimes in Member State and prospective members that have been, or are being, developed very much in the shadow of the EU regime, and are therefore very much shaped by it.

The nine criteria that form the basis for the taxonomy in Table 4.2 reflect the pressures for regulatory reform discussed above. The first four were prompted by questions about ideological and economic reasons for reform. These points also reflect the institutional characteristics of each political system. The next four criteria reflect more specific points about the role of agencies and institutions and regime-specific factors. The ninth and final criterion reflects the importance of the immediate political reasons for, and the goal of, reform: to maintain the system through regulatory reform, to replace the old system with a new one or to develop a system where there was none (or only a weak one). As Table 4.2 illustrates, questions concerning telecommunications regulation do not always yield a single set of dichotomous answers.

- The economic philosophy, or culture, behind each model is classified as laissez-faire or interventionist. The shift to the agency approach would suggest a shift towards laissez-faire inasmuch as it was driven partly by rejection of interventionism and activist industrial policy. However, the approaches still differ considerably.
- Each regime is classified according to whether its approach to regulation is predominantly legal or administrative. To be sure, the agency approach is centred on the notion of independent agencies and competition authorities, both of which require rules. Yet the British and French regimes retain administrative regimes, featuring ministerial discretion.
- The regimes tend to reflect concern either with competition *per se* (neo-Austrian economics) or as a means to achieve economic efficiency (neo-classical economics) (Sturm and Wilks 1997). This is reflected in the difference between rule-based and effects-based approaches to regulation respectively, though some regimes include elements of both, e.g. the form-based merger rules in the Restrictive Trade Practices Act of 1976 (Bridgeman 1996).
- The primary justification for regulation tends to be either economic or social (Ogus 1994). The shift to the agency model is associated with a shift to increasing focus on economic reasons for regulation, though social and public-service concerns remain prominent in some cases.
- The degree of independence from executive control varies considerably. Some NRAs and competition authorities can be overruled by the relevant ministers.

- Most NRAs are accountable either to government departments or to the judiciary (or, on some matters, to competition authorities). However, in reality the British regulators are more accountable to the market and the press than to parliament (Prosser 1994; Wilks 1997).
- The extent of concurrent powers, i.e. the question of overlap and shared competencies between NRAs and competition authorities, varies considerably across the six regimes. Most NRAs share competence with competition authorities, at least on competition matters, while in the EU regime DG IV is the de facto regulator in the telecommunications sector (Schaub 1996; Sturm and Wilks 1997).
- Every regime contains a degree of discretion. The question is where this lies, i.e. who has the power of discretion and whether this power is considerable, moderate or limited.
- The final question concerns the process of regulatory reform. In most cases it represents an effort to improve the system, to develop a new system or to adapt to the EU regime. However, the UK's centralised system of government permitted unusually radical reform.

The dynamics of EU telecommunications liberalisation: toward a new regulatory regime?

A considerable body of literature on European integration assumes, implicitly or explicitly, a link between integration and convergence, or even harmonisation (on telecommunications see, e.g., Sauter 1997). Briefly, convergence theories suggest that if the obstacles to integration represented by differences among Member State can be overcome, then convergence would follow. In other words, European integration is not so much based on convergence as actually causing a process of convergence. Hence the debate over whether integration has decreased economic disparities in the Mediterranean Member States (Leonardi 1993; Keating 1995, Leonardi 1995a; 1995b). The assumptions of convergence have shaped much of the debate on Economic and Monetary Union, where meeting the convergence criteria has become economic policy orthodoxy in the 1990s, and the prospect of a single currency has raised questions about wider convergence of fiscal policy.[3] Similarly, with the Single Market programme, the EU saw a shift toward laissez-faire economic policy across the board. This included the decline of Member State and EU-sanctioned industrial policy, increasing EU action against state aid, and increased assertiveness on the part of DG IV. 'Competition policy is thus the most direct example of the industrial policy of the 1970s being replaced by a neo-liberal free market policy in the 1990s' (Wilks 1996a: 545). However, in the 'problematic' sectors (gas, electricity and telecommunications) the completion of the single market has been less a process of integration and convergence than one of accommodating differences. Nowhere is this clearer than in the case of electricity, where

Table 4.2 A taxonomy of approaches to competition policy and telecommunications regulation in the US and Europe

Country	Philosophy	Legal or admin. approach to regulation	Basis: competition or economic efficiency	Goals: economic and/or social	Independence from executive	Account-ability	Concurrent powers with competition authorities	Power of discretion continuity	Reform: radical or continuity
USA	Laissez-faire	Legal	Competition Form-based	Economic	Very independent	To the judiciary	FCC, some overlap with FTC and states on anti-trust	Limited	Continuity, but break-up based on anti-trust laws
UK	Laissez-faire And 'popular capitalism'	Administrative Negotiated RPI – X	Economic efficiency Effects-based (1998 bill may cause change)	Predominantly economic	Independent in effect, but subject to ministerial approval	To parliament, but in effect to ministers, still more to press, the City (+ EC)	Oftel shares with MMC and OFT (Competition Commission)	Considerable lies with Oftel and the minister	Radical reform
Germany	Laissez-faire	Predominantly legal	Economic efficiency Effects-based	Mixed economic and social	Independent	To the judiciary and DGIV/ECJ	Reg TP shares with BKA, which ministry can overrule	Limited, lies with the minister	Paced reform through competition law and corporatism
France	Intervention and Public service	Administrative	Economic efficiency Effects-based	Predominantly social	Limited independence, final say and sanctions with minister	Judiciary, but in effect to the minister with DG IV/ECJ	ART regulates CC advises, control by minister (esp. mergers)	Considerable, lies with the minister	Paced reform, partly influenced by Single Market
EU regime	Undeclared, but laissez-faire assumptions	Legal	Competition Form-based	Predominantly economic	Independent, but DG IV can be overruled by the full Commission	To the judiciary, i.e. the ECJ based on the Treaties	DG IV, subject to approval by the full Commission	Moderate, first at DG IV, then more with the full Commission	Syncretism
EU 'second wave' and prospective members	Laissez-faire driven by Single Market Programme	Predominantly legal	Competition Mixed, but form-based due to EC influence	Predominantly economic	Independent, though minister/ department can overrule	Mixed, judiciary and ministry, and DG IV/ ECJ	NRAs, competition authorities and/or ministry	Considerable, lies with the NRAs and the minister	Fairly radical, influenced by EC reform Syncretism

Sources: Forrester Norral & Sutton for the European Commission, *The Institutional Framework for the Regulation of Telecommunications and the Application of EC Competition Rules* (Luxembourg, Office for Official Publications of the European Communities, 1996); World Wide Web pages of the NRAs, competition authorities and national ministers.

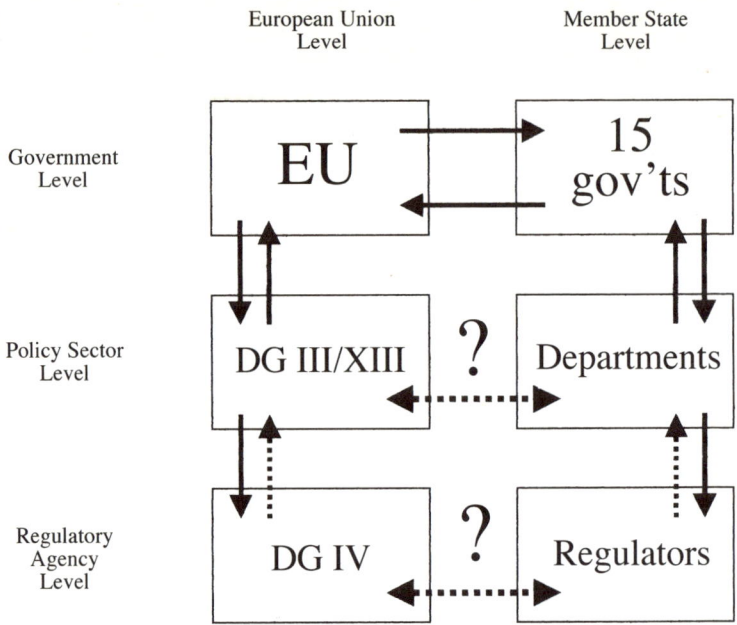

Figure 4.1 Relationship between key actors in the regulatory reform

van Miert's open rejection of the 'single purchaser model', the Commission's Article 90 powers, and the provision for Qualified Majority Voting in the Council of Ministers did not prevent a compromise that essentially permitted France to maintain Electricité de France's domestic monopoly (Van Miert 1994; CMEU 1996). It is of course entirely possible (and quite likely) that in due time this will give way to complete liberalisation, because partial liberalisation is unstable and generates its own momentum for further liberalisation (Hunt and Shuttleworth 1996). But, so far, some Member States have fought hard to project their institutional traditions onto the EU regime, or at least to secure their survival through flexible solutions. Hence our rejection of the teleological baggage, and our suggestion that the actors and institutions involved in the policy-focus warrant further study. Figure 4.1 indicates the relationships between the key actors in this process. The government level has attracted considerable attention, as have most of the vertical relationships (represented by the solid arrows). The broken arrows represent questions that have attracted somewhat less attention, but which warrant analysis given institutional diversity.

- The relationship between Member State government departments and the Commission DGs on the policy level has increasingly become the subject of academic analysis. Policy networks and policy community approaches have focused on the actors involved at this level and their relationships. However, the system of committee decision-making remains opaque, the infamous subject of 'comitology' (Sauter 1997: 207–10). Particularly in the telecommunications sector, the direction of impact depends on which country is considered, e.g. the leaders in the sector are more likely to escape EU influence, or even shape the direction of the development of the EU policies. The 'second-level' states, which develop policies in response to the EU, are far more likely to be influenced by it. The UK's development of its own ISDN standard, ahead of Euro-ISDN illustrates the point.

- The same holds for the relationship between DG IV and the Member State competition authorities and telecommunications regulators. Again the relationship varies across the Member States. For example, the UK telecommunications and competition authorities have not been heavily influenced by DG IV, though this is in the process of changing, the government considering bringing UK competition authorities and policy into line with the EU regime. The other side of the coin has been Franco-German efforts to influence the shape of EU competition policy, and the Mediterranean states adoption of EU-style regimes.

- The relationships between the independent agencies and the departments are of increasing importance in the telecommunications sector. DG IV's use of Article 90 has illustrated the extent to which agencies (the Directorate now operates much like an agency in many ways; Wilks 1992) can contribute to shaping the regime and policies. This is of considerable potential relevance given Europe's new NRAs, most of which have been established in states with little or no tradition of independent regulators. Though it remains unclear whether the NRAs or ministries will prove the dominant force, the EU-level experience suggests that the question is at least open.

Therefore, developments at Member State level cannot be explained thoroughly without reference to developments at the corresponding EU level, and vice versa. In the telecommunications sector the pressure has not come mainly from Member State governments or the College of Commissioners, let alone from the major non-governmental actors demanding integration, though all have mattered. Rather, it has been driven by regulatory reform at the Member State level, Davignon's initiative and DG IV's metamorphosis into an independent agency and the extensive use of actual or threatened action on the part of the Competition Commissioners.

However, Figure 4.1 contains one major omission – the telecommunications operators. Wilks' suggestion that the firms that are the targets of regulation be included in analyses of regulation (Wilks 1997), warrants an extension of Figure 4.1 to Figure 4.2. Telecommunications operators have undeniably exercised considerable influence over the shape and form of liberalisation, and even the nature of regulation, inasmuch as it is the product of negotiation in cases such as the UK. This is particularly relevant given the Commission's negotiate-or-we-will-legislate approach, which was used recently in Employment Commissioner Flynn's moderately successful attempts to persuade the 'social partners' in the sectors excluded from the Working Time directive to negotiate rules covering their sectors. This 'Social Dialogue' was written into the Social Chapter. The Commission's Auto-Oil programme, which represented a major effort to involve the two industries directly in developing new environmental regulation and standards, is a case in point. This consultation-based approach has also dominated the Commission's approach to telecommunications.

Again, in Figure 4.2, the broken arrows denote the problematic areas that may require further investigation, while the solid arrows indicate the less controversial flows of influence. The flanking arrows indicate the industry's conventional lobbying of EU and Member State institutions, including departments, DGs and the executive and legislative branches of government. The vertical arrows downwards from the regulatory agencies to the target of regulation are hardly controversial, as the regulators' task is to influence the targets. However, the possibility of the firms influencing the regulators raises three significant questions about the agency–operator relationship.

- To what extent are the telecommunications operators shaping the process of liberalisation, or at least its trajectory? Lawson recalls that the government's original preference was to break up BT, but that it was persuaded to privatise the company intact by its newly appointed chairman, George Jefferson. The government could not afford to add management opposition to the workforce's bitter opposition to privatisation (Lawson 1992: 222).
- Why do operators comply with regulation? Compliance is based to some extent on the legitimacy of the rules and procedures, and partly on self-interest because of image and reputation, or even fears that regulatory regime will be tightened (Wilks 1997: 287). Here the EU regime faces inherent *sui generis* problems of legitimacy: 'when firms choose to ignore, evade or defy European regulatory requirements, they do so with a stronger moral justification and with more public (and official?) sympathy than when they flout national regulations' (Wilks 1996a).
- How involved is the industry in drawing up the rules for the new regulatory regime, or setting the norms for enforcement? This entails a potential danger that regulation may be used to keep competitors

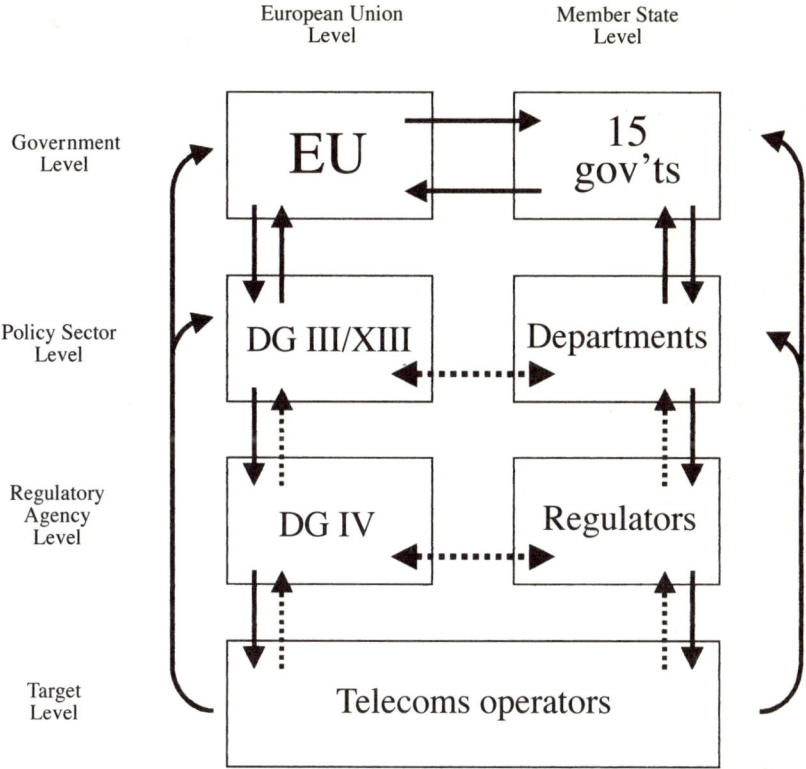

Figure 4.2 Extended model of relationship between key actors in the regulatory
reform

out of the market, as in the case of France's defence of its gas and
electricity monopolies. Agency capture has been of less concern in the
telecommunications sector.

In conclusion, two points should be made. First, the process of
liberalisation and regulatory reform of the telecommunications sector
in the European Union is anything but uniform. Although much of
the pressure for reform may have hit the EU symmetrically, and the
Commission provided a unifying force, institutions at Member State
and EU level shaped the path of reform and thus contributed to the
differences in their agency mechanisms. Rather than seek to harmonise
these, the EU approach to regulatory reform and liberalisation has been
based on accommodating institutional diversity. The outcome has therefore been a drive toward a new regulatory regime based on independent
agencies, which, although it appears unified compared to the previous

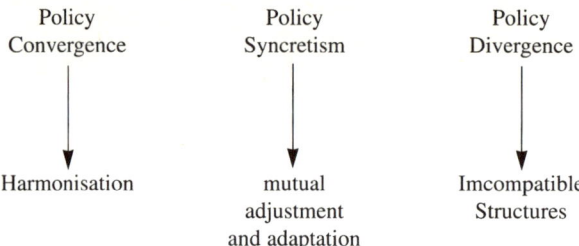

Figure 4.3 Approaches to European integration

PTT-based regime, contains several agency models rather than one single model. Interestingly, the current UK Competition Bill indicates that this *might* change in the long run. But theory does not demand that this must inevitably happen.

Second, this analysis offers a possibility of going beyond the teleological theories of integration, to emphasise the pluralist and unpredictable nature of EU integration in policy sectors. Hence policy syncretism. This concept has been used in a variety of disciplines such as comparative religion, philosophy and psychology, and refers to a general meaning of 'attempted union or reconciliation of diverse or opposite tenets', where 'the resulting system may lack coherence and contain contradictions and or inconsistencies' (OED 1993; PDP 1985). In fact, it is related to pluralist analysis of liberal democracy, where the focus on incremental decision-making relaxes the rational element of public policy (Lindblom 1959; 1979). Collective decision-making and partisan mutual adjustment thus replace rational games: 'it is a process where decisions are reached without an agreed consensus about matters of substance' and 'policy-makers advocate and pursue their own special concerns in a disjointed way' (Dunleavy and O'Leary 1987: 56). Hence the unpredictable outcome, a compromise that may not be completely rational, yet commands acceptance as a universal compromise because the different actors interpret its significance in a different light.

Reports of the death of the Luxembourg compromise might or might not be exaggerated, but its spirit certainly stalked the minds of Member State and Commission officials pursuing the liberalisation of telecommunications, gas and electricity markets. In the telecommunications sector, the outcome has been a move *toward* a single new regulatory regime, but one that accommodates a series of variations on a theme. There is, as of yet, no single model of European capitalism and no single model of European regulatory agencies, and the two are of course inextricably linked. The case for policy syncretism is clear: mutual influence and adaptation *where necessary*, but divergence or maintenance of differences *where possible*.

Notes

1 The authors wish to thank Steve John, the editors and the London School of Economics and Political Science Regulation Seminar for helpful comments on a draft version of this chapter.
2 Lord Lawson of Blaby was Financial Secretary to the Treasury 1979–81, Secretary of State for Energy 1981–83 and Chancellor of the Exchequer 1983–89.
3 Common tax measures were discussed at the 20–22 March 1998 informal meeting of EU Finance Ministers in York, *Financial Times*, 24 March 1998.

5 The European Union content regulation in the converged communication environment

Patrizia Cincera

Introduction

This chapter concerns both the regulation of multimedia sector content, including traditional broadcasting, as well as the new communication and information services, and the accompanying European Union framework legislation. The aim is not to draw conclusions on what the converged environment will be like, nor to analyse the sectors' interaction in the convergence process. Neither will issues of network and terminals regulation be addressed. Rather, the focus will be on the regulation of the content in the nascent multimedia environment at the European level and on the hindrances to progress currently facing the Information Society. The first part of the chapter sets out the initial attempts of the European Community to regulate media-sector content through the 'Television Without Frontiers' (TWF) Directive. We shall examine why and how the Community regulates, and what have been the results of TWF. The second part of the chapter focuses on the regulatory framework process with regard to the content aspects of the converged environment. The questions raised here concern activities at EU level and their purpose, why regulation is needed at EU level, and the possible consequences of such regulation for the development of the Information Society. Finally, we draw some conclusions on the attempts of EU content regulations and reflect on the difficulties of regulating media as compared to tele-communications.

In the last decade, the European audio-visual landscape has developed considerably with regard to privatisation, new communications technologies and content diversification. The audio-visual industry has also become increasingly important to the EU in terms of job creation, economic growth, consumer choice and cultural diversity. Its market, which is already the largest in the world, is expected to grow rapidly in the coming years. This expansion stems mainly from the emergence of new communication and information services, made possible by digital technology which has enabled more programmes to be transmitted over the same infrastructure (cable TV, satellite transponders, terrestrial spectrum). In the new communications infrastructure we find many services like programme bouquets,[1] thematic channels, video-on-demand, and pay-per-view. In addition the 'digital channel' can deliver other services in the form of data, graphics, moving pictures or combinations thereof. Hence, end-user choice is increased. Previously, broadcasting, telephony and on-line computer services were separated and operated on different networks. Today, digital technology enables those services to use the same networks and consumer devices, which has meant that the IT, telecommunications and media sectors are converging technologically towards a global communication world. However, these revolutionary advances are not necessarily associated with overall convergence. Markets, content, and the regulation authorities themselves, are all components of the Information Society which remain divergent to date.

EU intervention in the content regulation of the media and multimedia sector

The European Community justifies its intervention in the audio-visual sector in the application of the Treaty of Rome, which aims at the creation of a single market, and which is based on the principle of free movement of goods and services between Member States. This internal market also includes the broadcasting industries, as was made clear in the Commission's memorandum 'Television Without Frontiers',[2] published June 1984, which set out that EEC rules relating to the achievement of the common market also apply to products of the press, television and radio programmes, and to the activities of broadcasting and telecommunications bodies.

In addition to the economic objective of creating a vast internal market for European broadcasting industries, the European Community also wants to promote cultural policies, and to stimulate the creation of consensus between European cultures with a view to further European integration. After 1987, EEC cultural action has no longer been based simply on EEC treaty rules and on economic requirements. Instead, it has become a political need within the double perspective of internal market creation and the advancement of European citizens towards the European Union.

Furthermore, the EU has intervened in the media sector because, in light of the single market of 1992, it was imperative to understand the stakes of the new information technologies which represented a huge economic and commercial potential in the production of communication equipment (cable, satellite, fibre optic, HDTV), and also in the production of content (programmes, movies). Thus, the EU has advocated the setting up of an industry and market capable of competing with the United States and Japan. The new information technologies represent a high-value-added sector and their rapid expansion will boost the economy, as well as increasing the possibilities of new employment in the service sector. It is primarily for these reasons that the EU is active in trying to eliminate obstacles to the free circulation of programmes, to harmonise differing national legislation current in the Member States, and to narrow all the technical arrangements with regard to broadcasting.

From 1989, the European Community developed a plan to curb the alarming situation of the European audio-visual industry.[3] The EC set up two main objectives: the first was to set up and ensure the functioning of a European market for audio-visual products; the second to develop a new strategy for the strengthening of the European industry both in audio-visual hardware and software. These ambitions are organised along three main lines: a technological line which aims to settle the HDTV norm;[4] the regulatory line with the adoption of the 'TWF' Directive (upon which we will focus); and the third line which concerns the programme 'MEDIA' set up by the Commission to support the European audio-visual and cinema industry.

The Directive 'Television Without Frontiers'

Satellite and cable technology have abolished the frontiers of communication and, as the development of these new technologies will considerably increase the possibility of television programmes distribution, have rendered certain national broadcasting rules pointless. In the early 1980s, there was an increase in the demand for television programmes, which again lead to a subsequent increase in audio-visual production. The sudden interest of the EC in this sector is due to the alarming situation of the European broadcasting sector, which is lacking far behind the United States and Japan.

The TWF Directive, adopted by the Council on 3 October 1989, bound Member States to incorporate the regulations into their own laws. The main objective of the TWF directive is to create the necessary conditions for free movement of television broadcasts, and to this end it sets out the legal framework for television broadcasting in the single market. It also aims at creating the basis for a true European audio-visual area by implementing the free circulation of services. In addition, by co-ordinating national regulations in a number of fields relating to the provision of broadcast services, it attempts to provide a minimum set of common rules concerning advertising, protection of minors, moral standards, events of major importance to the public (particularly sports), right of reply and promotion of European works with the quotas of European programming. Member states must ensure that broadcasters under their jurisdiction respect the rules and must refrain from any restriction on reception of broadcasts coming from other Member States. Thus the Directive applies to programmes transmitted by ground relay stations and also to those transmitted by satellite and cable.

Among the areas covered by the Directive, the promotion of the distribution and production of European works represents an important point for the European Union. The Quotas measure aims at protecting European cultural and linguistic diversity. It states that Member States have to ensure, 'where practicable and by appropriate means', that broadcasters reserve a majority proportion of their transmission time for European works, excluding the time appointed to news, sports events, games, advertising, teletext services and teleshopping (Article 4). Member States must also ensure, where practicable and by appropriate means, that broadcasters reserve at least 10 per cent of their transmission time, or alternatively at the discretion of the Member State, at least 10 per cent of their programming budget, for European works created by producers who are independent of broadcasters (Article 5). The quota principle advocates the promotion of the distribution and production of European works, which means that each Member State has to take appropriate steps to ensure that television companies set aside the larger part of broadcasting time for European works.

The implementation of the Directive 'TWF'

The implementation of the Directive is based, on the one hand, on the extent to which the EU is legally allowed to intervene in the media sector, and on the other hand, on the effectiveness of the directive itself.

The principle of subsidiarity

EU cultural activities are subject to a set of judicial rules[5] and to the principle of subsidiarity. Audio-visual regulation is largely national in scope and the regulation of broadcasting is essentially determined at national level. Nevertheless, as we have seen, certain features are harmonised at European level through the TWF Directive, which represents the core of media regulation at the EU level.[6] The amendments to the EC treaty agreed at Maastricht formalised the principle of 'subsidiarity', which ensures that for 'the areas of joint competence, the EU should only act where the scale or effects of a particular policy area make action at that level more effective than individual action by the Member States' (Article 3B).[7]

The Directive's weaknesses

The Directive has been weakened by various obstacles to its implementation, and by the general questioning of the real need for its implementation at all. The main reason behind this has been the fierce opposition of some Member States towards its very existence. The audio-visual sector is a sensitive issue, reflecting as it does the national and regional cultural identity of the Member States. Perhaps not surprisingly, therefore, EU intervention in this sector was perceived by some of them as an intolerable incursion. The German Länder (States) are a good case in point. Culture is one of the main preserves of each individual Land, so that, especially with regard to broadcasting, they fought fiercely to defend their independence and to resist EU interference.[8] Consequently, the German delegation insisted on the Council attaching a written state-ment to the Directive describing the provision as 'politically' rather than 'legally' binding. This change made the Directive open to interpretation and, furthermore, effectively prevented the Commission from bringing Member States to court for failing to reach quota goals, and thus breach-ing the Directive.

The evolution of the Directive

In March 1995, the EU Commission approved the revision of the TWF Directive by a clear majority in order to reassert the legal framework favouring the development of television broadcasting activities in the single market. While the scope of the new Directive remains the same, i.e. point-to-multipoint broadcasting services, it also takes market trends, especially those due to technological advances, into account. New services are dealt within a separate Green Paper, i.e. the Green Paper on Convergence.[9]

This new Directive 'Television Without Frontiers' of 5 May 1997, comprises three new areas:

- Broadcasting of major events (Article 3a), which states that Member State are to recognise lists of major events (e.g. the Olympic Games, the football World Cup), drawn up by each government, which cannot be transmitted in coded form. This applies in particular to major sporting events, which MEPs wanted to ensure that the general public would have access to without having to subscribe to particular channels or on a pay-per-view basis.
- Use of the V-chip electronic filtering device (Article 22b). Within one year, the Commission, in liaison with the appropriate Member States authorities, would investigate the possible advantages and drawbacks of measures which would provide parents with technical methods for viewing control. The study will involve, *inter alia*, establishing appro-priate rating systems, encouraging family viewing policies and other educational and awareness measures.
- The issue of independent producers. According to the European Commission, the EU should give more support to independent

producers to encourage the production of European works. It was therefore important for the Member States to define the term 'independent producer'. The Directive holds that Member States should take appropriate account of criteria, such as the ownership of the production company, the amount of programmes supplied to the same broadcasters, and the ownership of secondary rights.

The new Directive was not originally intended to cover the new on-line multimedia services such as the Internet and video-on-demand, but the evolution, particularly of the latter, has made it necessary to extend EU regulation to these services. The next TWF Directive will require legislative amendments to take account of the changes occurring in the new communication world.[10]

EU content regulation adaptation to multimedia

At first, communications services were distinct, with broadcasting, voice telephony and on-line computer services all offered separately. Each operated on different networks using different technological 'platforms' such as TV sets, telephones, and computers, and each was regulated by different regulators at the national level. Today, with the advent of digital technology, a higher capacity of traditional programmes and new services can be transported over the same networks, even using integrated consumer devices for telephony, personal computing or television. Thus, media now comes within the scope of a broader communications framework, using telecommunication and other IT technologies. Currently, therefore, all three sectors utilise digital technologies[11] wherever possible and are able, on an increasingly international scale, to offer services outside their traditional sectors.

This growth potential, linked to the rapid development of a wide range of new audio-visual products and services, and boosted by information and communication technologies, has drawn the attention of national governments and EU policy-makers alike. Consequently, both, but specifically the latter, are trying to find the optimum regulatory framework to promote the information society, covering telecommunications, broadcasting and other electronic services.

Towards the regulatory framework of the digital age

Within the Commission several DGs are working on the setting up of the Information Society in Europe. DG IV is responsible for competition, DG III for industrial co-ordination, and DG XV for the internal market. DG X is in charge of the European audio-visual policy and DG XIII is active in the technical aspects of the communication industry: digital TV, telecommunications liberalisation, piracy and decoders standards. The major concern of the DG XIII has been the harmonisation of technical standards. While all these DGs have produced various directives concerning digital television, attention here will be on those which deal with the content aspects of the broad communication environment, that is primarily DG X, in collaboration with DG XIII. These have worked on three main action plans: the Green Paper on the protection of minors and human dignity in audio-visual and in the context of on-line services;[12] the Communication on illegal and harmful content on the Internet;[13] and the report on copyright and related rights in the Information Society.

In order to prepare the optimal approach to adapt the regulatory framework to the developing multimedia environment, the European Commission has produced a Green Paper on 'The regulatory implications of the convergence of the telecommunications, audio-visual and information technology sectors.[14] DG X set up a department to follow through the work on the Green Paper, which should be seen as a basis for discussion upon which the future regulatory framework of the new communications and information services can be built. In the Commission's view, this framework must be settled 'progressively' and 'by appropriate methods', and it is too early to lay down specific regulations at this stage of development of the new communications and information services. However, at the present stage of development, the temporary regulatory framework, with regard to content, encompasses the following objectives as seen from point of view of the EU:[15]

- Services must not be regulated according to the method of delivery. Convergence enables different types of networks to carry the same services. The focus on regulation would not be on the nature of the delivery system, but rather on the impact, 'public-ness', and degree of consumer control over the content.
- Regulation must encourage the market competitiveness, and must therefore be flexible enough to favour the emerging Information Society. However, public interest objectives (privacy and freedom of speech, pluralism, cultural diversity, taste and decency) will still be needed. Regulatory safeguards must intervene in case the market fails to ensure their fulfilment.
- Public and commercial broadcasters must participate in the digital venture and encourage the switching-off of analogue systems for the benefit of digital technology. Public-service broadcasting has been recognised as being the guarantor of high-quality content production; it should enter in the new communication services providing that its financial situation becomes completely transparent.
- The computer/on-line industry, in Europe and world-wide, does not support shifting broadcasting regulations to the on-line world. Their preferred approach to content issues is 'self-regulation'[16] (technology-based filtering and rating systems). Consumers should

be empowered to manage questions of content and policy-makers should rely on existing laws to address criminal activity on the Internet. Concerning the Internet, 'self-regulation' has been recommended.

- Priority should be given to European content. The benefits of the sector should be reintroduced in the content production. Reasonable obligations to favour such investments are recommended. The presence of powerful communication groups in Europe is required. The setting up of European rights catalogues is an important asset for the audio-visual industry.

- Regulatory authorities, numerous in Europe, should better co-ordinate their work to avoid overlap and inconsistencies (e.g. Oftel, the regulatory authority for telecommunications in the UK, and ITC for broadcasting, will be merging their guidance into one document. Oftel has set up 'Guidelines for regulation of digital television services').

- Privacy and data protection are specific objectives of public interest which need to be met in order for new communication services to develop properly. For users to have confidence in the security of information passed over the networks they use, they must be assured that their privacy is adequately protected. Therefore, the EU has addressed the data protection issue in a Directive[17] which will be complemented by specific rules governing data protection and privacy in telecommunications.

- Intellectual property rights (IPR) need a clear and robust regulatory framework in order to stimulate content creation and promote investments. Protection is required throughout frontiers, both for large firms and small and medium enterprises.

The role of EU intervention in the content regulation of the global communication environment

The actors involved in the convergence regulation process are the governments, policy-makers, broadcasters, satellite and cable operators, computer software and hardware companies, telecommunications operators, audio-visual producers. All are in the 'digital race' and seek to defend their own interests. The major and most difficult task is to find the right regulatory framework for the future of the digital convergence.

The need to regulate media

The European Union's attempts to regulate media are based on the following general reasoning: the media sector has a pervasive influence on people and plays a key role in the formation of public opinion. To achieve this objective, the media have to guarantee ideological plurality by offering content that covers a broad spectrum of ethical and political beliefs, and represents a wide range of interests. Media is a powerful tool with social, cultural and political foundations. It therefore requires regulation, which aims to safeguard general public interest and protect the consumer (human dignity, protection of minors, etc.), to strengthen competition, pluralism, and democracy, to preserve and promote European cultures (including minority of cultures), to avoid monopolistic positions, and to guarantee open access to networks for content providers. All these assumptions and normative evaluations are, however, part of a much larger public debate about freedom of speech and democracy which will not be discussed within the framework of this chapter.

The regulation at the EU level

Before the advent of cable and satellite television, and digital technology, traditional television was a scarce national resource (due to its use of frequencies for transmission) and its use was regulated by the state. When broadcasting was dominated by public channels, it was not difficult to control and to safeguard the general public interest. The liberalisation of the European television markets, and the development of new communication and information services, have diminished the influence of the public-service broadcasters. Additionally, the dawn of digital technology has made the boundaries between broadcasting and other media and communications services unclear. Today, broadcasting is closer to the world of telecommunications and computer delivery systems, and comes within the scope of the broader communication environment, commonly known as the Information Society.

Media is increasingly becoming a transfrontier phenomenon: cable and satellite operators are broadcasting across Europe and communications networks, such as the Internet with its inherently transborder nature, are disseminating information not just at the European level but world-wide. Given this global perspective, it is more appropriate to legislate at the European, or even better, at international level. But to date, the media market is still largely organised within national boundaries, as is associated legislation. This situation affects the establishment of a single European market in the audio-visual market, endangering the emergence of the Information Society and risks increasing the gap between the United States and Europe in such developments.

The next question then becomes to what extent the EU is able to regulate the content of the global communication environment, and what danger the latter could encounter through such regulation.

Since the electronic services, particularly the Internet, know no frontiers, we assume that content regulation at EU level is already an outdated need. On-line services can shift geographical location, they can be provided from almost anywhere with the consequence of putting them beyond the jurisdictional reach of member countries. Foreign programmes can export values that are alien to national and European viewers, and can be considered, therefore, as a cultural threat. Seeing that digital programmes are not a European phenomenon but an international one, the setting up of international treaties could be more effective in regulating world-wide on-line services and audio-visual broadcasting.

Concerning the 'European cultural identity', the same reasoning applies: imposing quota rules or even controls on electronic information access might be useless, since they can be easily circumvented by satellite television and the Internet. Rather than banning non-European programmes, a more efficient solution might be to encourage the production of European audio-visual and cinema industry development. Furthermore, the European cultural protectionism goes against the World Trade Organisation's (WTO) provision relating to the free movement of information services. This also, in the view of the European Commission, represents a threat to the development of European communication industry and could increase the already existing gap between the United States and Europe. Regarding these latter points, the right assumed by the EU to settle quotas in programming and to prevent European audiences from watching only non-European production if they wish, has to be questioned. In sum, to what extent is this provision in the 'TWF' Directive really efficient?

A further comment regarding the extent to which the EU is able to intervene in the content regulation concerns the nature of the regulation itself. Indeed, we have seen that content regulation is a domestic matter, in many countries mainly concerning regional and local authorities. In order to have a better understanding of regulation at the different levels, it is helpful to distinguish between the two fields of content regulation: the first concerning legal aspects, the second, cultural and social aspects. In the issue areas related to the control of information legally enforced by laws (e.g. computer crime, extreme gratuitous violence) where supranational consensus can be achieved, the EU should, in their own view, be allowed to regulate for the reasons given previously. However, for those issues of an inherently local, regional or national nature, such as political broadcasts or programmes which are culturally sensitive, the intervention of the EU should accordingly be limited to advice and support, but without any legally binding provision. Indeed, as the EU is an administrative giant involved in many different issues, it cannot expect to be aware of all local needs across Europe. Decentralisation in such areas, therefore, is seen by the EU to be essential to protect European cultural diversity.

At this stage, it is difficult to come to any fixed conclusion over whether EU intervention is needed or not, and if it is, to what extent. What can be said is that EU intervention in content regulation does not pose a threat as long as it acts in the interests of the consumer. The emergence of the

Information Society will not be jeopardised if the EU resists the temptation to replace national intervention, and rather remains a 'European agora', i.e. providing a forum where Member States can meet to discuss their views.

The aim of EU intervention in the multimedia regulation

The aim of the EU intervention in the regulation of multimedia is threefold:

- To encourage the development of a competitive European audio-visual contents industry, and by so doing increase economic growth and employment opportunities;
- To meet general public interest objectives (IPR, plurality of ownership, fair and effective competition, free speech, data protection, etc.), increase consumer choice and promote cultural diversity;
- To improve the functioning of the single market in this area whilst avoiding any fragmentation.

The EU legislation includes the principle of free movement of services in the Community, which presupposes the removal of unjustified barriers and the harmonisation of national legislation when needed. While the free movement of broadcasting services in the Community is secured by the TWF Directive, the transfrontier movement of other audio-visual and information services is covered by the general rules of the internal market, particularly the freedom to provide services. The aim of the European Commission is to ensure that measures adopted are not discriminatory (that freedom of providing services is respected) and that their application is in proportion to the objective pursued. The EU intervenes to ensure the free movement of services and undertakes harmonisation in order to ensure that the legal framework allows general public-interest objectives to be met. The philosophy of the EU is to co-ordinate national rules, but only to the extent necessary, according to the principle of subsidiarity.

Complex challenges

Adapting content regulation to the whole converged communication environment is not an easy task. Among all these questions, one answer at least can be given: convergence will occur in a rather long transitional period. Policy-making at the level of the European Union is faced with opposing objectives. On the one hand a market-led approach characterised by the desire to encourage economic priorities of industrial competitiveness is advocated, while on the other hand, there is the need to maintain public general interests (which require content regulation intervention). An additional consideration is the desire to promote a European cultural identity and content production (irrespective of their commercial success). Certainly it is not clear whether market forces can meet the latter objectives, and by regulating, there is a risk of stifling the development of the converged environment. However, leaving the market to its own devices is no solution either, as this leaves sensitive issues like the protection of minors, taste and decency, media concentration, and even the expansion of the European media industry, unresolved and exposed to potentially harmful developments. Not surprisingly, therefore, EU policy-makers have not yet been able to find the right balance between these contradictory objectives.

Meanwhile, the stance of the Commission has evolved towards a more liberal approach, especially DG XIII, which advocates that quantity will ensure diversity and that competition is good for digital television and services. DG X, however, tends towards the over-regulation of European broadcasting, making the sector dependent on EU subsidies. In their decisions, European policy-makers have inevitably been influenced by developments in the United States and the speech of the American vice-president Al Gore on the 'Global Information Infrastructure' (GII). Notwithstanding concerns for Europe to keep abreast of developments in the USA, European policy-makers should keep in mind that the European situation is largely different and, therefore, any regulation will have to be adapted to the European situation.

Why it is so difficult to regulate media (content) compared to telecommunications (conveyance)?

Telecommunications and broadcasting have quite different regulatory traditions because of their different social role. The telecommunications sector has been 'carrier-regulated' with the obligation to ensure universal service, to provide non-discriminatory access and not to interfere with content. Media has been highly regulated with controls on the content of the broadcast. In telecommunications, the flow of communication is interactive and one-to-one. By contrast, in broadcasting, communication flow is traditionally one-to-many and non-interactive. These characteristics are determinant in shaping the regulation. While telecommunications has nothing to do with content regulation since it handles voice telephony which comes within the scope of privacy, broadcasting is completely public and can therefore influence its audience. It is more difficult to regulate media compared to telecommunications because one needs the content to be regulated, the other simply does not.

The telecommunications sector in the run towards full liberalisation has to achieve the conditions for market entry (common framework for market entry), the maintenance of public interest (framework guaranteeing the provision of universal service, data protection and privacy), the interconnection and interoperability of services and networks, and fair allocation of resources. The focus of the regulatory framework for telecommunications has been on networks and service provision but not on the content regulation carried over those networks. A public telephone network has to provide universal service, which means that all citizens have the right to benefit from this fundamental social service, considered to be among the basic element of the freedom of expression. All users are treated alike in terms of prices and provision of service quality. In the broadcasting sector, again, the situation is more complicated. All users are not treated alike. Content regulation takes account of the different needs expressed by the audience: children, cultural minorities, religious beliefs and so on. Here as well, media regulation is more complicated compared to telecommunications because television has more to do with social, cultural and political concerns, and therefore the same regulation cannot easily be applied to everybody. By contrast, the telecommunications sector has to achieve objectives of a practical nature characterised by economical and technological aspects which are the same for everybody.

The second dimension in which media encounters greater difficulties in regulation compared to telecommunications, is the geographical aspect. We have seen that regulation in the audio-visual sector has political, social and cultural grounds. Broadcasting is highly regulated because it has to ensure general public interest, and provide unbiased information, educational programming, cultural promotion, programming for minorities, etc. Such issues are essentially determined at the national level. Therefore, audio-visual policy is largely national in scope in contrast to telecommunications (with the exception of the TWF Directive, which represents the first regulatory framework for the audio-visual sector at the European level). Additionally, it is worth noting that media regulation in some European countries is elaborated at the regional level, as in Belgium and Germany. This increases the difficulty when it comes to harmonising some aspects of content regulation at the supra-national level. The ubiquitous validity of telecommunication policies makes it easier to harmonise legislative measures at the EU level.

In sum, the key dividing line between the two sectors is the regulatory framework for content intended for the broadcasting sector, and the regulatory framework for activities relating to the delivery of content meant for the telecommunications sector. Thus, in the converged world of telecommunications and media, telecommunication operators eager to launch digital television programmes and/or on-line services will have to learn how to deal with the sensitive issue of content regulation.

Conclusion

It is important in the view of the European union to harmonise legislation at EU level because differences between Member States can generate disproportionate barriers to the free movement of audio-visual and information services within the Community. The main objective of the TWF Directive seeks precisely that thorough the establishment of a legal framework for the free movement of television broadcasting services and the development of a single market in broadcasting, production of television and cinema programmes and advertising. However, the Directive has not been efficient in developing a single market for European television mainly because of the loophole created by the change from a 'legally' to a 'politically' binding status, which weakened the effect of its implementation. Furthermore, the revised version of the Directive in 1997 still asks for majority European programming 'where practicable', despite the flexibility given in the implementation of the provision. Finally, it did not really take sufficient account of the rapid development of new television services so that it is already outdated and insufficient to respond to the challenge of digital technology. The broadcasting time principle, on which the present Directive is based, will also become meaningless because of the increasing individual choices offered by digital television. The quota issue, aimed at promoting European works, has not been adequately defined, and this could, in effect, aggravate rather than help the European audio-visual industry. The US entertainment industry should not be seen as a threat, but rather as complementary. For example, 'blockbuster' movies are mainly produced in the US and are in demand for pay-per-view or video-on-demand services. Finally, the 'paternalistic' approach of the EU could stifle content creation which seems to need adequate competitive, industrial policies more than subsidies.

Concerning attempts to regulate the multimedia services, it is hard to claim that a regulatory framework exists at the EU level. DG X is in charge of the content issues, whereas distribution of content comes within the purview of DG XIII. Despite their divergences (the first being more public-interests oriented, the second more liberal in its approach), the two DGs are collaborating over regulation but things are still at an early stage. Even if some content regulatory endeavours have been taken in the multimedia sector at EU level, a lot remains to be done before convergence can be truly discussed. In fact, the Commission and other working groups have already raised a myriad of questions in trying to untangle the complex situation of the converged environment, which shows that it is still too early to settle on a definitive regulatory framework. This will undoubtedly happen, but only gradually, and in the long term.

In the Green Paper on Convergence, it is stated that 'approaches to content regulation in the context of convergence need to be reassessed'. This presupposes that convergence exists, but convergence as it has been defined in the text is not yet a reality. The only form of convergence existing at the present is the technological one. However, even in this area a lot of progress remains to be made before full convergence is achieved (e.g. the diversity of European standards). In addition, although the word convergence is used here, there and everywhere, on closer inspection a range of divergences concerning content, regulatory authorities, and even the devices used in the IS can be detected.

Concerning the role of the EU in content regulation, we have seen that the extent to which the EU can intervene is geographically limited. The rest of the world – especially the United States – is also active in the regulation process, and the multimedia sector is exported world-wide. Therefore, international regulations are required so that the EU has to co-operate with multinational bodies like the OECD, the WTO and the United Nations in order to settle an efficient regulatory framework. The second limitation on EU intervention comes from the member countries eager to preserve and promote their cultural sovereignty. Areas related to social and culturally sensitive issues need to be tackled initially at the local, regional, and national levels, and only thereafter at the EU level. The current aim of the EU, however, is to encourage the development of a competitive European audio-visual industry, to protect general public interest objectives, to promote cultural diversity by, for instance, offering financial support, and to ensure the functioning of the single market in this area.

In the last part of the chapter we have tried to explain why it is more difficult to regulate media compared to telecommunications. Media encounters greater difficulties because the sector requires content regulation while telecommunications face problems of a more practical nature characterised by economical and technological aspects. Additionally, media is a national matter while the telecommunications sector is a transfrontier service. This means that media content regulation deals with a lot of different regulatory levels. In conclusion, content regulation is a sensitive issue because of its pervasive influence on people and its role in the formation of public opinion. All these social, cultural, and political aspects are absent in the telecommunications sector which make the mission of its regulation easier.

The new communication and information services are rapidly becoming thriving economic sectors, which will flourish in the context of a world-wide market. Businesses use the scale of the EU market to compete effectively around the world. A correctly designed regulatory framework at EU level could lead the European entertainment industry to become a thriving production sector. In order to do so, the right balance must be found between regulation on the one hand, and competition on the other. It appears unlikely that an optimal regulatory framework of the global communication world will be forthcoming in the near future. The new communication world is still in its infancy and regulation will probably be an issue-by-issue process.

One point is at least sure, policy-makers and regulators should bear in mind the most important question: how can quality content be promoted to best serve our 'Information Society'? Most of the attention has focused on the medium rather than on the message. What are we going to do with a thousand new channels if there is no content to be conveyed? Regulatory bodies, at whatever level, strive hard to regulate the existing content on the different communication and information services, and this is necessary for the reasons already presented. But what is also necessary, and widely lacking, are policy strategies to help the entertainment industry develop. The convergence between media, telecommunications and computer-based services is a matter of time, but the real emergence of the Information Society does seem to depend on the expansion of content creativity.

Notes

1 Programme bouquets means a group of programme channels allowing viewers to access programmes like news, sport, movies, etc. when they wish to see them, rather than waiting for the appropriate segment broadcast by the generalist TV.
2 Livre vert sur 'L'établissement du marché commun de la radiodiffusion, notamment par satellite et par câble', COM (84) 300 final.
3 The European audio-visual and cinema industry is in a serious economic deficit situation in comparison with the United States. The European audio-visual industry also suffers from a great lack of programmes. This situation is due to the rise in the costs of production of programmes and to the increase of the daily broadcasting time. The fragmentation of the European audio-visual market – because of national cultural and linguistic diversity – aggravates Europe's negative audio-visual trade balance with North America, which benefits from a large market that makes investments profitable. European countries cannot redeem their production investments because their internal market has too low an absorption capacity.
4 Beginning in 1993, the EU will abondon analog HDTV for digital technology.
5 Article 128 §5, newly inserted in the Maastricht Treaty for EU cultural policies, provides for the Co-decision institutional procedure provided for in article 189B.
6 The EU Treaty, however, contains a large number of articles relevant to the autio-visual policy, including free movement of goods (Art. 9, 12, 30 and 31), freedom of movement of workers, right of establishment and freedom to provide services (Art. 48 to 66). Article 127 provides for professional training projects, Article 128 for promoting culture and Article 130 for industrial policy initiatives. Competition rules and common commercial policy also play a significant role in this sector.
7 'Traité sur l'Union européenne', Commission des Communautés européennes, Office des publications officielles des Communautés européennes, Bruxelles, 1992.
8 However, the European incursion in national and regional cultural policies is greatly limited by the Council's obligation to make unanimous decisions.
9 'Green Paper on the Convergence of the Telecommunications, Media and Information Technology sectors, and the implications for regulation', COM(97)623, Brussels, 3 December 1997.
10 We have seen that the amendment of the Directive 'TWF' in 1997 takes into account some aspects of the evolution of the communications industry. How-

ever, it still remains inadequate and DG X has supplemented several draft and adopted measures adapted for the new communication and information services. Among them we find: a draft 'Conditional Access' Directive that aims to protect broadcasting and Information Society services that are offered to the public on a subscription; a proposal for a Council Recommendation on the Protection of Minors and Human Dignity; the 'Transparency' Directive, which sets in place an administrative procedure that will apply to Information society services, to promote the smooth functioning of the internal market; and a directive on the use of standards for the transmission of television signals.

11 Examples of technological convergence are numerous: Internet services delivered to TV sets via systems like Web TV; using Internet for voice telephony; webcasting of radio and TV programming on the Internet; e-mail and World Wide Web access via digital TV decoders and mobile telephones.

12 Green Paper on the Protection of Minors and Human Dignity in audio-visual and information services, COM(96)0483.

13 Commission Communication on Illegal and Harmful content on the Internet, COM(96)0487.

14 Green Paper on the 'Convergence of the Telecommunications, Media and Information Technology sectors, and the implications for regulation', COM(97) 623, Brussels, 3 December 1997.

15 We shall present here the major results following the Green Paper. These are the views of the EU Commission and of various working groups co-operating with the latter.

16 Traditional television and on-line services do not have the same regulations. The fundamental difference between the Internet and broadcasting is the question of liability. In broadcasting the liability is clear: The broadcaster is liable for the content and can always be identified because of the controls based in the home country. In contrast, liability rules on the Internet are not clear. Who should be held responsible: the infrastructure provider, the service provider, the access provider or the content provider?

17 Directive 95/EC of the European Parliament and Council on the protection of individuals with regard to the processing of personal data and the free movement of such data, OJ L281, 23 November 1995, COM (90)314, OJ C277, 15 November 1990.

Part II

National strategies in some EU countries

Mark Thatcher discusses in Chapter 6 how regulatory reform in Britain since the early 1980s has been characterised by the legacy from privatisation of BT, where behavioural regulation was centred on BT. The form, speed and extent of the liberalisation process were to a large extent determined by the decisions of a regulator wishing to ensure effective competition. The reform has not resulted in 'deregulation', nor in the 'rolling back of the state'.

Raymund Werle argues in chapter 7 that relevant German advocates of liberalisation – including the Federal Ministry of Economic Affairs and, to some extent, the Ministry of Posts and Telecommunications – have been instrumental in initiating reforms both at the national and European level. Recently, a significant degree of liberalisation has been achieved in the German telecommunications market, but the dominant position of Deutsche Telekom is still a reality.

Winston Maxwell demonstrates in Chapter 8 the status of one of the most important issues for competition, namely licensing. The regulator has been reluctant to give out new operating licences, and has also showed 'interventionist tendencies' under the auspices of universal service obligations. There are signs, however, that procedures are improving, and that the ART is exercising its authority to a greater extent in favour of new entrants.

6 Liberalisation in Britain

From monopoly to regulation of competition

Mark Thatcher

The British experience of telecommunications regulation in the 1980s and 1990s provides a particularly appropriate and important case study of 'liberalisation'. Britain was one of the earliest countries in Europe to undertake privatisation, the extension of competition and the establishment of a new regulatory regime. A period of more than a decade has provided evidence of the factors influencing liberalisation and sufficient time for its impacts to be seen. Moreover, Britain has constituted an important pressure and example for regulatory changes at the European and national levels.

Analysis of events in British telecommunications in the 1980s and 1990s indicates the importance of carefully specifying the concept of 'liberalisation'. Frequently it is associated with privatisation, 'deregulation', replacing 'the state' with more of 'the market' and the 'rolling back of the state' (see, for example, Swann 1988; Wolf 1988; Toffler 1990). However, liberalisation can also be seen as the introduction of greater competition, which involves continuing state involvement and regulatory reform (see Majone 1989; Cawson *et al.* 1990; Majone 1994; Wright 1993; S. K. Vogel 1996).

Examination of the regulation of telecommunications in Britain shows that these aspects of liberalisation offer differing conclusions. Ending monopolies and allowing competition in supply can coexist with vigorous activity by regulators. Indeed, instead of asking whether 'deregulation' has occurred, the chapter suggests that it is more profitable to analyse the form of liberalisation and accompanying regulation that have been introduced. Of particular interest is the replacement of detailed sector- specific rules with the general regulation that applies to economic activity.

The chapter therefore looks at 'liberalisation' in telecommunications in Britain, both in terms of the extension of competition and the changing nature of regulation. It argues that the characteristics of telecommunications regulation were influenced by the new institutional framework established in the 1980s and by the inheritance of privatisation. Initially, regulators engaged in detailed controls over British Telecom, applying their institutionally-provided powers and instruments. However, in the 1990s, as competition developed, there was a degree of movement towards more general competition rules. The result of the process is a national market with a powerful supplier, but one that has become increasingly open to competition, supported by a mixture of detailed sector-specific rules and the more recent application of broader regulatory controls.

Reform of the institutional framework of telecommunications regulation

The 1980s saw the end of the traditional 'posts and telecommunications model' in which both services were supplied by a government department. The process of reform had begun in 1969, when the Post Office had become a public corporation; it gained its own legal identity, being headed by a Board, and its staff were no longer civil servants but were employed under ordinary contracts. Reform continued in 1981 when British Telecommunications (BT) became a separate public corporation and the link with postal services was severed. Nevertheless, as public corporations, the Post Office and then BT remained subject to ministerial intervention and particularly to Treasury controls over investment and required rates of return.

The major change took place in 1984: the government privatised BT, selling 51 per cent of the shares to private investors; the remaining public stake was sold in 1990 and 1993. A new regulatory regime was established in the place of public ownership. Legislation ended BT's monopoly, replacing it with a system of licences. A new, industry-specific regulator was created, the DGT (Director General of Telecommunications), who was appointed by the government but enjoyed a measure of independence. The DGT headed an office that became known as Oftel (the Office of Telecommunications), although powers were vested in the DGT as an individual and not in Oftel.

The legislation divided functions and powers over licensed suppliers between several regulators. The government (specifically, the Secretary of State for Trade and Industry) had the power to issue licences, whilst licence terms were enforced by the DGT. Modification of licence terms was possible via two routes. First, a licence change could be made by agreement between the DGT and the licensee; however, the Secretary of State for Trade and Industry had the power to block the proposed change. Second, the DGT could refer a matter to the MMC (Monopolies and Mergers Commission), an independent general competition regulator setting out the need for a licence modification; if the MMC report were favourable, the DGT could impose a licence change on the licensee. General competition law applied to telecommunications, but many powers were held concurrently by the DGT and the Director General of Fair Trading.

The extension of competition was not the central reason for the privatisation of BT and the establishment of a new regulatory regime. Rather, the reforms were undertaken for reasons of fiscal pressure, party political advantage, dissatisfaction with the previous nationalised industry arrangements, new ideas about competition and the role of the private sector, and the example of the United States (Moon *et al.* 1986; Hills 1986). Insofar as the prospect of extensive competition did play a role, it was used to justify privatisation, notably through the arguments that a publicly-owned BT would be vulnerable in competing with privately-owned suppliers or that fair competition would be impossible (cf. Beesley 1981).

The fact that liberalisation was not the central thread in the reforms of 1984 was reflected in the new institutional arrangements. The duties of the Secretary of State and the DG were very broadly defined. Their primary ones were to ensure that supply satisfied 'all reasonable demands' and that suppliers could finance such provision of services. Maintaining and promoting 'effective competition' was only a secondary duty and, moreover, liable to conflict with the other primary and secondary duties listed in the Telecommunications Act 1984. The new regulatory framework lacked detail and left great discretion in the hands of the regulators over the central aspects of competition and the future nature of regulation. Thus, for instance, the legislation did not define which services would be opened to competition, nor did it lay down detailed substantive criteria for the Secretary of State in issuing licences or determining licence terms. It also said little about interconnection terms or the procedures to be followed by the DG or Secretary of State when deciding their overall approach to regulation.[1] Perhaps most important in indicating the modest place of liberalisation was that BT remained one company, despite strong support for its break up from the Prime Minister, Mrs Thatcher, and Conservative backbenchers. Instead, faced by fierce resistance by BT management to splitting the company, and in order for the sale to go ahead on time and without obstruction from BT's senior management, BT was sold as a single, integrated company that supplied the infrastructure, voice telephony, advanced services and customer premises equipment (pers. comm.).

The regulatory regime introduced in Britain in 1984 thus stands in contrast to that of other countries in Western Europe, such as France and Germany: reform took place much earlier; it was unrelated to the EC or other developments in Europe; the new regime was very broad, with major decisions left to the regulators, notably over the issuing of licences and their terms. The institutional framework of regulation remained largely unchanged between 1984 and 1998.[2]

The central actors in regulation and their strategies 1984–1998

After 1984, regulatory decisions were dominated by three actors who occupied the centre of the 'regulatory space' in telecommunications: the government; Oftel; and BT (Scott *et al.* 1997; cf. Hancher and Moran 1989). Each had its own strategy, although that strategy was modified over time, especially in the 1990s.

During the process of privatisation, the government wished to protect BT by limiting competition. This was due to several factors, notably the government's desire to maximise proceeds from the privatisation of BT and BT management's pressure to enjoy protection from 'cream-skimming' by new entrants and to have time to prepare for competition. However, after privatisation, the government gradually extended competition, albeit only reaching the fixed-line infrastructure in the 1990s. The government thus sought to give BT time to adapt to a new competitive environment. Moreover, it supported measures that would aid BT's expansion overseas, including EU liberalisation and access to the US market.

Oftel, under its first director general, Sir Bryan Carsberg (DGT 1984–92), rapidly placed competition at the centre of its approach to regulation. It developed a 'conceptual framework' that justified the choice of this secondary duty as the central 'guiding principle' for regulation (see Oftel Annual Reports 1984, 1985; Carsberg 1989, 1991). It claimed that competition would benefit consumers and was compatible with its other duties. At the same time, regulatory action was needed to ensure that competition was fair and effective, thereby providing a basis for many measures to regulate competition. However, where competition was not possible, Oftel suggested that in order to produce similar incentives and pressures to those offered by competition, it needed to establish a regulatory framework that 'mimicked' a competitive market.

In the 1990s, under Don Cruickshank (DGT from 1993), Oftel changed its emphasis, concentrating instead on withdrawal from detailed regulation through 'prescriptive' licence conditions, as effective competition developed. It argued that it was transforming itself into an industry-specific sectoral competition authority, applying 'simple over-arching principles' backed up where necessary by guidelines derived from general UK and EC competition law (Oftel Annual Report 1995).[4] It thus sought, to some extent at least, to replace *ex ante* regulation (via detailed licence conditions) with broader, *ex post* regulation (policing competition as it developed). Oftel claimed that its new approach matched changed market conditions, notably the development of 'real competition' in some market segments. Intrusive regulation carried dangers of limiting choice and innovation and hence 'the regulator must not meddle more with the market than is justified in ensuring fair competition' (Oftel Annual Report 1996, 1995 pp. 1–2).

On privatisation, BT found itself a vertically integrated supplier with almost 98 per cent of the UK market operating under a detailed licence that contained many conditions governing its decisions. It faced the legacy of past policies: a relatively backward network (due to years of limited investment), problems with technological development (notably digital switching) and the choice of intermediate technologies. Its tariffs, internal organisation and culture reflected its previous status as a public corporation. In response, BT's strategy was twofold. On the one hand, it took advantage of its new status to undertake measures designed to transform itself into a competitive private sector firm. It increased capital spending to modernise its network, particularly by introducing digital switches and optical fibre cables. Staff numbers were reduced, and a series of organisational changes were introduced, together with attempts to alter the 'culture' of BT to one seen as more appropriate to an aggressive business (Pitt 1990; Willman 1994). Prices were 'rebalanced' to bring them closer to costs and to meet pressures from competitors (actual or potential). BT internationalised, through alliances (notably Concert) and purchases (sometimes unsuccessful) of foreign firms.[5] On the other hand, in relation to the regulators in Britain, BT sought removal of controls on its behaviour. Rather than attacking the principle of wider competition, it argued that it should be allowed to compete (notably in broadcasting transmission) and be freed from regulatory restrictions, and that its competitors, especially foreign ones, should not enjoy unfair advantages.

The interaction of the strategies and decisions of the government, Oftel and BT influenced the division of roles and the relations between the actors in the process of liberalisation. The government set the boundaries of competition through its licensing decisions, albeit often relying heavily on advice from Oftel, but did not intervene in the day-to-day regulation of telecommunications in Britain. In contrast, BT and Oftel engaged in almost constant communication and sparring. Oftel embarked on vigorous activity in a two-pronged strategy: first, taking action to protect consumers; second, undertaking measures that promoted competition. Given BT's dominance in the UK market, most activity concerned the interpretation and modification of BT's licence conditions. Over the period 1984–98, a series of modifications of BT's licence were made, covering almost all aspects of its business, from price controls to fair trading and information provided to the regulator. A form of 'game' developed (cf. Veljanovski 1991): BT and Oftel undertook detailed discussions on a possible licence change; in the background (and sometimes in the foreground for contentious issues) existed the threat that if they did not reach agreement, the DGT would refer the matter to the MMC; such a reference would result in a period of uncertainty for BT and carry the danger that the issue of breaking up BT would reappear; hence, almost all licence modifications were agreed between Oftel and

BT.[6] The lack of references to the MMC, togther with Oftel's strategy in the 1990s of positioning itself as a sector-specific competition authority, meant that the general competition authorities, notably the MMC, were not active participants in regulation. Instead, over the period 1984–98, Oftel became established as a powerful force for greater competition, central to regulation of the sector.

Liberalisation in practice: from regulation of monopoly to regulation of competition

The extension of competition

The ending of BT's monopoly over supply and the licensing of competitors had begun before privatisation, but the process was greatly accelerated and extended after 1984. The government issued licences for value-added network services and authorised the sale of all types of customer premises equipment in the mid/late 1980s. Competition was extended in mobile and satellite communications: a duopoly in analogue mobile telephony had begun in 1982; several licences were given for other mobile networks (Personal Communications Networks and one-way 'Telepoint' services in the late 1980s, and then digital GSM (Groupe Service Mobiles) services in the 1990s); paging also saw the entry of several operators and satellite services were opened up to competition in the late 1980s.

Competition in fixed-line voice telephony and infrastructure had started with the establishment of Mercury, largely owned by Cable and Wireless, in 1982. On the privatisation of BT in 1984, the government widened Mercury's licence. However, it also promised investors in BT that resale of transmission capacity for public voice telephony would remain prohibited for five years and that the BT–Mercury duopoly over the infrastructure and fixed-line voice telephony would not be broken for at least seven years. When the time periods ended, the government, strongly supported by Oftel, lifted the limits on competition: unrestricted resale of spare capacity was allowed in 1989; the BT–Mercury duopoly over fixed-line infrastructures in the United Kingdom ended in 1991, when the government announced that it would license other applicants, with a presumption that licences would be granted unless there were good reasons not to do so (although no legislative changes were made to give applicants the right to a licence) (Department of Trade and Industry 1991). Indeed, Oftel and the government actively encouraged competition in the infrastructure, and new suppliers entered the long-distance market, often using the networks of other utilities such as the railways and electricity companies, and in the local loop, where competition was driven by the cable television companies. The final element of duopoly was terminated in 1996, when the government allowed competition in international communications.

Ensuring effective competition: interconnection

Although licences were issued to suppliers by the Secretary of State, effective competition required suitable regulation of behaviour, a task to be performed by Oftel. Interconnection between networks was central to competition. BT's licence contained conditions whereby BT was to provide connection with other public telecommunications operators, licensed systems and apparatus, with clauses allowing the DGT to determine interconnection terms in the event of a dispute. Oftel rapidly became directly and deeply involved in setting conditions and tariffs (for an overview until 1994, see Cave 1994). After BT and Mercury failed to reach agreement on interconnection terms in 1984, the DGT (Sir Bryan Carsberg) made a 'determination' (Oftel 1985). He ruled that there should be full interconnection between the two networks, so that users of either network could call each other.[7] Moreover, the tariffs charged by BT were based on its fully allocated historic costs, plus a percentage decided by Oftel, rather than its retail tariffs; nevertheless, few details were given of the calculation on which the determination was based and the coverage of the charges (notably concerning social costs) was not clear, nor were different types of costs distinguished.

The end of the duopoly in 1991 resulted in pressures for change. One question was the basis for interconnection determinations. In 1993, a new determination excluded certain categories of BT expenditure that could be included in its cost base. In 1995, as part of inter-connection and accounting separation, BT was obliged to allocate costs to different parts of its network activities, information used by Oftel in calculating interconnection charges. Then, as part of price controls from 1997, the basis for interconnection charges was altered to long-run incremental costs, thereby seeking to 'mimic' an economically efficient competitive market, rather than allowing BT to recover its past expenditure.

Another issue was BT's claim that it made a loss on certain services and, in particular, on providing access to the network, since prices for access were below actual costs. In 1991, the DGT modified BT's and Mercury's licences to set out more explicit rules and powers over inter-connection charges and social costs. The licence changes empowered the DGT to impose additional interconnection charges known as 'access deficit contributions' (ADCs) to cover these costs, although as part of Oftel's policy of 'entry assistance', the DGT was also given the power to grant waivers of ADCs.[8] In practice, however, the DGT continued to waive ADCs for almost all operators (Gillies and Marshall 1997: 143),[9] whilst BT continued to argue that it was bearing costs, notably of universal service, that it was not able to recover through its charges. In 1994–95, Oftel reviewed ADCs as part of its work on BT pricing and the cost of universal service and in 1997 decided to end them, with any costs of universal service being met by a special fund rather than interconnection charges (see p. 104; see also Oftel 1993, 1994a).

The entry of new operators after 1991 called into question Oftel's detailed involvement in price-setting through annual 'determinations' if the operators failed to agree on interconnection terms: the process was slow and contrary to Oftel's desire to become a 'competition authority'. In response, Oftel loosened controls on interconnection rates (see Oftel 1994a, 1995c, 1996, 1997a, 1997b). From 1997, it ended the previous system of setting particular rates for interconnection in annual 'determinations'. Instead, price controls were removed from services opened to competition. For services that were likely to become competitive ('prospectively competitive services'), price controls would be ended when competition occurred; in the meantime, a cap of RPI–0 was set.[10] For 'bottleneck' services (notably call termination services – i.e. from the local exchange to their destination on the local loop) and for services not opened to competition, Oftel set price caps, but in the form of baskets, thereby allowing price rebalancing.[11] Thanks to the development of competition, the network charge cap only covers around 45 per cent of BT's wholesale revenues (Bell 1997). Furthermore, BT became freer to decide its prices: it set interconnection charges, albeit within the constraints imposed by specific price controls. However, Oftel retained many powers to intervene in the case of disputes between operators and if it believed that anti-competitive behaviour was occurring. Moreover, BT was required to publish indicative maximum prices and minimum tariffs ('floors and ceilings') based on costs, according to a methodology established by Oftel. These indicative prices provided guidance to BT and interconnecting operators and also offered Oftel data to use in deciding whether anti-competitive behaviour was taking place (for details, see Oftel 1997c). Oftel was able, thanks to the new 'fair trading' conditions in licences, to act against anti-competitive behaviour, and breach of the indicative tariffs would represent weighty evidence of anti-competitive action.

Regulating anti-competitive behaviour

As a vertically-integrated dominant supplier, BT was in a powerful position to distort competition. In order to prevent this, conditions in BT's licence prohibited it from showing 'undue preference or discrimination' and from undertaking measures that would give it an unfair advantage as network operator in markets for other services, such as linked sales or exclusive deal arrangements. After privatisation, Oftel was responsible for ensuring observance of these licence clauses, notably in relation to cross-subsidisation and BT not favouring its subsidiaries in purchases.[12] Enforcement, therefore, was highly dependent on appropriate information being available on BT's internal practices, especially concerning cross-subsidisation. However, BT was an integrated company, with operating divisions established for business purposes and producing commercial accounts. Following pressure by Oftel, in 1995 BT introduced 'Interconnection and Accounting Separation', providing regulatory accounts ('financial statements') designed to offer information in a form suitable for Oftel's regulatory decisions (see Oftel Annual Report 1995: 29–31; Oftel 1993, 1994a). In particular, BT had to produce separate accounts for different businesses on a regulatory basis, for instance, distinguishing its access, network, retail, and supplemental services and apparatus supply. Moreover, BT had to 'unbundle' costs, setting out which costs were apportioned to which business and explaining the basis for so doing. Using this information, Oftel determined interconnection charges and checked that BT was not unfairly discriminating in access to its network against third parties who were competitors downstream.[13]

With its desire to become a 'competition authority' and the extension of competition in the 1990s, Oftel sought major modifications to the conditions under which anti-competitive behaviour was regulated. It decided to alter BT's licence conditions in 1994–5 to include a broad prohibition of anti-competitive agreements and abuse of a dominant position, these clauses being modelled on Articles 85 and 86 of the Treaty of Rome. Oftel argued that in a fast-moving competitive market, it was not appropriate to have licence conditions to cover specific individual types of anti-competitive behaviour (Oftel 1994b, 1995a). Although BT bitterly opposed the licence change, it ultimately chose to accept it as part of the new 1997 price controls, rather than face a reference to the MMC. Similar conditions are being placed in the licences of other operators. Moreover, in 1998, a Competition Bill is being considered by parliament which would take the statutory framework for regulating competition closer to that of the EC; it would enable the DGT to levy fines for anti-competitive behaviour by suppliers (Department of Trade and Industry 1997).

Retail price controls

The most visible form of consumer protection was through price controls on BT's retail services (for economic analyses, see Vickers and Yarrow 1988; for a legal/historical overview, see also Prosser 1997: 66–71). They were included in BT's licence conditions (and hence were open to modification by Oftel) and took the form of a price cap on certain services using the formula of changes in the retail price index minus a certain percentage (known as 'RPI–X'), set for a number of years. On privatisation, a price cap of RPI–3 per cent was set on a basket of services covering local and trunk calls, together with access charges, for a period of five years; in addition, BT accepted a 'voluntary' limit for rentals of RPI+2 per cent. Over the following decade, however, price caps were extended: by the early/mid-1990s, the basket included operator calls, directory enquiries and international calls; individual price caps were placed on connection charges, rentals and leased lines (for details, see Armstrong *et al.* 1994: 223–30). Thus, by the mid-1990s, 64 per cent of BT's revenues were covered by price controls, whilst a variety of sub-caps existed on individual services (Oftel Annual Report 1996: 3; Oftel 1996). Moreover, the caps appeared to tighten, with the overall cap on the main basket of services being RPI–7.5 per cent for the period 1993–97.

Oftel's role in price reviews was central. Each modification of the price controls (1989, 1991, 1993 and 1997) saw prolonged discussions between Oftel and BT; the threat of a reference to the MMC by Oftel was averted by agreement with BT. In the absence of detailed substantive rules governing the renewal of price controls, Oftel enjoyed considerable discretion in establishing a framework for its decisions. In the 1980s, it argued that regulation should create incentives for BT to increase its efficiency without allowing it to earn 'excessive' profits by 'mimicking' a competitive market: in the long run, BT should earn only 'normal' profits, but it could exceed this level between price reviews by producing additional efficiency gains. As a result, the determination of price controls became a complex matter: Oftel looked at BT's profits, rate of return, comparable rates of return, expected future investment and possible efficiency gains. Many of these matters involved considerable judgement, thereby increasing Oftel's discretion. Moreover, within the control of BT's overall prices lay the issue of tariffs for individual services, a vital matter in a competitive market. Oftel explicitly supported tariff 'rebalancing' by BT so that prices moved closer to costs (notably by long-distance prices falling relative to access and local charges) (see, for example, Carsberg 1986: 2; Oftel 1988: 22). This process was made possible by the price caps, which were either in basket form or which permitted increases above the RPI for access charges. Thus Oftel became closely involved in many aspects of pricing policy by BT, from tariffs (overall and for individual services and groups) to issue of rates of return, costs and efficiency gains.

The mid-1990s saw some reversal of the trend towards increasingly extensive and specific price controls over BT's retail services. In 1996, Oftel and BT agreed to end the specific price cap on residential line rentals (of RPI+2 per cent), replacing it with reference prices; BT was therefore able to offer a wider range of discount packages, covering both rentals and call charges (see Oftel 1995a). The most radical change came in the 1995–6 price review (taking effect in 1997).[14] Oftel argued that high-spending users had 'disproportionally' benefited from previous price controls and were protected because they had access to effective competition (see Oftel 1996). On the other hand, smaller users, notably most residential customers and small businesses, had benefited less and still did not enjoy sufficient choice through competition. Oftel therefore sought to concentrate retail price controls on segments of the market in which competition was less strong, whereas BT's prices in other areas could be regulated through competition; in addition, Oftel could apply its new powers under 'fair trading' conditions in operators' licences (which formed part of the agreement with BT on price controls from 1997) (Oftel 1996). The scope of formal price controls on BT for the period 1997–2001 was therefore reduced. A price cap of RPI–4.5 per cent applied to BT, but only to its tariffs for residential customers in the form of a basket of rental charges and calls based on the spending patterns of the lowest 80 per cent of residential users; hence, the weights of rental and local call charges would increase, and the reduction in charges would be concentrated on lower-spending users. As a result, only 26 per cent of BT's revenues would be covered. BT promised that bills (for equivalent usage) for small businesses would not rise in real terms, and that 'reference prices' would be the same as for residential customers.[15] Two services were removed from the price cap (specially-tariffed voice telephony services and directory enquiries). Moreover, Oftel stated that it was 'confident' that effective competition at the retail level was not far away and that the 1997–2001 price control would therefore be the last one for BT's retail services (Oftel 1996: paragraph 2.12).

Provision of customer information and quality of service

Oftel also undertook wide-ranging action over quality of service. It collected and published statistics concerning BT's quality of service, obliging the company to resume publication of its internal data on quality. It then ensured that information was available on other operators, so that by the mid-1990s it was able to offer comparable figures on many aspects of quality of service, from faults to bill accuracy (see Prosser 1997: 72–4). Providing such information can be seen as necessary for fair and effective competition, but Oftel also sought to use it in protecting customers. Thus, for instance, in the late 1980s it put pressure on BT to set quality of service targets and to give subscribers contractual rights of compensation for poor service. Oftel's actions were strengthened by the 1992 Competition and Service (Utilities) Act, which gave it powers to regulate quality of service and deal with inadequate performance, including the powers to impose standards of performance and complaints procedures on suppliers, and to determine disputes over poor service and compensation.

Social objectives

Oftel's DGs have put competition at the heart of their regulatory strategy, arguing that it is the best method of protecting users and meeting the needs of different customer segments (see, for instance, Oftel Annual

Report 1996: paragraph 1.4; Oftel 1997d: paragraph 4.19). In their view, social needs should be met in ways that encourage competition and Don Cruickshank argued that measures required for social or environmental policy objectives that conflicted with competition (for instance, because they required subsidy or cross-subsidisation between users) ought to be explicitly laid down by ministers and parliament, rather than the DGT.

Nevertheless, Oftel has taken decisions to protect certain groups of users or particular services that involve operators, especially BT, in providing loss-making services. BT's licence contained conditions used to limit its freedom to maximise profits. It had a general duty to meet 'all reasonable demand' for voice telephony services and other services consisting of transmitting messages (Condition 1). It was forbidden to engage in 'undue discrimination', which Oftel interpreted to mean that the same tariffs had to apply throughout the UK. Moreover, it was to maintain at least the level of public call box provision as existed in 1984, only being allowed to remove public call boxes under specified conditions and often needing Oftel's approval (Condition 11); Oftel pressed BT on issues of availability and especially repair of call boxes in the 1980s. Finally, price controls allowed Oftel to restrain losses for certain groups; indeed, the review of price controls for 1997–2001 explicitly sought to target price cuts on low-spending users.

The means of ensuring universal service became a more explicit social issue in the 1990s, with the end of the duopoly in 1991 and continuing price rebalancing. Oftel examined the scope of universal service and decided that it included connection to the fixed-line network, the availability of restricted services at low cost and reasonable geographic access to public call boxes across the UK at affordable prices.[16] It looked at the cost of such services and methods of meeting it. After prolonged discussions, Oftel argued that the costs of universal service borne by BT were low – £65–85m in 1995–6 for uneconomic areas, customers and public call boxes (Oftel 1997f: 28). However, BT enjoyed many benefits from providing universal service, such as attracting customers who would become profitable later in their lives, ubiquity and positive corporate reputation. As a result, Oftel decided that the benefits to BT offset the estimated costs and hence that universal service was not an undue burden on the company. It therefore decided to end ADCs as part of the new price controls that began in 1997 and not to establish a universal service fund or make payments to BT until further study had shown the costs and benefits of providing universal service (Oftel 1997g).

Oftel also undertook specific measures for certain universal services. It targeted price controls on the lowest-spending users (see pp. 101–3). It persuaded BT to encourage schemes for low-spending customers (such as the 'low user' and light user' schemes, and the 'lifeline' scheme offering incoming calls only), to introduce alternatives to disconnection for non-payment and to provide services for the disabled. Oftel increased local involvement in decisions by BT concerning the removal and siting of public call boxes (ibid.).

Thus despite Oftel's protestations that social policy was for elected politicians and that its role should be that of a competition authority, in practice, it has been greatly involved in limiting the effects of competition to promote the protection of certain groups and services.

Conclusion: explaining the form of liberalisation in British telecommunications

By 1996, the entire UK telecommunications market was opened to entry. By 1998, there were some thirty licensed public telecommunications operators, with five offering national services across the UK, six providing services mostly in London and another four offering regional services (Bell 1997).[17] Competition had developed in almost all segments of the market. In the fixed-line infrastructure and voice telephony market, which remains the largest segment of the market, PTOs were competing with cable companies (including in the local loop)[18] and a host of resellers for national and international services. Mobile telephony was also growing rapidly, with 5.7 million cellular telephone subscribers by end 1996, and offered significant competition to fixed-line operators (Oftel Annual Report 1996: 144). By the mid-1990s, BT's market share was falling steadily – overall, it had reached 70 per cent by 1997; whilst it remained overwhelming in terms of access revenues and local calls, it was below 50 per cent for international calls by business users.[19]

Although competition developed in Britain in the 1980s and 1990s, it did not mean 'deregulation' or any 'retreat of the state'. On the contrary, it was accompanied and impelled by vigorous activity by regulators – notably the government and Oftel – and the establishment of a host of rules governing supply. Public ownership and monopoly supply of telecommunications were replaced by regulation of the activities of privately-owned suppliers. The British experience suggests that, rather than analysing whether competition increases or decreases regulation (a question that assumes the amount of regulation can be measured or compared), it is more valuable to examine the form of liberalisation, i.e. the extension of competition, how competition was regulated and the reasons for the form that it took.

In the period between 1984 and the early 1990s, competition was extended only gradually in telecommunications in Britain. It involved the setting of often detailed rules, in the form of licence conditions, that were generally designed for one supplier, BT. The enforcement and modification of licence conditions saw continuous activity by Oftel; in contrast, the general competition authorities played little direct role, with the MMC representing a background threat in licence-modification negotiations between BT and Oftel. The extent and detail of Oftel's involvement in regulating supply increased after 1984. By the early 1990s, it covered prices (both baskets of services and often individual services), interconnection charges and terms, relations amongst BT's different parts and services, information provided for customers and, for itself as regulator, quality of service and the provision of services for non-economic objectives – to name but the most prominent of Oftel's regulatory activities.

The 1990s saw some modification in the regulation of competition. Oftel laid greater emphasis on replacing detailed rules with more general ones and on moving from acting as an intermediary or arbiter in relations between market actors to adopting a 'policing' role over those relations to prevent abuses (cf. Prosser 1997: 76). The modification remained modest, with regulation still being centred on BT and consisting largely of detailed *ex ante* controls. Nevertheless, the new direction of regulatory developments did become evident in the 1990s. However, it has not meant an end to regulation: the regulators remain central in the market through the establishment and application of general rules for competition[20] and their capacity to intervene in particular instances in which anti-competitive behaviour may have occurred.

How can the processes of decision-making and the path followed in liberalisation of telecommunications in Britain be explained? Factors applicable to telecommunications in all industrialised countries can be advanced; in particular, attention can be given to the changing technological and economic nature of telecommunications, which allowed greater opportunities for competition and increased the economic importance of the industry for other sectors. However, unless tight technological determinism is adopted, these factors are better adapted to explaining why liberalisation took place rather than why it took its particular form in Britain, especially as liberalisation in other countries has taken other paths.[21] Moreover, it is noteworthy that, to date at least, European legislation has played little part in liberalisation in Britain: changes were made before EC legislation and largely for domestic reasons (for a discussion and the argument that current detailed EC legislation on ONP and on licensing potentially have implications for regulation in Britain, see Hunt 1997; see also Scott and Audéod 1996). Instead, two factors specific to Britain can be underlined.

First, the inheritance of privatisation exerted a continuing influence on the form of liberalisation. The decision to sell BT as a single, vertically integrated company with a dominant position in the UK market meant that behavioural regulation was chosen instead of 'structural regulation' and that regulation was centred on BT (for an economic critique, see Vickers and Yarrow 1988). Moreover, the desire to ensure a successful sale and to protect BT limited the pace at which competition was extended. Furthermore, BT arrived with the consequences of its past history as a public corporation. In particular, its prices often differed from costs, its organisation and internal information were not prepared for a regulated competitive market and its culture was that of a public monopolist. Given these circumstances, detailed measures in pursuit of the goal of extending effective competition were needed in order to prevent BT abusing its dominant position, to obtain the information needed to regulate competition and to ensure BT's gradual transition from monopolist to supplier in a competitive market.

The telecommunications market evolved, however, modifying the effects of the inheritance of privatisation. Effective competition grew and BT adjusted to its new position. Large powerful suppliers entered the market (for instance, AT&T and the Baby Bells via cable television companies). Better information, suitable for regulation, was obtained. The changed regulatory environment provided by competitive supply in telecommunications aided alterations in regulation. It became easier to move the focus of regulation away from detailed regulation of BT and towards more general rules applicable to other suppliers. Very specific price controls could be limited to segments of the market not subject to effective competition. *Ex ante* controls could be partially replaced with *ex post* controls.

A second key factor for the path of liberalisation in Britain was the institutional framework established after 1984. The privatisation of BT, the relative lack of legislative provisions over licensing and the existence of an industry regulator, Oftel, influenced the speed and extent of the extension of competition and the establishment of detailed rules to ensure that competition was effective (for a comparison with France, see Thatcher 1994). The government was free to choose when to license new suppliers and to decide to offer licences to almost all applicants. Oftel's powers and its rapid expansion of its expertise, allied with the weakness of general competition law in Britain, facilitated the development of sectoral rules rather than the application of general competition law by competition authorities. Oftel's ability to modify licences was crucial in its capacity to growing competition and to adapt regulation to changing market conditions. The breadth of Oftel's duties and the existence of the DGT as a powerful single head in whom powers were personally vested, provided Oftel with discretion and flexibility, permitting it to use its powers to expand the range of its activities and achieve a central role in the regulation of telecommunications. Then in the 1990s, under a new DGT, Oftel was able to modify its role in regulation, redefining itself as a competition authority through, for example, the alteration of BT's licence to include general conditions prohibiting anti-competitive behaviour and the modification of the scope of price controls.

Between 1984 and 1998, the institutional framework interacted with the (changing) effects of the inheritance of privatisation, resulting in the pattern of liberalisation seen in Britain. On the one hand, greater competition encouraged and facilitated the development of the regulation of competition. At first, this centred on the establishment of detailed regulations to govern relations between BT and entrants and to ensure that BT, as the principal supplier, did not abuse its dominant position. Later, regulation was modified to include the application of more general rules of competition. On the other hand, regulation aided the development of competition and protected its effectiveness.

Notes

1 Insofar as procedural matters were laid down, they concerned precise categories of decision, such as enforcement orders.
2 The most important modification was the 1992 Competition and Service (Utilities) Act which provided legislative grounding for minimum standards of service and compensation terms for inadequate service; in 1998, the new Labour government is conducting a review of utility regulation and is also undertaking legislative reform of general competition law with a Competition Bill that is likely to have significant implications for telecommunications.
3 Thus, for instance, in 1997, when BT was seeking approval from US regulators to take over MCI, British officials lobbied US regulators and the government ended its 'golden share' in BT that gave it the right to block a takeover, thereby removing a possible obstacle to approval of BT's takeover.
4 See especially the section in Oftel's Annual Reports headed 'Oftel as a Competition Authority'.
5 The most important were stakes in Mitel, MacCaw Communications and MCI; the stakes in the first two were sold, whilst BT's attempted takeover of MCI appears to have failed.
6 The two major exceptions were on Chatlines in 1988 and number portability in 1995.
7 Even if this meant that Mercury's network was only used for the trunk section of the call, which would originate and terminate on BT's local network.
8 Depending on market shares won by a new operator and BT not falling below an 85 per cent market share; see Oftel 1991a and Oftel 1991b.
9 The only major contribution was from Mercury, ending in 1996.
10 These services included 'inter-tandem conveyance' (corresponding to transmission between trunk switches as a 'tandem exchange is one that routes calls between exchanges but is not linked to end users) and international direct-dialling services. For a detailed list, see Oftel; (1997c) Annex A.
11 There were three separate baskets – for call termination services, general network services and interconnection services; the RPI–X formula was continued, with 'X' set at 8 per cent.
12 For action to enforce licence conditions (of BT and other operators), see Oftel Annual Reports and recent Competition Bulletins; the number and range of decisions by Oftel appear to be increasing, especially in the mid-1990s.
13 The most important example was that BT Network had to offer the same terms for use of the network to BT Retail as to other operators.
14 Oftel issued two consultative documents, both entitled Pricing of Telecommunications Services from 1997 (London: Oftel, 1995c and 1996).
15 The increasing array of discount packages makes it difficult to even establish what tariff's exist for particular services, leading to BT nominating baseline or 'reference' tariffs.
16 Other elements included free emergency services and access to operator

assistance, directory information, itemised billing and selective call barring. Universal Telecommunication Services (Oftel 1994b, 1995b, 1997e).

17 The most important national PTOs were Mercury, now part of CWC, Energis and Ionica.

18 By end 1996, cable companies had passed a quarter of residential homes. Oftel, Annual Report 1996: 8.

19 For detailed figures, see Oftel, Market Information Updates.

20 Even the new fair trading condition of operators' licences, which was presented as a 'deregulatory' measure, involves a host of tests to be used in its application, ranging from determination of the 'relevant market' to whether a supplier has a dominant position. See Oftel 1997h.

21 Comparison with regulation in the United States, with features such as the involvement of the courts, state and federal regulators, the break up of AT&T and the maintenance of monopoly over local area telephony until the mid-1990s, or with other European countries examined in this volume, show that many regulatory arrangements have been adopted in the face of similar technological and economic developments in telecommunications.

7   Liberalisation of telecommunications in Germany[1]

Raymund Werle

From public administration to private competition

In the 1980s Germany was no driving force concerning deregulation and liberalisation of the telecommunications market. As in some other countries, a corporatist complex of actors from business, politics and the trade unions tried to obstruct any reform. Originally, it was the PTT, a powerful postal union, and a handful of companies producing technical equipment for the telecommunication network who in effect 'joined forces' to oppose a fast transition from the old order of a public telecommunications monopoly to a competitive mode of service provision through private firms (Schneider and Werle 1991; Schmidt 1991).

This does not mean, however, that Germany only reacted or adapted to European pressure towards liberalisation. Early on, relevant German advocates of liberalisation – including the Federal Ministry of Economic Affairs and, to some extent, the Ministry of Posts and Telecommunications – tried to initiate reforms both at the national and European level. Indeed, the Commission's famous Green Paper on telecommunications (European Commission 1987; Ungerer 1988), which coincided with the publication of a concomitant report from a German government commission (Witte 1988), was already significantly influenced by the German reformers. If at the time the German government did challenge a directive of the Commission aiming at a liberalisation of the market for terminal equipment, it was more out of formal jurisdictional reasons than a dissenting view of the need for reform (Schneider and Werle 1990).

With the emergence of a European telecommunications policy network, the German supporters of liberalisation gained leverage *vis-à-vis* those who tried to uphold the status quo. While this latter group stressed the social benefits of the old order in its national confines for the private users of telecommunications services and the staff of the PTT, the reformers rather emphasised the need to transform the system in a way that would make it competitive in a globalising market economy. This view of the reformers was shared and reinforced by the European Commission and other actors in a policy network that provided supra-national and cross-national support (Schneider *et al.* 1994). The policy network relied on common values and convictions concerning the benefits of liberalisation, and these were referred to in the political debates about this issue in Germany.

However, it took years until the transition from a public administration providing telephone and data services to a system of (potentially) competitive provision of a variety of telecommunications services by private enterprises was complete. That the road to liberalisation was long was due to two reasons. The first can be identified in the political and legal institutional structure of Germany. The old order was rooted in a specific provision of the German Constitution (Basic Law, Article 87), which determined that the operation of the network and its services was an exclusive task of a federal administration, thereby creating a public monopoly. Corporatisation, as well as privatisation, of network operation and service provision was ruled out by Article 87. In the federal structure of Germany, constitutional provisions can only be changed if there is a broad consensus, i.e. a two-third majority is required in the federal parliament (Bundestag) and in the federal council (Bundesrat), which represents the individual German states (Länder). This stipulation guarantees political minorities a strong veto position.[2]

The second reason why the process of change was comparatively slow can be seen in the already mentioned constellation of vested interests in the area of telecommunications. In the early 1980s, core actors in this constellation enjoyed a rather comfortable position. After decades of deficit and shortage the PTT had turned into a profitable public enterprise that, despite its obligation to subsidise the postal services and to transfer a fixed share of its revenues to the federal budget, could mobilise the resources needed for the modernisation and digitisation of the telecommunications infrastructure. In addition, the PTT could provide a high degree of job security for its staff, represented by a postal union which had strong links to the PTT Ministry and the Social Democrats.[3] Also, PTT's decision to purchase digital switches (the central components of the future ISDN network) from Siemens and SEL/Alcatel was more than a symbolic action, rather it indicated an interest in the stabilisation of a national club of manufacturers with traditionally strong ties to the PTT. The manufacturers of telecommunications equipment, especially exchange and transmission technology, also benefited from the consolidated business of the PTT. This mixture of a corporatist and clientelist arrangement was completed by the direct involvement of the PTT Ministry combining political control, regulatory authority and operational responsibility for the PTT under one roof, which was a situation the majority of the Länder governments expressed no intention to change. The PTT's commitment to universal service and uniform rates was regarded as an asset, particularly by the less industrialised or peripheral Länder.

However, vested interests and institutional barriers to change only retarded rather than blocked reforms. Initiated and perpetuated by a number of factors, the reform process began in the second half of the 1980s, and gained momentum during the 1990s. At the national level, the Federal Ministry of Economic Affairs (traditionally under the leadership of the neo-liberal Liberal Party, the FDP), large users, top business associations, and computer manufacturers were all early advocates of reform. Also, European actors, particularly the Commission, gained leverage in the debates and deliberations on telecommunications.[4]

The reform process had three stages. First, the 1989/90 *Postreform I* established three separate operational units for the provision of postal services (Postdienste), banking services (Postbank) and telecommunications services (Telekom). All three units of the former Bundespost remained as separate branches under the auspices of the Bundespost, which was a holding company rather than an organisation providing services. Another feature of the new law – in line with the provisions of the Green Paper – was a separation of regulatory competencies of the Ministry of Posts and Telecommunications from its operational functions, which in the past were included in the PTT Ministry. In the reform, PTT Telekom lost its monopoly in the market for terminal equipment and telecommunications services, other than that of telephony. This 'liberalisation at the margins of the market', as it was denounced by the proponents of more radical reforms, was supplemented by an announcement from the PTT Minister that a license was to be granted to a private competitor of Telekom in the emerging market for digital cellular telephony.[5]

The second stage, *Postreform II*, was approved in 1994. After the German Unification the pressures for reform accelerated, one reason being Telekom's need of capital and entrepreneurial autonomy in order to build a modern telecommunications network in the former East Germany. In this context, but also *vis-à-vis* international developments in the markets for telecommunications, key actors of Telekom came to believe that corporatisation and, eventually, privatisation could secure the resources and the flexibility needed (Schmidt 1996: 55). Other actors producing telecommunications equipment, particularly Siemens who relied on exports of transmission and switching technology, understood that competing in the more and more liberalised export markets was not compatible with defending a public monopoly enterprise in Germany. The political debates focused on privatisation and further organisational reform of the PTT complex, whereas additional steps towards liberalisation and deregulation played only a minor role and were eventually postponed.[6]

At the beginning of 1995, each of the three enterprises overseen by the Bundespost were transformed into independent joint-stock companies. All the shares, managed by a holding company, have been retained by the federal government and cannot be traded on the stock exchange until the year 2000. Even then, the government is legally obliged to keep a majority of the shares, and any attempt to change this would require legislation, i.e. a decision of the Bundestag and the Bundesrat. Those shares of Deutsche Telekom AG (DTAG) which were offered to the public in autumn 1996 served to expand the capital stock of DTAG, i.e. they were not owned by the government but were new shares. Through this transaction the percentage of government-owned DTAG shares decreased from 100 to 74 per cent.

In the third stage, *Postreform III*, the Telecommunications Act (Telekommunikationsgesetz TKG) adopted in 1996 removed the public monopoly of the cable-based telecommunications network and the telephone service (effective 1 January 1998). According to EU directives, the Act (discussed in more detail in the next section) also establishes a National Regulatory Authority (NRA) and other elements of the new regulatory regime in German telecommunications. The Telecommunications Act, which is intended to complement German competition law, draws a distinction between areas needing sector-specific regulation, in order to control market power and guarantee universal service, and areas where general competition law already applies (cf. Knieps 1997a). However, the TKG does not specify in detail the mode of co-operation between the NRA and the Federal Cartel Office (Bundeskartellamt), the guardian of competition in Germany.[7] Thus it can be argued that the TKG diminishes the authority of the Cartel Office in the telecommunications market.

During the process of reform, many actors modified their convictions and beliefs concerning the advantages and disadvantages of a competitive order of telecommunications provision, and in this sense the process was a learning one. But interest positions also changed as it became obvious that the old order would not be sustainable and a new order, if designed appropriately, would provide many new opportunities.[8] Many former opponents of reforms recognised that co-operation and participation in the European telecommunications policy network might be the only way to direct the process towards a stable institutional equilibrium. This is why the German regulatory model was designed in close co-operation with European actors and why it has implemented many requirements stipulated in European directives (cf. Thorein 1997).

Regulation and co-ordination – towards a competitive market?

Just in time for monitoring the emerging market for telecommunications networks and services, on 1 January 1998, the German National Regulatory Authority (NRA) for Telecommunications and Posts was established (see Figure 7.1). It assumed the regulatory functions of the former Federal

Ministry of Posts and Telecommunications (BMPT), which was dissolved at the end of 1997, with parts of its functions being transferred to other ministries. Management of the Federal Holdings, including the majority of the shares of the Deutsche Telekom AG (DTAG), has been shifted to the Federal Ministry of Finance (BMF), while the Federal Ministry of Economic Affairs (BMWi) deals with the basic policy issues in telecommunications. The BMWi has also taken over from the BMPT the powers to issue ordinances specifying the provisions of the Telecommunications Act (TKG) and related legal rules.[9] As a government agency, the NRA is part of the BMWi's scope of business, i.e. the agency is independent but accountable to the Ministry of Economic Affairs.

Expectations that the new NRA would be shaped as a 'lean' agency, regarding the scope of regulation and the number of people employed, have not been met. As the Federal Office for Posts and Telecommunications (BAPT), a government agency in the area of technical regulation and standardisation, has been incorporated in the NRA, this organisation has started business with more than 2,700 employees. The Telecommunications Act (TKG) restricts the scope of regulation to the areas of:

- technical regulation (e.g. standards, allocation of frequencies and telephone numbers)[10]
- universal service provision (e.g. telephone and related services at affordable (reasonable) cost)
- pro-competitive market regulation (e.g. market access, interconnection, control of dominant firms)

However, the TKG does not invariably determine the organisational framework of regulation or the size of the NRA. Institutional path dependencies may well lead to excessive regulation (cf. Knieps 1997b). Such tendencies might be reinforced by the fact that the new German regulatory agency recruited its staff by simply transferring the civil servants from the BAPT and the BMPT to the NRA. This includes the agency's president who was head of a department of the BMPT.[11]

Decisions of the NRA are taken by independent decision-making chambers set up by the Minister of Economic Affairs.[12] The members of the chambers are higher civil servants of the NRA, and legal complaints (actions) against any of their decisions can be filed at Administrative Courts. An Advisory Council, comprising nine members of the Bundestag and nine members of the Bundesrat, has monitoring functions *vis-à-vis* the NRA.[13]

From the point of view of deregulation and liberalisation, the crucial area of regulatory action is that of pro-competitive market regulation. The Telecommunications Act has established a rather liberal *licensing regime*. However, licensing is not restricted to areas in which technical or other constraints might suggest a need for central co-ordination.[14] Of the

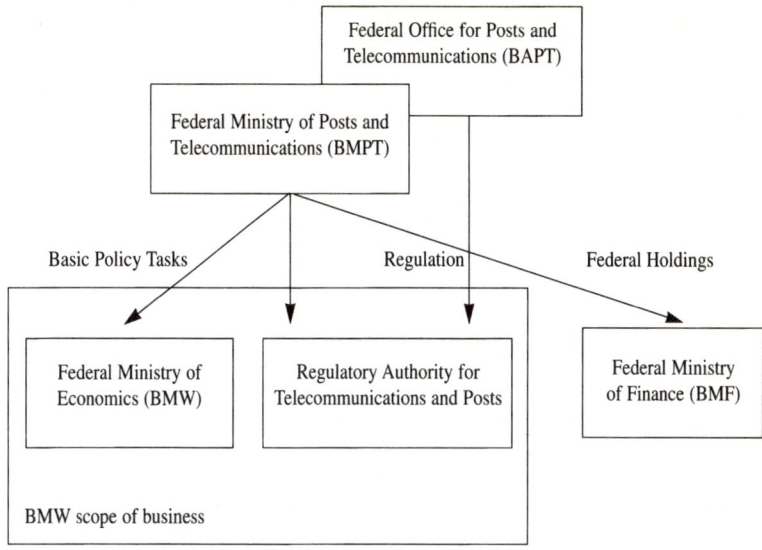

Adapted from the NRA (http://www.regtp.de/English/regtp.htm)

Figure 7.1 Establishment of the regulatory authority

four classes of licences granted by the NRA, only Class 1 (mobile radio) and Class 2 (satellite transmission) cover domains in which unregulated action may lead to a sub-optimal outcome.

• Class 1 licences are for operating mobile radio transmission networks. A licence is only required if the lines are used by the licensee or others to provide public services.
• Class 2 licences refer to the operation of satellite transmission lines. Again a licence is only required if public services are offered on these lines by the licensee or others.

The other two classes of licences refer to business domains where free (unregulated) access to the market could be allowed without necessarily impairing the market functions. Until the end of 1997, Deutsche Telekom had a monopoly in these domains. Licence requirements in former mono-poly areas are an advantage for the incumbent firm.

• Class 3 are licences for operating fixed (i.e. not mobile or satellite) networks. A licence is only required if the network is used by the licensee or others to provide public services.

- Class 4 licences refer to the provision of voice telephony services over a self-operated network.

Thus a licence is needed for the operation of all kinds of telecommunications networks or lines if they are used for the provision of public services (i.e. Classes 1–3). A licence for telephone services is only obligatory if the services are offered over a self-operated network. As most of the potentially big new players in the German telecom market will operate networks and provide telephone services, they are required to have at least a Class 4 and a Class 3 licence. A licence can also be restricted to a particular part of Germany if a firm plans to operate in a geographically smaller market segment. The NRA can only refuse granting a licence if the applicant is not 'qualified' (concerning skills, qualification, technical equipment, reliability etc.) to provide the respective service or if – in case of Classes 1 and 2 – no frequencies are available. In principle the number of licences is not limited, and foreign ownership is not ruled out.[15] Where technical reasons call for a limitation of the number of licences they will be granted through tender or through competitive bidding (auctions). No licence requirements are imposed on firms who offer telephone services without operating their own network (voice resale)[16] or who provide any other telecommunications service. However, these providers are obliged to register with the NRA which keeps a public list of registrations.

The licensing regime is only one element of market regulation. Another crucial element is *open network provision and interconnection of networks*. Most of the provisions of the Telecommunications Act (TKG) dealing with these issues are exclusively addressed to dominant firms – which means, in fact, that they are addressing Deutsche Telekom.[17] Referring explicitly to the European regulations concerning open network provision (ONP Framework Directive, June 1990) the Act obliges the dominant network operator:

- to grant competitors access to its public and internal services on a non-discriminatory basis;
- to grant competitors unbundled access to all parts of the network including access to end user terminals – if necessary on a customised basis (special network access);
- to facilitate network access and interconnection according to European interface standards.

If the dominant network operator denies access on equal non-discriminatory conditions the NRA can be requested to intervene. Experiences from the past indicate that future conflicts in this area will not arise because access is denied, rather they will focus on the rates DTAG intends to charge competitors for the use of its facilities and services. In 1997, when the telecommunications market was still regulated by the Ministry of Posts and Telecommunications, the Minister fixed the rate for the use of the lines of DTAG at an average of 0.027 DM per minute. That was above the price Mannesmann ARCOR – one of the competitors of DTAG – offered to pay (0.02 DM) but significantly below the 0.06 DM DTAG wanted to charge. Another recent conflict arose because of the fees DTAG announced it wanted to charge for technical provisions necessary to switch customers to the networks of competitors. The competitors with their own networks turned to the NRA for intervention because they considered the fees for both connecting subscribers to their networks and keeping DTAG-assigned telephone numbers too high.[18]

As the dominant firm in the market of cable-based networks, DTAG is obliged to grant competitors access to its network and services. As a rule, competitors reject the rates suggested by DTAG and submit the issues to the NRA. This means that DTAG might be subject to continuous control and intervention in this area, whereas competitors enjoy some freedom to act. If they operate public networks they are also obliged to grant other network operators access, but they can negotiate the conditions of access with the other firms. The NRA only gets involved if network operators do not reach an agreement.

Although the DTAG's interconnection rates will be a major concern to the NRA and the general public, a particular feature of the German regulatory regime in the area of open network provision may turn out to become equally significant. It relates to the requirement of unbundled access to the local loop and has its roots in American regulatory history rather than in sector-specific directives of the EU. Unbundled access to a network provides the opportunity for competitors of the network operator to offer services with as many self-produced features as possible. The competitors rent the plain transmission capacity of a subscriber line and add their own multiplexing, signalling, and switching devices.[19] These functions are also provided by the network operator who usually bundles them in the services offered to the subscribers. Competitors benefit from the unbundling requirement because they only have to rent the network operator's basic transport medium and can add as much value as possible on top of it. This will certainly stimulate competition in the local loop, which, however, will very likely be confined to services and service features. Unbundling provides little incentives to invest in networks, i.e. transport capacity, which is generally regarded as being not very profitable (cf. Noam 1994; Gong and Srinagesh 1997). From this point of view, it comes as no surprise that Deutsche Telekom AG (DTAG) tried to preclude competitors from unbundled access to the local loop (Schuler and Meyer 1998: 12–13). DTAG only offered bundled services, but gave in after an Appellate Administrative Court arranged a provisional agreement among contending parties. As a result, the actual conflict was reduced to a controversy over the price of access, which developed in the familiar pattern: DTAG wanted to charge 28.80 DM per month for unbundled access to the standard subscriber line but the NRA fixed 20.65 DM as an upper price limit.[20] The basic conflict, however, remains to be resolved, as DTAG challenges the unbundling requirement as a violation of fundamental property rights of network operators. A court decision is still pending, and it might well be that the final decision has to be taken by the Federal Constitutional Court.

Another element of market regulation is the *regulation of tariffs for voice telephony*. The Telecommunications Act provides for a different treatment, depending on the market position of firms, and only dominant providers are subject to regulation. Their tariffs – local and long-distance, including discounts for special users – must be approved in advance by the NRA.[21] Recently, the NRA approved a tariff scheme of DTAG – effective 1 March 1998 – with moderately reduced rates for national long-distance calls and significantly lower rates for international and transatlantic calls. The scheme does not provide for any reduction of the rates for local calls. This 'unbalanced' scheme was heavily criticised by the president of the Federal Cartel Office (Bundeskartellamt) who suspects that DTAG abuses its dominance in the market for local calls. At the same time, the criticism was addressed to the NRA because – although expected by the TKG to do so – it did not ask the Cartel Office to file an assessment of the tariff scheme.

The last section of the Telecommunications Act (TKG) to be discussed here deals with universal service provision. Universal services are determined by ordinances of the federal government, and must be approved by the Bundestag and the Bundesrat. At present the TKG only requires voice telephony to be universally provided at affordable cost. The Universal Service Ordinance specifies the quality requirements (basic telephony with ISDN capabilities) and adds some features linked to basic telephony such as provision of public telephones and telephone directory services.[22] Although the TKG does not determine a particular network operator to provide the service, every operator with a market share of at least 4 per cent is, if necessary, obliged to contribute to the service. The NRA, however, can impose the obligation to provide the service at an affordable price on a dominant firm, if it so wishes. If this price does not cover the operator's costs, the firm will be compensated from fees levied against the other operators if their share exceeds 4 per cent of the market.

Although addressed in a different section of the TKG (§ 43), issues such as number portability and free selection of operators can be seen in the context of universal service provision. According to the law, users have the right to keep their telephone numbers if they switch to another operator. Moreover, every operator must grant access to other operators' networks and services on a pre-selection, as well as on a call-by-call basis through an access code.

Assessing the Telecommunications Act is difficult because one has to speculate about future effects of a law whose provisions concerning the NRA have just been implemented. The TKG is considered 'an enormous step forward' towards competitive provision of networks and services (Knieps 1997a: 2; see also Wieck 1997). When the law was prepared, many prominent advocates of liberalisation pleaded for the establishment of a regime with asymmetric regulation (e.g. Monopolkommission 1996: 26–7) because, with symmetric regulation,[23] the incumbent network operator would keep a de facto monopoly, even after the legal barriers of entry to the market had been removed. Some provisions can indeed be regarded as asymmetric. They include the requirement for *ex ante* approval of the rates for voice telephony and the rules governing access and connection to the networks and services of Deutsche Telekom (DTAG).[24] Some observers doubt that DTAG has a monopoly in the long-distance market in the sense that this market is not contestable. Therefore they suggest switching to symmetric regulation or avoiding any regulation in this area (Knieps 1997a). Also, in some instances, the style of regulation has been criticised. It is argued that, as a rule, the NRA will only (reactively) intervene in the market when market failure becomes obvious (Knieps 1997b). Although in this sense *re-active intervention* is the dominant pattern in the law we also find *pro-active* elements, as in the case of rate regulation for Class 3 and Class 4 licensees, if they have a dominant market position.

The crucial problems concerning the German regulatory setting relate not only to the Telecommunications Act and the potential jurisdictional conflicts between the NRA and the Federal Cartel Office in the area of competition, but also to Germany's federal structure and the convergence of telecommunications and electronic media. The commercial provision of telecommunications services (including transmission) to third parties is subject to federal regulation (TKG §3). However, regulation of radio and television broadcasting, including content and market regulation (but excluding transmission), is part of each individual Länder's jurisdiction. Usually the Länder enter into negotiations concerning broadcasting in order to provide uniform rules, which are laid down in an Inter-Länder Treaty (Staatsvertrag).[25] This does not preclude some individual regulatory provisions being adopted in the Länder. Without going into detail, one can say that the situation is even further complicated by the co-existence of public and private providers of broadcasting services, and different regulatory agencies and traditions concerning the public and the private domain. Also, the dominant position of DTAG in the market for cable TV transmission must be taken into consideration. DTAG controls the technical side of the network but has no right to select which TV and radio stations can use the transmission capacity. This decision is taken by regulatory agencies of the Länder, and which programs can be received via cable varies from Land to Land.[26]

With the convergence of mass media and telecommunications, new services and, in parallel, new problems concerning the jurisdictional confines of the federal government and the Länder governments have emerged. Both sides tend to define their jurisdictions extensively. A conflict in the area of what is called *teleservices* (information and communication services) was brought to a temporary solution in July 1997 by the adoption of the Teleservices Act (Teledienstegesetz – TDG). The act covers services such as telebanking, telegames, access to the Internet or access to databases. It includes provisions on liability, privacy and digital signatures. According to the Act, the jurisdiction over teleservices is granted to the federal government. Unlike telecommunications services, teleservices neither have to be licensed nor registered with the NRA or any other regulatory agency. A service provider is responsible for the content of its services but not generally for the content of other providers who can be accessed via these services.

In the political deliberations, teleservices are distinguished from what is called media services and, in parallel with the TDG, they have been specified in an Inter-Länder Agreement. Media services include video-on-demand, access to online news and teleshopping and are offered to the general public in a similar way to traditional radio and television services. As media services, they are subject to licensing and other regulations at Länder level in the mass-media domain. The distinction between teleservices and media services evolved as a compromise between the federal and Länder governments. The example of teleshopping in particular indicates that it might turn out to be extremely difficult to draw a clear distinction between these two types of services. If organised as an individualised interactive service, the screening of retailer databases and electronic ordering via a PC is treated as a teleservice, whereas using a shopping channel on television and ordering via telephone is regarded as the use of a media service.

The federal parliament acknowledged the difficulties of drawing clear distinctions between the two types of services and therefore asked the federal government to evaluate the impact of the TDG after two years and, if necessary, propose revisions and amendments. In conclusion, if we include the provision of electronic mass-media services and the grey area of teleservices and media services in the analysis of the German telecommunications market, the situation is multifaceted and complicated. Depending on the specific type of service, provision can be subject to different legal regulations and to different regulatory authorities at the federal and the Länder level. Liberalisation of the telecommunications market has to be assessed in the context of the overall regulatory setting. This multidimensional multilevel regulatory setting has remained complicated and might well turn out to be a barrier to entry, not only for foreign but also for German firms.

The evolving telecommunications market: many new actors – few new products

The German telecommunications market is one of the largest in the world. The market for technical equipment and services in tele-communications and information technology is estimated at a volume of US$100bn (184bn DM) and about 1.2m jobs. While information technology has traditionally been an unregulated industry,[27] deregulation of the telecommunications market did not begin until the early 1990s, and has only proceeded slowly. Telecommunications has been controlled by Deutsche Telekom (DTAG), which, according to the latest ranking of telecommunications carriers, ranks second in the world. International revenues in 1996 were estimated at US$6.96bn, and total revenue amounted to US$40.95bn. In 1996, 201,060 employees worked for DTAG.[28] As a result of its monopoly, DTAG is strongest in the market for telephone services and for cable TV transmission networks, although only the telephone market is profitable.

Essentially all segments of the German telecommunications market are growing. Most spectacular are the growth rates in the area of mobile telephony, which was a competitive market from the start, with initially two and later three carriers. In 1997 the total number of subscribers exceeded 7 million. T-Mobil, a subsidiary of DTAG, reports more than 3.5 million subscribers in the (digital) D1 network and the analogue C network. Mannesmann Corporation has more than 3.3 million subscribers in the D2 network, and is leader of the digital market. The third player, E-Plus, who was a latecomer in the market, reports more than 700,000 subscribers. Another licence has been granted to a consortium, which is about to start the E2 network. Parallel to the growth of the Internet, the number of subscribers to online services is growing rapidly. T-Online, a subsidiary of DTAG, reports 2 million, America Online (AOL) 500,000 subscribers. A dozen larger access providers link their customers directly to the Internet.

At the beginning of 1998, the first carriers started to offer public telephone services in Germany. That will not necessarily result in tremendous competition in the very near future. On the other hand, as liberalisation in some market segments was initiated well before 1998 (e.g. public data communication services), many companies could gain experience in network management and operation, and could prepare themselves for the new opportunities in the evolving market. Data from the NRA indicate how the number of carriers and service providers has developed. If we look at the licences granted and telecommunications services registered we find that within two years (January 1996 to February 1998) the number of licensees increased from 88 to 269. Over the same period, the number of registered services only rose from 892 to 997, which is a comparatively slight increase.[29] The figures indicate that in the area of operation of networks for public services and provision of telephone services in self-operated networks, the former monopoly of the DTAG was an effective barrier to market entry.[30]

Many experts expect that Deutsche Telekom will be able to keep its market share in the former monopoly segments up to a level of 80 to 90 per cent because DTAG had enough time to prepare for competition. Digitisation of the network has been completed, many long-distance lines are optical fibre cables (more than 115,000 km), and the number of ISDN subscribers is growing much faster than in other countries (16 per cent of the telephone channels are ISDN channels). At the same time DTAG forged alliances with international partners[31] and became involved in the East European market for telecommunications networks and services. This, however, has not prevented DTAG's potentially largest competitors from attacking the former monopoly directly in its core business: networks and telephone services.

Table 7.1 gives a sample of competitors in the German tele-communications market and shows that a variety of network operators and service providers are active. At present, some carriers such as Colt or WorldCom only offer business services; others such as Mobilcom or Talkline do not operate networks but try to get a share of the telephone market by offering attractive rates for long- distance telephony (resale).

Another group of firms, e.g. ISIS or Netcologne, can be classified as regional carriers because their activities (and the respective licences) are concentrated in certain regions, although they offer complete service packages, i.e. long-distance and local services. Customers often have the choice of using the services of a firm on a call-by-call basis, to pre-select the firm as their regular long-distance carrier, or completely switch to a firm for local and long-distance services (direct access).

Observers of the German market suggest that the three companies referred to as national carriers in Table 7.1 are likely to be the most serious competitors of DTAG. Arcor, Otelo and Viag Interkom emerged after a turbulent time, in which many alliances were set up, reshaped, dissolved, or created anew, and have just started offering services for private and business customers. A few of the big utilities with stakes in the race for the telecommunications market, such as RWE, (parts of) Veba or (parts of) Viag and others who enjoy regional monopolies in the production and distribution of energy, have been prepared to bear the initial deficits of infrastructure investments and start-up costs,[32] and, as such, have been resourceful players. A special object of desire was the telecommunications subsidiary of German Rail (DBKom) because an alliance with this company would open access to the telecommunications network of German Rail – the second largest German network after the DTAG network.

Figure 7.2 gives an up-to-date impression of the shape of the alliance, including moves to set up links which eventually failed.[33] From this we can

Table 7.1 Sample of Deutsche Telekom competitors

Company	Self-operated network	Services (at present)	Date of provision
		National Carriers	
Arcor	Yes	Call by Call (long distance)	Jan 98
		Preselection (long distance)	
Otelo	Yes	Call by Call (long distance)	Apr 98
		Preselection (long distance)	Apr 98
Viag Interkom	Yes	Call by Call	May 98
		Regional Carriers	
ISIS	Yes	Preselection	Jan 98
		Direct Access	
Netcologne	Yes	Direct Access	Jan 98
Tesion	Yes	Call by Call (nationwide)	Feb 98
(previously CNS)		Preselection	
		Direct Access (business only)	Jan 98
		Service Providers	
Mobilcom	No	Call by Call (long distance)	Jan 98
		Preselection	Mar 98
Talkline	No	Call by Call (long distance)	Jan 98
		Preselection (long distance)	Jan 98
Telepassport	No	Call by Call	Jan 98
		Preselection	Jan 98
		Specialised Carriers for Business Services	
Colt	Yes (in selected cities)	Direct Access	Jan 98
RSL COM	Yes (International)	Preselection	Jan 98
		Direct Access	
WorldCom	Yes (in selected cities)	Preselection	Jan 98
		Direct Access (additional carrier needed for local calls)	

see that DBKom is part of Arcor, a consortium lead by Mannesmann who operates the profitable mobile network D2. Also, RWE and Veba's Otelo with E-Plus, and Viag and British Telecoms's Viag Interkom with E2, either control or have strong links with operators of cellular telephony networks. That means that they are ready to compete with DTAG in all segments of the telephone market. This market, indeed, appears to be the most promising. Certainly, with the exception of Internet services, it is more attractive than other market segments for new products. Strategic actions of many new firms aim at what has been called 'cream skimming' or tariff arbitrage in the telephone market. Some smaller firms only offer services to business customers, other full-service providers attract business customers with special tariff packages and reduced rates for long-distance and international telephony. It seems, therefore, that there

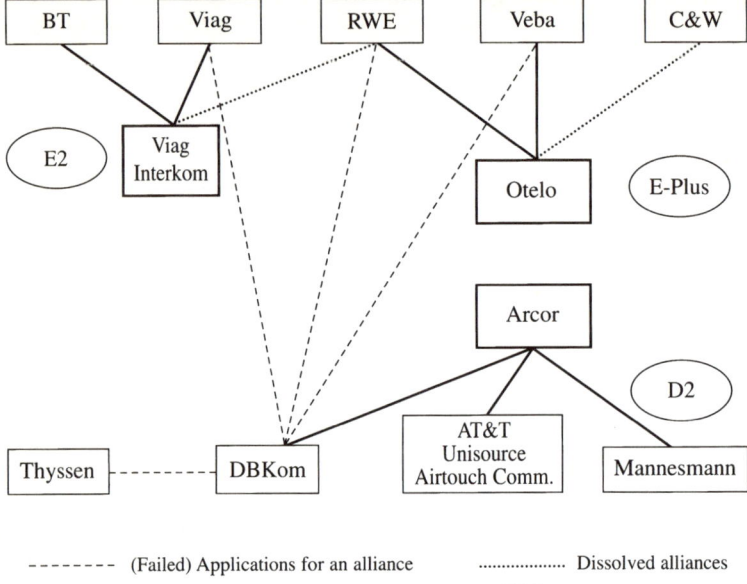

-------- (Failed) Applications for an alliance   .... Dissolved alliances

- DBKom opted for Mannesmann in July 1996
- Separation of RWE and Viag Interkom in October 1996
- Separation of C&W and Otelo in February 1997

Figure 7.2 Telecom-alliances and their links to providers of cellular phone
services

will be growing competition in the long-distance market for business
customers but that it will take some time before new products will be
available for the mass market.

Competition, however, not only takes place in the telecommunications
market. Parts of the battle for market shares have been transferred to the
regulatory arena – in Brussels as well as in Bonn – and at the same time
new corporate actors have appeared on the stage. One example is the
Verband der Telekommunikationsnetz- und Mehrwertdiensteanbieter
(Association of providers of telecommunications networks and value
added services – VTM), a trade association which was set up as a political
alliance of about thirty new players – including all the big competitors of
DTAG. In the bylaws of this association it is stated that deregulation and
liberalisation in Germany and Europe is a central goal, and that the
association will initiate and co-ordinate actions in the political and regulatory arena. Other business and trade associations, such as the association
of private radio, television and telecommunications services providers
(VPRT) and a new multimedia association (DMMV), have moved in the
same direction (cf. Werle 1996). This indicates that the corporatist and

clientelist structures of the German telecommunications sector have been replaced by a more pluralist network, which links actors in the over-lapping industries of telecommunications, electronic mass media and multimedia services, and complements the competitive market structure.

Conclusion

Liberalisation of telecommunications in Germany took eight years and three waves of legislation, and it was only recently that (almost) all barriers to entry to the telecommunications market were removed. This has not meant the abolition of all sector-specific regulation, although examination of the new regulatory regime, with the National Regulatory Authority (NRA) as a central actor, does suggest that a significant degree of liberalisation has been achieved. The provisions of the German Tele-communications Act are so much in line with the directives of the EU that the Commission's 'Third report on the implementation of the EU tele-communications regulatory package',[34] published in February 1998, lacks any criticism of Germany.[35] From the point of view of a liberal regulatory regime, the size of the NRA, elements of the licence requirements, and the tendency towards pro-active (*ex ante*) regulation of dominant firms, may appear too rigid. Also the role of the Federal Cartel Office, and its relation to the NRA, needs further clarification.

If the German regulatory regime is to be assessed appropriately, regulations in the area of broadcasting must be included. Due to the convergence of telecommunications and electronic media, the two regula-tory domains collide and overlap. This problem is aggravated because regulation of broadcasting is part of the jurisdiction of the individual Länder (states). Terminological compromises, such as the distinction between teleservices and media services, which are meant to help separate one jurisdiction from the other, do not provide a sustainable solution.

It is certainly too early to evaluate the effects of the Telecom-munications Act on the German market. Many firms are about to offer services in competition with the former monopoly Deutsche Telekom, and business-related services, especially long-distance telephony, will see tremendous competition. However, the dominant position of Deutsche Telekom which had time to get well prepared for competition will not be jeopardised in the near future.

Notes

1 I am indebted to Alberta Sbragia, Marcel Haag, Jette Steen Knudsen and the editors of this book for valuable comments on an earlier version of this paper. I also want to thank Ulrich Müller who did more than just assist with the research underlying this paper.
2 Another element of the federal structure – the constitutional provision that regulation of broadcasting lies within the jurisdiction of the federal states

(Länder) – might make it even more difficult to adapt the regulatory framework in this area to new technological and market opportunities.

3 The union also claimed to represent the interests of private users.

4 For a broader assessment of the role of the Commission and the Council in telecoms liberalisation, see Schmidt (1997a; 1997b).

5 The PTT Minister traditionally had the right, but was not obliged, to grant licences. But not until licensing cellular telephony carriers did he use the right as a means to stimulate competition.

6 It should be noted, however, that a Regulatory Board (Regulierungsrat) was established to secure participation of the federal parliament and the federal council in regulatory issues. It started business in 1995.

7 According to §82 TKG the two agencies have to exchange information touching upon each other's jurisdictions. They must reach an agreement if the dominance of a firm in the telecommunications market is to be determined. In addition, the regulatory authority must consult the Cartel Office in several other matters.

8 The PTT Ministry provides a good example. Initially only the minister (Schwarz-Schilling) and a few of his friends in the ministry struggled for liberalisation. But after Postreform I the number of supporters of reform increased, particularly in the telecom department of the ministry.

9 The ordinances include licence fees, provision of universal services, regulation of rates, technical type approval, privacy and consumer protection. Most of them were issued by the Minister for Posts and Telecommunications in the last couple of years before 1998.

10 Details of technical regulation will not be discussed in this paper.

11 For details concerning the contentious appointment of the president, see Schuler and Meyer 1998: 5–6.

12 This legally qualified decision-making procedure only applies to specific areas such as network access and interconnection, universal service provision, and the allocation and awarding of licences for frequencies if they are scarce.

13 This council upholds the tradition of parliamentary control of telecommunications which traditionally was not very tight but rather symbolic (cf. Werle 1990). It is the successor of the Regulatory Board established in Postreform II.

14 For a discussion of different modes of technical communication and the need for co-ordination on a global scale, see Krasner 1991.

15 The NRA charges licence fees.

16 This includes Internet telephony.

17 Concerning the general definition of market dominance the TKG refers to German competition law (Gesetz gegen Wettbewerbsbeschränkungen).

18 A final decision has not yet been taken. However, some smaller enterprises and also the Competition Directorate of the EU criticised the way the NRA initially handled this case. Instead of hearing both sides and taking a decision afterwards, the decision-making chamber charged with this case initiated a round-table with the contending parties in order to reach a compromise. If this doesn't work, the chamber will have to decide. The opponents regard the round-table initiative as an invitation to the participants to set up a kind of oligopolist forum which might reach compromises at the expense of smaller competitors in the market.

19 The idea of unbundling is related to models of layered communication networks. Using layering techniques helps to partition complex tasks into smaller simpler ones which interact. The famous Open Systems Interconnection (OSI) Reference Model, for example, distinguishes seven layers (physical, data link, network, transport, session, presentation, application) (see Schmidt

and Werle 1998: 39). Another model in the context of the Open Data Network Architecture promoted by the US Computer Science and Tele-communications Board (1994: 47–9) differentiates four layers: the bit-level transport (bearer) service, the end-to-end transport service, the higher-level functions (middleware) as a toolkit for application implementors, and the applications level (for typical users) (see also Honda *et al.* 1995).

20 In contrast to the NRA, but in line with some competitors of DTAG who argued 15 DM would be adequate, the Federal Cartel Office suggested 14.30 DM to be a reasonable price.

21 In principle, all licensed services (Classes 1–4) are to be priced by dominant operators on the basis of cost of efficient provision. But only voice tariffs have to be approved *ex ante.*

22 This ordinance also demands that a minimum set of leased lines, according to the definition in Annex II to the respective ONP directive, is to be provided.

23 According to Shankerman (1996: 5) symmetric regulation means 'providing all suppliers, incumbents and new entrants alike, a level playing field on which to compete: the same price signals, the same restrictions, and the same obligations'.

24 It can be argued that the TKG also includes elements of assymmetric regulation which are beneficial to DTAG. The licensing regime provides an example.

25 According to Länder agreements, the prevailing definition refers to broad-casting as the electric/electronic provision and transmission of presentations of all kinds of speech, sound and picture for the general public. This includes customised (individualised) services such as video-on-demand.

26 In 1997, DTAG reported a deficit of 1.1 billion DM in the cable business which was never profitable. This fact, together with the lack of control over access to the cables, accounts for DTAG's hesitation in upgrading the net-work. On the other hand, DTAG also strictly rejects political demands to sell the network.

27 At the same time it was a focus of industrial policy for decades.

28 Source: Communications Week International 'Top 50 International Carriers' (http://www.totaltele.com/cwi/195/Top100carriers.html). A recent DTAG report shows total revenues of about 68 bn DM in 1997 and a further reduction of the number of employees to 191,000 (http://www.dtag.de/untern/ kurzprofil/index.htm).

29 This is partly a result of updates and revisions of the figures in this area.

30 By February 1998, exactly fifty-nine Class 3 licences (operation of cable-based networks for public services) and forty-four Class 4 licences (provision of public telephone services on self-operated networks) were awarded.

31 Most prominent is Global One, the alliance of DTAG, France Télécom and US-Sprint which, however, still yields high deficits on the side of DTAG.

32 Otelo reported 1.2 bn DM including cellular telephony in 1997. Profits are only expected by 2002.

33 Not included are the Otelo group's ongoing negotiations with the US carrier Bell South.

34 IIP/98/165; Brussels, 18 February 1998.

35 This leaves the question open, if the European rules provide the most adequate and liberal institutional framework for the telecommunications market or if a tendency to over-regulate deregulation prevails.

8 French licensing and interconnection[1]

Winston Maxwell

Introduction

The first six months of French liberalisation were fraught with difficulties. Would-be new entrants faced a series of obstacles, delays and complications in obtaining their licences. The situation has improved markedly since the middle of 1998. New licences are now being issued within time periods consistent with the European Licensing Directive.[2] The problems of interconnection, however, are just now beginning. The *Autorité de régulation des télécommunications* (ART) has just published its first annual report (ART 1997). The report, which can be ordered on the ART's web site,[3] summarises action taken by the ART and the French government since 1 January 1997, and outlines priorities for the future.

Two years after enactment of the Telecommunications Law,[4] the time is right to take stock of what France has done right, and what it could be doing better, to stimulate a thriving telecommunications industry. The first part of this chapter summarises briefly some of the basic terms of the French Telecommunications Law. The second part examines certain practical problems encountered by new entrants in the licensing process, and in interconnection.

Basic legal framework

The French Telecommunications Law distinguishes between network operators and service providers, applying separate licensing and interconnection rules to each. Schematically, the law classifies networks and services as shown in Figure 8.1.

Network Operators (Art. L 33)

To 'establish and operate' a 'network' generally requires a licence.[5] The licensing regime applicable to network operators varies depending on whether the network is open to the public.

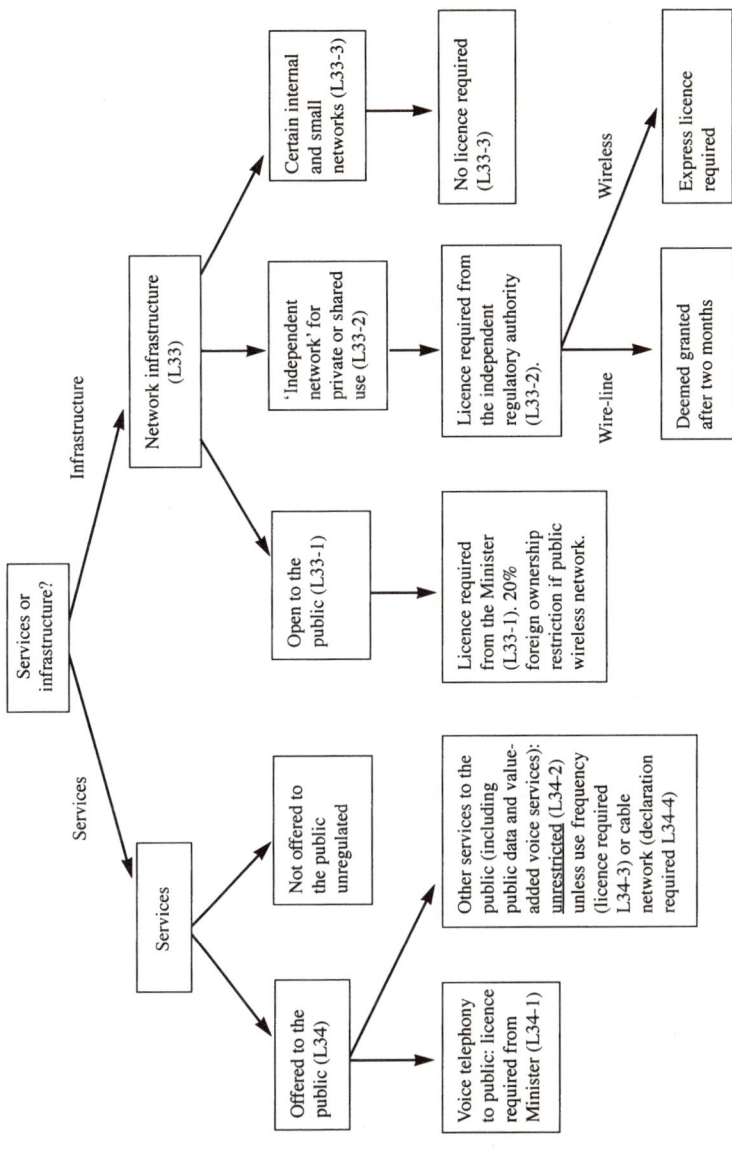

Figure 8.1 Schematic classification of networks and services in French telecommunications law

Networks open to the public (Art. L 33-1)

In a consultation document published in the Official Journal on 30 May 1997 ('Consultation Document'),[6] the ART set forth the licensing procedure applicable to networks open to the public. Notwithstanding debate as to whether it is legally binding on either the ART or the Ministry, the ART uses the Consultation Document as an internal checklist. Along with information presented on the Ministry's Internet web page (http://www.telecom.gouv.fr), these are sole sources to date (aside from the European Licensing Directive) that new entrants can rely upon when applying for a licence.

Licence applications for networks open to the public are first reviewed by the ART and then submitted to the Ministry for signature.[7] The Ministry (not the ART) issues the licence, which is then published in the Official Journal in the form of an '*arrêté*'.[8]

Licence fees are defined in the annual French budget law.[9] Initially, fees for the establishment and operation of a national network were equal to a one-time payment of FF500,000 for the application, plus FF1,000,000 per year.[10] On 30 December 1997,[11] these fees were increased more than three-fold. The fees for a network covering more than five administrative regions are now FF1,750,000, payable upon delivery of the licence, plus FF3,500,000 per year. The relatively high level of fees raises a question of

Table 8.1 Telecommunication operator fees

Network size	L33-1 Public Networks		L34-1 Service Provider (Public Voice)†	
	Filing Fee	Annual Management Fee	Filing Fee	Annual Management Fee
< 1000,000 people	50,000 FF*	100,000 FF†	50,000 FF	100,000 FF‡
≤ département	100,000 FF*	200,000 FF‡	100,000 FF	200,000 FF‡
≤ région	250,000 FF*	500,000 FF‡	150,000 FF	300,000 FF‡
≤ 5 régions	500,000 FF*	1,000,000 FF‡	300,000 FF	600,000 FF‡
> 5 régions	1,750,000 FF*	3,500,000 FF‡	750,000 FF	1,500,000 FF‡
exclusively satellite networks	250,000 FF*	500,000 FF‡	250,000 FF	500,000 FF‡

†When an extension of the coverage zone is requested, a modification file fee must be paid equalling the difference between the amounts provided for in the schedule before an after extension.
*Filing fees are doubled for tenders following the provisions of L33-1 V
‡Annual management fees, paid on December 1st of each year, are doubled if the operator belongs to the list provided by L36-7 7°. The amount for the first year of authorization fee is calculated *prorate temporis*
Holders of a combined L33-1/L34-1 licence must pay the annual and filing fees applicable to both licences

Table 8.2 French licences

Operator	Type of Licence	Prefix	Date Licence granted
9 Telecom Réseau/Netco	L.33-1 & L.34-1	9	18 December 1997
Esprit Télécom France	L.33-1 & L.34-1	6	12 March 1998
France Télécom	L.33-1 & L.34-1	8	12 March 1998
CEGETEL	L.33-1 & L.34-1	7	11 March 1998 Enterprises 18 December 1997 (TD)
OMNICOM	L.33-1 & L.34-1	5	18 December 1997
SIRIS	L.33-1 & L.34-1	2	18 December 1997
TELE 2	L.33-1 & L.34-1	4	16 April 1998
AXS Telecom	L.34-1	1616	17 June 1998
Belgacom Téléport	L.33-1 & L.34-1	1659	29 April 1998 7 February 1997
COLT Télécommunications	L.33-1 & L.34-1	1690	12 March 1998
First Telecom	L.34-1	1639	17 June 1998
Géolink	L.33-1 & L.34-1	1611	
INFOTEL	L.33-1 & L.34-1	1617	29 April 1998
Kertel (formerly Rhodium)	L.33-1 & L.34-1	1630	26 June 1998 16 April 1998
LDI Telecom	L.34-1	1688	17 June 1998
LEX 4-Auxipar Suez Lyonnaise Telecom	L.33-1 & L.34-1	1612	27 December 1996
MFS Communication	L.33-1 & L.34-1	1618 3678	16 April 1998
Phone Systems & Networks	L.34-1	1677	
Primus Télécommunications	L.34-1	1656	29 April 1998
Prosodie	L.34-1	1601	26 May 1998
RSL COM	L.33-1 & L.34-1	1661	12 May 1998
Viatel Opérations	L.33-1 & L.34-1	1623	5 June 1998
Western Telecom	L.34-1	1655	17 June 1998
Worldxchange Communications	L.33-1 & L.34-1	1678	17 June 1998
Aéroports de Paris	L.33-1 & L.34-1		
BT-France	L.33-1		6 October 1997
Eurotunnel Développments	L.33-1		28 May 1997
Hermes Europe Raitel	L.33-1		22 October 1997
Médiaréseaux Marne	L.33-1 & L.34-1		17 June 1998
Telcité	L.33-1		16 April 1998

Source: ART Web Site (http://www.art-telecom.fr)

compliance with the EC Licensing Directive 97/13.[12] Table 8.1 sets forth the licence fee schedule applicable in 1998.

Applicants for a network operator's licence must provide to the ART documents relating to the proposed network, the switching equipment to be used, the services to be offered over the network, and a business plan, including proforma balance sheets, income statements, cash flow and employment projections over five years.[13]

Except for operators holding a single-digit 'E' prefix (which have certain investment obligations), the investment and employment projections set forth in the licence application do not constitute binding licence obligations for the new licence holder.

Under the European Licensing Directive, the Ministry is required to issue the licence no later than four months after the date of application, longer for licences where the networks require the allocation of spectrum resources. Initially, the actual time period for allocation of licences was initially much longer than the four-month period mandated by European law. Recent experience suggests, however, that the ART and Ministry are now respecting the four-month period. Table 8.2 contains a list of the licences granted to date (through July 1998).

The Telecommunications Law limits the permitted level of foreign ownership of networks open to the public that use radio frequency resources to 20 per cent.[14] This limitation does not apply, however, to European Union Members States. Furthermore, it is subordinated to France's World Trade Organisation commitments.[15]

Independent networks (Art. L 33-2)

Networks not open to the public are referred to in the French law as 'independent networks'. The Law defines 'independent network' as follows:

> . . . a telecommunications network designed for private or shared use. An Independent Network is 'private': when it is reserved for use exclusively by the private individual or corporate entity which established it; An independent network is 'shared': when it is reserved for use exclusively by several private individuals or corporate entities who are members of one or more closed-user groups in order to exchange internal information within the same group.[16]

Independent networks can consist of VSAT networks, wire-line networks, microwave links or private mobile radio networks. Virtually all independent networks require a licence.[17] Contrary to licences for public networks, the ART, not by the Ministry, grants licences for independent networks. In addition, applications for independent network licences are available 'on-line' at the ART's web site (http://www.art- telecom.fr).

Independent networks can be operated for closed-user groups. However, the ART requires that the applicant for an independent network list in advance the names and addresses of the persons or entities that can be reached via the independent network.[18] Thus, an independent network is a good legal vehicle for a single organisation that wants to establish and operate its own telecommunications network to link its various corporate sites. The independent network regime is ill-adapted, however, to a telecommunications operator that wants to offer corporate voice and data services to a number of corporate customers.

Unlike public networks, there are no foreign ownership restrictions in connection with licences for independent networks.

Service Providers (L 34-1)

The 'supply of telephone service to the public' requires a licence.[19] The term 'telephone service to the public' means 'the commercial exploitation for the public of the direct transfer of voice, in real time, originating from and destined to public switched telephone networks, between fixed or mobile users.'[20] The Consultation Document explains that the word 'transfer' as used in the French law means 'the joint service of transport and switching.'[21] Providing switching services in itself does not constitute 'telephone services to the public'.

Services for closed-user groups do not require a licence because such services are not offered 'to the public'. Although not defined in the Telecommunications Law, the ART defines 'closed-user group' as a group that is based on a community of interests sufficiently stable to be identified and which pre-exists the provision of the telecommunications service.[22] Applying the ART's definition, most telecommunications services offered to business users fall within the 'closed-user group' category and therefore do not require a licence.

Services pursuant to which a user is connected by leased line also do not require a licence, for such services do not make use of the PSTN on both ends of the communication. Finally, although controversial, certain value-added services, such as calling-card services, fall outside the definition of 'telephone service to the public'.[23]

Licence fees for service providers were also increased on 30 December 1997. Table 8.1 illustrates that the new fees (for a service provider covering more than five administrative regions) are FF750,000 at the time the licence is issued, plus FF1,500,000 annually.[24]

The content of the application for a service provider (L 34-1) licence is similar to that for a network operator (L 33-1) licence.

In practice, applicants for a public-network operator's licence (L 33-1) generally request a combined network operator's and service provider's licence, which allows the network operator also to provide public voice telephone services over its network. Such a licence is referred to as a combined L 33-1/L34-1 licence. The holder of a combined L 33-1/L 34-1 licence pays the annual fees applicable to both licences, making the annual licence fee, for the holder of a combined L 33-1/L 34-1 licence covering more than five French regions, equal to FF5,000,000.[25]

Numbering

France has two systems for selecting a long-distance carrier: a single-digit prefix ('E' prefix), and a four-digit prefix ('16XY' prefix). Six new entrants have received an 'E' prefix: Netco (Bouygues Telecom), Telecom Developpement (Cegetel), SIRIS, Omnicom, Tele 2 France and Esprit Telecom (see Table 8.2). Because the single prefix is a scarce resource, the ART limited access to the 'E' to operators who undertake to build-out national networks.[26] A network operator with an 'E' prefix must pay an annual fee for the prefix (in addition to the licence fee) equal to FF3,000,000.[27] Long-distance carriers not qualifying for an 'E' receive a '16XY' prefix, permitting callers to select the carrier by dialling the carrier's '16XY' code prior to placing a call. The annual fee for a 16XY prefix is FF300,000.[28]

This dual system was challenged by AXS Telecom, a young European carrier, on the ground that the system created an illegal discrimination between two classes of new entrants. AXS Telecom also alleged that the manner of selecting candidates for the 'E' prefixes lacked objectivity and transparency. In an initial ruling on 30 March 1998,[29] the Conseil d'Etat enjoined the ART from further implementing its decisions on the 'E' prefix, indicating that there was a strong presumption that the procedure for attributing the 'E' would be held illegal for lack of transparency, and that the entire system of dual prefixes could be held to constitute illegal discrimination between operators. On 26 June 1998, the Conseil d'Etat reversed its prior decision, holding that the dual system for prefixes was not discriminatory because holders of the 'E' prefixes were subject to more burdensome obligations than those for holders of '16XY' prefixes, both in terms of licence fees as well as in terms of network build-out obligations.[30] Going against the recommendations of Advocate General Patrick Hubert, the Conseil d'Etat also held that the procedure for attributing the 'E' prefix (which consisted of selecting candidates who would then be permitted to participate in a drawing) was sufficiently objective, transparent and non-discriminatory to pass muster under Article 34-10 of the Telecommunications Law.

The ART's Decision no. 97–196 provides that carrier pre-selection will be available in France by 1 January 2000.[31] Beginning on that date, a consumer will be able to instruct France Télécom (or another local-loop operator) to route systematically all long-distance and international calls to a given long-distance carrier, without the consumer having to dial a special prefix, as is currently the case.

Holders of the 16XY prefix regret that the French government did not impose carrier pre-selection ('equal access') at the outset of liberalisation back in January 1998, as the German government did. Indeed, according to a 1996 inter-ministerial document, it would have been both technically and financially feasible to require that France Télécom implement the necessary software upgrades to permit equal access in 1998. That decision would have given rise to extra cost for France Télécom in 1997, but would have facilitated the development of new competition.

Interconnection

Operators who 'exercise a significant influence on a relevant tele-communications market'[32] must publish interconnection tariffs approved in advance by the ART. Those tariffs must be cost-based. The ART makes a list every year of those operators deemed to 'exercise a significant influence on a relevant telecommunications market.'[33] For the time being, only France Télécom is deemed to exercise a 'significant influence' on the relevant market. *All* operators (not just France Télécom) are required to interconnect with other operators under 'objective, transparent and non-discriminatory' conditions.[34] French decree no. 97–188 of 3 March 1997 sets forth detailed rules for interconnection, along the lines required by the EC Interconnection Directive 97/33. Interconnection agreements are filed with the ART, who may communicate their contents to interested third parties.[35] The ART has jurisdiction to arbitrate inter-connection disputes.[36] France Télécom issued an interconnection tariff for 1998 that was approved by the ART on 9 April 1997 and 30 July 1997.[37] The interconnection tariff for 1999 is currently under discussion.

The key elements of the 1998 interconnection tariff are set forth in Table 8.3.

Universal Service

For the time being,[38] the scope of universal service is limited to the supply of basic voice telephony at an affordable price, the free transmission of emergency calls, the supply of a directory assistance service and a telephone directory, and the supply, throughout France, of public phone booths.[39] The Telecommunications Law provides that the universal service obligation may be entrusted 'to any operator who accepts to provide [universal service] throughout the [French] territory and who is capable of assuming such obligation'.[40] The Law then provides that 'France Télécom is the public operator entrusted with the universal service obligation'.[41] Before the Telecommunications Law was enacted, prospective new entrants hoped that the Telecommunications Law would offer them a choice of either contributing financially to universal service, or assuming the universal service obligation themselves in a limited geographic area. The French Parliament rejected in large part this 'pay or play' approach to universal service, at least for operators of fixed net-works,[42] electing instead to entrust the entire universal service obligation to France Télécom and/or to another operator capable of assuming the obligation on a nation-wide level. It is hard to imagine any operator other

Table 8.3 Summary of 1998 France Télécom interconnection tariffs applicable to holders of a network operator (L.33-1) licence

Interconnect to Local (end-office) Switches		Interconnection to Transit Switches at 'PROs' (points de raccordement d'opérateurs)			Interconnect Link Tariffs*
			Per Minute		Link (*liaison de raccordement*) intra-ZT to the closest PRO
			SIMPLE TRANSIT (*to carry incoming or outgoing traffic within the same zone as the PRO*)	DOUBLE TRANSIT (*to terminate traffic to zones other than those covered by the PRO*)	
Annual	Per Minute	Annual			
FF34,450 for each 'primary digital block' (*bloc primaire numérique*) (2Mbit port)	FF0.0469 (FF0.0322 nights and weekends) for access to customers served by that local switch	FF47,590 for each 'primary digital block' (*bloc primaire numérique*) (2Mbit port)	FF0.1140 (FF0.0783 nights and weekends)	FF0.1677 (FF0.1151 nights and weekends)	Contracts for interconnect links must have a minimum duration of 2 years
	FF.0.1088 (FF0.0747 nights and weekends) for access to customers served by contiguous local switches which can be accessed without going through transit switch		An additional FF0.02 per minute for universal service	An additional FF0.02 per minute for universal service	*Access Fee:* FF17,000
	An additional FF0.02 per minute for universal service			Double transit not available for call origination ('indirect access')	*Per link:* • Fixed costs of 23,650–61,250 FF/year, depending on link length • For links longer than 1 km, a per km cost of 335–1,849 FF/year, depending on link length
					Groups of 9 or more links at 2Mbits benefit from an annual discount of 12,500–13,600 FF per link, depending on the number of links per group

*These interconnect link tariffs only apply to interconnect links to connect the operator's point of presence in the zone to the PRO within the same zone. 'Long Haul' interconnect links (covering more than one 'zone') are subject to normal France Télécom commercial rates (Transfix). Operator must bring traffic to, and pick traffic up from, the relevant PRO or end office in the provinces through 'three groups of unidirectional links supported by separate 2Mbit/s lines'. In the Paris region, the requirement is two groups of unidirectional links for connection to the PRO for the urban zone ('ZU'), and two separate ones for connection to the PRO for the periphery zone ('ZP').
Other costs: Research & Development: Operator must pay or contribute in kind to research, development and teaching an amount equal to 5 per cent of his investment in telecommunications infrastructure, equipment and software

Table 8.4 Summary of 1998 France Télécom interconnection tariffs applicable to holders of a service provider (L.34-1) licence

Interconnect to Local (end-office) Switches		Interconnection to Transit Switches at 'PRFs' (points de raccordement de fournisseurs de service))		Interconnect Link Tariffs*
		Per Minute		
		SIMPLE TRANSIT (to carry incoming or outgoing traffic within the same zone as the PRF)	DOUBLE TRANSIT (to terminate traffic to zones other than those covered by the PRF)	Link (liaison de raccordement) intra-ZT to the closest PRF
Annual	Per Minute			
No connection permitted to local switches	FF47,590 for each 'primary digital block' (bloc primaire numérique (2Mbit port)	FF0.1584 (FF0.1087 nights and weekends to carry incoming or or outgoing traffic within the same zone as the PRF) An additional FF0.02 per minute for universal service	Double transit is not available to service providers	Contracts for interconnect links must have a minimum duration of 2 years *Access Fee:* FF22,040 *Per link:* • Fixed costs of 25,513– 67,782 FF/year, depending on link length • For links longer than 1 km, a per km cost of 343– 1,895 FF/year, depending on link length Groups of 9 or more links at 2Mbits benefit from an annual discount of 12,500–13,600 FF per link, depending on the number of links per group

*These interconnect link tariffs only apply to interconnect links to connect the operator's point of presence in the zone to the PRF within the same zone.
'Long Haul' interconnect links (covering more than one 'zone') are subject to normal France Télécom commercial rates (Transfix).
Service provider must bring traffic to, and pick traffic up from, the relevant PRF or end office in the provinces through 'three groups of unidirectional links' supported by separate 2Mbit/s lines'. In the Paris region, the requirement is only for 'two groups of unidirectional links'.
Other costs: Research & Development: Operator must pay or contribute in kind to research, development and teaching an amount equal to 5 per cent of his investment in telecommunications infrastructure, equipment and software

than France Télécom being capable of assuming the universal service obligation throughout France, at least in the foreseeable future.

The ART determines annually the net cost to France Télécom that results from its universal service obligation. The cost is then approved by the Ministry and collected from operators in the form of additional interconnection fees and a contribution to a universal service fund. The costs are divided into two basic categories. The first (and by far the largest) category of costs relates to the loss caused by the currently unbalanced structure of France Télécom's rates,[43] and the loss associated with geographic balancing, i.e. the obligation to charge the same rate for basic telephone service in both high-cost (rural) and low-cost (urban) areas. This category of the universal service obligation is funded through an additional payment by each operator in addition to the per-minute interconnection charge. The amount of the additional per-minute charge in 1998 will be equal to approximately FF0.02 per minute, corresponding to a total cost estimated at approximately FF5 billion for 1998. The second category of universal service costs relates to public phone booths, and to the need to provide special discounts to certain needy user groups (handicapped or low revenue individuals, for example). This category of costs, estimated at approximately FF1.1 billion for 1998, is funded through contributions to a universal service fund managed by the Caisse des dépôts et consignations.[44]

Although the total cost of universal service for 1998 (both categories combined) is estimated at over FF6 billion, the majority of this cost will be borne by France Télécom itself. The cost is divided pro rata, based on each operator's share of traffic. Thus France Télécom will continue to bear the lion's share of the universal service cost. The ART expects that competitors will pay a total of approximately FF98 million in 1998 toward the FF6 billion universal service cost.[45]

Two associations of telecommunications operators[46] filed a complaint before the European Commission challenging the legality of the French universal service regime. The associations assert that the charges on new entrants are excessive, pointing out that France is the only country in the European Union to have levied a universal service contribution on new entrants. The method of calculating the cost of universal service is, according to the associations, illegal because the cost does not take into account the tremendous goodwill value to France Télécom of being the ubiquitous telecommunications provider in France. Finally, the regime does not comply with Article 5 of the Interconnection Directive,[47] which permits a Member State to levy universal service charges when it determines that the universal service obligations 'represent an unfair burden' on the incumbent operator. Because the French government has never determined that it would be 'unfair' to leave the cost of universal service with France Télécom, the universal service charge is illegal.

Education, Research and Development

French Decree no. 96–1175 requires licensed operators to invest annually, in the field of telecommunications research, development and education, an amount equal to at least 5 per cent of the operator's annual investments in telecommunications-related assets.[48] Operators do not need to pay this amount to an outside fund, but can satisfy the obligation by sending employees to continuing education programs, by funding university research projects, or other similar alternatives. This investment obligation is not foreseen in the EC Licensing Directive 97/13, and could pose a problem of compatibility with European law. While reaching the 5 per cent threshold should not be difficult for smaller operators, operators with large infrastructure investments could find the obligation burdensome.

Practical difficulties of implementation

With the preceding short overview of the Telecommunications Law as background, the following are some of the practical problems that have arisen in applying the Telecommunications Law over the last eighteen months.

Distinguishing between 'Network Operator' and 'Service Provider'

As mentioned above, the Telecommunications Law draws a fundamental distinction between 'network operators' and 'service providers'. This distinction is based on whether the operator owns and exploits its own transmission infrastructure. 'Own transmission infrastructure' means copper or fibre links owned and installed by the operator itself. The term also includes transmission links established 'via an optical connection service offered over dark fibre installed by a third party . . .'.[49] Transmission capacity leased from other operators is not considered to be an operator's 'own transmission infrastructure'.[50]

Thus the Telecommunications Law treats differently an entity whose network consists exclusively of leased circuits from an entity whose network consists partially of leased circuits, and partially of 'an optical connection service offered over dark fibre installed by a third party'.

The reason for the distinction is to encourage investment in transmission infrastructure. The effect of the distinction is to create a confused situation for new entrants. For example, small service providers generally use leased lines to connect their points of presence until traffic volumes, cash flow, and infrastructure prices warrant an investment in fibre. Yet under the French approach, such companies must choose at the outset whether to apply for a 'service provider's' licence or a 'network operator's' licence. If they choose the latter, they must show to the ART that they plan to invest in transmission infrastructure in addition to the circuits leased from other operators. The Telecommunications Law does not stipulate how much transmission infrastructure must be purchased, or where or when it much be purchased. The only guidelines that have been published relate to network operators who apply for an 'E' prefix. Those operators must reach a ratio of 30 per cent of their 'own' transmission infrastructure versus total transmission infrastructure within eighteen months. Other operators (i.e. those who do not have an 'E' prefix) must guess how much transmission infrastructure is necessary to be considered a 'network operator'. Applicants must discuss the issue with the ART on a case-by-case basis.

The difference in treatment between an operator who uses dark fibre provided by a freeway system, for example, versus an operator who rents leased circuits seems artificial, and is hard for new entrants to manage in practice.

Time periods for processing licence applications

The Consultation Document provides that:

> the maximum time periods foreseen between the receipt of a complete application and the attribution of the licence or the notification of refusal are as follows:
> Authorisation L. 33-1 and L 34-1: 4 months
> Authorisation L. 34-1: 6 weeks[51]

These time periods are longer if the licence requires the attribution of radio spectrum.

The six-week time period provided for the attribution of an L 34-1 licence complies with the EC Licensing Directive 97/13, which requires that Member States '*inform the applicant of its decision as soon as possible but not more than six weeks after receiving the application*'.[52] The Directive provides that the six-week period can be extended to four months for 'objectively justified cases'.[53] It is not clear why the attribution of a normal network operator's licence in France (L 33-1), without radio spectrum, constitutes an 'objectively justified case' for extending the normal six-week licensing period required by the Directive.

However, the problem faced now by new entrants is not whether the time period should be six weeks or four months. The problem is that until recently, both time periods were ignored. Some licence applicants waited ten months to receive a licence. Fortunately, these delays have recently abated, such that licence applications are now being processed within four months.

Another issue is when the six-week or four-month time period begins to run. The Consultation Document states that the 'ART acknowledges receipt of the application when it is complete, and when it is not complete, sends a written request for the additional documents'.[54] The document then states that the six-week or four-month time period begins to run only when an application is 'complete'. The ART seemingly has unlimited discretion to decide when an application is deemed 'complete'. The official 'receipt' from the ART, referred to in the Consultation Document, sometimes takes weeks, or even months, to obtain, even when an application contains all the materials listed in the Consultation Document. Sometimes the 'receipt' is never sent, leaving the applicant guessing when the six-week (or four-month) period begins to run.

A decree is being prepared that will hopefully set forth more clearly the time limits within which licences will be issued, and the point at which those time limits will begin to run.

Determining the applicant's 'financial capacity'

The French Telecommunications Law provides that the Minister may not refuse a licence:

> except to the extent required for the preservation of public order or the needs of public defence or security, by technical restraints inherent in the availability of frequency, or *where the applicant does not have the technical or financial capacity to satisfy, on a long-term basis, the obligations resulting from the conditions of exercise of its activity*, or where the applicant has been the object of sanctions under article L 36-11, L 39, L 39-1 and L 39-4.[55]

The ART interprets the language in the Telecommunications Law regarding 'financial capacity' to mean that the applicant must prove that he has the financial wherewithal successfully to complete its business plan, as set out in his licence application. Surprisingly, this burden even falls on service providers applying for a service provider (L-34-1) licence, and who have no plans to invest in fibre.

The task of furnishing proof of financial capacity is all the more difficult because there are no published criteria, raising an issue of transparency in the licensing process. In some cases the ART requires written financing commitments from the applicant's shareholders. In other cases the ART asks for documents evidencing private financing arrangements (commitment letters from banks, for example), evidence of capital increases, or other verifications of financial backing.

The intent of the 'financial capacity' provision in the Telecommunications Law is to protect the French public from unworthy 'fly-by-night' operators. However, the ART's current interpretation of this provision goes beyond the language of the Telecommunications Law, and seems contrary to Directive 97/13.

The ART has a tendency to judge financial capacity against the objectives set in the applicant's business plan and not against basic licence obligations. The two concepts are not the same. The French Telecommunications Law refers to the applicant's 'financial capacity to satisfy, on a long-term basis, the *obligations* resulting from the conditions of exercise of its activity'.[56] The EC Licensing Directive 97/13 refers to financial capacity only in the context of 'requirements relating to the quality, availability and permanence of a service or network'.[57] Under the language of both the Telecommunications Law and the Directive, financial capacity is linked to the obligations of the licence holder to respect criteria of quality, availability and permanence as set forth in the licence. Financial capacity is *not* related, however, to the applicant's ability to fulfil its own network development plans. Except for entities applying for an 'E' prefix, which have specific investment obligations as part of their licence, licence holders in France have no obligation under their licence to install a minimum number of points of presence within a certain time period, even if the licence holder says he hopes to achieve these objectives in his business-plan. Business plans change depending on cash flow, market conditions, the entry of new investors etc. In no case should a licensee's business plan objectives be considered an 'obligation resulting from the conditions of exercise of [the licensee's] activity'. Yet in practice, this seems to be the benchmark against which the ART judges 'financial capacity'.

This approach makes the licensing process difficult for small entrepreneurial companies, who rely on future cash flow to fund expansion. Such applicants would be advised, under the ART's current approach, to present extremely conservative business plans when applying for a licence.

Some of the world's most successful telecommunications companies started out as small businesses with little or no outside financial backing at the outset.[58] The ART's current method of applying a 'financial capacity' test in the licensing process creates an obstacle for small companies and also violates, in the author's view, the principles of proportionality and transparency imposed by the EC Licensing Directive 97/13.[59]

At a minimum, the ART should publish specifications setting forth what documents an applicant must supply to prove its 'financial capacity' and what criteria the ART will apply when evaluating the candidate's financial capacity.

Licence fees

As noted above, the fees for licences (both the application fee and the annual maintenance fee) increased dramatically on 30 December 1997.

The EC Licensing Directive 97/13 requires that fees 'seek only to cover the administrative costs incurred in the issue, management, control and enforcement of the applicable individual licence' and that they be 'proportionate to the work involved'.[60] It is hard to imagine that the FF750,000 application fee payable by an L 34-1 service provider covers only the administrative costs incurred in the issue of the individual licence, and is proportionate to the work involved (recall that an L 34-1 licence must be issued within 6 weeks after receipt of the application). If one estimates an hourly rate per ART (or Ministry) employee of FF1000 per hour (which rate should be sufficient to cover a pro rata share of overhead), the initial licence fee would correspond to 750 man-hours, which translates into three employees working full time on the licence application for the entire six-week licensing period. Using the same yardstick, the FF5 million annual fee required of network operators also holding a voice telephony (L 34-1) licence translates into three employees working 37 hours per week, 46 weeks per year,[61] in connection with the 'management, control and enforcement of the applicable individual licence'.[62] These annual fees relate only to the *licence*; they do not relate to the attribution and management of spectrum or numbering resources, which are charged for separately.

While every licence applicant will no doubt pay these licence fees initially, some applicants may be tempted to apply to the administrative courts for partial reimbursement of the fees, on the ground that they are excessive under the clear language of EC Directive 97/13.

Both the European Commission and the International Chamber of Commerce have issued strong warnings against using licence fees as a tool to raise general tax revenues.[63] Yet with enactment of its latest Finance Law, France seems to have departed from the principle of 'cost-based' licensing fees mandated by EC Directive 97/13.

Difference in treatment of service providers

Under France Télécom's current interconnection tariff structure, entities holding an L 34-1 licence will pay more for network access than will entities holding an L 33-1 (or a combined L 33-1/L 34-1) licence. Holders of an L 34-1 licence will also have the right to fewer interconnection services than holders of an L 33-1 licence. This difference in treatment between network operators and service providers does not seem justified by differences in the nature or costs of the services offered by France Télécom. Indeed, the description of the interconnection services offered by France Télécom to L 33-1 and L 34-1 licence holders appears identical. Both kinds of operators connect their points of presence to France Télécom points of interconnection ('POI') using a series of 2 Mbit connection links (*liaisons de raccordement*) that have the same technical characteristics. The call termination and origination services (*prestations d'acheminement de trafic commuté*) offered by France Télécom also appear identical. The only difference is that in the case of an L 34-1 service provider, France Télécom will not be requesting reciprocal interconnection services, as it would from an L 33-1 network operator who operates a local loop (France Télécom needing access to customers served by that local loop). During the initial period of liberalisation, most L 33-1 network operators will be long-distance operators, not local-loop operators. It is hard to find an objective reason to treat differently a long-distance operator and an L 34-1 service provider. For example, a network operator whose long-distance network consists principally of leased circuits, but who has achieved 'network operator' status thanks to investment in a few kilometres of dark fibre, can benefit from a lower per-minute call termination charge. The only explanation for the difference in treatment appears to be the industrial policy decision to encourage investment in transmission infrastructure. This reason is not legally sufficient (in the author's view) to justify the difference in treatment between the two categories of operators, under ONP and competition law[64] principles.

Cost is not the only issue. Service providers holding an L 34-1 licence cannot benefit from so-called 'double transit' call-termination service. To terminate a call in Marseille, a service provider holding an L 34-1 licence must bring the call to France Télécom's POI in the Marseille region. Holders of an L 33-1 licence can, on the other hand, hand over the same call to France Télécom's special POI in Paris for 'double transit' termination in Marseille. Moreover, service providers cannot transfer a call to France Télécom at the local-switch level. They must interconnect at the transit-switch level, naturally at a higher fee. Holders of an L 33-1 licence may, on the other hand, interconnect either at the local-switch level or at the transit-switch level. France Télécom and the ART are even reluctant to allow a service provider (L 34-1) to 'piggy back' on another network operator's (L 33-1) interconnection links with France Télécom.

How does this difference in treatment between network operators and service providers square with the provisions of French and European law? Article L 34-8 of the Telecommunications Law provides for the possibility of applying different treatment to different categories of operators, provided always that 'interconnection tariffs shall be cost-oriented and shall cover the effective cost of using the network'. Article 6(a) of Directive 97/33 provides that telecommunications organisations having significant market power 'shall apply similar conditions in similar circumstances to interconnected organisations providing similar services' and Article 7(3) of the same Directive indicates that 'different tariffs, terms and conditions for interconnection may be set for different categories of organisations which are authorised to provide networks and services, *where such differences can be objectively justified* on the basis of the type of interconnection provided and/or the relevant licensing conditions'.[65]

Based on these provisions, it appears that applying discriminatory tariffs and conditions to service providers would be justified only if the tariffs are 'cost oriented' and designed to cover 'the effective cost of using the network', and if the discriminatory conditions in general 'can be objectively justified on the basis of the type of interconnection provided and/or the relevant licensing conditions'.

Moreover, the burden of proof regarding the 'cost-orientation' of service-provider interconnection tariffs lies with France Télécom.[66]

The French Decree also specifically provides for interconnection at the local-switch level.[67] The failure of France Télécom to include in its interconnection offering the possibility for service providers to access local switches violates the plain language of Article D 99-15 of Decree no. 97–188.

Thus, while the ART-approved interconnection tariff has tilted the playing-field in favour of operators who invest in transmission infrastructure, the legality of this approach is not clear either under EC Interconnection Directive 97/33 or under the French decree on interconnection.

Obtaining copies of other interconnection agreements

Article D. 99-6 of Decree no. 97–188 provides that copies of all interconnection agreements (including those entered into between non-dominant operators) are transmitted to the ART and that the 'ART may, upon request, transmit to interested third parties information that [the interconnection agreement] contains, subject to information covered by *trade secrecy*.'[68]

The French interconnection decree unfortunately departs from the clear language of EC Directive 97/33, which provides (as regards agreements entered into by operators having 'significant market power') that:

> interconnection agreements are communicated to the relevant national regulatory authorities, and made available on request to interested parties, in accordance with Article 14(2), with the exception of those parts which deal with the *commercial strategy* of the parties. The national regulatory authority shall determine which parts deal with the commercial strategy of the parties. In every case, details of interconnection charges, terms and conditions and any contributions to universal service obligations shall be made available on request to interested parties.[69]

Article 14(2) of the Directive provides:

> With regard to the information identified in . . . Article 6(c) . . ., national regulatory authorities shall ensure that up-to-date specific

information referred to in those Articles is made available on request to interested parties, free of charge, during normal working hours. Reference shall be made in the national Official Gazette of the Member State concerned to the times and location(s) at which the information is available.

The French decree uses the term 'trade secrets' (*secret des affaires*) whereas the Directive uses the term 'commercial strategy' (*stratégie commerciale*). 'Commercial strategy' is arguably narrower than 'trade secret', and there is fear that the ART will, based on the 'trade secret' language used in the decree, exclude such elements as pricing and delivery terms from disclosure. Article 6(c) of the Directive is nevertheless quite clear: 'In every case, details of interconnection charges, terms and conditions . . . shall be made available'. The parts of an interconnection agreement that may be legitimately protected from disclosure are those aspects that reveal the geographic location of points of presence, the dates of deployment, and network capacity. Such items relate to the 'commercial strategy' of the parties. In practice, all individually-negotiated arrangements between a new operator and France Télécom are placed in a separate part of the agreement which is labelled as containing 'trade secrets'. This is obviously done in order to discourage the ART from disclosing the information contained in that section to third parties. However, this does not mean by any stretch of the imagination that all individually-negotiated arrangements with France Télécom are necessarily trade secrets.

Another interesting aspect relates to the form of disclosure. While the Directive requires that interconnection agreements be made available to interested parties, the Decree provides that the ART 'may . . . transmit to interested third parties *information that [the interconnection agreement] contains . . .*'. Thus the ART 'may' (not 'shall') transmit the information contained in the agreement, but need not communicate the agreement itself. While permissible under the language of the decree, such an approach would conflict with the terms of Article 6(c) of the Directive, at least when applied to agreements entered into by operators having significant market power.

The purpose of communicating interconnection agreements is to help guarantee non-discrimination, particularly by operators having significant market power. As recommended by the International Chamber of Commerce in 1995: 'interconnection agreements with operators subject to the regulatory interconnection framework should be open to public scrutiny, and not just the regulator's scrutiny. In certain instances the national regulator would benefit from market participants' evidence of hidden discrimination'.[70]

The ART can (and does) examine interconnection agreements to verify non-discrimination. However, discrimination can take many forms, and may be hidden in apparently innocent details. Operators involved in the details of interconnection negotiations, testing and deployment with an operator having significant market power should be in a position to judge for themselves whether they are being discriminated against by having at their disposal copies of other interconnection agreements entered into by the incumbent operator. Leaving the job of detecting discrimination solely with the ART has two drawbacks: first, it is unrealistic to expect the ART to ferret out every instance of discrimination. The task would be daunting. Second, by the time the ART discovers discrimination in an agreement, it will be too late to help the operator who has been harmed by such discrimination, particularly if the discrimination relates to delays in testing. To be useful, the information needs to be available at the time the relevant operator is negotiating interconnection conditions with France Télécom.

Part of the difficulty of implementing the French decree is that the filing and public-disclosure requirements under French law apply even to interconnection agreements entered into between two non-dominant network operators, whereas the Directive's filing and public-disclosure requirement apply only to interconnect agreements entered into by operators having 'significant market power'. The ART may be legitimately concerned about communicating to third parties commercial information contained in agreements entered into between two non-dominant operators. It may be appropriate, therefore, for the ART to develop two different approaches to the issue of communicating interconnection agreements to third parties: one approach – more discretionary – that would apply to agreements entered into between two non-dominant carriers, and another approach – in strict conformity with the Directive – that would apply to agreements entered into by operators having 'significant market power'.

Implementation of interconnection

It is too early to make a judgement about how interconnection is working in France. France Télécom has not (to this author's knowledge) allowed operators to begin interconnection testing or the negotiation of the inter-connection agreement until the operators have received their licence. Thus the interconnection process, as it regards public-network operators,[71] is just now beginning. Initial problems relate particularly to the implementation delays requested by France Télécom between the time an order is placed for interconnection circuits and the time the order is filled. Contractually, France Télécom retains the possibility to take up to eighteen months to fill an order for interconnect links. There are also no penalties if France Télécom is late in delivery.

Other issues relate to the difficulty of satisfying certain tests which are required to comply fully with the French 'SSUTR2' switching protocol, and limitations imposed on new operators regarding the use of compression, etc.

The ART can arbitrate disputes relating to interconnection under Article L 36-8 of the Telecommunications Law. To date, the ART has acted under this provision only in connection with a dispute between two French cable operators and France Télécom regarding the upgrading of the France Télécom-owned cable infrastructure.[72] The cable operators sought to force France Télécom to allow upgrades on the network so as to permit the cable operators to offer Internet access services to their subscribers.

The ART has not yet, to the author's knowledge, rendered a decision involving an interconnection dispute between a new entrant and France Télécom, even though, based on similar experiences in other countries, such a dispute is highly foreseeable. This is understandable. For a new entrant, it would be foolhardy to bring an arbitration before having signed the interconnection agreement with France Télécom and placing initial orders for interconnect links. An arbitration could delay the ordering and provisioning process.

Conclusion

The ART is trying to encourage new operators to establish their hub in France for international telecommunications traffic. To achieve this goal, the ART is liberalising access to irrevocable rights of usage in submarine cables.[73] However, France's licensing procedure, with its high licence fees and its emphasis on 'network operators' with 'financial capacity', favours large companies to the detriment of small entrepreneurial firms, whom many view as offering the greatest potential for innovation, growth and employment in France.

The ART should not underestimate the effect of licensing procedures on telecommunications investment decisions. The International Chamber of Commerce, in a recent position paper, underlined the risk of creating heavy licensing procedures:

> liberalisation has generally been accompanied by a proliferation of licensing requirements, covering a wide range of operators and service providers. Excessive resort to licensing can stifle emerging competition at birth, particularly competition in international service[74]

Making the licensing process long, difficult and expensive will inevitably favour the development of European telecommunications hubs in other European countries, where the licensing process is less burdensome.

To the ART's credit, the licensing process has improved markedly since June 1998. New entrants hope that this trend will continue and that the

ART will exercise its authority vigorously to make interconnection conditions better for new entrants. For example, the ART is focusing on promoting local-loop competition through wireless technologies. One of the top priorities for new entrants, however, is to obtain access to the unbundled elements of France Télécom's local loop, which is not yet possible.

Notes

1 Portions of this chapter appeared in an article written by the author in *Communications & Strategies*, IDATE, Issue 29, First quarter, pp. 57–77.
2 Directive 97/13/EC of the European Parliament and of the Council of 10 April 1997 on a Common Framework for General Authorisation and Individual Licences in the Field of Telecommunications Services, OJEC No. L 117/15. 7 May 1997.
3 http://www.art-telecom.fr.
4 Law No. 96-659 of July 26, 1996, OJ 27 July, 1996.
5 Art. L 33-1, Telecommunications Law. Certain very small networks, or networks located solely on private property, do not require a licence. See Art. L 33-3, Telecommunications Law.
6 OJ 30 May, 1997, p. 8361.
7 Art. L 36-7 1°, Telecommunications Law.
8 Arts. L 33-1 and L 34-1, Telecommunications Law.
9 Art. L 33-1-Iq), Telecommunications Law.
10 Art. 36, Finance Law of 1997, No. 96–1181 of December 30, 1996, OJ, 31 December, 1996, p. 19496.
11 Art. 22, Finance Law of 1998, no. 97–1269 of December 30, 1997, OJ, 31 December, 1997.
12 See *infra* p. 164.
13 Internal ART Document entitled: 'Documents à fournir dans le cadre d'une demande d'autorisation'; see also Annex II, Consultation Document, OJ, 30 May, 1997, p. 8364.
14 Art. 33-1 III, Telecommunications Law.
15 Fourth Protocol to the General Agreement on Trade in Services, Schedule of Specific Commitments, European Communities and Their Member States, World Trade Organization, 15 April 1997, p. 155.
16 Art. L 32 4°, Telecommunications Law.
17 Wire connections of less than 30 metres can be established without a licence.
18 ART 1997 Annual Report, p. 193.
19 Art. L 34-1, Telecommunications Law.
20 Art. L 32 7°, Telecommunications Law.
21 Consultation Document, OJ, 30 May, 1997, p. 8361. Although the European directive employs the terms 'switching and transport' the definition of 'transfer' in French is the equivalent of the two terms.
22 1997 Annual Report, p. 211.
23 Communication by the Commission on the status of implementation of Directive 90/388, OJ, C 275/2, 20 Oct. 1995, p. 6; see also 'Téléphonie Vocale – le marché des services de la voix', Etude de la Direction Générale des Posts et Télécommunications, IDATE December 1994, p. 25.
24 Art. 22, Finance Law for 1998, no. 97–1269, OJ 31 December 1997, p. 19266.
25 Previously, the holder of a combined licence paid only the fees applicable to the more expensive L33-1 licence. Art. 36, Finance Law for 1997, no. 96–1181

of December 30 1996, OJ, 31 December, 1997, p. 19496. Thus, the holder of a combined licence covering the entire French territory previously paid FF1,000,000 per year, versus FF5,000,000 per year under the current law.

26 ART Decision no. 97–196, OJ, 2 August, 1997, p. 11518.

27 Arrêté of December 30, 1997, OJ, 31 December, 1997, p. 19439.

28 Arrêté of December 30, 1997, OJ, 31 December, 1997, p. 19439.

29 Decision dated 30 March 1998, Conseil d'Etat, requêtes AXS TELECOM no. 194151 and 194152.

30 Decision dated 26 June 1998, Conseil d'Etat, requêtes AXS TELECOM and ESPRIT TELECOM no. 194151, 194152, 195427, 195428, 195429 and 195430.

31 ART Decision no. 97–196, OJ, 2 August, 1997, p. 11519.

32 Art. L 36-7 7°, Art. L 34-8 I, Telecommunications Law.

33 Art. L 36-7 7°, Telecommunications Law.

34 Art. L 34-8 I, Telecommunications Law.

35 Art. D 99-6, Decree no. 97–188 of March 3, 1997, OJ, 4 March, 1997, p. 3439, Telecommunications Law.

36 Art. L 36-8, Telecommunications Law.

37 ART Decision no. 97–88, OJ, 10 May, 1997, p. 7121; ART Decision no. 97–242, OJ, 20 August, 1997, p. 12347.

38 There is periodically talk of extending the scope of universal service to cover new services including Internet access. The Telecommunications Law requires a periodic review of the scope of universal service to take into account 'developments in telecommunications technology and services, and the needs of society'. Art. L 35-7, Telecommunications Law.

39 Art. L 35-1, Telecommunications Law. The entity entrusted with providing universal service must also provide certain 'obligatory services' throughout the French territory, including ISDN access, leased lines, packet-switched data services, advanced voice services and telex services. Art. L 35-5, Telecommunications Law.

40 Art. L 35-2, Telecommunications Law.

41 Art. L 35-2, Telecommunications Law.

42 Mobile operators benefit from a limited 'pay or play' option. In exchange for undertaking to cover major roads throughout France beginning 1 January 2001, mobile operators are exempted from financing the part of universal service destined to compensate France Télécom for its currently 'unbalanced tariff structure'. Art. L 35-3 II 1°, Telecommunications Law.

43 France Télécom's flat monthly fee for subscribers is lower than it should be, based on costs. France Télécom is currently 'rebalancing' this rate structure, and has until 31 December, 2000 to do so. At that time (at the latest), new entrants will cease having to make payments for this element of the universal service cost. Art. L 35-3 II 3°, Telecommunications Law.

44 Art. L 35-3 II 2°, Telecommunications Law.

45 ART press release dated 27 October, 1997.

46 The 'AOST' (Association des Opérateurs de Services de Télécommunications) and the 'AFOPT' (Association Française des Opérateurs Privés en Télécommunications).

47 Directive 97/33/EC of the European Parliament and of the Council on Interconnection in Telecommunications with Regard to ensuring Universal Service and Interoperability through application of the principles of Open Network Provision (ONP) of June 30, 1997, OJEC, 26 July, 1997 L 199/32.

48 Decree no. 96–1175 of December 27, 1996, OJ, 29 December, 1996, p. 19438.

49 Consultation Document, OJ, 30 May, 1997, p. 8363.

50 *Id.*

51 *Id.*

52 Article 9(2), Directive 97/13.
53 *Id.*
54 Consultation Document, §II-3(2), OJ, 30 May, 1997, p. 8362.
55 Art. L 33-1(I), Telecommunications Law (emphasis added).
56 Art. 33-1 I, Telecommunications Law (emphasis added).
57 Directive 97/13, Annex, par. 4.8.
58 MCI started in 1967 out of a radio repair shop in Joliet, Illinois.
59 Art. 3(2) of Directive 97/13 provides that licensing conditions 'shall be objectively justified in relation to the service concerned, non-discriminatory, proportionate and transparent'.
60 Art. 11(1), Directive 97/13.
61 Three employees × 1,000 FF/hour × 1,700 hours = FF5.1 million.
62 Art. 11(1), Directive 97/13.
63 European Commission, Green Paper on the Convergence of the Telecommunications, Media and Information Technology Sectors, and the Implications for Regulation, COM(97)623, December 3, 1997, pp. 17, 23; International Chamber of Commerce, ICC Policy Statement on International Telecommunications Licensing Policies (Document no. 373/291, 3 March 1998).
64 Arrêt de la Cour d'appel de Paris dated September 9, 1997 relating to the appeal of Héli-Inter Assistance SARL in connection with the exploitation of the héliport de Narbonne, OJ, 7 October, 1997, p. 693.
65 Art. 7(3), Directive 97/33 (emphasis added).
66 Art. 7, Directive 97/33: 'The burden of proof that charges are derived from actual costs including a reasonable rate of return on investment shall lie with the organization providing interconnection to its facilities.'
67 Article D 99-15 of Decree no. 97–188 provides '. . . these operators must in particular offer in the interconnection offering, an access to: their local switches; their higher-level switches to an equivalent technical solution.'
68 Art. D 99-6, Decree 97–188 of March 3, 1997 (emphasis added).
69 Art. 6(c), EC Directive 97/33 (emphasis added).
70 ICC Statement no. 373/246 of June 13, 1995 on the European Commission's Green Paper on the Liberalisation of Telecommunications Infrastructure.
71 France Télécom has entered into interconnection agreements with certain operators holding other kinds of network operator licences.
72 Decisions no. 97–209 and 97–210 of July 10, 1997, OJ, 7 September, 1997; Decisions 21 and 22 of April 28, 1998 of the Paris Court of Appeals (reprinted in the ART Annual Report, p. 232).
73 ART Decision no. 97–455 dated December 17, 1997.
74 ICC Policy Statement on International Telecommunications Licensing Policies (Document no. 373/291, 3 March 1998).

Part III

Liberalisation policies outside the EU framework

In Part III we look at countries outside the European Union, countries that to a large extent have managed their liberalisation within the framework of bilateral agreements, or with a perception of the competitive structures being formed within the WTO.

As Zdenek Hruby shows in Chapter 9, we find the same issues and conflicts in the Czech situation as in various European countries. The question of ownership and control of operating companies ranks high on the list, and is difficult to solve because it lies at the heart of the role of the state and how it should create welfare for its citizens. Financial difficulties, however, are only part of the problem. As important is the need for the domestic industry to engage in global alliances.

The Israeli situation, as described by David Levi-Faur in chapter 10, is in itself a very interesting case study in how a traditionally 'etatist' governed sector has been liberalised 'from above'. It reflects the importance of the national-level reform process wherein state officials were possibly *the* most important driving force for liberalisation. As global regimes develop, however, the need for co-ordination increases.

Prasit Prapinmongkolkarn (Chapter 11) demonstrates how Thailand's need for a new infrastructure has led the authorities to open up the market for new entrants. It also lays down some crucial factors for the future success of the regime, especially with regard to the nature of the new private-sector participating enterprises.

9 Privatisation and competition of telecommunication markets in transition countries

The case of the Czech Republic

Zdenek Hruby

The Czech Republic is an example of a country in transition in Central and Eastern Europe (CEE). It has a population of approximately 10 million and, in 1996, its GDP per capita was US$3,500 whilst its GDP per capita in purchasing power parity was 55 per cent as compared to the EU (Cullen Int. 1997).

As a result of the dissolution of the Czechoslovakian Federation, the Europe Agreement signed between the EU and Czechoslovakia on 16 December 1991 had to be renegotiated. A new agreement with the Czech Republic was signed in October 1993 (effective 1 February 1995) and the Czech Republic formally applied for EU membership on 17 January 1996.

With regard to telecommunications, the Czech Republic has signed and ratified the WTO agreement on Basic Telecommunications, thereby agreeing to implement liberal telecommunication principles and open all its telecommunications markets by 1 January 1998 (with the exception of voice telephony markets which will be opened 1 January 2001). With this in view, in August 1994, the Czech Republic introduced 'The Main Principles of the State Telecommunication Policy' (Ministry of Economy CR 1994) which, amongst others, included statements of intent concerning:

- a liberal regulatory environment
- licensing two GSM mobile telephone networks
- partial privatisation of the national carrier SPT Telecom with a strategic partner and a voice long-distance and international monopoly until the year 2000
- introduction of competition, by licensing local telephony operators in sixteen localities
- more than doubling the number of main telephone lines between 1994 and 2000
- maintain integrity of SPT Telecom
- a minimum 51 per cent state share of SPT Telecom

Table 9.1 Network development statistics

Main lines per 100 inhabitants	27% (1996)
Average waiting for a telephone	1.9 years (1996)*
Total growth of main lines over the period 1990–1995/6	growth from 16.6 lines (1990) to 29.0 lines (1997) per 100 inhabitants
Network digitisation	33% of SPT Telecom's customers are being served through digital exchanges
Penetration of mobile subscription as percentage of population	2.5%
Percentage of population covered by mobile radio	End of 1996: EuroTel Prague 74% Radiomobil 40% EuroTel Prague (NMT-450) 96%
Penetration of Internet as percentage of population	Number of hosts per 100,000 inhabitants connected to the Internet in the Czech Republic: 428 (July 1997) In 1995 there were 7.4 PCs per 100 households
Radio-paging coverage as percentage of population	99% (Radiokontakt Operator)

Source: Czech Telecommunications Office, Prague 1997
*With considerable differences among regions depending on the state of modernisation of switches.

Prior to this, in 1991, a network development program called First Tele-communications Project (SPT Telecom 1994) had been launched. The restructuring programme aimed primarily at the expansion of SPT Telecom's capital stock, the reform of its management structure and practices, and the implementation of a comprehensive investment programme. In addition, it was to expand and modernise the public telecommunications network, and to improve the quality of services.

The first phase (1992–4) saw the successful implementation of a national digital overlay network (DON). The second phase (1995–8) is to extend the DON and local networks, and to move gradually from analogue to digital technology at all levels of the network. With additional funds from its strategic partner since 1995, Telsource, SPT Telecom plans to complete the second phase of the First Telecommunications Project, which includes increasing mainline penetration to over 35 per cent, by 1998 – two years ahead of schedule – and to digitise 60 per cent of the network by the year 2000. The current situation is shown in Table 9.1.

SPT Telecom in the voucher privatisation

As a first step towards privatisation and in order to let the company take part in the second wave of 'Voucher Privatisation', SPT Telecom was transformed into a joint-stock company in 1994 with a total of 23,512,565 shares. Following a decision by the government, 26 per cent of the equity (6,113,267 shares) was floated and has been traded on the 'quoted' market of the Prague Stock Exchange since June 1995 (SPT Telecom 1995). Table 9.2 contains the percentile division of ownership with and without the strategic partner in the company. However, voucher privatisation does not bring any new money to the equity of the company involved and, consequently, SPT Telecom did not benefit financially from privatisation. This was not a problem particular to SPT Telecom, but of the voucher privatisation scheme in general (Frydman, Rapaczynski and Earle 1993). It should also be noted that the decision to undertake voucher privatisa- tion was probably more influenced by political than economic necessities.

Choice of strategic partner

On 10 August 1994, the Czech government accepted 'The Main Principles of the State Telecommunication Policy', which implied entrance of a strategic partner into SPT Telecom. The Minister of Economy underlined the necessity of international capital for speedy modernisation, as shown by the analyses of various international consulting firms, and it was clear that an equity injection into SPT Telecom would be cheaper for the company than debt financing, even though part of the profits would be lost abroad (Hruby and Seda 1995).

The necessity of a foreign partner had been discussed widely in the Czech Republic and a strong opposition, led by representatives of the Association of Small Shareholders of SPT Telecom,[1] was mounted in the months preceding the final decision (*Ekonom* 21/1995). Their arguments raised several points against the adoption of a strategic partner; these were: the ability of mainly domestic banks to cover the financing

Table 9.2 Breakdown of shareholders position in SPT Telecom

	w/o strategic partner	w/strategic partner
CR National Property Fund	70.00%	51.10%
TelSource (strategic partner)	0.00%	27.00%
Investment and Share Funds	22.00%	16.06%
Individual Owners	4.00%	2.92%
Restitution Investment Fund	3.00%	2.19%
Endowment Investment Fund	1.00%	0.73%

Source: The 1994 Balance Report and author's computations.

of any future development; the strategic importance of the sector; the disproportional rights that the strategic partner would possess; and the technological ability of domestic producers. Nevertheless, the final decision was in favour of a strategic partner for three reasons. First, because of financial resources and aspects of modernisation. Second, global trends were identified as moving towards multinational alliances, in the expectation of further liberalisation of telecommunication markets. Third, the nature and degree of challenges expected by top management in implementing the changes necessary to reform SPT Telecom, with its partially socialist work ethic, into an efficient and productive company (*Hospodarske noviny* 03/28/1995, p. 4).

In addition, the Minister of Economy indicated that the strategic partner option was the cheapest and least risky venture. If only domestic financial resources were used, development would be slower and would, consequently, disadvantage the Czech Republic in light of the fast development of the competitive environment expected in European telecommunications markets. Eventually, the selection of the strategic partner was organised by the Ministry of Economy and the final choice of the partner made by the government.

The search for a strategic partner for SPT Telecom was considered to inaugurate one of the largest capital transactions in Central Europe. Begun in October 1994, a decision was reached some ten months later, in June 1995. The strategic partner, chosen after a long selection process and some legal struggles, was the consortium TelSource, consisting of PTT Telecom Netherlands and Swiss Telecom, backed by American telecommunications giant AT&T. TelSource paid US$1.32bn. (CZK35.64bn) for the 27 per cent stake in SPT Telecom and also agreed to provide the Czech company with managerial, software and other services worth US$131m (CZK3.54bn) making the total value of the TelSource offer US$1.451bn (CZK39.18bn). The transaction was the biggest foreign direct investment in the country so far and put the company at the centre of attention for actors in the European telecommunications sector.

After the establishment of TelSource as SPT Telecom's strategic partner, their joint goal was to fulfil the following requirements:

- from 1995, 35 per cent of requests for lines must be satisfied within one year
- by the year 2000, 95 per cent of requests must be connected
- call completion rate should go up from 60–65 per cent to 97 per cent by 1998

TelSource wants to modernise the telecommunications infrastructure in the Czech Republic as quickly as possible. By this they mean the swift elimination of telephone shortages, and the creation of a new image of SPT Telecom as a fully customer-oriented company (cf. AT&T

participation in TelSource). In order to retain the multinational customers, international tariffs must be cut, which will entail a rise in local tariffs, although the inflation targets of the Czech government will have to be considered. Above all, these changes should be made within five years.

According to TelSource the main reason for strategic partnership is the opportunity it presents to participate in the international telecommunications trade. The winning firms already operate a regional network in Hungary and are active in the Ukraine. Liberalisation introduces profound changes to the European market. The number of operators will probably decrease to a handful of large corporations that will operate profitable long-distance and international calls and data transfers. In addition to these, there will be small local-network operators which are less profitable. The middle-size firms will most probably either merge with the long-distance giants, or disappear.

New competitors on the Czech fixed telecommunications market

Institutional framework

In principle, entry into the local networks was not precluded even prior to the decision of the government in 1994 to open the market to tender. According to the Telecommunications Act's 1992 (Act No. 1250/1992) amendment, the state was allowed to grant licences for providing basic telephony services to operators other than the SPT Telecom in 'exceptional circumstances'.[2] However, the conditions for granting licences were not defined and the government was reluctant to support any introduction of even limited competition, given the decision about the entry of a foreign strategic partner into the main company, SPT Telecom. It was believed that competition might weaken the bargaining position of the Czech government in pending negotiations or even discourage entry altogether. In November 1993 the Economic Committee of the Czech Parliament ruled explicitly that entry into the local markets was possible and, immediately, two companies applied for a licence.[3] Both of the projects were approved in principle in January 1994.

In August 1994, the government adopted the Main Principles of the State Telecommunication Policy. Besides ensuring a monopolistic position for the current operator, SPT Telecom, on the domestic market for long-distance and international basic telephony services until the year 2000, the principles assumed the entry and specified the conditions for such an entry for the new operators in selected local circuits, thus laying the ground for introducing limited competition into local networks. The two successful companies, Dattel and Kabel Plus, received their licences in 1995 and were to serve as pilot projects for the future tender of local operator licences.

By the end of 1995, the Czech government had completed the tender and six companies were granted licences for providing telecommunication services in selected regions of the Czech Republic. The six winners of the tender will enter the market representing some 5 per cent of the total number of direct exchange lines (DELs) in the country. The main conditions for entry into the local networks can be summarised as follows:[4]

- The government will designate a limited number of local networks in which entry of a second operator will be licensed.
- The entrant can be either a joint venture with the incumbent SPT Telecom (with a share of SPT Telecom of at most 51 per cent) or an independent company with a share of foreign capital of no more than 34 per cent.
- The entrant can operate in public-switched local telecommunication networks and can transmit information, not only in the form of voice telephony but also in some other ways (data networks); it is obliged to provide additional services such as telex and telegraph, and circuit leases.
- The individual local networks can be interconnected exclusively via the SPT Telecom network, even where they are operated by the same operator.
- The entrant is obliged to provide long-distance and international calls in co-operation with SPT Telecom, as well as other common services such as telephone delivery of cable messages.
- The entrant will charge a single tariff in the entire selected region and is subject to the same tariff regulation as the incumbent company.
- The entrant should sign an interconnection agreement with SPT Telecom within six months after its licence is issued, otherwise the interconnection charges will be specified by the regulator (the Czech Telecommunications Office) or the Ministry of Finance.

The decision to open the local circuits to competition has threatened the current monopoly position of SPT Telecom and is likely to change the situation in the Czech telecom market.

Characteristics of the designated local circuits and the entrants

Sixteen local circuits were selected by the government, based on the investment projections of SPT Telecom (SPT Telecom 1994). Generally speaking, these local circuits were amongst the most underdeveloped in the country, at least as far as the telecommunications infrastructure was concerned, and no major investment was being planned there by the main operator.

As can be seen from Table 9.3, with the notable exception of the Benesov and Ceska Lipa circuits, the penetration rate in all the selected regions is well below the country's average. The excess demand, although high with respect to the installed capacity, is also not particularly concentrated in these regions.[5] The areas are also rather small and geographically dispersed, the largest having only about thirteen thousand direct-exchange lines. Despite the fact that the winners of the tender will generally receive licences for two adjacent areas, integration, even where feasible, is precluded by conditions of the tender.

All six companies participating in the tender were successful in at least one region. Also, each firm, with the exception of Opatel, attempted to enter several regions, with one company, Telop, applying for a licence in all designated circuits. The companies participating in the tender were either established cable TV operators or suppliers and designers of the telecommunication equipment (local switches). One company, Opatel, is a joint venture with the incumbent SPT Telecom, two others are joint ventures with the US Global Telecommunications, and the rest

Table 9.3 Characterisation of the designated local circuits

Region	Penetration rates[a] 1995	Total number of lines[b]	Waiting list[c] 1995
Horsovsky Tyn	12.96	3620	2046
Benesov	16.96	6060	3017
Votice	14.36	1507	886
Sedlcany	15.08	1310	2608
Uhlirske Janovice	17.00	1477	932
Litomerice	15.00	6534	3166
Lovosice	11.98	2959	1592
Novy Bor	15.28	4395	2148
Ceska Lipa	18.45	13,875	3938
Frydlant v Cechach	11.19	2599	1584
Moravske Budejovice	10.67	2437	1762
Valasske Klobouky	10.05	2243	1634
Jesenik	8.57	3639	1033
Zabreh	7.32	3943	765
Opava	10.71	10,223	7681
Bilovec	9.43	3222	1365
Czech Republic	21.9	2,391,000	640,000

Source: Czech Ministry of Economy, SPT Telecom, 1996
a) Number of direct exchange lines per 100 inhabitants
b) Direct exchange lines installed and operated by SPT Telecom
c) Total number of unmet requests, SPT Telecom

supported their applications with intentions to co-operate with foreign partners.

One could conjecture that these foreign firms are trying to create a foothold in the Czech telecommunications market ready for its future liberalisation in line with EU policy after the year 2000, and that they are interested in long-term strategic investment rather than early returns (Hruby 1997). Hence, even the relatively unfavourable tender conditions were not completely disconcerting. In the case of the joint venture with SPT Telecom, the latter holding a controlling portion of the shares, SPT will transfer its current equipment in the local circuit, as well as its staff to the joint venture, while the other parties will secure financing for network development. The result will, therefore, be a continuation of the monopoly, albeit now held by a joint venture company. This is in clear conflict with the original aim of introducing competition.

What could result from the introduction of competition?

The decision of the Czech government to allow entry of private tele-communication companies to the local-services market is often presented as proof of a fast and cohesive strategy of liberalisation of the tele-communication sector in the Czech Republic. However, even the keenest supporters of the measure admit that entry is not likely to have a significant effect on the sector, given the small number of local circuits offered and their wretched technical and commercial state. The whole exercise is thus burdened with several, often competing, goals.

First, the introduction of competition has been claimed to serve as a disciplining device for the incumbent SPT Telecom. Second, it is meant to increase penetration of telephone lines and improve the quality of overall service, in at least some regions, as rapidly as possible, and without excessive drain on the resources of the dominant firm in the sector. Third, and most interesting, SPT Telecom was later allowed to influence the choice of regions offered, thus managing to shed its least profitable and most neglected regions. The new, private firms, however, are expected to deliver services quickly in these areas, whereas SPT Telecom was previously unable or unwilling to do so. The result is a mixed set of expectations concerning what the current experiment can deliver and what is beyond its reach.

The companies plan to compete with SPT primarily in the speed of network expansion, and by providing a wider range of value added services (voice mail, conference calls, etc.). This implies the need for a significant investment and the use of modern technologies, so all local companies are planning to invest very rapidly in the first years. The estimated cost of one telephone line in the year 1995 fluctuated around US\$2,670 (CZK80,000). Eventually, as the major switching equipment is installed, all the firms expect a significant drop in their cost (in some cases rather implausibly) to less than US$135 (CZK4,000) per installed direct exchange line. (SPT Telecom estimates its marginal cost of one additional line at about US$470, i.e. CZK14,000).[6] Table 9.4 presents some estimates of future investments and installation of the direct-exchange lines by the winners of the tender.

The conditions of the tender did not, in the Czech case, offer any advantages to the entrants in comparison with the incumbent company, SPT Telecom. The companies will operate in small local markets but will be subject to the same tariff regulation as the SPT.[7] All their long-distance and international calls will have to go through the SPT Telecom's network and companies will have to negotiate interconnection fees with a much stronger bargaining partner. They will, moreover, be constrained in the use of cross-subsidisation, which is widely practised by SPT Telecom. Despite the recent changes in tariff structures (see Erbenova and Hruby 1995), the Czech tariffs are still rather unbalanced compared to the standards of developed countries.

The structure of the customers is another important factor that might influence the potential outcome of competition in local markets. The typical split in the OECD countries is 20 per cent business and 80 per cent residential DELs. By 1994 the total number of DELs in the Czech

Table 9.4 Investment plans of the new entrants

Company	Region	Planned investment until 2000* (thous. CZK)	Approximate planned number of DELs 2000
Alias	Ceska Lipa	430,000	13,500
	Frydlant	202,000	6,300
	Novy Bor	215,000	6,700
Kabel Plus	Litomerice	430,000	13,500
Tel	Lovosice	190,000	6,000
KT Jesenik	Jesenik	291,000	9,700
	Zabreh	342,000	11,400
Opatel	Opava	851,000	25,800
Telecom 21	Horsovsky Tyn	171,000	5,700
	Moravske Budejovice	150,000	5,000
	Sedlcany	114,000	3,800
	Votice	99,000	3,300
Telop	Benesov	65,000	4,300
	Bilovec	69,000	4,600
	Uhlirske Janovice	21,000	1,400
	Valasske Klobouky	77,000	5,100

Source: Czech Ministry of Economy, author's own calculations, 1996
*Estimate using the average cost of DEL from the individual projects.

Republic had reached approximately 2.1m, implying a penetration rate of 21 per cent. Concerning the line structure, 32 per cent of all DELs were business and 68 per cent residential, generating 77 per cent and 23 per cent of the total call revenue, respectively (Doyle, Hruby and Mueller 1993). This suggests a continuing bias in favour of business lines compared to OECD countries. On the other hand, as the Table 9.5 implies, the investment plans of new entrants reveal different intentions. The local operators expect a structure of telephone lines much more in accordance with OECD standards than with the SPT Telecom's pattern. The share of residential lines is expected to reach 80 per cent well before the year 2000, and then to stay above it. Given the low revenue-generating pattern of the residential telephone lines in the Czech Republic (the average call revenue of SPT Telecom per direct-exchange line in 1994 was US$270, i.e. CZK8,116). It remains to be seen whether the estimates of future revenue streams are not over-optimistic. The new entrants plan an average revenue per DEL of between CZK6,000 and 12,500 (US$200–417) in year 2000. They also estimate their average cost of installing a direct exchange line at between CZK15,000 and 33,000 (US$500–1,100). These differences reveal the uncertainty with which some local operators enter the competition.

The incumbent's position in the Czech Republic will be comparable to BT's situation in the UK. The regions selected for independent operators represent only 5 per cent of the total number of telephone lines in the Czech Republic, and their market share is even lower. Furthermore, SPT Telecom will still play an important role in these regions – it is even one of the three shareholders in one of the 'independent' local operators, Opatel. In addition, SPT Telecom has launched a large investment program in the Liberec region, where Kabel Plus has recently invested under the pilot project, despite it's promise not to invest in the selected regions until 1998. This case may indicate the potential predatory behaviour of SPT Telecom towards new entrants.

Table 9.5 Estimated structure of DELs in the sixteen designated circuits

Year	1996	2000	2004
Total number of DELs	17,605	81,436	90,096
business – absolute	4,419	14,696	14,696
relative	25.1%	18.0%	16.3%
residential – absolute	13,064	66,272	74,917
relative	74.2%	81.4%	83.2%
public payphones-absolute	122	468	483
relative	0.7%	0.6%	0.5%

Source: Ekonom 48/1995.

GSM deployment

Mobile characteristics in transition countries

In countries, such as those of the former eastern bloc, where there is an acute need for a fast improvement to the previously unsatisfactory level of communication services and equipment, development plans for fixed networks tend, naturally, to be ambitious (Kubasik 1995). However, their realisation will require massive reconstruction taking, realistically, at least ten years and the investment of billions of dollars. Unfortunately, this time horizon does not match the desired development and actual changes in the society and economy of these countries (Hruby 1995).

In the Czech Republic, where the waiting list for telephone lines is currently 650,000, this long-running deficit situation has lead to the partial use of mobile networks for the most urgent telecommunications needs. Indeed, as the time for implementation and technological supply indicates that mobile services are markedly more flexible and faster to implement than fixed systems (implementation within months as opposed to several years, and investments in the order of millions of dollars rather than billions) their use is of growing importance.

However, there is no global indication of mobile telephones being used as a substitute for poor fixed networks; in fact the countries with the highest penetration rates for mobile phones tend also to have the highest penetration rates for fixed telephone connections. Rather, mobile telecommunications have largely complemented existing fixed services. That said, in Central and Eastern European countries a suitable environment for the partial use of mobile networks could be created, although predominantly in short-term implementations and, considering costs, mostly for expanding businesses. The availability of mobile telecommunications could also act to depress waiting lists for fixed DELs, reducing the externalities associated with waiting, and thus benefiting the economy.

GSM tender

The Czech government, having decided to increase competitive pressure in the still monopolistic mobile telecommunications industry (Doyle 1993), declared through its Policy Principles that no more than two GSM permits would be issued in the immediate future. Presently it is not known whether a third spectrum in the range 900MHz will be available for GSM use. Based on current policy, the government announced in 1995 that a tender for one free GSM licence would be organised, and that its winner would form a joint venture with CRa (Ceske Radiokomunikace, the radio communications company) based on further specified conditions (Ministry of Economy CR 1995). The second licence was awarded to EuroTel based on an existing contract from 1991.[8]

CRa has a dominant position in national and regional radio and TV broadcasting, and is a regulated business with stable revenues, and some profit margins. Furthermore, CRa has a monopoly in radio-relay transmissions and satellite services, and is a 25.5 per cent owner of Radiokontakt Operator, the monopolistic paging operator in the Czech Republic. However, CRa is a small firm compared with giant SPT Telecom and, although CRa is chosen to be the majority partner in the GSM joint venture, it is unlikely to match the other partner's cash contribution. CRa's main advantage is that it owns several hundred locations throughout the country suitable for the installation of GSM equipment. However, it is not unique in this. Also, it has the disadvantage of not being a retail-oriented company and, consequently, not having the medium- or high-capacity billing centres necessary for GSM joint-venture operations. From this point of view, others, such as energy distribution companies, could be more appropriate partners.

GSM tender results

The winner of the tender for partnering Ceske Radiokomunikace, selected in March 1996, was TMobil consortium. This is jointly owned by DeTeMobil, Germany (84.5 per cent), STET, Italy (12 per cent), the rest being owned by the Czech companies, Telekomunikacni montaze Praha, PVT, and Sporitelni investicni spoleènost (Stadnik 1996). TMobil has management control over the GSM joint venture (known as Radiomobil) and will invest US$204m, operating one of the lowest tariff regimes in Europe. This is said to be the main reason the group won the licence against other bidders. The government had put a weighting of about 50 per cent on the affordability of the new service and had identified rapid coverage, quality of the new service, and the funding of the joint venture as other important areas for consideration. Starting in September 1996, Radiomobil will cover 90 per cent of the population by the year 2000.

Since the introduction of competition in mobile services in 1996, the tariff situation has changed rapidly. The new competitor, Paegas, introduced much lower tariffs and the incumbent Eurotel also lowered its tariffs. As a result, some tariffs in mobile services in the Czech Republic are comparable with those provided by the PSTN operator SPT Telecom, particularly with regard to high-usage schemes and long-distance calls.

State ownership

State ownership plays a significant role in both fixed and mobile network telephony. On the GSM market, 26 per cent of EuroTel is owned by the state, 49 per cent by US West and Bell Atlantic (Bell Atlantic and US West operate through a holding company based in the Netherlands, called Atlantic West BV), 13.7 per cent by TelSource, and 11.3 per cent by remaining shareholders (mostly investment funds). However, it is not a public company, as it is a joint venture between SPT Telecom[9] and US West with Bell Atlantic. The recent privatisation of CRa in the second wave of voucher privatisation resulted in 69.4 per cent being temporarily[10] owned by the National Property Fund, 1.0 per cent by the Foundation Fund, 3.0 per cent by the Restitution Investment Fund, 0.1 per cent by employees, and 26.5 per cent by individual shareholders (83 per cent are investment funds). Thus, state ownership in the GSM joint venture amounted to 35.4 per cent.

The high percentage of state ownership both of EuroTel and the GSM joint venture leads to a natural question: what is the state's policy in this situation, where its shareholding position makes it something of a double-headed dragon? Can the state allow the two heads to fight together? The situation is somewhat paradoxical: on the positive side, the state's revenues support social welfare, and also consumers benefit from the competition. However, because the state owns a minority of the future mobile operators, it can only absorb part of the consumers' loss in its budget. By this reckoning, the state should encourage EuroTel and the GSM joint venture to engage in marketing wars, particularly to improve social welfare. Alternatively, and perhaps far better, the state should dilute its shareholding in EuroTel and CRa to a minimal level, thus avoiding this unpleasant policy-making situation.

Tariff regulation

In countries in transition, tariff regulation and tariff reform operate in different circumstances compared to those of developed countries. Besides the introduction of new regulatory approaches, there is also a general trend of rebalancing and increasing tariffs. Rebalancing is a result of distorted tariff structure as well as of technological development in the industry. Increased tariffs result from:·

- long-term unchanged, low tariffs in telecommunications at the beginning of transition·
- higher inflation rates in transition countries (Hruby 1992).

These must be compensated for in order to meet investment requirements in dynamically developing telecommunications in transition countries.

Table 9.6 demonstrates the general trend of tariff reform in the Czech Republic. The previously very low tariffs, unaltered since 1979, changed relatively rapidly from 1992 to 1996. Overall, inflation during this period was 58 per cent but the most noticeable increase was in local calls (280 per cent). The other increases in tariffs for impulse and trunk calls are not so high when inflation is taken into account, while the 52 per cent increase in rental fee is, in reality, only an inflation adjustment, and unchanged

Table 9.6 Tariff development in PSTN, domestic services, as of 1992 and 1996, CZK, VAT included

Indicator	1992	1996	Difference %
tariff	1.05	2.00	90
local call 6 min peak	1.05	4.00	280
trunk call I peak 1 min	1.05	2.00	90
trunk call II peak 1 min	2.10	4.00	90
trunk call III peak 1 min	3.15	6.00	90
payphone call	2.00	2.00	0
connection fee residential	2,100	2,100	0
connection fee business	5,250	5,250	0
rental fee	52.50	80.00	52

Note: Inflation rate 1996/1993 58 per cent
Source: Author's own calculations, 1997

tariffs for payphone calls and connection fees should be interpreted as a considerable decrease.

Price regulation applied to telecommunication services since 1997 is different from those generally used in the past. For example, it now relates the change in the price level of telecommunication services to the level of inflation for the period until 2000. This came about when, after long and often confusing debates (Czech Telecommunication Office 1994), the Czech government proclaimed its intention to switch from the annual ritual of tariff-setting negotiations to a price-capping regulation. This commenced in April 1997, initially with the formula set for 1997–2000. This long-term tariff development was initially fiercely opposed by the Ministry of Finance, mainly because of the high uncertainty involved in forecasting future telecommunication revenue and the cost of the telecommunication development programme. Nevertheless, a classic formula was eventually agreed upon.

As far as the rule for weighting different services is concerned, a commonly used criterion is the previous year's revenue.[11] The price-capping method leaves the operator with a considerable flexibility to rebalance its tariff structure. The adopted version of the regulation, however, contains a number of further 'sub-caps' for specific services, whereby the Ministry of Finance attempts to influence individual caps for rental charges, local and international call tariffs. This could result in excessively limited pricing flexibility, even under the proclaimed price-capping framework, and would complicate rebalancing of tariffs.

Bearing the above facts and arguments in mind, the resulting price-capping formula can be assessed as a half-hearted attempt to abandon the maximum-price-setting mechanism. Further, the Czech government has so far been reluctant to enshrine the formula in law. Therefore, there is still a possibility of changing rules well within the period of their proposed validity. Nevertheless, the very intention to switch to the price-capping framework shows that the regulation environment in the Czech Republic is changing in favour of a more appropriate framework (Erbenova and Hruby 1995).

Conclusions

Financial resources were not the only decisive reason for opting for a strategic-partner solution to the problems of the privatisation and restructuring of the Czech Republic's telecommunications systems. The connection to global alliances, strengthening of the competitiveness of SPT Telecom in the face of increased competition within the framework of liberalisation of the European telecommunication market, know-how transfer, as well as managerial influence on the behaviour of the company, were also important.

This chapter has attempted to shed some light on the current process of the, as yet, very limited liberalisation of the Czech telecommunication market. However, even this simplified and limited approach has brought about striking peculiarities. The Czech government has selected, under the undeniable influence of SPT Telecom, the least attractive and also the least developed regions. It has specifically precluded any possibility of price competition, and has not allowed the local companies into the lucrative long-distance and international calls market. Nevertheless, a number of private firms competed for the privilege of entering the market long abandoned by SPT Telecom. All have been promising a rapid increase in penetration, quick and massive investment, and all expect a profitable return within five to six years, provided that their estimates of (high) future revenues and (low) future cost are not overestimated.

This seems almost to be too good to be true. Perhaps the local operators are not fully aware of the potential threats and opportunities, or are promising unrealistic results in order to secure a contract, or that the current monopolistic provider, SPT Telecom, had failed to extract profit from its position in the past. If the least attractive sixteen regions will be able to generate profits after two to three years of massive investment, what potential is then hidden in the remaining 95 per cent of the Czech telecommunication market?

There is one further, rather more sophisticated explanation possible. As the majority of local operators comprise at least one foreign tele-communication firm, it can be argued that these firms are building a foothold in the Czech market. This could explain their rather relaxed attitude towards the expected profitability and returns on investment. Foreign firms could underwrite even significant losses if they expect to gain insider knowledge and a position which could give them an advantage after the year 2000 when the Czech telecommunication market is expected to be fully liberalised.

Five years of monopoly in the operation of mobile cellular services in the Czech Republic brought high tariff levels and relatively low number of subscribers. Thus, the introduction of competition into the market was very desirable and, considering the small size of the market, as well as the low average income levels and limited purchasing power of the population, the decision to adopt a duopoly position for GSM services economically reasonable. However, there are several particular features of the mobile market in the Czech Republic which make the emerging duopoly unusual.

The extraordinary exclusive rights included in the incumbent mobile operator EuroTel's licence in 1991 created important conditions for the GSM tender and for future competition. According to EuroTel's contracts, it automatically has the right to be awarded any licence issued for mobile voice services in the Czech Republic on equal terms with any other tendering party. Consequently, only one GSM licence was to be granted.

According to a pre-tender decision of the government, a 51 per cent share of the second licence is held by the CRa. Moreover, the tender has been limited to just a 49 per cent share of one of the two licences issued. Although there were rational basic requirements of service-operating experience for tender participants, it is not clear why the CRa was selected to be a majority owner in the GSM joint venture, especially as it has no obvious advantages enabling it to meet the challenges of GSM competition. The incumbent position naturally also gives EuroTel better entry conditions as well as costs advantages.

Direct as well as hidden state ownership in all companies operating in the mobile sector in the Czech Republic is another source of potential interest conflict. The substantial size of state ownership of both EuroTel and the new entrant Radiomobil entails a dilemma regarding its independence in the regulation of the market. Moreover, the state's revenues contribute positively to social welfare, whereas increased competition is also seen to do so, but from another source. The two sources are in constant conflict. As the state is only a minority owner in the operating companies, it can only absorb a part of the consumers' loss into its budget. Conflicting interests should lead the state to divest its shareholding in the two companies to a minimal level, to avoid irreconcilable dilemmas in the policy-making situation.

A rather asymmetric competition situation arises from the current ownership structure. Both GSM operators need to reach interconnection agreements with the almost monopolistic operator, SPT Telecom. However, SPT Telecom is a majority owner of one of its competitors, EuroTel. Clearly, this situation creates a difficult task for any regulator at the very least. Tariff regulation is another issue. Theoretically, mobile tariffs are not regulated, yet in practice they are, through the Conversion Penalty paragraph included in Radiomobil's contract.

Despite previously mentioned limits in the development of GSM services, there has been a high level of interest by well-established mobile operators in the Czech Republic's GSM tender, and the issue of two licences for GSM services has already considerably improved the quality of mobile services in the country. One very important positive effect has been the lowering of tariff levels through price competition. This was considerably encouraged by the government's approach in making the low tariff scheme the most important criterion used for tender, and by setting the licence fee suitably low. Visible positive results through the introduction of lower tariffs and more flexible new tariff schemes, together with rapidly increasing numbers of users, were recorded immediately after introduction of the GSM duopoly.

The general trend of tariff reform has been for an increase in tariffs as a result of their very low level at the beginning of transition. This trend has been accompanied by changes in the tariff structure, e.g. the radical increase of local tariffs versus lowering of international tariffs. The introduction of a price-cap formula has been another positive step toward effective regulation.

Notes

1 The association comprises mostly individual shareholders from the voucher privatisation.
2 Amendment to the Telecommunications Act No. 150/1992.
3 Dattel applied for a licence covering selected districts in downtown Prague and intended to serve chiefly business users located there. Kabel Plus, the largest cable TV operator in the Czech Republic, planned on providing its services in Liberec, a growing financial centre in Northern Bohemia.
4 See Main Principles of the State Telecommunication Policy (Zasady statni telekomunikacni politiky).
5 The total number of direct-exchange lines in the sixteen regions represents some 5 per cent of the total capacity of SPT Telecom, while the (registered) waiting list there corresponds to about 6 per cent of the total excess demand.
6 For instance, Kable Plus Tel expects its costs to be CZK83,000 (US$2,770) per line in 1996, around CZK8,000 (US$270) in 2000 and only CZK3, 100–3,200 (US$105) in 2005.
7 Since 1997 the tariffs are regulated using the CPI–X formula, value-added services are not subject to any tariff regulation. For a description of the price regulation in the Czech telecommunications, see Erbenova and Hruby (1995).
8 For an in-depth discussion of EuroTel contracts, see Detecon's 1994 study. Also, EuroTel has a monopoly in NMT 450 to the year 2011. These rights are an attempt to control future Czech mobile communication markets, because all new services can only be introduced (through a licence) with EuroTel participation. This holds not only for GSM, but also for PCN and mobile services in local loop. Regarding the GSM tender, EuroTel had the right to negotiate licence conditions prior to open tender, and has substantial financial advantage in the assessment of tender fee as it will obtain 51 per cent of the licence rights free of charge and its original US$10m deposit, together with

accrued interest, will be charged towards the rest of the licence fee (money was deposited in 1991 – the size of the charge may differ depending upon the size of licence fee).

9 Other than US West with Bell Atlantic, shareholders of EuroTel were pro-rated based on SPT's Annual Report.

10 This could mean five years and more.

11 As, for instance, in the case of British Telecom.

10 The dynamics of liberalisation of Israeli telecommunications[1]

David Levi-Faur

In the Israeli telecommunications sector, with the exception of the local loop and cables, the most important markets have already become intensely competitive. In 1999, competition is expected to be introduced into these two remaining markets also (see Table 10.1). This is a radical change from the etatist past and a relatively impressive success for the Israeli policy-makers. The most impressive changes have doubtless been the enforcement of competition in the cellular and international communications markets, which resulted in a radical expansion of these services, while bringing prices down at the same time. The Open-Sky Policy, announced in August 1997, now promises to liberalise the satellite market for the provision of analogue and digital multi-channel radio and TV broadcasting. Telecommunications equipment, business systems and value-added services are also under competition. The vitality of the services markets is reinforced by a dynamic equipment and software industry that extends the telecommunications community. The contrast with the recent past, where the state controlled services and provided the financial resources (rather than Wall Street), and where military, not civilian products, dominated exports, could not be greater. In fact, Israel's telecommunications sector is experiencing no less than a revolution.

The rapid liberalisation of Israel's telecommunications sector and its achievements raise questions that form the basis for this chapter's inquiry into the dynamics of change in this sector. These questions arise owing to three basic traits of Israeli polity and economy which seem to suggest that the extent and direction of change should have been less radical and less liberal than they actually are. First, the Israeli tradition of etatism suggests that the state would resist change in general and liberalisation in particular, and would attempt to retain its control over this sector. Second, Israeli polity is overburdened with problems of national security, with intense political and social cleavages, and with periodic waves of mass immigration (Horowitz and Lissak 1989). These problems would seem to suggest strict constraints on market liberalisation and an impairment of the overall performances of the system. Third, being located outside the European-wide market and having to function as 'a country without a region', the benefits of liberalisation of tele- communications services that Israel seems likely to gain from the world's new telecommunications markets are relatively limited. In order to examine the dynamics of Israeli policy-making and provide a framework in which it can be assessed, the chapter divides the period since the arrival of telephony in the country into three policy regimes: the old regime (1920–84), the intermediary regime (1984–94) and the new regime (1994–). While the old regime was an etatist monopoly, the current (new) regime is one of (regulated) competition. Between the old and the new regime it is possible to identify an intermediary regime that was characterised by corporatisation and (partial) privatisation. In considering these regimes, attention is paid to the dynamics of interaction between politics, economics and technology, in the making and remaking of governance mechanisms. The final part of the chapter discusses the political economy of the process and, by characterising the process as liberalisation from above, sheds light on the particular Israeli trajectory of liberalisation.

The old telecommunications regime

As in most other countries, the Israeli telecommunications sector was dominated by a state-administered monopoly. The Israeli government served as the policy-maker, regulator, and provider of telecommunications services. The origins of the Israeli etatist regime date back to the early 1920s when the first civil telephone network was established by the British government in Palestine. Considering the British origins of the system, it is hardly surprising that the organisation of the telecommunications regime, and the economic, political, cultural and social principles governing its introduction to the country, followed the European etatist PTT model.

The only scholarly account of the old Israeli telecommunications regime is a short study by Noam (1992). Yet, even without an authoritative study of the old regime, it is sufficiently clear that several important characteristics of the current regime were shaped as early as the 1920s. The first and the most important among these was perhaps the tendency of the system to fall short of the demand for telephones from its very inception (Anglo-American Committee 1946: 869). A second characteristic is the organisation of the sector according to the classic PTT model, whereby post, telegraph and telephony are all organised under the same department. A third characteristic of the system which originated under the British Mandate is the practice of cross-subsidisation. Telephone subsidised the post, long-distance calls subsidised local ones, and international calls subsidised domestic ones. This marginalised economic considerations and cost-benefit analysis in favour of

Table 10.1 Milestones in the Liberalisation of Israeli Telecommunications

Legislation
1982 – The Bezeq Law (corporatisation)
1994 – A new general licence is issued for Bezeq's operation. This new licence allows the introduction of competition
1997 – Israel is one of the signatories of the WTO telecommunications accord

Organisation of government
pre-1984 – Government serves as the provider of services, regulator, and policy-maker
1984 – Government acts as the regulator and policy-maker
1995 – The Antitrust Commissioner takes an increasingly active role in the sector
1996 – Government approves the creation of an independent regulator (not yet implemented)

Corporatisation
Bezeq was corporatised as a fully owned state company in 1984

Privatisation of Bezeq
1990/1991 – 24 per cent of the shares were sold in the Tel Aviv Stock Exchange
1997 – an additional 12.3 per cent of the shares were sold to the Merrill Lynch
1998 – another sale of 10 per cent of the shares on the Tel Aviv Stock Exchange

Divestiture
Bezeq is required to operate through subsidiaries in the markets for cellular telephony, international calls and customer premises equipment

Regulatory walls
*Cables are not allowed to enter telephony or provide Internet services
*Bezeq and other telecommunications operators are not allowed to lay cables
*Bezeq is constrained in offering Internet services

Competition in the international calls market
In July 1997 the market was opened up to two new operators, which together with the incumbent Bezeq International have an exclusive concession till 2002

The creation of the cellular telephony system
*Bezeq and Motorola establish Pelephone (in operation since 1986)
*Cellcom – The second mobile telephony operator started to operate at the end of 1995
*Partner – The third operator is expected to start its operation in 1998

Cable and satellite policy
1986 – The provision of cable TV is regulated by an amendment to the Bezeq Law
1989 – An amendment to the Bezeq Law prohibits transmission through satellites without government approval
1997 – Government decision to open the cable market when concession ends (2002–2006)
1998 – Communications Minister is authorised to allow multi-channel TV by DBS

Competition in the local loop
January 1997 – Government decision to open domestic communications (transmission, infrastructure, telephony) to competition no later than January 1999

government's social and national preferences. A fourth characteristic of the regime, existing since the early days of telephony, is the contribution it makes to the government budget. Using surpluses as a source for enlarging government revenue was a typical practice from the very first days of telephony, and still is in many countries. A fifth characteristic, which originated in the Mandatory period and has had an effect well into the 1990s, is the proliferation of unions among telephone employees and their incorporation into a larger umbrella organisation of (junior) civil service employees. The multiplicity of the labour organisations, as will be demonstrated later, created a dynamic of internal competition and, in turn, made the leading unions important actors.

The British withdrawal from the country in 1948 and the ensuing war between Jews and Arabs, caused the destruction of important parts of the network but, as in other parts of the Israeli economy, reconstruction was rapid. The annual average growth rates of the system, as measured in the number of subscribers, was around 15 per cent between 1951 and 1960 and 19 per cent between 1961 and 1970 (Bezeq 1995). This period in Israeli history is one of economic nationalism and rapid development (Levi-Faur 1998), the values of both being reflected in the governance and provision of its telephony. Indeed, telephony was used by the government to nurture the creation of a national telecommunications industry as a means of import substitution, so that instead of importing terminals, switching and cables, a national industry was established. Thus, since the 1950s, two manufacturers of telephone and switching equipment and two manufacturers of cables have dominated the Israeli scene.

Despite the fast growth of the system in the 1950s and 1960s, and the rapid catching-up with major European systems, there was widespread public dissatisfaction with its performance, and especially with the quality of its service. From the early 1960s, dissatisfaction was also evident among insiders and policy entrepreneurs who pushed for corporatisation of the telephone services into a government owned-company (Gorel 1997: 49). Corporatisation was then perceived as a tool to promote efficiency, encourage work motivation and end the practice of allocating jobs as a prize for political loyalty. It was also considered as a tool with which to mobilise private loans and even as a form of private investment (the possibility of selling the telephone services to private investors was raised in the 1960s but it was never taken seriously as a real policy option). In 1963 the Dinstein Committee recommended corporatisation of the telecommunications services but it took at least three more committees (all recommending corporatisation) for the government finally to approve the decision (19 August 1979). Four more years were needed before the new corporation, Bezeq, was ready to take legal and practical responsibility for the telecommunications sector.

Corporatisation took place against the background of a severe performance crisis in the system and the changing ideological mood in

Israeli politics and society. Growing budgetary constraints in the early 1970s and a severe physical crisis following the 1973 war and the oil crisis severely affected the country's economy. This had its effects in poor performances of the system. While the gap between Israel and West Germany in penetration of telephony in 1974 was about 20 per cent in 1974, it grew to 35 per cent in 1979 and to 36 per cent in 1984.[2] Instead of catching up, Israel's telecommunications at the time were in stagnation. From 1970 to the corporatisation of the telecommunications services in 1979, the average growth rate of supply lagged behind the growth of demand (Bezeq 1995), so that the gap between supply and demand became immense. Between 1971 and 1980, the growth of demand (measured as standing applications) was double that of supply. The major reason for the delays and the crisis of supply was constraints on the government budget, hence on investment in the sector. The outcome was a decline in public support for the state monopoly in the sector and a crisis of confidence among the employees and managers. In addition, a combination of political change in Israel and a 'paradigm shift' among the economic elite in the world led to a re-examination of the government role in the telecommunications sector. Thus, in 1977, and for the first time in Israel's history, the combination of a new right-wing government and the spirit of deregulation were able to legitimise the corporatisation of telecommunication services.

Corporatisation had to be hard fought for by government officials (among whom officials of the Ministry of Finance played an important role) against the labour unions. The battle over corporatisation antici-pated the basic characteristics of future stages, when privatisation and liberalisation would be on the government agenda. With the backing of the Histadrut, the sector's labour unions proved to be major actors which had to be taken into account. Only when their demands for significant benefits were met (in the form of wage raises, stability of work, and more influence in the day-to-day management) did corporatisation become possible. Thus, when corporatisation was finally implemented, it was the product of a compromise between the two most powerful actors of the sector: the bureaucrats and the unions. Both sides had reason to be satisfied at the time. Working conditions were improved and the government achieved corporatisation of the sector. This ensured the conditions for future efficiency benefits; however, as will be shown below, agreement over the sector's structure and goals did not lead to long-term consensus among the policy actors.

The intermediary telecommunications regime

The Telecommunications Law of 1982, and the operation of the new corporation, Bezeq, after February 1984, radically transformed the struc-ture of the old regime. In the new regime, policy-making, supervision and regulatory functions, which were kept in the hands of the communications ministry, were separated from service provision, which was handed over to Bezeq. Changes not only occurred in the sector's structure but also, most remarkably, in its performance. The improvements were partly due to a new business culture in Bezeq and partly due to a growth in the investment in the sector. Noteworthy too is the partial privatisation of Bezeq in 1990 and 1991. Paradoxically, the impressive success in improving Israeli telecommunications performance did not contribute to the legitimisation of the regime. Pressures for a more radical reform, which would promote competition and not merely privatisation and efficiency, began to be felt from the late 1980s. They were expressed most clearly in a major report by the Boaz Committee, published in April 1991, which called for immediate liberalisation of the telecommunications market (except for the local loop). These recommendations were subject to intense and sometimes violent conflict which resulted in the victory of the proponents of competition in March 1994. Thus, a new regime of regulated competition replaced the intermediary regime.

The radical improvements in the performance of the Israeli telecommunications sector following the corporatisation of Bezeq are primarily evident in the rapid reduction in the number of standing applications for telephone lines, from a record 257,000 in March 1984 to 41,000 in 1989 and 18,000 in 1991. The growth in the supply of telephony, measured as the annual average increase in number of subscribers between 1984 and 1994, was 7.5 per cent. While it took more than sixty-four years to install the first million telephone lines in the country, it took only ten more (1984–94) to double this number. While only 72 per cent of Israeli families had telephones in 1984, the figure ten years later was 95 per cent. An increase in the number of lines per hundred people improved the penetration rate of telephony in comparison with Europe after more than a decade of the gap widening. The technological capacities of the system radically improved too. A large investment raised digitalisation of the system to a rate of 81 per cent in 1994. Digitalisation carried with it value-added services, and these opened a new source for revenue for Bezeq.

While performance greatly improved, the first years of Bezeq's corporatisation were followed by a crisis of governance in the policy and regulatory capacities of the Communications Ministry. Now that the ministry had changed its role from an operating department to policy-maker and regulator, it had to develop new skills to reorganise its functions and to change its role perceptions. The problem was especially severe because many of its skilled workers left for Bezeq, which could provide better salaries and also a stable working environment (in terms of job protection), while also offering the challenging task of renewing the country's telecommunications. The reorganisation of the ministry, which was conducted mainly by the Minister Amnon Rubinstein and his

Director-General, Yoram Alster, proved to be a slow and energy-consuming process, which is not yet over (cf. Waxe 1995). The initial stages of this process can best be observed in two spheres of action: institutionalisation of the 'type-approval' process and the promotion of efficiency under a regime of rate-of-return regulation.

The type-approval process that was institutionalised after the corporatisation of Bezeq allowed the communications ministry to approve, under certain conditions, the import, supply and connectivity of terminal equipment to Bezeq's network. The type-approval process allowed the creation of a market in telecommunications equipment for the first time in the history of the system. Amendment 5 to the 1982 Telecommunications Law, put before the Knesset by the communications minister, Amnon Rubinstein, in March 1987 and approved in July 1988, institutionalised the process. From then on, importers and manufacturers of terminal equipment could release their products to the market, providing they had been approved by the ministry's technical laboratories. True, the market for terminal equipment was marginal in Bezeq's overall revenues, and the type-approval process did not open the door to fair competition in this market (the provision of the first telephone was still bundled by Bezeq, and the type-approval process was very restrictive).[3] However, the process allowed to the ministry to consolidate its control over Bezeq and, for the first time, the general public could enjoy some of the benefits of competition in this sector.

The partial recovery of the state's policy-making capacities towards the end of the 1980s is also evident in the movement from rate-of-return regulation to incentive regulation. In the first years of corporatisation, tariffs were calculated on the basis of rate-of-return, i.e. tariffs were determined by Bezeq's costs, and on this basis the company was allowed to make profits to be used to finance its investment plans. The great disadvantage of this regime was that it gave Bezeq incentives to raise its costs, or at least did not give it the incentive to become more efficient. The growth in state capacities in the second half of the 1980s is evident in the establishment of a new tariff regime, which included a mechanism of incentive regulation. In December 1987, the communications minister, Gad Ya'acobi, nominated a committee headed by Aaron Fogel, a former Ministry of Finance official, which was asked to recommend a tariffs policy for Bezeq's services. Instead of rate-of-return regulation, this committee devised an incentive-regulation regime.[4] The committee, which submitted its recommendations in September 1989, introduced a system of regulation in which Bezeq was required to reduce its prices at an annual rate of 3.5 per cent, which was supposed to exert pressure for more efficient provision of services. At the same time, price regulation was confined to services in which Bezeq enjoyed more than 60 per cent of the market. The new regulatory regime introduced by the Fogel Committee did not prevent the Ministry of Finance from raising the issue again in

1991 and demanding new price reductions. In September 1993, a new committee was nominated to investigate Bezeq's tariffs. This committee, chaired by Doron Shorer, recommended, in November 1993, raising the efficiency factor from 3.5 to 6.5 per cent. The pressure for more efficient operation is still evident today. In January 1998, the Gronau Committee was established and is expected to construct the new regime for regulating Bezeq's wholesale (interconnection) and retail tariffs.

Examination of the process of tariff regulation clarifies the extent and importance of economists in the Ministry of Finance in pushing for reforms in the sector. These 'eco-bureaucrats', who were predominantly graduates of the Department of Economics at the Hebrew University, had played an important role in policy-making since the early 1950s. However, after 1985, when the success of the economic stabilisation plan normalised the formerly hyperinflation and the state budget deficit, their role in policy-making was even more critical (Keren 1995). This is also evident in the process of the privatisation of Bezeq, which was already declared an official government goal in 1977 with the rise to power of the first Likud government. But only in 1990 and 1991 were 25 per cent of the corporation's shares transferred to private hands on the Tel Aviv Stock Exchange. This partial privatisation did not proceed further for the next six years for four reasons. First was the vehement opposition of labour to further privatisation. Second was the indecisiveness of Bezeq's management about selling control to foreign telecommunications companies. Third were the security considerations that the state faced over transferring control to foreign investors. Fourth was the growing recognition among policy-makers that further privatisation, as such, was not a panacea for the Israeli economy in general and the telecommunications sector in particular (Arnon and Preschtman 1992).

Some time was needed before the distinction between privatisation and competition appeared very clearly on the decision-makers' agenda in the sector. This is most clearly observed by examining the process in the second half of the 1980s in which new cellular telephony and cable broadcasting technologies were accommodated into the intermediary regime without challenging the interests of its major stakeholders. The new cellular telephony technology, which was first launched on a commercial basis towards the end of the 1970s, arrived in Israel through the Israeli subsidiary of the American multinational, Motorola. Yet to provide the service, Motorola had to fight the telephone monopoly of Bezeq or join forces with it. The venture, under the commercial name Pelephone, was granted exclusivity until 1994. The new cellular technology, which might have broken, or at least constrained Bezeq's monopoly, instead served to strengthen it.

The intermediary regime, then, promoted privatisation with the development of competition being only a marginal goal. This is evident in the accommodation of cables into the Israeli telecommunications sector.

After several decades of restrictive policy, which de facto prevented the diffusion of cable broadcasting, a policy change was evident in the mid-1980s. An amendment to the 1982 Telecommunications Law allowed the Communications Ministry to grant exclusive franchise for the provision of multi-channel broadcasting through cables (Katz 1992; Gandal 1994). The operators were all private companies and there was wide agreement between the legislators and policy-makers that the public purse should not provide the heavy investment needed for building the cable infrastructure.

The intermediary regime was not about change in the distribution of power in comparison with the old regime, but about reassertion of its power in changing circumstances and pressures for improvement in its performances. This is evident in respect of Bezeq's senior management, the interests of the equipment industry, and the power of Bezeq managers. Outside the constraints of civil service regulations, Bezeq's senior management won wage conditions and managerial autonomy it had not experienced before. The rapid expansion of investment in the sector, under conditions of protectionism and generous government subsidies for R&D and investment, had a positive impact on the equipment industry's revenues and profits. At the same time, the reality of technical change at a time of economic expansion allowed newcomers to enter the closed circles of the Israeli telecommunications industry. The labour unions that at first opposed corporatisation later negotiated an attractive deal (which included better working conditions, higher wages, and did not reduce employment stability). From 1984 to 1994 their wages constantly rose higher than the average rise in the economy as a whole (Bank of Israel 1995: 90). Cuts in the labour force were hardly painful as they were based on voluntary retirement under conditions of highly attractive financial incentives.

Considering the desirability of the intermediary regime for labour and business, as well as the successful accommodation of new technologies and the great improvement in services, it is quite puzzling to see that already by the end of the 1980s, and soon after it was established, it faced serious challenges. It took a while for the opponents of the intermediary regime to change the rules of the game, but at last they had their way after bitter and, at one point, even violent conflict. The new regime of competition was designed and enforced by the state, particularly through co-operation between the bureaucrats of the Communications Ministry and the 'eco-bureaucrats' of the Ministry of Finance. These policy entrepreneurs worked in a changing environment which helped them carry out the reforms and to bring about a regime change.

A critical turning point in the life of the intermediary regime came with the appointment of the committee for 'The Examination and Re-organisation in the Structure of the Telecommunications Sector' (Boaz Committee). The new committee was established in February 1990 by the

Minister of Finance, Shimon Peres, and the Communications Minister, Gad Ya'acobi. It was chaired by David Boaz, head of the powerful Budget Department in the Ministry of Finance. The committee's recommendations, which were published in April 1991, placed the issue of competition at the top of the regime's agenda. They called for the liberalisation of supply and installation of telephone equipment, and for opening up international telephone services, cellular phones, data transmission and value-added services to competition. The committee also recommended that Bezeq's monopoly over the operation of the local system not be changed, but that to guarantee fair competition and avoid cross-service subsidies, substantial parts of its operations be organised as autonomous subsidiaries (CM and MOF 1991).

These recommendations were a subject of bitter conflict between the Communications Ministry on the one hand and Bezeq's management and labour union on the other. The first to react was the labour union, which took its grievances to the communications minister, Refael Pinhasi. However, the minister was not easily impressed either by the unions or the management, and preferred to follow the advice and goals of his officials. Despite Bezeq's objections, a new licence was signed by Pinhasi on his last day in office, just before the new labour government took over. For a few days after Pinhasi's move, it seemed that the road was clear for a new regime change. Yet under the pressure of 200 activists of the Bezeq labour union and a few legal questions raised about the new licence, the new communications minister, Moshe Shahal, suspended the licence. A new committee was appointed to examine the issue, this time chaired by the economist Ilan Maoz. This committee's recommendations, which were published in September 1992, in general reasserted the recommendations of the Boaz Committee on competition and again opened the door for a regime change in Israeli telecommunications (CM 1992).

The political machine of the labour government thereafter moved more rapidly, with the intensive involvement of the late Prime Minister, Yitzhak Rabin. In December 1992, an amendment in the Bezeq law to end Bezeq's monopoly control over international calls and cellular phone services was placed before the Knesset. After a struggle, Bezeq's labour union and its supporters in the Labour Party Knesset faction lost and the amendment to the law was approved. This allowed the communications and finance ministries to move on to draft a new general licence for Bezeq. In March 1994, after a long delay owing to changes at the head of the Communications Ministry (of both the minister and the director-general) the new general licence was signed by the Communications Minister, Shulamit Aloni. Bezeq fought the new general licence in the Israeli high court of justice but, in June 1994, the court upheld the new general licence and so opened the door for a new regime of 'regulated competition' in Israeli telecommunications.

The new telecommunications regime

The decision of the Israeli high court of justice brought the intermediary telecommunications regime to a symbolic end. Yet it took more than legislation and a court verdict to restructure the Israeli market. Liberalisation, as will be shown, proved to be a piecemeal and slow process. The new general licence, drafted in 1994, required that Bezeq's monopoly services, which were unrelated to infrastructure, be organised under fully independent subsidiaries. Since then, Bezeq has come under intense pressures of competition. After years in which its labour force was well protected, the company is now experiencing the very difficult process of dismissing 20 per cent of its 8,400 workers. In the next two years the Israeli government will most probably reduce its shares in Bezeq to less than 50 per cent, the first 25 per cent of Bezeq's shares having been offered to the Israeli public in 1990 and 1991. In 1997, another 12.3 per cent of the shares were sold to the American investment bank Merrill Lynch, which intends to resell them in 1999. In March 1998 the government sold another part of the company and now holds about 60 per cent of the shares. The remaining shares are held by the public (20 per cent), Cable and Wireless (10 per cent), and Merrill Lynch (10 per cent). While Cable and Wireless is certainly a candidate to acquire control over Bezeq, the issue in not yet settled.

A recommendation to create an independent regulatory authority in the style of the Federal Communications Commission had been raised in various reports since the mid-1980s. On 31 August 1993, the government decided to establish a committee of experts to present recommendations for the establishment of a telecommunications regulatory agency. The committee recommended that the Communications Ministry be dissolved and most of its responsibilities transferred to a new National Tele-communication Authority (NTA). This was to be headed by up to seven commissioners and to be responsible, like the FCC, for tele-communications and for the media field (CM and MOF 1996a). A government decision of 29 May 1996 gave a green light to the preparation of draft legislation by December 1996. However, the political upheaval that brought the right-wing government to power in mid-1996 was a pretext for delay in the establishment of such an authority. Yet, judging by the general consensus on the issue, as expressed in various reports, it seems fairly certain that in the next couple of years such an authority will be created.

As mentioned, 1994 was a critical year, not only in regard to the symbolic act of the new general licence but also in regard to the enforcement of competition in important markets. The first to be liberalised was the terminal-equipment market. Indeed, initial steps towards the opening of the equipment market were taken during the first years of the inter-mediary regime. Yet the most meaningful step was taken in July 1994, when, for the first time, the Communications Ministry forced Bezeq to allow new customers to choose who would supply their first telephone set. At the same time, the type-approval regime is becoming more and more flexible. Now, manufacturers and importers of terminals can test their equipment in private laboratories, they are no longer required to test for quality (only for compatibility and safety) and test results from Europe and the US are recognised unilaterally by the authorities.

Although the equipment market was the first to be liberalised, the benefits of liberalisation were first widely observed by the Israeli public in the cellular market. The policy-makers of the old regime gave the first cellular operator a monopoly over the provision of the service until 1994. Following the recommendation of the Shiloh Committee, a tender for a second cellular operator was published in November 1993. The winner, Cellcom, a joint venture of BellSouth, the Safra Brothers and Discount Investments, started to offer its services to the public in December 1994. The entry of this second operator radically transformed the sector. While prices fell to a quarter of their previous level, the penetration rate increased by an even greater factor. The current penetration rate is 30 per cent (that is, 30 out of 100 people have mobile phones), a usage rate which is second only to the Nordic countries. In February 1998, a third operator, Partner, won the first GSM licence in Israel and is expected to start its operation during 1998. Recent estimates are that the penetration rate of cellular phones in Israel will reach 60 per cent in four to five years.

The outstanding growth in the cellular market, following the entry of Cellcom, made the benefits of competition in the international market clearly visible to both policy-makers and the public. This in turn encouraged the Ministries of Communications and Finance to continue in their liberalisation plans. The next target on the government agenda was the market for overseas calls, which represented about 30 per cent of Bezeq's revenue (about US$700m in 1996) and about 40 per cent of its net profits (CM and MOF 1993). To make liberalisation possible, Bezeq's labour union opposition had to be hammered out. From July 1992, when the new labour government took office, to June 1995, Bezeq's workers were engaged in bitter, and to some extent violent, conflict with the Ministries of Finance and Communications. This conflict only became manageable with the promise of the late Prime Minister, Yitzhak Rabin, and the Ministers of Finance and Communications that the 'financial solidity' of Bezeq would be preserved.[5] Even then, Bezeq's workers engaged in strikes aimed at obstructing the opening of the market for international calls.[6] Yet the state officials eventually had their way and, in October 1995, a tender for two licences to operate international services was finally launched.

Six groups entered the competition. The two winning groups represent joint ventures between first-class international actors and local business. The first winner, Golden Lines, is a consortium of Israel's Orek,

Globescom and the industrialist Cahan family, the Texas-based Bell company Southwestern and Italy's STET. The second winner, Barak, is a consortium comprising Israel's Clalcom and Matav, together with the Global One Alliance partners, Deutsche Telekom, France Télécom and Sprint. The new companies started to offer their services on 1 July 1997 and immediately revolutionised this segment of the telecommunications market. Prices of international calls fell by an average rate of 60 to 70 per cent and, overnight, the Israeli public found itself enjoying one of the lowest rates, if not the lowest, for international telephony. Moreover, the market grew by 50 per cent and in two months Bezeq International lost about 45 per cent of its share. At present, Bezeq International holds 55 per cent of the market and the newcomers, which are less than a year old, hold 30 per cent (Barak) and 15 per cent (Golden Lines).

The next stage in the liberalisation and introduction of competition to the Israeli telecommunications market aims at opening the local loop for competition. The policy process in this regard moved ahead during 1996 when Communications Minister, Shulamit Aloni, and Minister of Finance, Avraham Shohat, charged their respective Directors-General, Shlomo Waxe and David Brodet, to examine whether the national infrastructure should be exposed to competition, and if so, when and under what terms.[7] The committee's report was published in December 1996 and included recommendations (a) to open the Israeli domestic market to competition from January 1999 and (b) to open multi-channel satellite broadcasting to competition (Communications Ministry and Ministry of Finance, 1996b). The 1998 agenda of the Communications Ministry is devoted to setting the rules for regulation of competition in the local loop. While a major decision has been made – new operators will not be able to use the current network but will have to build their own – much still has to be decided. Many questions are open, such as the scope for operation of the new service provider (regional or national), the numbering policy, the definition of universal service, the availability of an electromagnetic spectrum, the right-of-way for the new operators, the ability of cable companies to supply telephony services in competition with Bezeq, and the scope and authority of the new regulatory agency for telecommunications. Many of these issues are now under discussion, but it would be overly optimistic to assume that by the 'official day' of opening the domestic market to competition they will have been resolved. Considering many of these issues need legislation, long delays are expected before the restructuring of the Israeli telecommunications market is complete. This is of course hardly surprising when we recall that earlier stages in the liberalisation of the market were handled in the same way.

Liberalisation from above – political economy analysis

The liberalisation of Israeli telecommunications can be seen as a battle-field in the intensive war that is fought between the major forces which govern the Israeli political economy. The state, the labour unions and the business community were the protagonists in this 'policy battle' during the making and remaking of the three regimes. When the conflict was over, four major outcomes became clear. First, through inter-ministry and inter-departmental co-operation, some state officials had triumphed and reinforced their dominant political position.[8] In this co-operation the senior partners were the economists who, despite their lack of expertise in telecommunications, proved their reform-making capabilities.

To understand the power of the economists, one must go back to the period of turbulence and hyperinflation of 1977–85. This period of crisis came to an end in July 1985, when a stabilisation programme was announced and successfully implemented, almost immediately checking inflation. This programme, which incurred only (relatively) minor costs in unemployment, had been designed and managed by professional economists, and was their most remarkable success in Israel's economic history. Alongside the decline in the prestige of politics and politicians in Israeli society, it helped to secure the dominant status of the economics profession among Israeli policy-makers (cf. Keren 1995). That is not that Israeli economists were negligible policy actors before 1985, but after this period they enjoyed critical advantages over other policy actors.[9] The rise in their status, influence and power is clearly reflected in the liberalisation of Israeli telecommunications. One episode concerning the establishment of the Boaz Committee may illustrate their power. The establishment of the Boaz Committee was forced on the Communications Minister by David Boaz, a senior eco-bureaucrat in the Ministry of Finance. Boaz, in his position as head of the powerful budget department, used his budgetary controls to put pressure on the Communications Minister to establish the committee.[10] This was justified by David Boaz on account of the likely partiality of the Minister (and politicians in general), as against his own impartial behaviour (and that of bureaucrats in general) which would better support general interests.[11]

The ability of the Ministries of Finance and Communications' bureau-crats to act in such an assertive and entrepreneurial way should also be understood against the background of the French-style etatist tradition in Israel. The Israeli trajectory of state-building under intense warfare, its unique mixture of nationalism and socialism, and its late-industrialisation, all contributed to the formation of a strong state. The entrepreneurial role played by eco-bureaucrats in their mission of liberalisation does not seem to be so different from that played by the old political guard that led the process of state- and economy-building. The paradox of the Israeli case stems from the incongruity between an etatist tradition on the one hand,

and enforcement of competition by the state on defiant market actors on the other. Not only can we now see how, under certain conditions, regulation and competition complement rather than contradict each other, it also seems that a strong state tradition is conducive to market restructuring and the enforcement of competition. Here, Gerschenkron's argument, linking the timing of industrialisation to the particular advantages of the strong interventionist state, can be invoked (Gerschenkron 1962).[12]

A second outcome of liberalisation is that some business actors, despite their marginal role in the process, had their way cleared to the highly lucrative and expanding market of telecommunications. Business, which had clear advantages to gain from liberalisation, whether as users of telecommunications, manufacturers, service providers or importers of its equipment, played a relatively negligible role. Business Users Groups (BUG), which played an important role in legitimising the liberalisation of telecommunications and in providing support for government officials in the United States and the United Kingdom, did not take an active part in the Israeli process. The salience of the business community is evident, although to a lesser extent, in the case of equipment manufacturers, who profited much from the old and intermediary regimes. While they certainly opposed liberalisation, they did not launch an offensive against it, and were relatively passive. Business, one must recall, was relatively weak in the formative period of the Israeli political economy (Zionism was never a profitable venture) and against this background it is hardly surprising that it was minor actor. However, things are changing in telecommunications, as in other sectors of the Israeli economy, and the new policy community is replete with aggressive and well-positioned businesses that most probably aim to translate their economic power into political power. Yet it is not yet clear how far these expectations about the power of business will be realised, and thus how much they can transform the traditional role of business.

A third outcome of liberalisation is that the unions and workers were losers in the process. The labour union of Bezeq, as well as the labour unions of the privileged equipment industry, increased, or at least preserved, their power in the intermediary regime as they were able to provide job security and raise wages at the same time. But the movement towards competition changed this picture of union power. While Bezeq's labour union is still the most important actor which challenges liberalisation, it clearly lost the war and is now engaged in battles to minimise the damage but not to change the picture. Bezeq's workers no longer have the privilege of job security and face massive layoffs. They are also increasingly unable to gain wages unlinked to their corporation performance so that they are becoming ever more dependent on management. In short, after a long period of decommodification and a bitter struggle against liberalisation, the state has finally succeeded in comodifying the telecommunications sector work-force.[13]

The fourth major outcome of liberalisation is that the benefits of changes in telecommunications are highly widespread and are enjoyed by the Israeli public and not only by business. It implies that tele-communications will be used as a 'paradigm case' by the proponents of liberalisation in order to extend it to other spheres and sectors. Unlike other sectors in the Israeli economy, where liberalisation did not realise its promise to bring visible benefits to consumers, in telecommunications they are highly visible and impressive. The sector may well serve as a symbolic case on which future developments in Israeli politics and economy will be modelled. In this respect, developments in the sector are highly important to the Israeli economy at large. It is, however, doubtful whether the telecommunications success can be reproduced in other sectors.

Conclusions

The success of liberalisation is evident in almost every corner of the sector: from competition in the provision of services through lower rates, better services and growth in demand, to the booming equipment and software industry. This success guarantees that the rate of innovation, and extent of competition, will also be high in the future. Yet the success is only relative to European performances, and the European policy process can hardly count as an efficient or a target-oriented process. Its most problematic aspect is its need for unanimity, or at least very wide agree-ment. This style of decision-making has its price in immobilism in some sectors and delays in liberalisation in others. If the liberalisation of European telecommunications is a success, it is only a relative success as compared to sectors such as energy and electricity where immobilism prevailed (cf. Schmidt 1997a). It took almost fifteen years for the Euro-pean telecommunications market to be legally proclaimed an open sector, and it may take a few years more for competition within it to become common practice. Thus, in comparison to Europe, Israeli performances, so far, are good.

The process was characterised as 'liberalisation from above' because of the critical role played by state officials in promoting the process, defeat-ing the opposition and designing the new competitive regime. Scrutiny of the patterns of liberalisation in Israeli telecommunications highlights the paradox of liberalisation. More competition is evident in almost every segment of the market (even in the local loop, where cellular telephony serves as the alternative for the fixed network), yet this 'rise of the market' has not necessarily entailed a 'retreat of the state'. The scope and the depth of the state's involvement in the enforcement of competition in the Israeli telecommunications market leads to the interpretation of this market's liberalisation as 'regulated competition'. Thus, the market is structured, restructured and maintained by the state, so the relations between the two are critically positive-sum rather than zero-sum relations.

Against this background, Israeli policy-makers can be seen to be facing difficulties at the moment in designing a suitable regulatory regime. Such a regime is necessary in order to promote and protect current achievements and in order to deal with the challenges of the expected convergence of media, computers and telecommunications. The future of the reforms depends on the creation of a regulatory authority which will replace the Communications Ministry. The promotion of this regulatory authority has been on the official agenda at least since 1993, but the wagon is moving so slowly that policy-makers continue to rely on improvisation and lag behind in the cultivation and nurturing of new policy instruments. The administrative problems of governance are also expressed as a problem of co-ordination in labour relations. This darker side of the reforms is evinced in the massive layoffs in Bezeq amounting to almost 20 per cent of all employees. Sadly, although the necessity to reduce the workforce has been evident for at least five years, state officials, managers and labour unions still find it easier to engage in conflict and to delay decision-making than to co-operate in a process that will ease the inevitable shock for the employees.

Notes

1 This study profited from the co-operative attitude of the practitioners in the field. I am indebted to David Boaz, Joseph Gandai, Arie Gorel, John Graiber, Shemuel Klepner, Menachem Ohali, Daniel Rosenne, Haim Sakharovich, Avi Teitelman, Shlomo Waxe and Ofer Weiss. This research profited from the very able research assistantship of Ornit Egosi.
2 Measured as the number of telephone lines per 100 people.
3 Bundling is the tying of the supply of one service or product to the supply of others.
4 Incentive regulation is based on 'rules that encourage a regulated firm to achieve desired goals by granting some, but not complete, discretion to the firm' (Sappington and Weisman 1996: 2).
5 The government made commitments to reduce the rate of royalties that the corporation pays to the government from 8 to 5 per cent. The annual efficiency factor which is used to calculate the rates of Bezeq was reduced by 3 per cent.
6 Their refusal to connect the new operators delayed the beginning of competition for four days.
7 Moshe Leon joined the committee after the rise to power of the right-wing government in 1996.
8 To some extent this was a reflection of co-operation between the engineers and legal experts of the Communications Ministry and the economists of the Ministry of Finance and the Department of Economics in the Communications Ministry.
9 An indication of their growing power may be seen in the rise of the autonomy

of the Bank of Israel and in the new autonomy and authority given to the Monopolics Authority under the new law of 1988.

10 On the powerful position of the Budget Department, see Drey and Sharon (1994).

11 Interview with David Boaz.

12 An example of the advantages of a strong state in the process of liberalisation is the attempt by Cable and Wireless to take over Bezeq. This move was resisted by the Israeli government, which treated it as hostile takeover and immediately set out to enact legislation to prevent further moves by Cable and Wireless.

13 Decommodification occurs when a person can make a living without reliance on the market.

11 Privatisation of telecommunications in Thailand

Prasit Prapinmongkolkarn

Introduction[1]

The history of Thailand's telecommunications begins as early as 1883 when the Departments of Post and Telegraph were founded. These were merged in 1898 to become the Department of Post and Telegraph. The first telegraph line was built from the mouth of Chao Phaya river, in the Samutprakarn province, to Bangkok to monitor the incoming ships. From 1934, following the Telegraph and Telephone Act of the same year, the Post and Telegraph Department (PTD) held the monopoly for telephone services, but in 1954, under the Telephone Organization of Thailand (TOT) Act, telecommunications were transferred to the control of the TOT. This body was responsible for installing and operating telephone services, including other value-added services. In 1977, the Communications Authority of Thailand (CAT) Act of 1976 was passed which created a new state enterprise responsible for international communication and the postal services.

Though the TOT and CAT are both state enterprises, their functions overlap so that in some areas they are in competition with each other. This was highlighted in 1986 when the TOT established the first NMT 470MHz cellular telephone network and then a year later, the CAT set up its own AMPS system using 800MHz. Recently, CAT launched a digital cellular phone service called Personal Communication Service (PCS) at 1800MHz, using Code Division Multiple Access (CDMA), competing with the TOT's Global System for Mobile Communications (GSM) at 900MHz. Total Access Communications (TAC), a subsidiary of United Communications Industry Plc (UCOM), and Advance Info Service (AIS), a subsidiary of Shinawatra Computer and Communication Plc (SCC), were given the concession to operate the cellular phone service by the CAT and TOT, respectively. At present, the total number of subscribers for all types of cellular mobile telephones is more than three million.

Following the recommendations of the fifth National Economic and Social Development Board (NESDB) plan (1987–91), the government of Anand Panyarachun invited the private sector to invest in and operate part of the nation's telephone services. Since the existing outdated telecommunication laws, which empowered the TOT as the sole authorised telephone operator, were not changed, all telephone concessions to private-sector companies are based on the Build, Transfer, and Operate (BTO) principle. In 1991, TelecomAsia (TA), a subsidiary of the Charoen Pokphand Group with a 13.5 per cent shareholding by the Nynex Corporation, won a concession to install two million telephone lines in Bangkok Metropolitan, which includes five surrounding provinces, and to operate them for twenty-five years. According to the contract, all lines were to be in service by 1997, and TelecomAsia undertook to pay 16 per cent of line revenues to the TOT for the duration of its concession.[2]

In 1992, the Thai Telephone and Telecommunication Corporation (TT&T),[3] was awarded a concession to install one million telephone lines in provincial areas, and to operate them for thirty years, with the TOT receiving 43.1 per cent of revenues for the life of the contract. However, in 1997, this high revenue sharing scheme proved difficult to operate, mainly due to negotiation problems between the TT&T and TOT in converting the revenues into equity shareholdings.

In addition, the increasing question of globalisation has necessitated the development of a quality telecommunications infrastructure on a multilateral basis, to support and promote free world trade, market opening, competition and human interactions. This quality network provision is important at both domestic and international levels. As a result, nations committed to trade liberalisation, as set out in the World Trade Organisation (WTO) treaty, need to plan major restructuring and adjustments to the services involved, particularly those of telecommunications. Thailand is no exception and, since the Thai government signed the WTO treaty in February 1997 agreeing to the liberalisation of Thailand's telecommunications business by the year 2006, it has taken several major steps towards the restructuring and privatisation of its telecommunications industry.

One of the first steps was the commissioning of Coopers & Lybrand by the TOT, in 1994, to study the restructuring and privatisation of Thailand's telecommunications industry. In the resulting report, Coopers & Lybrand *et al.*[4] have taken into account some likely changes in the policy environment in which TOT will have to operate. First, that competition will be introduced across all basic telephone services; second, the government will set up a regulatory authority;[5] and third, the regulatory powers previously held by the TOT and CAT will be withdrawn – including, for example, the power to grant concessions. In all, six potential missions were identified for the TOT, of which a combination of two, 'Domestic Market Leader' and 'Public Service Providers', would seem to be the most likely and attractive ones for the TOT to adopt.

Prior to this, the CAT had commissioned the Thailand Development

Research Institute (TDRI), together with Chulalongkorn University, to study its future direction.[6] The results of the TDRI study, published in 1993, recommended the separation of telecommunications and postal services, and presented three possible scenarios whereby this could be accomplished:

- The division of the CAT into post (Post Authority of Thailand) and telecommunications (Telecommunications Authority of Thailand); both corporatised without a regulator.
- The corporatisation of the CAT with a separate regulator.
- The division of the CAT into post and telecommunications (as set out in the previous option) but with only the Post Authority of Thailand (PAT) being corporatised. The Telecommunications Authority of Thailand (TAT) would be merged with TOT.

Following the signing of the WTO treaty in February 1997, the Ministry of Transport and Communications (MOTC) set about drafting the Master Plan for Development of Telecommunications Activities. Published in 1997, the plan set the framework for the privatisation of both the TOT and CAT and defined the function and organisational structures of a powerful national regulatory body, the National Communications Committee (NCC). According to the plan, a model of a common holding company will be used, with the TOT privatised to become the TOT Co. Ltd, and the CAT split into separate post and telecommunications divisions, which will be privatised to become the CAT Post Co. Ltd and CAT Telecommunications Co. Ltd., respectively. Also, under the plan, a holding company (under the MOTC) will be set up to be in charge of investment in these companies. Initially, the government will hold all the shares with plans for later divestment (see Figure 11.1). As a guide, it is planned that domestic telecommunications will be liberalised by 1999 and international telecommunications by 2000.

The MOTC has also submitted a bill to Parliament, which if passed, will become the new Telecommunications Act, replacing the several existing and outdated ones.[7] The intention of the new act is to encourage free competition and attract private investment in the former state-monopolised telecommunications business. Indeed, international tele-communication service providers, such as NTT and Nynex are already stakeholders in private telephone service providers, such as the TT&T and TA. Singapore Telecom has also been a shareholder operating and providing services on the X.25 data network, Datanet, under the licence of the TOT, and holds 20 per cent of the shares in Shinawatra Paging. In addition, Motorola invested 28 per cent in World Phone, a cellular mobile phone service operating under Total Access Communications (TAC), a UCOM Group company.

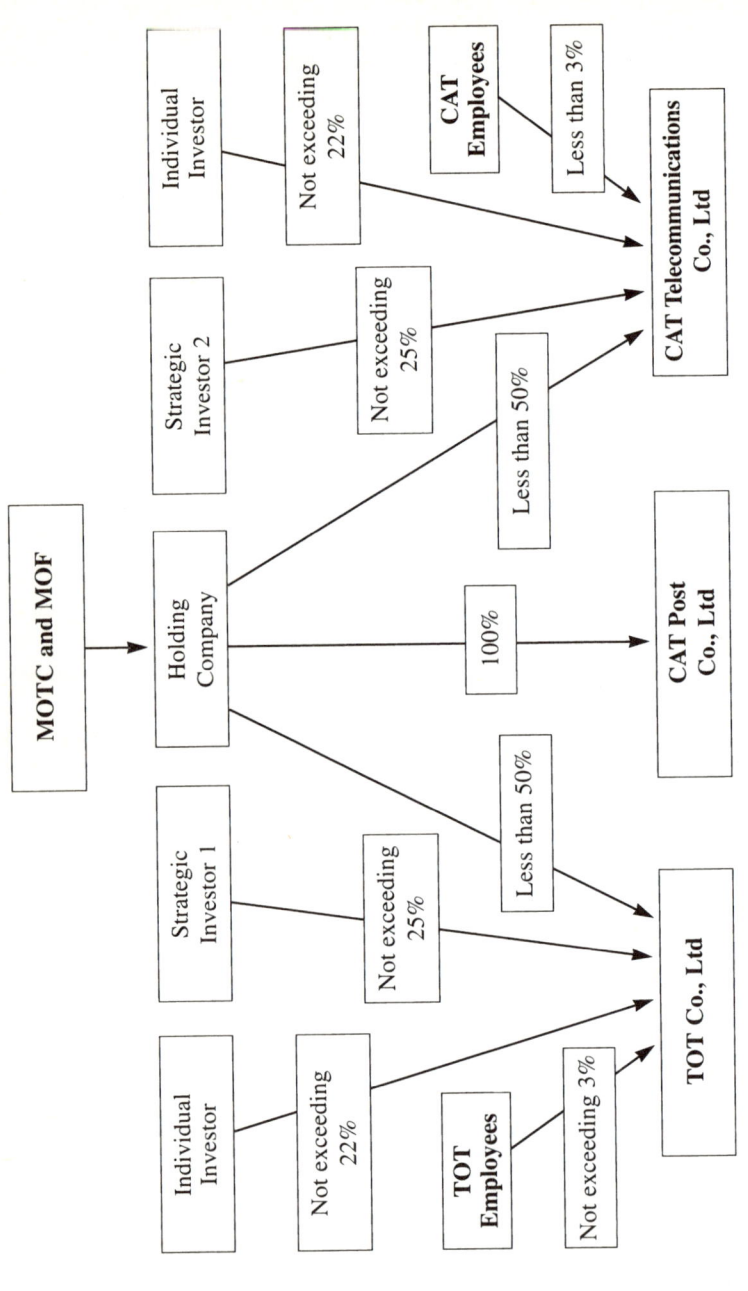

Figure 11.1 Divestment scheme of the holding company

Privatisation – the evolving paradigm

In the 1980s, Thailand's economy enjoyed double-digit growth, which increased the demand for telephone lines and added enormously to the already acute shortage. In order to meet the demand quickly, the TOT introduced the innovative Build, Transfer and Operate (BTO) scheme for telephone service concessions to the private sector. As a result, TA and the TT&T were awarded a twenty-five year concession to build two million telephone lines (with 16 per cent revenue sharing) in the metropolitan area of Bangkok, and a thirty year concession for 1 million telephone lines (with 43.1 per cent revenue sharing) in the provinces.[8] At present, Thailand has approximately 6 million telephone numbers, which represent approximately 10 lines per 100 inhabitants – a remarkable improvement in telephone density from the 2–3 lines per 100 inhabitants of the early 1990s.

However, the concept of concessions will not be sufficient for coping with the rapidly changing telecommunications environment resulting from the restructuring and privatisation of the former state monopoly. From the Coopers & Lybrand consortium study, the advantages and disadvantage of three other possible privatisation structures were compared. These were: regionally-based, customer-facing, and service-line-separation structures. Of these, the TOT management decided to adopt a customer-facing structure. Examples of privatisation structures adopted by other telecommunications organisations are shown in Table 11.1.

Privatisation approaches

Once the structure of privatisation had been determined, a decision had to be taken over implementation. Currently there are five approaches used in the telecommunications industry.

- Domestic Initial Public Offering (IPO)
- Domestic IPO with an international tranche
- Global IPO with a dual-listing structure
- Strategic sale followed by IPO
- Project Finance Schemes (BTO/BOT etc.)

Due to the large size of IPO compared to the local capital markets, the first approach, domestic only IPO, has not been frequently used. The domestic IPO with an international tranche, however, has the advantages of an equity offering with a listing on the Stock Exchange of Thailand. In addition, a significant portion of the offering (likely to be over 50 per cent) would be sold to domestic investors, while the international investor base would be accessed through an international tranche structured as a standard Euro-style offering. An alternative would be a US offering,

Table 11.1 Examples of the world's telecommunication privatisation structures

Telecom Service Providers	Regionally Based	Customer Facing	Service line separation	Remarks
AT&T			1984	
British Telecom		1991		
DBP Telekom (Germany)		1993		
France Télécom				Corporatised
NTT (Japan)			1992	
Pactel/Air Touch			1994	
PTT Telecom Nederland		1992		
Telecom Corp. of New Zealand	1988	1993		
Singapore Telecom		1994		
Tele Denmark		1985–1988		
TOT (Thailand)		2000		

which would take the form of a 144A private placement to Qualified Institutional Buyers (i.e. the largest US institution). Even though the offering size may be limited, and valuation as well as liquidity of trading would likely be lower than a Global offering,[9] the initial disclosure and ongoing reporting requirement are less stringent than a dual-listing structure with a NYSE (New York Stock Exchange) listing. The registration process is also simpler and quicker than a NYSE listing. Examples of IPO for the telecommunications industry are shown in Table 11.2.

The TOT Board decided to use public stock offering in Thailand and internationally, and to reduce state ownership to below 50 per cent. The Coopers & Lybrand consortium had evaluated three privatisation/restructuring strategies based on five key financial criteria, namely, market share, profitability, operating efficiency, gearing, liquidity and valuation. Set against a Base Case of no significant restructuring/BTO, the three strategies considered were, (1) geographical/IPO, (2) customer-facing/IPO, (3) strategic-partner. The decision was taken in favour of strategy (3) for the following reasons.

- Increased operating efficiency before IPO
- Government financial burden reduced more quickly
- Likely to provide highest valuation of shares, both in initial sale and subsequent IPO
- Added credibility when accessing international markets
- Provision of technical expertise
- Quality would be evaluated against international standards
- The TOT would be suitably positioned for future expansion (e.g. into

Table 11.2 Examples of IPO for the telecommunications industry

Telecommunications Service Providers	Offering Size (US$/mm)	Divestiture %	Domestic IPO with an International Tranche %		Global IPO with a Dual Listing Structure %		Project Finance Scheme	Date
			Domestic	International	Domestic	International		
British Telecom	4,668	50.2			86.2	13.8		December 1984
Compania de Telefone de Chile	98.3	14.5	0.0	100				July 1990
Hong Kong Telecom	538.5	8.0			65.8	34.2		December 1988
Indosat	750	35.0			n/a	n/a		Pending
PTT Nederland	3,675	36.0			33.3	66.6		1994
New Zealand Telecom	818	30	47.5	52.5				July 1991
Singapore Telecom	2,758	11.1	61.5	38.5				October 1993
Telecom de Argentina	1,241	30.0	71.1	28.9				February 1992
STET – France Télécom SA								
Telecom Asia	472.5	No meaning	50.0	50.0				1993
TeleDenmark	2,975	38.9			20	80		April 1994
Telefonica de Argentina SA	848	30	43.4	56.6				December 1991
Telefonos de Mexico	2,174	15.0	60.0	40.0	7.2	92.8		May 1991
TT&T	287						BTO to TA and TT&T	1993
TOT		No meaning						1993

Source: Coopers & Lybrand Consortium: The TOT Restructuring and Privatisation Study

other countries in Indochina) with either a strategic partner or other like linkages developed through a strategic partner

The disadvantages of this strategy are that the TOT may lose some influence with the government and have to face reductions in its labour force. The main differences between the strategies in term of company restructuring and privatisation are summarised in Table 11.3.

Legal issues

In order for privatisation to happen, certain legislative measures are necessary. First, an amendment of the Telegraph and Telephone Act, which would eliminate the government monopoly for telecommunications services provision, is required. Second, the Telephone Organisation of Thailand Act, which would enable some form of TOT corporatisation, and perhaps even private-sector ownership needs to be passed. An alternative approach, as mentioned earlier, is the new Telecommunications Act proposed by the MOTC to replace, amongst others, the obsolete Telegraph and Telephone Act of 1934, the TOT Act of 1954 and the CAT Act of 1977. Following the Coopers & Lybrand consortium study, it has been recommended that the TOT should apply for 'Class A' state enterprise status as quickly as possible, which would give it the flexibility of determining human resource policies, salaries and bonus, as well as procurement, and certain accounting rules, without requiring approval from the Ministry of Finance (MOF). In addition, the TOT needs to obtain a comprehensive licence granted by the new NCC, although the state will be given restricted veto rights through its 'Golden Share'. However, to achieve privatisation, the TOT must first be converted to a corporation, which can be achieved under existing private and public company law. The result could be a holding company or, alternatively, the TOT could create a corporate subsidiary through which it could effect privatisation. The holding company will facilitate the corporatisation process and gradual divestment at the government's discretion but at the cost of loosening the control of the subsidiary through the holding company. While direct privatisation of the TOT involves lengthy assets valuation and legal procedures, international IPO with a strategic partner is easier. Nevertheless, in either case, the TOT will need the prior approval of the Cabinet and of a committee established under the Prime Minister's regulations.

Telecommunication policy and regulation

Another influential factor in the process of liberalising telecommunications policy in Thailand have been the varying policies of the different governments. For instance, when Mr Chuan Leekpai took office as Prime

Table 11.3 The main differences between the strategies in terms of company restructuring and privatisation

Strategy	Form of Restructuring	Legal Features	Business Philosophy	Management Process	Privatisation Structure
Base Case	Status quo	Basic licence granted to TOT	Status quo	Status quo with limited change following introduction of 'Class A' status in 1997	7.1m line expansion through further BTO schemes
'A'	Regional organisation. Strong marketing and commercial disciplines in regions. Devaluation of authority from HQ	Comprehensive. licence granted to TOT, defining its right and obligations. The state given restricted veto rights through 'Golden Share'	Public service provider with greater emphasis on meeting customer needs but still inhibited by strong functional orientation	Reduced standardisation and specialisation. Greater individual accountability and reward of performance	Public stock offerings in Thailand and internationally to reduce state ownership below 50%
'B'	Customer-facing organisation. Functionally-based organisation disappear and TOT's culture fundamentally changes	As 'A'	Public service provider and leading domestic operator mission. Emphasis on meeting the needs of each customer group	As 'A' but with additional changes in the sales and marketing area. Use of specific marketing objectives and of market driven approach to new product development	As 'A'
'C'	Probably customer-facing organisation. Strategic partner group formally involved in management of TOT	As 'A'. In addition a management contract would define the roles and responsibilities of the strategic partner group (or experienced operator member of the group)	Public service provider and leading domestic operator mission. Emphasis on meeting the needs of each customer group Strong commercial focus	As 'B' but processes are likely to be changed more rapidly. 'Best practice' processes, skills, tools and software will be imported from the strategic partner group. Greater emphasis on training	Sale of stake to a strategic partner. Subsequently public offerings of stock in Thailand and internationally. Possibly, sale of stake to a non-governmental public organisation

Source: Coopers Lybrand and Consortium: *The TOT Restructuring and Privatisation Study*

Minister and announced his telecommunications policy to Parliament on 21 October 1992, the major points were:

- To develop an infrastructure for transport and communications as would sustain economic and social growth in the future by promoting the private sector to participate in the investment and service of transport and telecommunication activity.
- To develop the telecommunication network nation-wide, and to modernise it by introducing new technologies which would facilitate new and better services to enable and support Thailand as the regional centre of economics and finance.

The Chaun Leekpai government did liberalise foreign currency control and introduce the Bangkok International Banking Facilities (BIBF) in order to enable Thailand to become the centre of finance in this region. Unfortunately, after five years, it was these very measures which were cited as major cause for the ensuing economic crisis and the downfall of the Thai economy.

When Mr. Banhan Silpa-archa replaced Mr Chaun and announced his telecommunications policy to Parliament on 26 July 1995, the major points were:

- To develop, improve and expand telecommunications services using equipment and modern technology; to provide services at a reasonable, low price nation-wide; and, in particular, to install public exchanges in every district and to even expand telephone services at the village level.
- To promote the use of modern telecommunications system for the benefit of national defence and economic growth.
- To develop Thailand as the centre of telecommunications in Southeast Asia.

Two years later, when Prime Minister General Chavalit Yongchaiyudh announced his intentions to Parliament on 11 December 1997, an important part of his policy on transport and communication was 'to accelerate the Master Plan for the Development of Telecommunications and improve the relevant laws in harmonised accord'.

The Master Plan is based on the seventh NESDB plan (1992–6), which has set a target of a minimum teledensity of 10 per 100 inhabitants. In the Master Plan, however, it is proposed to increase the number of telephone lines by 1.9 million lines by 1998. This includes an earlier project to add 1.1 million lines nation-wide by the end of 1996. Overall, 600,000 lines and 500,000 lines were given as a concession to TA and TT&T, respectively, while the TOT is currently building the remaining 800,000 lines through its contractors. The plan also calls for the liberalisation of the tele-

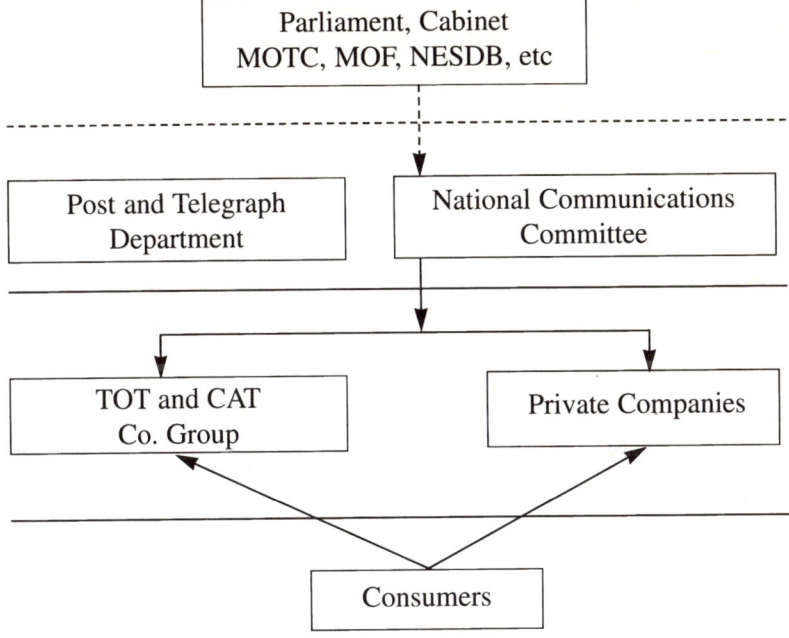

Figure 11.2 Flow chart of regulations by National Communications Committee

communication business, with preparation underway to promote fair competition in the telecommunication sector by abolishing the existing, outdated telecommunication laws and implementing the new telecommunication business laws. The essence of the plan is to privatise the TOT and CAT, separate postal services from the telecommunication services of the CAT and set up a neutral body, the NCC, whose functions are similar to the Federal Communications Commission in the United States. The relationship of functions and regulations of the NCC with others organisations is shown in Figure 11.2.

According to the eighth NESDB plan (1997–2001), another six million telephone lines will be installed and the concession for them will be divided into six zones. However, if the demand for telephones service continues to grow at the current rate, by 2001, twelve million telephone lines, not six, will have to be available.

The regulatory body which will play a vital role in telecommunications liberalisation, the NCC, was originally designed to consist of fifteen members appointed by the Cabinet, with proposals from the Minister of Transport and Communications. Five members were to be permanent,[10] while the other ten members were to be experts drawn from the telecommunications sector and other fields,[11] one of whom was to be chairperson. The proposal for the NCC was approved by the Cabinet on 23 June 1998[12] but the structure was changed from fifteen members to just eleven, comprising the Secretary General of the NCC as secretary of the committee, and another ten elected independent members. Whatever the eventual composition of the NCC, the TOT will have to apply for a licence and negotiate its terms with the NCC to ensure its own competitiveness and investor attractiveness.

Conclusions

From various possible approaches to restructuring and privatising the TOT, the most feasible integrated programme for ensuring that the TOT achieves its aim is to structure it as a customer-facing organisation, and to privatise it through public stock offering with international tranche. The TOT will need a strategic partner, both in the case of setting up a holding company or as a directly privatised company. At the same time, the TOT will need to convince the NCC to implement price-capping regulations as soon as possible, not just because it is significant for the TOT's profitability, but also because potential investors will expect a price-capping regime. In order to fulfil its missions of domestic market leader and public service provider, the TOT must be able to sustain its market share growth through more effective marketing and much higher operational efficiency. It is also important to change the TOT's culture from that of being a state-owned company to one of free enterprise, in the light of which, the TOT must compete, attract investors and fulfil its social obligations.

General concerns over the liberalisation of telecommunications in Thailand include the degree of customer-mindedness which will be involved, and the pricing and quality of services. Consequently, measures will have to be taken to avoid the problems that may arise changing from a state monopoly to a private-sector one. Because of the devaluation of the Thai baht and other Asian currencies, which resulted in heavy private sector debts and foreign exchange losses in most Asian countries, the strategic partner is most likely to come from the western world. Thus, it is only a matter of time before foreign investors and service providers will become major investors and strategic partners in Thai telecommunications businesses. The TOT should therefore adopt prudent tactics and strategies to attract the right strategic partner so that the privatisation process can be implemented with the best interests of the nation and in such a way that it can also fulfil its social obligations.

Notes

1 The author would like to express his heartfelt thanks to Professor Kjell A. Eliassen, Norwegian School of Management, for his kind encouragement and

support, and to Verona Christmas, Friedrich Schiller, University of Jena, and colleagues at the conference held at the Centre for European and Asian Studies in Oslo, March 12–14, 1998, for their comments on this paper. Due thanks are given to Telenor for their generous financial support.

2 TelecomAsia met the 1997 deadline.

3 A joint venture among Nippon Telegraph and Telephone Corporation (NTT), Jasmin International Plc, Loxley Plc, Phatra Thanakit Plc, and Italian Thai Development Plc.

4 Coopers & Lybrand, TISCO, Merrill Lynch, Skadden Arps Slate Meagher & Florm and Chula Unisearch.

5 This became the National Communications Committee (NCC). The Cabinet recently approved the establishment of the NCC as Thailand's regulatory authority.

6 Thailand Development Research Institute, 'Future Direction of the Communications Authority of Thailand,' September 1993.

7 Telegraph and Telephone Act in 1934, the TOT Act in 1954 and the CAT Act in 1977.

8 This was later increased by an additional 600,000 and 500,000 telephone lines, respectively.

9 Various instruments of global offering were discussed in Prasit Prapinmongkolkarn's paper presented at the Interregional Workshop on Development Project Financing, ESCAP, Bangkok, 25–27 June 1997. See also, J.F. Marshall and V.K. Bansal, *Financial Engineering*, chapter 17–18, New York Institute of Finance, 1992.

10 These were to be the Permanent Secretaries of the MOTC and MOF, the Secretary General of the NESDB, the Director General of the PTD, and the Secretary General of the NCC itself.

11 These ten members were to be governed by a system of rolling membership and to comprise three experts from telecommunications, two from the judicial profession, one from accounting and finance, one economist, one engineer, one manager, and one sociologist.

12 The cabinet renamed the NCC as the National Communications Commission.

Part IV

Technology and its consequences for industry

Knowledge about the technological possibilities (as well as the development to date) is crucial for the understanding of the regulatory challenges we are facing.

The chapters on mobile technology (Chapter 12) and future infocom systems (Chapter 13) both stress the interdependence between new technological possibilities and new lifestyles, characterised by high mobility and the demand for access of information independent of geographical position. In Chapter 12 Ulf Körner discusses, in particular, how future infocom systems will be characterised by four factors: broadband communications, mobility, wireless communication, and multimedia and internet technologies.

Christer Englund demonstrates in Chapter 13 how mobile services grow at an amazing pace, especially in Asian markets. The rapid speed of technological development and diversification necessitates a combination of economies of scale and differentiation in companies. Englund concludes that the consequence will be an upsurge of new niche markets, which will be functionally rather than geographically defined.

The building of the Information Society has consequences for the industry, where new models of value creation are needed to understand the functioning of the sector. In Chapter 14 Øystein D. Fjeldstad presents a model for thinking about how value is created in network systems. There is a tension between the opening up of the old monopolised industry and offering investment protection for the creation of new networks, and we might see a situation where it becomes paramount to allow firms to protect new investments made in diffusing new contract sets.

12 Future infocom systems

Ulf Körner

Introduction

Since the beginning of 1998 the established telephone system operators in Europe have been exposed for the first time in their history to competition in their core business, i.e. voice telephony. This means that they must be more efficient and show more consideration to their customers, as citizens now have the choice of accessing the most efficient, reliable and reasonably priced operator. The new competition is expected to bring jobs, growth and innovation to the citizens of EU countries. However, many of the traditional telephone administrations, not only in Europe but all around the world, are now collapsing, pushed by political, technical as well as social forces. The political forces lie in deregulation and privatisation based on a free-market ideology. Liberalisation is there to pave the way for the information society of the next millennium. Even if liberalisation is dictated by economic common sense, the tremendous technical and technological achievements within telecommunication and computer systems have, to a major extent, pushed this development.

Computers and telecommunications used to rank as separate fields, now they are moving closer and closer together – irreversibly. Today these two areas form part of a joint multimedia service platform only made possible by the digitisation of telecommunications and the networking of computer technology. During the last two decades we have seen tremendous developments within the computer and communication industry. The ever-increasing density on silicon, the increasing transmission speeds on fibre-based systems as well as twisted pairs, the revolutionary development in the wireless area and of course the Internet have all led to many opportunities for new service developments. The main technical forces are the innovations in fibre optics and microelectronics that have increased transmission capacities and processing powers considerably for the last fifteen years. Moore's Law holds that the processing power, at any given time, doubles every eighteen months or so, whilst the price of a given level of computing power decreases at the same dramatic rate. This development means that, even without liberalisation laws, it is impossible for an operator to maintain its former monopolised position.

Even where there exists a monopoly in a country, new operators will take parts of the market for themselves. For instance this happened to European operators many years ago, initally in the market for international calls. There were two reasons for this. First, international calls were, in most cases, subsidising national and local calls. With the rapid development of particularly optical fibre, the cost of carrying a call from Europe to the US was dramatically decreased and this consequently became a very lucrative market for competitors of the monopolists. Today it is, in many cases, not much more expensive to carry a call from Europe to the US than to carry a local call as, during the last couple of years, we have seen that the cost for carrying a call has become less and less dependent on the distance. In most countries local calls are becoming more expensive while international calls decrease in price. The second reason that competition started with international calls was, of course, that no national monopoly could prevent transport of telephony which took part beyond their own frontiers.

The current telecommunications market will change dramatically during the next decade. The change will be mostly towards the incorporation of new technologies as defined by the current and future Internet. With the term 'Infocom' systems, we often refer to new systems and services that will arise from the revolution of new communication technologies, and what will come out of the merging of communications and computing technologies with media, i.e. multimedia and broadcasting services. Many of these new services (which range from telelearning to online shopping) require broadband connections in order to transmit high-quality voice (sound in general) and video in real time. They will be moving along the so-called Information Super Highways (ISH), where these refer to telecommunication systems with vast transmitting and switching capacities. The term Information Super Highways arose originally from the Clinton National Information Infrastructure plan (NII), which draws up lines for the second-generation Internet. Today the initiative of the Clinton administration on the NII can be deemed as a success. This was seen clearly by the international efforts on the Global Information Initiative launched by the Group of Seven some years ago. The NII, lead by vice president Al Gore, is there to raise strategies for the next generation Internet, a network that should be 100-1000 times faster than that of today.

There are a couple of very clear trends when it comes to which technologies these Information Super Highways are built upon and which types of services they should forward. The key words for these Highways are: broadband, mobility, wireless, multimedia and Internet technologies.

Wireless systems

These systems will to a large extent be used by those who require to reach and be reached regardless of their geographical position. Thus these ubiquitous information and communication networks of tomorrow must provide mobility services to the users. Wireless access is one of the most important future technologies to provide this. Within the next few years, completely new demands will be put on the wireless systems. As individuals and companies change how and where they work, wireless end users will expect to have access to Internet or corporate intranets and LANs virtually everywhere. They will also expect the systems to handle video and other multimedia applications. The next devices to reside on wireless networks are commodity devices such as stereo systems, cameras and other household and commercial appliances residing in 'smart' offices and houses. These terminals and the services they will utilise require much higher bit rates than that of today's mobile telephone systems. Third-generation systems should support a substantially wider and enhanced range of services than those supported by second-generation systems. This enhancement includes interactive multimedia services. This naturally means that mobile telephony systems will be required to handle large amounts of high-speed data.

Already today, wireless computing and communication is part of the infocom revolution. The public cellular systems like the first- (NMT, AMPS, TACS) and second-generation (GSM, D-AMPS, PDC) mobile telephone systems were originally designed for voice, but are today also used for data and also to some extent for wireless Internet access even if the bandwidth offered is narrow. These systems show at present a significant penetration of the global infocom community, and of a large number of different terminals, not only mobile phones, but also laptop computers and digital assistants which are miniaturised enough to work as mobile terminals accessing these networks. In January 1998 there were more than 210 million mobile phones world-wide and we foresee that this number will grow to 850 million by the year of 2003. Besides these public mobile telephone systems, wireless LANs offering higher bit rates are already at hand, making mobile multimedia already a reality.

The wireless systems that we see today were designed under the assumption that the spectrum was very limited, and these systems were therefore designed with channels as narrow as possible. The second-generation mobile systems normally provides around 10kbps. Long before the third-generation systems (the UMTS or IMT-2000) are to hand, possibly two years from now, today's system will increase these present access rates by offering more than one 'channel' per user. In addition, many of the GSM operators plan to introduce the new GSM-standard GPRS (General Packet Radio Services) in their networks in less than two years from now. GPRS will give user-access rates of up to 384kbps. The next step will be the implementation of EDGE (Enhanced Data rates for the GSM Evolution), also known as Evolved GSM. EDGE is one way to make it possible for existing GSM operators to meet the requirements of next-generation wireless systems using the same frequency bands as today; 900, 1800 and 1900MHz. This will be possible to achieve with comparatively small upgrades of hardware and software.

About ten years ago the ITU formed a study group that was to evaluate and specify future wireless standards for the delivering of many new services like high-speed data and multimedia. These systems, the third-generation mobile systems, now go under the name of IMT-2000 (International Mobile Telecommunication). In Europe, the third-generation system is called Universal Mobile Telecommunications System (UMTS) and the standards for this system have just been established by the European Telecommunication Standards Institute, ETSI. The entire 'third-generation' discussion is all about evolution, not revolution. Today's second-generation wireless networks have provided the foundation on which third-generation services will be built, and these will protect the investment already made by operators.

Another factor is the desire to make more efficient use of the available radio spectrum. Each wireless network operator is allocated a specific set of frequencies within which its network must function. As more and more people want mobile phones, so it becomes increasingly difficult to accommodate them within the existing frequencies, even with new radio engineering techniques that boost network capacity. UMTS will give bit rates up to 384kbps for wide-area coverage and 2Mbps for indoor or certain other locations, including many enhanced services from narrow-band voice to wide-band real-time multimedia. There will be support for high-speed packet data for many Internet applications and real-time audio/video applications. The second- and third-generation systems will co-exist for many years to come and there will be roaming possibilities between the two systems. The enhanced services involve additional requirements on the fixed-network functions needed for mobility support. Meeting these requirements should be achieved according to an evolution path that capitalises on the investments, both currently in place and planned, for second-generation systems in Europe (e.g., GSM) while maintaining a system view.

Within the coming years we will see many satellite-based systems designed to enable users of hand-held wireless phones and other terminals to communicate with one another from any two points on earth. Already this year, two of these systems, Iridium and Globalstar, will be put into operation. Many of these systems will have a world-wide coverage while others will just cover large regions. Thus users will, for the first time, be able to communicate using one single terminal world-wide even in areas not covered by land-based cellular systems and where your 'own' cellular system does not exist. With the LEO-systems (Low Earth Orbit) like

Iridium, the introduced transfer delay will be quite acceptable, in the order of 10ms. The terminals for these systems are under development (some already exist), and even if the costs for these are quite high today, they will of course drop considerably in the years to come. The total system costs for these satellite-based systems are quite high, for Iridium more than US$5 billion, but even so, airtime charge per minute will in a couple of years from now exceed normal long-distance charges only marginally. Wireless will be one of the dominating access principles in the future. As the number of utilised frequencies increase, the severe bandwidth limitations disappear for there is plenty of bandwidth in the higher bands. However, the systems of tomorrow must still be designed for efficient use of bandwidth, as users will require 2Mbps, 5Mbps, 10Mbps or more locally to fully utilise mobile multimedia, entertainment and video in general. These systems must also be very cost efficient as they should offer mobile multimedia at a cost comparable to that of today's POTS (Plain Old Telephone Systems). As for POTS, these costs just cover the end-to-end connection and not the costs for the required multimedia services. The latter costs are of course subjects to the multimedia service providers. Wireless LANs for high-speed applications are here already today. We now plan for wireless LANs with very high capacities. In years to come private LANs could also be used as access systems for those wanting to communicate globally. With low costs, almost every PC connected to a network, a fixed network like an Ethernet or a wireless LAN, could work as a base station for many users that perhaps want global access. These local networks will then have connections to the networks of one or several public operators.

The introduction of GSM in Europe was one of the first and major initiatives to allow European users to really choose between different operators. When GSM was launched in the early 1990s at least two operators were given frequencies with which to operate in most countries. Of course, in most cases, the former monopolists operator was one of them, but the second operator was either a private company or a major operator from another country. Now, more than five years after the introduction of GSM in Europe we can see a diversity of operators, many of them with US companies as owners. It is evident that GSM has pushed the liberalisation of the European mobile telecom market, but more than this, it has also had a large impact on liberalisation of the fixed telecom market as well. From a user's perspective, the competition is there to lower the fees and to give better service. However, until now we failed to see a dramatic decrease of the tariffs; operators seem to compete more with giving good service to the users. With the introduction of GSM 1800 there is now a handful of different GSM operators in many countries, and this combined with the fact that GSM 1800 can carry much more traffic in densely populated areas, will undoubtedly lead to lower costs for the users. In a few years from now the tariffs for using GSM should not be higher than those for the fixed network today.

Broadband systems

ITU-T defines broadband systems as those providing switched connections of more than 2Mbps to end users, and equivalent, broadband services are those requiring at least this capacity. Today public systems, i.e. the PSTN (public switched telephone network), are not able to provide this capacity and thus most of applications today make do with less. However, many of the new services such as multimedia, switched video, high-resolution graphics and Internet surfing, as well as LANs, will require broadband connections. B-ISDN (Broadband Integrated Services Digital Networks) is a concept that was devised in the 1980s. These normally public networks should be able to handle all sorts of communications from narrow-band voice services of say 64kbps to any application requiring up to several hundreds of Mbps. ATM (Asynchronous Transfer Mode) has for a long time been seen as the transmission and switching technique to build up large public Broadband-ISDN systems that will provide users with broadband connections upon demand. These systems may give individual users hundreds of Mbps but also, and this is important, they can give users dynamic variable switching and transmission capacities according to the bit-rate variations of the applications. A multimedia connection requires high bandwidth when for instance a video is started, but a short while later, when the video is not being used, it requires less. This is not unique to ATM. Variable bit-rate is naturally provided by any system sending information in packets. When a high bandwidth is needed, more packets are sent per second, and when the need for bandwidth is lower, fewer packets are sent.

A great deal of effort by researchers, in terms of development and standardisation, has been extensively devoted to the ATM technology. In ATM-based networks, all information is transferred by dividing the digital bit stream into fixed-size packets (so-called cells). Each cell consists of five octets (each octet is eight bits) of a header and 48 octets of a payload (segmented information). The fact that all information is packed into fixed-size cells of a single format is one of the advantages of ATM networks compared to conventional packet-switching networks such as Ethernet and older X.25 networks. Moreover, the ATM network is a connection-oriented network by virtue of a notion of virtual circuits called VPs (Virtual Path) and VCs (Virtual Channels). Each connection is assigned its unique VP and VC identifiers, called a VPI (Virtual Path Identifier), and a VCI (Virtual Channel Identifier). At the ATM switch, cells are switched based only on VPI/VCI so that an overhead for interpreting cell headers is kept to a minimum. Thus, switching can be implemented in hardware because all information is transferred in fixed-size cells, and because cell routing at the switch is quite simple due to connection-oriented communication. For these reasons, the ATM technology can make gigabit-class networks a reality, which had been considered difficult with conventional packet-switching technology. Very cost efficient ATM systems can be built up, at least as a backbone network, and can meet various Quality of Service (QoS) demands regarding, for instance, delays, jitter delays and blocking of data, from very high demands to a 'best effort' service like in the Internet. In fact, different applications require different QoS. Real-time services like video and voice transmissions are very sensitive to delays in general, but even more to jitters in cell transmission delays. Many of these real-time services are, however, tolerable to small losses of information, especially if strong encoding methods are used. But other applications like data transfers are on the contrary very sensitive to cell losses and not at all sensitive to delays or jitter delays.

Today most of the larger operators run ATM networks even if there are relatively few users requiring 100Mbps single session connections. However, even if these operators carry among others Internet traffic in their ATM networks, the TCP/IP protocol suite used in Internet is not that compatible with the transfer mode used in ATM. IP networks built on Internet technologies are severe competitors to ATM networks. The high-capacity routers (these are the 'switches' in the IP networks) from Cisco and others are used to build up IP networks that are very cost efficient. This is definitely so for all sorts of access networks, where Gbit Ethernets running the IP protocol are most probably unbeatable when it comes to fixed local area networks, even if there are a number of ATM products at the market for LANs. Also, most future terminals will have at least parts of the TCP/IP protocol suite implemented and the applications they run will also respond favourably to TCP/IP-based connections. Also the wireless networks will to a large extent carry IP traffic. ATM networks will though have a substantial part of the backbone market.

If one can give users high-capacity connections in the networks, new services will naturally appear, especially as high-speed connections will be offered at prices compared to those of today's telephony. The multimedia services of tomorrow will to a great extent be built up on interactive video and the quality of that video will be limited only by the capacity of the networks. When new technologies give higher bandwidth, it will certainly be used. It is also important to point out that with packet-switched techniques like ATM and that based on IP technologies, the network resources are not used by the consumer at idle times during his or her connection. Thus the consumer will be charged only when he or she really sends or receives information, and not for the entire duration of the connection. It will almost be possible to have a constant connection to an Internet service provider, for example.

Internet

Internet is definitely here to stay for many years to come. It is not a new network and has been in existence for many, many years. However, it was not until web browsers like Netscape first became available, less than five years ago, that the Internet was really recognised outside universities and other research organisations. The Internet grew out of Arpanet, originally a research program by the US Department of Defense to build a packet switching network that was robust enough to withstand a nuclear attack. When Arpanet was set up in the late 1960s just a few educational, research and military sites were connected with which to build up an understanding of how this type of packet switched network could work. From those humble beginnings the Internet has grown to encompass millions of users and thousands of smaller networks.

Today the Internet and its communication protocol suite TCP/IP are not only well recognised within the telecommunications community but will be one of the major networks and protocols building up the 'Super Information Highway'. There are today more than 20 million computers all running TCP/IP connected to Internet, a network that is built up of tens of thousands of heterogeneous networks all using the IP protocol. We also find more than one thousand Internet Service Providers (ISPs) giving service to about 60 million users. There is no reason to believe that the Internet has reached the peak of its development. Its size doubles every nine months, according to BT. A recent report from International Data Corporation, expects the number of individuals and businesses using the Internet in Europe alone to grow from 8.9 million at the end of 1996 to 35 million by the year 2000. At this point, European Internet access revenues will be worth some $3 billion. Sales on the Internet reached US$21.8 billion in 1997. Based upon historical data and current Web growth, Web-generated revenues are predicted to exceed US$1.2 trillion by 2002. Mean monthly sales were over US$18.000 per site in 1997, up from US$4.200 in 1996 as web users became more accustomed to shopping online. Sales of US$1 million per month were not uncommon among leading sites in 1997. The upward growth of sales generated by the Internet is only just beginning in 1998.

Today's Internet suffers from its ability to give guaranteed Quality of Service particularly with regard to transfer delays. The Internet gives just a 'best effort' service, which means that when the network is highly loaded users have to cope with long delays, but also with varying delays during a session (often referred to as delay jitter). During the last few years there have been great efforts within the Internet community to come up with protocols that can handle the question of allocating transmitting capacities to individual users or at least to services requiring low transmitting delays and jitter delays. Protocols like the RSVP, a protocol that was proposed to handle these situations, have failed or at least have not been adopted by the Internet community. It is most likely that these situations may be solved by over-provisioning of Internet transmitting and routing capacities.

Many of the protocols used in the Internet, like TCP/IP, were developed many years ago and the growth of the Internet, as well as new applications like mobility, require new protocols. IPv6 (Internet protocol version 6) is one of these. IPv6 not only gives a large address space, needed because the address field in IPv4 is too short, but it will also facilitate mobility. Already today there is a lack of IP addresses and this need will increase as every terminal (in the very widest sense – stoves in each household, each power outlet, etc.) will require an IP-address. Mobile IP is another standard that will let users, with both wired and wireless access, move around from one access point to another and even from one network to another, without disconnecting a set up session. Mobile IP is an Internet protocol which enhances existing Internet protocols to be able to handle mobility.

The integration of wireless networks with the Internet, and especially with corporate Intranets, will revolutionise the way millions of people around the world conduct their business and use their leisure time. The Internet has the potential to serve as a common interface for a host of wireless applications, ranging broadcasting, tele-conferencing and distance learning. In particular, wireless Internet access offers new opportunities to increase access to education, to support fresh and innovative teaching strategies, and to help forge closer links among educational institutions, government, and industry.

Most telecom operators today feel threatened by Internet technologies. These operators might, in the near future, have a fixed digital infrastructure that is not competitive. However, public telecom operators stand to benefit from a number of opportunities offered by the Internet. Many operators have already tried to regain the initiative by building up Internet networks offering IP services, thus introducing the elimination of the substantially more beneficial traditional telephony. Many of the leading operators in the world will, within a couple of years from now, carry more traffic on their IP networks than on their traditional networks. And this is not only data traffic, but also real-time traffic like voice and video. Within, say, three to four years, half of the traffic carried by these operators might be based on Internet technologies.

The tremendous growth in the number of Internet subscribers and remote Intranet users illustrates the dynamic of this market. The TCP/IP protocol suite is expected to evolve into a communication platform for various applications: today Web and e-mail, tomorrow telephony and video services. It is not expensive to implement novel telecommunication services in IP networks, but they have to offer the same high quality as conventional telephony.

Some years ago, video on demand directly to the home was *the* service that motivated the building of new broadband-access networks. At that time, optical fibres to the home provided the technology that these networks were supposed to be based on. Today, we see a number of other technologies like broadband over the telephone copper cables (ADSL: Asymmetric Digital Subscriber Line) and over cable-TV networks etc. Today, we see that people's desire to have a fast access to the Internet from home will be one of the major forces behind the building of new broadband access networks. As the use of the Internet and its services grow, and this will surely be the case for many years to come, it will be of utmost importance for an operator to both carry this traffic and to act as an Internet Service Provider. This lucrative market will inevitably expand the competition further among established and new operators.

Conclusions

It is very clear that the future Information Super Highways will be built up of a variety of inhomogeneous systems and networks. We will see ATM networks form the backbone of these, sometimes carrying IP traffic, but also pure IP networks. The access networks will, to a large extent, be based on radio access. This is so for both narrow-band services like voice and for broadband services like video, data traffic and multimedia. However, the copper cables that have been the access cables for telephony ever since the first telephone systems came into use, will also be used for high-speed access to the backbone networks. New modem techniques that go under the acronym ADSL (Asymmetric Digital Subscriber Line) and similar will give users fixed connections of many Mbps. Thus over the telephone line, users may have video and telephony to the home and, at the same time, surf the Internet at high speeds. Also the cable networks, originally used for distributing TV channels to households are today used to provide high-capacity data connections. Moreover, power companies, traditionally delivering electricity to households, will use their networks to provide video, multimedia, data and telephony.

There are many reasons for the variety of new access networks that exist today. Some are the result of new technologies, but most of them are encouraged by the new liberalisation of the telecommunications market. Many of the old monopolists in Europe still rely on the telephone copper-cable access networks. For new operators it is very expensive to build up new access networks based on copper or fibre to the households. To reach these households via radio or existing networks like cable TV networks, or by power networks, is very cost efficient compared to the drawing of copper or fibre to the homes. Here liberalisation is providing momentum.

The Infocom systems of tomorrow will lead to dramatic changes in everyday life. Thanks to global networking, a third of all office workers will spend at least half the week at home working on their own computers. Also, since development projects are being carried out at different places simultaneously, innovation cycles are becoming shorter. When technicians in Europe finish work for the day, they send their data to their American colleagues, whose day is just beginning. Higher and continuing education will also increasingly take place at home. Virtual schools and universities will soon be a widespread phenomenon. Experts predict that by the year 2006 consumers will be ordering a third of their food and clothing with a click of a mouse.

Metcalfe's Law says that the value of a network is equivalent to the square of the number of nodes. In other words, as a network grows, the utility of being connected to the network not only grows with the number of users, but does so exponentially.

13 The global mobile market and regulatory aspects

Christer Englund

Introduction

The growth rate of the global mobile communications market has surpassed, by a substantial margin, any other form of communications except Internet- and WWW-based computer communication. The dynamics of the rapidly expanding markets is characterised by the exceptionally short life-cycles of wireless handsets and constantly decreasing prices. In the wireless network and service provision sector, the installed user base, as well as the number of new entrants, has soared all over the world. Under these circumstances, management of technologies, marketing, and regulatory regimes pose a great challenge to the equipment manufacturers, service providers and regulatory administrations. In this chapter we shall briefly consider the developments of the global wireless communications markets including its history and envisaged future directions with regard to standards and regulatory considerations.

Evolution towards personal communications worldwide

Although the cellular concept had been invented in 1947 by Bell laboratories, the technology was not ready for commercial exploitation until the microprocessor had been invented. Thus, the history of mobile cellular communications really dates back to the late 1970s, with NTT from Japan being the first to provide cellular services in 1979 (Rappaport 1996). Other forerunners of cellular telecommunications were the Scandinavian countries, which introduced analog cellular services in 1981–2 based on the common Nordic Mobile Telecommunications (NMT) standard. It took a few more years to launch the services in the USA in accordance with the US AMPS (Advanced Mobile Phone Service) standard. From the very beginning, the demand for cellular services has exceeded all forecasts, and been without precedent in the history of telecommunications.

NMT was followed by other analog (i.e. first-generation) systems in Europe, such as the Total Access Communication System (TACS) in the

UK and C-Netz in West Germany. The growth rate of wireless subscribers yearly exceeded that of fixed network lines by a significant margin, but it was not until digital GSM (Global System for Mobile Telecommunications), the first second-generation system, was launched for public service provision in 1992 that the market exploded. In the early days of cellular telecommunications, mobile stations were rather bulky and mainly used in vehicles. In the late 1970s, portable handsets were launched, which started to change the inherent nature of mobile communications into personal communications.

GSM was initially adopted only by European countries but soon spread world-wide so that there are now more than 200 GSM operators in over 100 countries. In the USA, the first digital system, DCS 1900, based on GSM technology was launched in 1995 by US Sprint subsidiary, American Personal Communications, and, after two years of operation, the number of subscribers exceeded 1 million. Commercial exploitation of the DCS 1900's strongest rival, CDMA (code-division multiple access)-based IS-95 systems, started in 1996. The start-up of TDMA (time-division multiple access)-based D-AMPS or USDC (US Digital Cellular), which was developed as a direct digital replacement for analog AMPS, has not progressed at the same pace. Now a full-fledged roll-out of these cellular systems based on three different standards is underway. Besides North America, IS-95 is spreading to countries such as China, Korea, Russia, and Chile. The Japanese Pacific Digital Cellular (PDC), launched in 1993, has been outstandingly successful, but only in Japan.

In the 1980s, so-called low-cost cordless phones, based on a simple analog CT-1 technology, were introduced. Despite the fairly modest quality of service, these gained a substantial market, particularly in the UK. However, its digital successor, CT-2, failed in the UK, bankrupting some of the operators before subsequently gaining success in Singapore and South Korea. In 1993, cordless phone systems or low-tier systems based on a common European DECT (Digital European Cordless Telecommunications) standard were launched and subsequently gained moderate success. The Japanese Personal Handy Phone System (PHS), however, which was introduced a year later, proved to be outstandingly successful. As a further refinement of PHS, the American PACS (Personal Access Communication System) standard was launched in 1996, representing the most modern cordless technology. At present, PACS is deployed in the US Virgin Islands and Taiwan (Wu-Jhy *et al.* 1996). Currently most cordless systems also support the reception of incoming calls with handover and roaming capabilities. Therefore, the distinction from macro-cellular high-tier systems is based on factors such as limited geographical coverage, vehicular use possible at lower speeds only, low-cost, simple short-range radio ports, and lightweight, simple and cheap handsets with excellent speech quality, low transmitted radio-frequency (RF) power, and low battery-power consumption.

Mobile satellite communications have served specific needs, such as maritime ones. Inmarsat was the first satellite operator to introduce mobile satellite services (MSS) in 1982 on a near-global basis. MSS are two-way voice and data communication services accessed by a user over a satellite link. Albeit many MSS satellites have been launched since then, the market has remained quite limited due to expensive bulky terminals, high service charges, and long transmission delays (Nourouzi 1997).

Mobile-phone market and market outlook

At present, the growth is concentrated on rapidly evolving digital cellular and Personal Communication Services (PCS) markets, the largest of which are GSM, including its derivatives DCS 1800 and DCS 1900 and CDMA-based IS-95, with versions available for both 900MHz and PCS bands, whereas analog cellular markets are on the wane.

When it all started in the 1980s, the adoption of the cellular telephone far exceeded the wildest expectations. Once supply appeared, a strong unsatisfied need turned into a very strong demand. The benefits of using mobile phones, such as better customer service, increased sales and more effective use of human resources, were great enough to justify the initial

Table 13.1 Major cellular and cordless systems around the world

Standard	Launched initially	Type	Geographic distribution	Frequency Band	Access Technology
NTT	1979	Analog cellular	Japan	400/800MHz	FDMA
NMT-450	1981	Analog cellular	Scandanavia, Europe	450–470MHz	FDMA
AMPS	1983	Analog cellular	Americas	824–894MHz	FDMA
C-450	1985	Analog cellular	Germany	450–465MHz	FDMA
E-TACS	1985	Analog cellular	UK, Hong Kong	900MHz	FDMA
NMT-900	1986	Analog cellular	Scandanavia, Europe	890–960MHz	FDMA
JTACS	1988	Analog cellular	Japan	860–925MHz	FDMA
CT-2	1989	Cordless	Europe, Asia,	864–868MHz	FDMA/TDD
GSM	1990	Digital cellular	>110 countries	890–960MHz	TDMA
USDC (IS-54)	1991	Digital cellular	USA	824–894MHz	TDMA
DECT	1993	Cordless	Europe	1.88–1.90GHz	TDMA
IS-95	1993	Digital cellular/ PCS	USA, Asia, Latin America	824–894MHz 1.8–2.0GHz	CDMA
DCS 1800	1993	PCS/cordless	Europe	1.71–1.88GHz	TDMA
PDC	1993	Digital cellular	Japan	810–956MHz 1429–1513MHz	TDMA
PHS	1993	Cordless	Japan	1895–1907MHz	TDMA
PACS	1994	Cordless	USA, Taiwan	1.85–1.99GHz	TDMA
CDPD	1993	AMPS overlay	USA	824–894MHz	FH/packet
DCS 1900	1994	PCS	USA	1.85–1.99GHz	TDMA

Source: Rappaport, 1996

high equipment and service costs. Besides sales and marketing personnel, physicians, social workers, lawyers, company executives, service personnel and truck-drivers were among early users, i.e. users for whom it was vital to be attainable 24 hours a day, regardless of their whereabouts. Subsequently the cellular phone has become a commodity affordable to almost any consumer.

Cellular phone penetrations and future directions

At the start of 1998, cellular phone subscriber penetrations ranged from 37 to 43 per cent in Finland, Norway, and Sweden, with Denmark and Iceland lagging slightly behind. Israel, Japan and USA came next with 27, 22.8 and 20.3 per cent. Other European countries with penetration levels of more than 15 per cent were the UK, Italy, The Netherlands and Luxembourg. New European subscribers amounted to 20 million in 1997 raising the average penetration to 14.4 per cent. By the end of 1998, the European subscriber base (currently around 55 million) is expected to grow by slightly more than 20 million new users.

Cellular phones have diversified enormously during their eighteen years existence. Low-end consumer terminals with only the basic functions have emerged, as well as high-end smart phones with versatile mobile computing capabilities, and all kind of variants falling between these extremes. The main competitive factors have been size, overall weight, fashionable design, user-friendliness, operational usability, i.e. stand-by and talk time between battery recharging cycles, and value-added features such as voice mail and call forwarding. A broad range of different accessories plays an important role for most users. The availability and affordability of mobile phones have increased significantly due to rapidly slumping prices and value-added services, such as prepaid calling-card services. The latter services have opened new market segments, such as temporary usage (business travellers, tourists etc.), users lacking financial credit, users not wanting to sign up and low-usage users using the phone for emergency calls only. At present, multiband and multimode terminals are being launched in the marketplace. Such terminals have a market opportunity, particularly in the US market, where only AMPS provides an almost nation-wide coverage.

General market trends world-wide

According to the latest statistics, the installed base of mobile-phone users amounts to 200 million subscribers, including cellular and cordless-phone users. In 1997, 101 million mobile phones were sold, of which around 30 per cent were replacements for existing subscribers (Nokia expects this number to grow to 50 per cent by 2000) and the overall annual mobile-phone market was worth US$25bn. Regardless of a continuous price

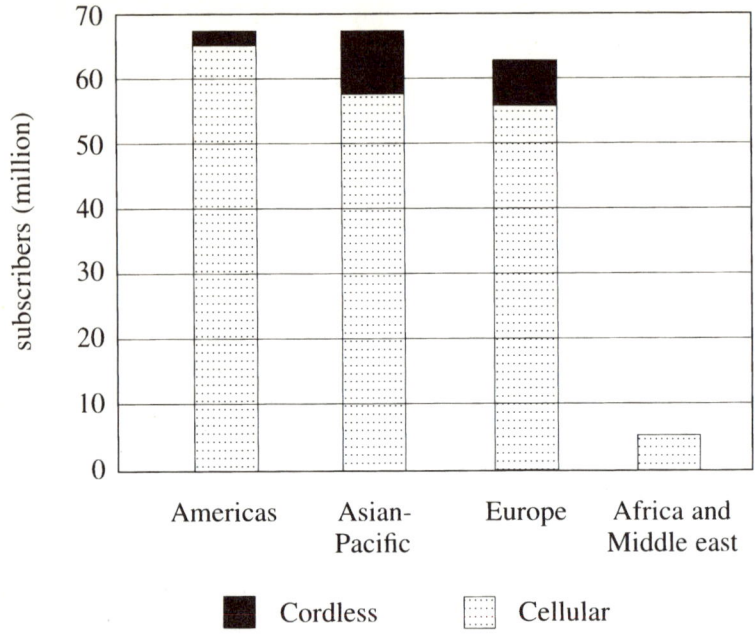

Figure 13.1 Installed base of mobile-phone users. January 1998
Source: Strategis Group 1997

erosion, the market volume is expected to rise to over US$50 bn by the year 2000.

The number of mobile-phone subscribers in Europe is around 55 million. For US markets, the number is slightly higher (Cellular Tele-communications Industry Association Web site, 1998), while those of Latin America consist of around 11 million subscribers, with a growth rate of 40–50 per cent. The US market has grown approximately 25–30 per cent annually, which is much less than in Europe (40–50 per cent annually) and in the Asian-Pacific area, where the growth rate has been notably higher (60–80 per cent). In February 1998, the installed base of Asian cellular phone users was close to 60 million and that of cordless-phone users was around 10 million. Africa, including the Middle East, greatly lags behind the other market areas.

In conclusion, the number of mobile-phone users world-wide in January 1998 was around 210 million total. Figure 13.2 illustrates the projected subscriber base in 2002 when, as can be seen, the total number of mobile-phone subscribers is expected to reach 500–600 million.

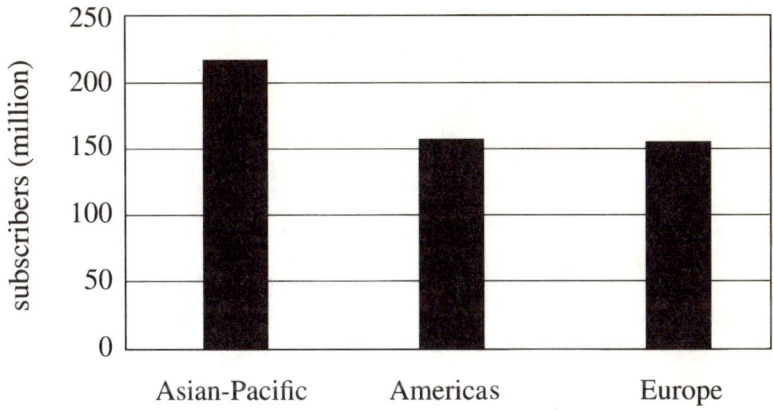

Figure 13.2 Projected mobile-phone markets by 2002
Source: Strategis Group

Asian-Pacific market and market outlook

Influence of the Asian financial crisis

The telecommunications market of the Asian-Pacific area will have a deep impact on the evolution of wireless communications world-wide. According to Coopers & Lybrand, the projected telecom investments in the area are a staggering US$331bn during the period 1995–2000. The predicted Chinese share alone is an enormous US$120bn (Thomas 1997). The Asian financial crisis is expected to slow down the growth somewhat and, since Japan and China are in a dominant position, the decline will depend decisively on the economic development of these two heavy-weights. At present, investments have slumped in countries such as Indonesia, Korea and Thailand due to substantial devaluation of their currencies. The fact that the overwhelming portion of cellular phones, as well as digital cellular network equipment, are imported goods, is also an important factor. Only Korea is better placed, because of its semi-conductor and domestic CDMA-based cellular manufacturing industry. The current market size of the Southeast Asian countries most affected by the financial crisis is relatively low.

India, the other Asian country with a large population, has so far escaped the same financial turmoil. In contrast to China, the Indian mobile-communications market is still in an early phase, reflected by a user base of one million users. In the medium and long term, the potential is huge but it cannot be unleashed rapidly because of regulatory hindrance and the undeveloped market.

In sum, the outcome of the latest developments in Asia on mobile

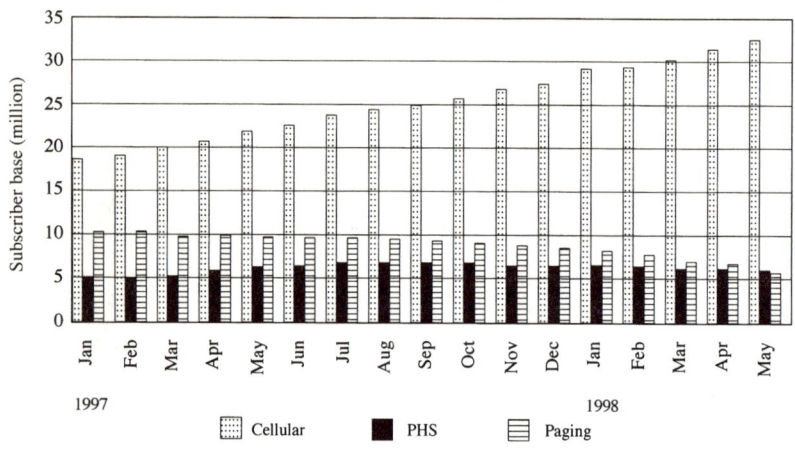

Figure 13.3 Evolution of Japanese mobile markets in 1997–98
Source: Ministry of Post and Telecommunications Japan

markets is presently obscure. In the worst case, ramifications could be fatal for the whole world economy and shame all the forecasts. A more likely alternative is a temporary slowdown with relatively little influence on the long-term growth trend.

Chinese and Japanese cellular markets: explosive growth

At the end of 1997, the shares of the Chinese and Japanese mobile-communications markets of the total Asian-Pacific market were 23 and 48.8 per cent respectively. However, the enormous long-term potential of the Chinese market makes it by far the most important. Regardless of a slump in growth, the Japanese cellular market grew by over 50 per cent in 1997, resulting in a penetration of 22.8 per cent by the year's end.

In contrast, by the end of 1997, the Chinese cellular phone market was only 1.1 per cent of the total population. Yet the growth rate in 1997 was around 100 per cent, amounting to 6.78 million users, and market studies (McClelland 1996; Strategis Group 1997) have predicted that by 2002, China will outstrip all other countries, including the USA. In a recent press release, Ericsson expected the sales of mobile phones in China to total between 12 and 14 million in 1998. Given that 25–30 per cent are replacements of analog mobile terminals, the predicted growth of the subscriber base falls within the 8–10 million range, suggesting a growth rate of 60–75 per cent. The confidence of leading manufacturers in the Chinese markets is apparent. Recently Motorola established a CDMA

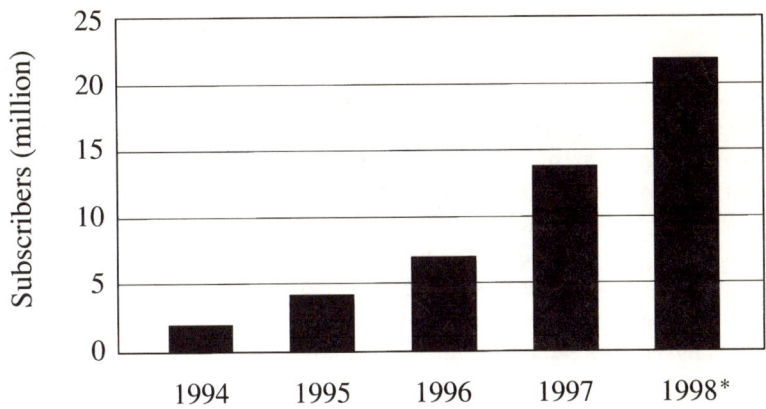

Figure 13.4 Evolution of cellular markets in China
Source: MPT of China *projected

plant in Hangzhou as a joint venture with two Chinese companies. AT&T
Bell Labs have also set up R&D facilities both in Beijing and Shanghai,
and Nokia has done the same in Beijing. The research is, among other
things, focused on wireless local-loop (WLL) technology, which is a clear
signal about the future expectation of the prime WLL market.

Cordless systems markets and demographics

As far as the other East-Asian countries are concerned, Hu *et al.* (1996)
emphasise that there is a market need for low-tier systems, such as PACS.
These countries, in particular Hong Kong, Singapore, Taiwan and Korea
are also likely to act as market drivers for the Chinese market. Taiwan has
already decided to provide PACS for wireless local loops in 1997 and a
public PACS network in 1998 (Wu-Jhy *et al.* 1996). Recently, China has
announced that it will adopt both PHS and PACS for WLLs. Therefore,
there are very strong signs that China and the other Southeast Asian
countries will play an important role in the deployment of PACS. There
is, however, a snag in this scenario. No supply is yet available and the
market opportunity of PHS and PACS is threatened by cellular systems,
which are enhancing their competitive advantage. Macro-cellular systems,
such as DCS 1800, with a relatively small cell size, are becoming strong
rivals to PACS and PHS, although high access fees have slashed the
profits of the latter (Strategis Group 1997) which means that PHS is not
ready to encounter tough competition just now. The terminal subsidising
policy adopted by PHS operators further undermines their ability to
respond to price competition. As macro-cellular systems support much

wider geographical areas and vehicular operation at relatively high speeds, attractively priced cellular services would, therefore, beat the cordless ones in both versatility and utility.

The Chinese urban population (approximately 350 million people) represents most of the rapidly growing purchasing power. In urban areas, cellular networks are being launched in large quantities. This is a natural course of development because of the huge supply of terrestrial wireless networks based on regional cellular standards. However, cellular networks are not suitable for meeting the communication needs of all user groups. In particular, low-income workers and young people look for paging or cheap mobile-phone services. As the social status of a user improves, they migrate from a pager to a cellular phone and from a cellular phone to a smart phone. Some analysts characterise this process as the 'food chain'.

In Japan, PHS was first adopted by young people with an above average social status. The market research of PHS user profiles in Japan indicated that a typical PHS-user is a young male, well educated, and with an income well above average (Ishii 1996). The PHS handset is acquired basically for private use, while Japanese companies as a rule provide cellular phones for their employees and pay the service charges. Fashionable design of the handsets and low service charges were major factors encouraging private use. Half of the PHS-users had a PC of their own, which is more than twice the average 20 per cent PC penetration in Japanese households. These demographic results suggested a paradigm shift towards low-tier wireless systems and nomadic lifestyles. Now the recent decline of PHS indicates that the PHS user profile is also changing to low-income users. In addition, the business market of PHS has not yet taken off in Japan. Availability of dual-mode phones supporting both PHS and PDC is important for this market segment. The decline of PHS has not been investigated yet but it seems that the unexpected downturn is not a temporary slide. Complaints about bad quality of service (QoS) suggest that the PHS operators have had problems in managing the extremely rapid growth. PHS image as a yuppie phone service has also faded due to heavily subsidised PHS phones. This policy has now started to backfire, because many users have rejected PHS in favour of PDC, the latter one having higher status-symbol value. However, it is premature to draw too far-reaching conclusions let alone to judge the utility and future of low-tier systems based on the latest PHS market developments. Cellular systems maintain their position as a high-end solution for nomadic users, whereas cordless systems serve low-income users and young people, and act as a replacement for the fixed local loop. The latter is an incumbent market, which may grow heavily in the near future, particularly in China, India, Pakistan and other densely populated countries with undeveloped subscriber copper networks.

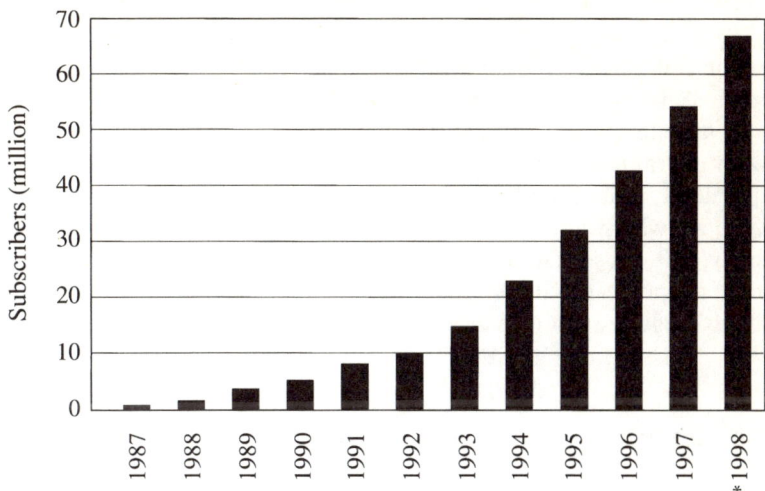

Figure 13.5 US mobile-phone users
*estimate

US and European cellular phone markets

The growth rate of the US mobile-user base has slowed down gradually (see Figure 13.5). Furthermore, the US cellular markets differ significantly from those of Europe and Asia. According to the 1995 CTIA survey, 57 per cent of US cellular phone users use their phone for outgoing calls only and one third used it only in emergency situations. We lack respective data from Europe and Japan, but it is likely that personal safety plays a minor role in the decision-making of Japanese and European consumers. The lack of prefixes specific to wireless networks has profoundly influenced the US markets because a mobile subscriber will be charged for the incoming calls. The law prohibits charging a POTS user for a mobile terminated call under circumstances when the access number cannot be distinguished from a normal local telephone number, since a flat rate is commonly applied to local calls. This is probably the main reason for the high number of users using the mobile phone for outgoing calls only.

The available market research studies (Meyers 1997) suggest that low service charges, wide geographic coverage and sound quality are the most important factors boosting the adoption of mobile phones. Therefore, subsidising terminal prices at the expense of high service charges, a policy widely adopted among US service providers, does not meet users' expectations. Subsidising cellular phones with service charges and charging recipients also for incoming calls have contained the diffusion and kept the utilisation rate at a fairly low level of 125–150 minutes per user per month, roughly half the average monthly cumulative call time in Europe.

This may also explain the high number of users in the USA who use their mobile phone mainly for outgoing calls. Usually this user group has got a pager for call-back request messages. In North America, the geographic coverage is fuzzy, as seen from the end-user perspective, due to fragmented mobile markets and different standards. One particular system does not guarantee operation in all places of the continent. Users moving around need a dual-mode phone or at least a pager to be attainable anytime, anywhere.

Finally, all these factors are likely to retard development of US markets, despite rapid deployment of versatile digital PCS services keeping the average growth rate at a notably lower percentage than in Europe and Asia.

Evolution towards third generation systems

Mobile data communication markets

Currently, mobile data communications constitute only a fraction (2–2.5 per cent) of the total wireless communications market, but this share is likely to soar in the near future due to increased demand and new technical developments. Most of the existing mobile data markets concentrate on the USA, currently dominated by proprietary systems ARDIS (Motorola) and RAM MOBITEX (Ericsson), and lately CDPD, an overlay technology of AMPS. They support data transfer at only relatively low bit-rates. According to the market forecasts of Giga Information Group (Blodgett 1997), by the year 2000, the number of US mobile data users will increase from 1 million (1996) to 9 million, which is close to the 9.9 million projected by the Yankee Group. The Web and e-mail are widely considered to be the killer applications for high-speed wireless data.

The reason, then, for the slow take-off of mobile data in the USA, as well as elsewhere, is a fragmented market due to lack of common standards and application protocols. However, the situation will soon change as leading manufacturers of mobile phones have decided to develop jointly a standard for wireless application protocols (WAP) together with application and service providers. This will enable economies of scale for mobile-aware data applications.

In Europe, circuit switched GSM data at bit-rates up to 9.6 kbps and Short Message Service based on GSM signalling channels are being deployed. The development path from GSM to third-generation systems goes through GSM phase 2+ (Blodgett 1997; Berg 1996; Hämäläinen 1996). The European Telecommunication Standards Institute (ETSI) has issued standards on HSCSD, high-speed circuit switched data, GPRS, general packet radio service in GSM, and wideband GSM (EDGE,

Enhanced Data rates for GSM Evolution) as Phase 2+ extensions. Actions have been undertaken in the USA to develop respective extensions for EIA standards IS-54 (Hooper and Sicher 1996) and IS-95 (IS-95A, IS-95B, and IS-95C) (Emmett 1997). The Internet and forth-coming interactive digital television have activated the need for an asymmetric data transfer with high-speed reception capability. The tech-nology for meeting these needs is cheaper and simpler than full-fledged 2-way high-speed communications. Wideband downlink data on demand is the core service of low-earth orbit (LEO) satellite-based Teledesic (Stuart 1996). Cordless systems are now capable of offering data access of a much higher speed to the Internet than the cellular systems. Therefore, rapid kick-off of wireless data services and markets might enhance the market opportunity and competitive edge of PHS and DECT against their strongest rivals, the cellular systems, but time is running out.

Although European companies such as Ericsson and Nokia are very strong in terrestrial mobile systems, especially in digital technologies, their Achilles heel is the IP technologies. Therefore, they need to establish joint ventures with US companies to develop the next generation fast packet radio technology. Since the third-generation systems will encounter very tough competition from the existing digital mobile systems, an evolutionary approach is more likely than a revolutionary one (Berg 1996). The key factors steering the migration will be:

- versatility of services with high quality and integrity conforming to those of the fixed network to meet the needs of different markets
- seamless interoperability with the applications and services provided in the existing wireless and wireline networks including the Internet
- increased bandwidth, in particular for downlink
- more efficient modulation and flexible bearer capabilities for air interfaces to improve spectral efficiency and enable high traffic den-sities
- improved security and advanced functional capabilities, which bring additional value to a user
- improved audio and video coding technology fit for low bit-rate channels (e.g. MPEG-4)

The long-term technological development is likely to concentrate on WCDMA-based systems in accordance with the forthcoming ETSI third-generation standards.

Mobile satellite systems

The market share of personal communication satellites is relatively small compared to terrestrial systems. Nevertheless, a number of ambitious projects are underway and satellites intend to increase their market share substantially. However, the European Commission has expressed its concern at the modest European commitment to LEO and intermediate circular orbit (ICO) mobile satellite technologies and systems (EU Action Plan: Satellite communications in the Information Society).

Integrated access based on wide-area overlay networks

Currently, no single wireless technology exists which would be fit for diverse operational conditions. Therefore, a combination of different technologies is needed, even after migration to third-generation systems, leading to the conclusion that multi-mode operation, in some form or another, is inevitable if the user's expectation of being accessible anytime anywhere, is to be realised. This would mean utilising the virtues of each technology, which is of course economically difficult. At one end we have satellites as wide coverage high-tier systems and at the other, Wireless LANs and low-tier cordless systems with limited coverage and low mobility (Madani 1996; Noerpel 1996). On the way to a global standard, all the systems mentioned above need to be integrated seamlessly into one functional entirety. The fundamental idea of the third-generation-systems architecture described above is demonstrated by a wide-area overlay network of the Berkeley University Daedalus project led by Professor Randy Katz (http://www.cs.berkeley.edu/~randy/Daedalus.html). In third-generation systems these technologies are expected to merge in such a manner that users can access wireless services anytime, anywhere, and at a reasonable cost, both in terms of end-user equipment and service charges. However, depending on circumstances, the accessed mobile system, available bit-rate, service variety, and QoS may vary. The resemblance with the flexible multifunctional-network concept included in the ITU system architecture for IMT-2000 is obvious.

Standardisation of third-generation systems

Standardisation work for IMT-2000 is a huge effort, which is underway in the ITU-R Task Group, TG8/1 and, for UMTS, in the ETSI Sub-Technical Committee SMG5. In the USA, a wideband CDMA (WCDMA) initiative called MediaOne has gained wide support. In January 1998, European countries reached a compromise based on two competing European proposals. Subsequently, the European Parliament has also given its support to the agreed concept, which relies mainly on WCDMA technology being used on paired frequency bands. The TDMA-based part will be used on single-frequency bands only. The ETSI proposal has also gained wide support in Asia, and among US GSM operators. The agreement was a remarkable success for European wireless industries and equipment manufacturers. There is no doubt that the set of UMTS standards, soon to be developed, is the strongest candidate for IMT-2000 and will gain superior world-wide market dominance, regardless of the US position. The final decision will be taken within the ITU in the autumn of 1998.

Implications from rapidly developing technologies and markets

Rapid development of core technologies, turbulence of the services market, increasingly tough competition and the short life-cycles of handsets, pose a great challenge to all-important sub-areas such as IMT-2000 standardisation, regulation, service provision and wireless terminal distribution and marketing channels.

The anticipated enormous diversification of user equipment creates the need to combine economies of scale with differentiation, i.e. a set of features customised to specific user needs. The same requirements are valid for services: mass-produced, cost-effective horizontal services need to be complemented by vertical applications tailored under user control to meet their individual interest profile. This trend will reflect inexorably on service provision and standardisation. A large number of new enterprises are expected to enter the service-provision markets, which aim at specialising in value-added niche markets. It is likely that the predicted course of development will enforce the National Regulatory Authorities (NRA) to separate access network provision from service provision to ensure balanced conditions and sound market development. The standardisation needs to be accelerated and modularised in alignment with decreasing life-cycles of new services.

The Internet phone revolution, which is expected to cause a shake-out in telephony, is likely to do the same in the wireless office domain as well. Signs of this trend are already visible as Nokia introduced its Wireless Intranet Office concept in the Hannover CEBIT fair in March 1998. A promising market opportunity is envisioned for Intranet-based wireless phone systems, which make use of IP- and LAN-based infrastructures. In the Nokia concept, GSM voice packets are conveyed over packet switched Intranet trunk lines to other GSM handsets and PC-based Internet phones. This technology is expected to provide an alternative to PBX systems with superior functionality and cost-effectiveness.

Regulatory framework for service provision

Need for regulation in wireless telecommunications

Past experiences have indicated that regulation should be kept to a minimum to let the market mechanism function properly and encourage competition. However, in a number of countries, a jungle of regulatory obstructions hamper competition and free entry to service provision, underpinning the incumbent operators' actions to protect their formerly exclusive rights for service provision. The general secretary of the ITU, Pekka Tarjanne, emphasised in a recent interview that the role of the ITU is to promote minimalist regulation, i.e. only those things should be regulated that really need to be regulated, and governments should stay out of the whole business (Cadwalader 1997). MIT professor Jerry Hausman has investigated the economic implications stemming from the Federal Commission of Communications' (FCC) regulatory actions and claimed that the FCC's indecision over allocating spectrum for AMPS in the early 1980s delayed the provision of cellular services in the USA by years, causing extremely large losses in consumer welfare (Hausman and Tardiff 1996). The foundation for a just licence allocation policy is that all licensees are treated equitably and free from any anti-competitive practices without undue delays. However, violation of these principles is not uncommon. For instance, in 1994 the European Commission intervened in the Italian government's licensing policy when a mobile telecom licence was awarded to Telecom Italia for free, whereas a fee of 750 billion lire was imposed on another entrant for a respective licence (Waverman and Esen 1997).

From the beginning of 1998, the ONP directive, including full liberalisation of voice services, came into effect in Europe. Official delays were granted to Greece, Ireland and Luxembourg, while the process of liberalisation has only progressed slowly in Austria, Belgium, Germany and Italy. While the EC directive serves as an overall policy guideline, national governments have to take appropriate action to establish a regulatory framework in their own countries to set prices and to stimulate competition under non-discriminative and equal terms (Waverman and Esen 1997). Kiessling and Blondeel (1998) argue that such measures are not effective enough to enforce competition. Therefore, they suggest that an independent European Regulation Authority, comprising representatives from NRAs, should be established.

The EC (Commission Directive 96/2/EC) has identified the need for regulatory actions in the following basic areas: licensing, terminal equipment, allocation of frequencies and numbers, service provision, network infrastructure, interconnection and interoperability with other networks, and universal service. Licensing policy should encourage competition by allowing free entry of licensees without imposing discriminative eligibility requirements. Globalisation of service provision has created multinational alliances, which implies that national frontiers no longer limit service areas. Leite *et al.* (1997) emphasise that MSS operation, versatility of service offerings, and functionality, such as international roaming, call diversion etc., reveal complex regulatory issues which require a high degree of co-ordination between NRAs, network operators and service providers. Therefore, a common international regulatory framework is needed for IMT-2000, in order to harmonise existing national regulatory practices. This work should be prepared by the ITU. Licensing is inter-twined with frequency allocation policy and service provision. Interoperability with other networks covers both other wireless networks (roaming etc.) and the fixed network. The regulatory framework should include general guidelines for steering roaming and interoperability agreements, the details and terms of which are for the market to decide. A numbering plan with prefixes unique for each wireless operator is essential for creating equitable conditions for service provision and furthering sound market evolution. Kiessling and Blondeel have claimed that the current regulatory framework of the EU does not optimally promote free competition and policy objectives for open service provision. For instance, the ability of NRAs to limit the number of licences on the grounds of scarcity of radio frequencies and numbering resources in favour of incumbent operators, restricts competition. Other problematic areas are the lack of an EU-wide transparent and harmonised cost-accounting system, as well as harmonised interconnection rules. For these reasons, Kiessling and Blondeel suggest that and an EU-wide licensing system and harmonised interconnection rules should be established. Promoting these ideas is also important for the sound evolution of third-generation mobile systems markets.

As a result of the lack of competition in local telephone business, the terms of providing transmission lines by an LEC to a wireless operator also need regulation. In Japan, NTT has collected healthy access fees for PHS lines, cutting the profits of PHS operators. Freedom to sell terminal equipment, and to use a terminal in any compatible system world-wide, are important objectives. Wireless universal service does not exist yet but needs to be catered for as a realistic possibility.

Frequency allocation issues of mobile systems

The radio spectrum is a valuable and scarce natural resource. The explosion of the digital cellular market has created a huge demand for frequencies, particularly in densely populated metropolitan areas of large markets such as the USA, Japan and China. New markets are envisaged due to the uptake of WLLs and other applications of low-tier systems. Under these circumstances, lack of radio frequencies may severely hamper the creation of a competitive market. Therefore, there is an urgent need to unleash new frequency resources for mobile communications, and to make effective use of the spectrum. The bandwidth required for a speech channel has decreased constantly due to technical advances and, at present, a half-rate channel of GSM consumes only one quarter of the bandwidth commonly allocated for radiotelephone systems before the cellular age.

Regardless of many bandwidth saving innovations, foreseen multimedia applications require a considerably wider bandwidth than ordinary speech. The expected rapidly growing demand for radio spectrum cannot be satisfied without allocating much higher, still unoccupied, frequencies for envisaged wideband services. For instance, two huge mobile satellite projects, Teledesic and Skybridge, share a 500MHz frequency block from the 28GHz band. WARC-92 of the ITU had allocated a frequency block of 230MHz from the 2GHz band (1885–2025, 2110–2200MHz) for IMT-2000. ITU has identified an additional block of 60MHz for satellite components of IMT-2000. The European Commission has reserved the bands allocated for IMT-2000 for UMTS.

The frequency bands allocated for IMT-2000 are currently occupied in some countries, for example in the USA for PCS systems, which is likely to hamper, more or less, the adoption of IMT-2000 on a nation-wide scale. Therefore, satellite-based third-generation wideband systems have better market opportunities on the American continent. For these reasons, the USA will probably choose its own course regardless of the forthcoming ITU-T resolution on third-generation technology.

The licence, i.e. the right to use a dedicated frequency band for the provision of wireless services, strongly influences the competitive environment. Due to bandwidth limitations, a free entry to the market may not be possible. In lucrative markets, the number of service provider candidates bidding for the available bands, is likely by far to exceed existing resources. Lotteries, i.e. random selections, used earlier as a just means to allocate spectrum rights, proved to have some serious drawbacks, such as checking the eligibility of hundreds of applicants, and a lottery winner making undue profit by selling the rights to a third party. For example, in 1989, an obscure alliance won the lottery of cellular phone frequencies for the Cape Cod area and subsequently sold the spectrum rights to Southwestern Bell for US\$41 million (Macmillan 1994). Later, Congress amended the Communications Act, 1993, in such a manner that allowed the FCC to open competitive bidding for exclusive spectrum rights, in particular for providing wireless services to subscribers on a commercial basis (Day and Trang 1997).

The forerunners of legislating spectrum auctions were New Zealand (1989) and the UK (1990) (Macmillan 1994). In the USA, the auctions based on open bids (English auction) have not only turned out to be a goldmine for the US Treasury, but they have been highly successful in US markets. English auction offers two distinct benefits compared to other options, such as sealed bid auctions:

- The process is more informative for the bidder and generates higher revenues for the seller
- The bidders having the highest use-value for frequencies will be identified (Macmillan 1994)

Auctions have downsides as well. Usually the spectrum rights are allocated for lengthy fixed periods of time, say seven to fifteen years. This leads to a very rigid status quo, which cannot accommodate rapid technological evolution. Therefore, the probability of inefficient utilisation of scarce frequency resources becomes higher. In addition, an auction may backfire if there are few bidders, i.e. no real competition materialises, whereas under fierce competition, auctions tend to overprice the spectrum rights. At present, auctions have not gained much support within EU countries as far as UMTS spectrum allocation policy is concerned, and the idea of sharing a common pool of frequencies between contending service providers has been rejected by European industry because of doubts as to whether it was technically feasible. Therefore, how the Commission will allocate UMTS spectrum rights remains unresolved (CEC: Strategy and Policy Orientations with Regard to the Further Development of Mobile and Wireless Communications (UMTS)).

Nevertheless, the allocation of UMTS and IMT-2000 spectrum rights is a crucial issue for future market developments and service uptake. A sound principle is that ownership of spectrum rights is awarded for a price corresponding to their economic value. Even if an auction does not guarantee this, particularly likely when there are only a few bidders, auctioning seems the least of evils in many European countries. To date, only the UK has adopted the auctioning policy.

Regulation of network interconnection and roaming

Besides spectrum rights, a wireless service provider needs digital transmission lines for interconnections between different sub-systems and gateways to the fixed network. Without any regulation, a local exchange carrier (LEC) having a monopoly could deny such interconnection or could dictate the prices in favour of its own subsidiary acting as a rival wireless service provider. To combat such predatory pricing practices, the US Congress included stipulations in the 1996 Telecommunication Act that require LECs to make agreements on terms that are just, reasonable and non-discriminatory. A regulatory framework should insure that competing wireless operators can rent lines on equal terms: the same applies to roaming agreements.

Regulation aspects of mobile satellites

Mobile satellites with world-wide coverage face a regulatory problem because approval needs to be gained from every country. Since many countries of the Third World lack a regulatory framework completely, this is very difficult. Also, the lack of frequencies allocated for MSS is becoming a problem. WARC-92 (World Administrative Radio Conference) allocated a 32MHz block from the 1.6–2.4GHz band for MSS, and the FCC decided that it can only support five systems, having already licensed three (Iridium, Globalstar and Odyssey; Nourouzi 1997). Although reservations have been made for MSS at the 2GHz band, shortage of frequencies at lower microwave bands is obvious. Spectrum is available mainly in much higher frequencies such as the 28GHz Ku-band employed by Teledesic and SkyBridge, but at the expense of higher cost, taking into account the technological state-of-the-art. Free circulation and trans border use of terminals is essential. The proper body for co-ordinating regulatory and policy issues on world-wide basis is the ITU.

Conclusion

The average growth rate of the global mobile markets is a staggering 40–50 per cent. For the time being, it is difficult to predict the impact of the Asian financial crisis on wireless services and equipment markets and, hence, the developments of the Japanese and Chinese markets are crucial. At present, the growth rates are 40–50 per cent in Japan and 70–80 per cent in China so that the most likely outcome is a temporary slowdown with relatively little influence on the long-term growth trend. The Chinese market is predicted to become the largest in the world by 2002, and also a driving force of low-tier systems needed for WLLs, wireless universal service, wireless PBX and Centrex. On a world-wide scale, GSM will dominate the cellular market, but IS-95, the strongest challenger of GSM, is likely to seize a lion's share in the USA, Latin America, and in some specific Asian countries, such as Korea. The uptake of third-generation systems is expected to start around 2002, but a common world-wide standard seems unlikely. The current standardisation procedures need to be upgraded in order to issue standards rapidly enough, otherwise the market opportunity may be lost. Mobile satellites will challenge terrestrial systems, but it is premature to assess the competitive advantage of mobile satellites, although they probably will mainly address the market segments of international business travellers and telephony services for rural areas of the Third World. Mobile data communications still only represents a fraction of the total market, but a rapid growth is envisioned in the next few years. It is also expected that mobile data markets will be driven by nomadic lifestyles, proliferation of notepad PCs, a new generation of wireless information appliances, high-speed Internet connectivity, applications such as e-mail, Web browsing and multimedia games. The WAP concept is likely to create system- and vendor-independent open markets for mobile-aware applications, bridging the gaps in the existing value chain. The transition to third-generation systems requires an effective regulatory framework on a world-wide scale to provide balanced conditions for service provision. Key areas for this are cross-border licensing, allocation of spectrum rights, and rules for interconnection, cost accounting and roaming. The enormous speed of development and diversification of both services and end-user equipment create the need to combine economies of scale and differentiation. As a consequence, a range of new niche markets of value-added services is expected to emerge.

14 The value system in telecommunications[1]

Øystein D. Fjeldstad

Introduction

Deregulation and technological innovation are driving dramatic changes in the global telecommunication industry. Investors, managers, public policy-makers and policy-enforcement officials have potentially different perspectives on the challenges and opportunities created, reflecting different objectives and vantage points. Regulators and public policy-makers are looking for governance regimes that promote efficiency, low prices and quality services, whereas telecommunication industry investors and managers are looking for profits and long-term competitive advantage. Actual industry performance will result from the actions and reactions of the different players, with both intended and unintended consequences. This chapter considers the perspective of the telecommunication firm seeking competitive advantage in a free market, and uses the Value Network model (Stabell and Fjeldstad 1998) to analyse value creation, industry structure and strategies of firms in the emerging tele-communication and mediations services industries.

The Value Chain (Porter 1985) has been the dominant model for characterising value creation and analysing competitive advantage, the latter defined as the ability to earn above normal profit (Barney 1991). The Value Chain model is based on the assumption that competitive advantage is found in the activities that a firm performs, and describes the manufacturing firm as creating value in a series of activities that transform inputs into products. However, profitability also depends on the attractiveness of the industry in which a firm operates. Suppliers, firms in the industry (producers), and customers all contribute to the value of the product as it passes through the extended Value Chain or Value System (Porter 1985). One can think of the firms along the extended Value Chain as co-producing the end product and the value created is assumed to be distributed among the co-producers. The Five Forces model (Porter 1980) is the dominant tool for the analysis of industry attractiveness which is seen as resulting from the collective bargaining power relative to suppliers and customers, the intensity of competition, the threat of new entrants and the threat from producers of substitutes. A firm can have a competitive advantage within its industry either in the value of its products or in the efficiency of its production (Porter 1980, 1985). The aim of regulation is to ensure both efficient and innovative industries (SEC 1996).

Assessing the firm from either the managerial or the regulatory perspective requires appropriate models of value creation and industry structure. Stabell and Fjeldstad (1998) have suggested that there are three distinct ways in which firms create value based on three underlying technologies (Thompson 1967):

- The Value Chain, which models firms using a long linked technology to make products
- the Value Shop, which models firms using an intensive technology to solve problems
- the Value Network, which models firms using a mediating technology to link customers

Firms within these broad industry categories share strategic properties and frequently co-produce value. As an example of the latter, consider the close relationship between banking and telecommunication in the provisioning of Internet-based electronic banking. Banking, Internet, and telephone are all mediation services. We propose that regulation should be specific to the three categories outlined above and as general as possible within these categories.

Telecommunication, banking, insurance, stock exchange and transportation are all examples of industries in which the firms use a mediating value-creation technology, and thus are modelled by the Value Network. The Value Chain model and the related Five Forces model (Porter 1980) do not reflect the strategic logic of mediators. In particular, the models fail to incorporate positive network externalities both as a source of competitive advantage and as a barrier to entry and innovation.

The competitive moves and positions attained, as a result of the current European liberalisation effort, may not be in line with the long-term objectives of telecom regulators. The presence of strong positive externalities requires large initial investments that may prove difficult to recover. On the other hand, the externalities may also lead toward monopoly once critical market share is reached. While the focus currently appears to be on opening established monopolies, the regulatory regimes must also consider the unique potential barriers to innovation that face mediators.

The value network applied to telecommunication[2]

Value networks[3] rely on a mediating technology (Thompson 1967) to link clients or customers who are or wish to be interdependent, such as telephone companies, insurance companies and postal services. The mediating technology facilitates exchange relationships among customers distributed in space and time. The firm itself is not the network, rather it provides a networking service.

The term value 'network' also emphasises that a critical determinant of value to any particular customer is the set, or network, of customers that are connected. Therefore, the value of a communication service depends on with whom it enables the customer to communicate.

The value-creation logic of mediators

Modern society is characterised by a complex set of actual and potential relationships between people and organisations. Linking, and thus value creation, in value networks is the organisation and facilitation of exchange between customers. The linking can be direct, as in a telephone service linking two or more parties in a call, or indirect, as in insurance, where one customer is not linked directly to another customer, but indirectly through a common pool of funds. The main distinctive attributes of a mediating value creation technology (Stabell and Fjeldstad 1998) are reviewed below.

Mediators act as club managers

One can think of managing a mediating firm as managing a club, whereby the mediating firm admits members that complement each other, and establishes, monitors and terminates direct or indirect relationships among members. Supplier–customer relationships may exist between the members of the 'club', but to the mediating firm they are all customers. By acting as an intermediary, bilateral interactions between the mediator and its customers are used to enable multilateral interactions between customers. Control of membership is via contracts which commit both the customer and mediating firm to a mutual set of obligations. Contracts specify price and actual obligations of both parties, and are also required to service 'on demand' mediation requests (which can be randomly distributed in time and space) efficiently. Service value is a function of demand side positive network externalities. Adding one more customer to a network directly affects the value of the service to other customers. (Katz and Shapiro 1985; Bental and Spiegel 1995). 'A positive consumption externality (or network externality) signifies the fact that the value of a unit of the good increases with the number of units sold' (Economides 1996) In telecommunications, each new customer added to the network provides for one more possible connection.

Value is derived both from service opportunity and from actual service

The customer may receive value from the value network without ever actually invoking the mediation service. Mediators typically charge customers separately for the linking opportunity and the actual use of linking services in terms of activities performed and capacity utilised. A subscription fee implies a commitment to servicing potential customer requests for the mediation service.

Mediation activities are performed simultaneously at multiple levels

A concurrent and layered set of activities is required for the efficient servicing of random need for mediation between a large number of customers. Service is only possible within a network of contracts with other customers and over an infrastructure that hosts the mediation between them, even if servicing individual customer transactions clearly involves a sequential set of activities. The simultaneous and layered performance of activities implies strong reciprocal interdependence between activities (Thompson 1967). Therefore standards are critical for the co-ordination of this reciprocity. Failure to synchronise activities may lead to a breakdown of the system, as when too many service requests bring a telecommunication system to a standstill.

Standardisation facilitates matching and monitoring

Standardisation enables the mediator to match compatible customers and to effectively maintain and monitor the interactions between them. Standardised addresses, e.g. telephone numbers, are used to direct mediation and to monitor the interaction for billing and accounting.

There are distinct life-cycle phases of rollout and operation

Positive network externalities introduce unique strategic challenges. A new service has relatively low value to its first customers, whereas costs are typically highest in the introduction phase. However, because the value of the service is dependent on who else adopts it, it may be difficult to target customers on an individual basis. Consequently, in many cases it is impossible to levy a realistic charge for the service or necessary equipment in this initial phase, leading to 'give away strategies' seen in areas such as cellular communications, browsers for the Internet and electronic cash cards. In other words, the rollout process manages the value of the service.

The industry value system consists of layered and interconnected mediators

Mediators frequently co-produce services in a layered system where the services of one mediator are provided over the network of another mediator. For example, network operators deliver the infrastructure for service providers in telecommunication who in turn serve as the communication infrastructure for payment services. Exchange relationships offered by a mediator can extend beyond its immediate customers to customers of other mediators. This leads to interconnected mediation networks. Interconnection is in some cases provided by firms that mediate between mediating firms. In summary, the business value system in a mediation industry is potentially a set of co-producing, layered and interconnected networks that enhance the range and reach of the services provided.

Telecommunication is the canonical mediator. What kind of mediator is a telecommunication service provider? The basic telephone service provides direct mediation between customers where the telephone number provides the basis for connecting and billing customers. Historically, delivery of the service meant establishing a direct, point-to-point link between clients. New technology (such as the Internet) has opened for more asynchronous and indirect (store-and-forward) mediation links.

Digitalisation, the use of programmed technology and other new technologies, have also opened up telecommunication service provisioning. These new technologies not only allow a much wider set of mediation services (voice, data, video) to be offered, but have also made the establishment of a more layered and a more distributed mediation service structure possible (Vialle 1998). As a result, we can no longer simply refer to the telecommunication mediator, but must consider an ever-increasing range of co-producing and more or less integrated mediation service providers, such as brokers, broadcasters and specialized mediation service providers.

Representation of value creation

The value network diagram is a tool for describing and analysing the competitive position of a specific mediator (see Figure 14.1).

A value configuration model distinguishes between primary and support activities: Primary activities are those that create value for the customers, which in the case of telecommunications are those involved in selling and providing a service. The primary activity categories capture the distinctive aspects of a mediation value creation technology. Support activities are engaged to perform effectively the primary activities of the firm. The primary activities of the value network are:

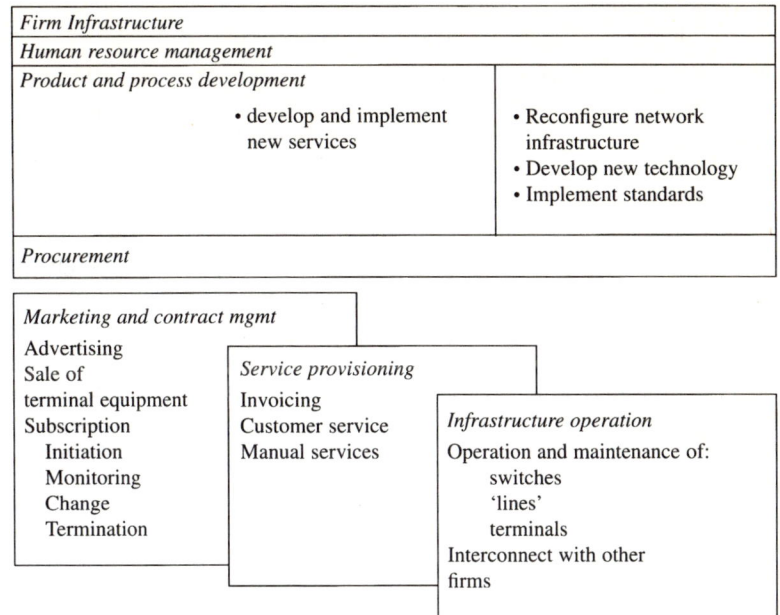

Figure 14.1 Value network diagram for POTS provider

- *Marketing and contract management,* which consists of activities associated with inviting potential customers to join the network, the selection of customers allowed to join, and the initialisation, management and termination of contracts governing service provisioning and charging. Contracts and contracting activities vary across networks, and the greater the commitment involved between mediator and customer, the more extensive the contract and contracting process, e.g. an application for a house loan is more extensively processed than an application for a telephone service. The marketing and contract management activity category in the Value Network differs from the sales and marketing activity category in the Value Chain in that selection of customers is as important as attraction.
- *Service provisioning,* which consists of activities associated with establishing, maintaining and terminating links between customers, and billing for value received. The links can be synchronous, as in telephone service, or asynchronous, as in electronic mail service or banking. Billing requires measuring customers use of network capacity both in volume and time.
- *Network infrastructure operation,* which consists of activities associated with maintaining and running a physical and information

infrastructure. The activities keep the network in an alert state, ready to service customer requests.

Figure 14.1 shows the activities for a generic telecommunication service provider (POTS). The three primary activity categories overlap in order to underline the concurrent inter-activity relationship across primary activity categories.

To summarise, some key points from the Value Network model are as follows. First, although some of the activities might be outsourced, a mediator includes all primary activity categories. Second, although costs are often considered to be primarily linked to heavy investments in infrastructure development, investments are equally associated with building up and maintaining a customer contract set. Third, in a setting with rapid technological innovations, the mediator's customer contract set may be the main value element in the mediator's offering. All these points apply to mediators in general but very much to telecommunication firms in particular.

Determinants of competitive advantage

Value configuration analysis is based on the assumption that competitive advantage is found in the activities that a firm performs. The cost and value behaviour of activities is determined by structural factors defined as drivers of cost and value (Porter 1985). Mediators offer value to their customers, both through the access option and the actual use of services. Hence, cost and value must be associated with both. The key drivers of cost and value in the value network model are reviewed below.

Scale and composition drive both cost and value

Value network services are characterised by demand side economies of scale resulting from positive network externalities (Katz and Shapiro 1985; Economides 1996). The value of the service to existing customers increases with each new customer added to the network. Network externalities exist for a variety of products, such as microprocessors, consumer electronics and software (Wade 1995). Mediation services offered by value networks represent an extreme case because the dependency among customers is the main product delivered. The services of a value network mainly deliver the customers' opportunities to exercise those dependencies. Size and composition of the customer base is therefore the critical driver of value in the value network.

Telephone service represents an extreme case of positive network externalities. Each new customer added to the network allows for one more possible connection. When network externalities are present, the value of the service provided is affected by the characteristics of customers that join the network (Bental and Spiegel 1995). Common industry standards are a prerequisite for inter-network connections virtually increasing the size of the firm. The evolution and diffusion of standards is therefore critical in the exploitation of demand side scale economies (Antonelli 1992).

Scale also affects accessibility in that a geographically extended network requires an extended infrastructure. This adds value because the number of access points available to customers increases (Domowitz 1995). Thus, while the externality effect of scale directly increases the value of the network to the customer, the size effect, in the form of increased accessibility, lowers the customer's costs of using the mediation service.

Capacity utilisation is closely related to scale and is both a cost and value driver, for while it may reduce unit costs, high capacity utilisation may also reduce service levels. Consider the case of heavy load for a communication service: it becomes difficult to get a line. Hence, in the value network, capacity utilisation is both a cost and value driver, while it is primarily a cost driver in the chain.

Inter-activity linkages affect synchronisation and dimensioning of simultaneous activities. First, both geographical coverage and capacity must reflect the composition of customers that are members of the network. Second, service provisioning capacity must be co-ordinated with customer recruitment and diffusion of new services. Stated differently, the switching and line capacity of a telephone company must reflect the customer base.

Learning takes place at both the firm and the industry level. Learning improves activities and interactivity co-ordination. In addition, inter-firm learning (spill-over) is critical in the diffusion of standards as the ability to interconnect value networks increases size and hence value.

A horizontally interconnected and vertically layered industry

Multiple firms contributing to the creation of a service or a product form a co-productive value system. In a co-productive[4] value system, implicit or explicit bargaining among the contributors takes place in the distribution of value. As noted earlier, in mediation industries co-production takes place both between horizontally interconnected firms and between vertically layered firms.

Unique structural properties of the telecommunication mediation industry following from the patterns of horizontal and vertical co-production, are critical to understanding the nature of competition. This chapter therefore develops in more detail the nature and implications of the distinct relationships that are involved.

Horizontal co-production

A telecommunication firm mediates between customers. It carries traffic between its own customers and between its own customers and customers of other telecommunication firms through interconnect arrangements. Similar interconnect arrangements are also found in other mediation industries, e.g. inter-bank transactions in banking. The horizontal co-production structure is illustrated in Figure 14.2.

Historically, telecommunication firms were restricted to national geographical domains within which they had exclusive rights to provide service. Interconnection enabled communication to take place between customers of distant, non-competing firms. Consider a simplified model of two firms, A and B, that serve discreet customer segments C_A and C_B. The value to one particular customer of subscription to firm A's services is a function of A's subscriber base and of characteristics of the service that A provides. Thus,

$$V_{Ai} = f(S_A, SC_A)$$

Where: V_{Ai} is customer i's value of subscription to the services of firm A S_A is the subset of potential customers in A's area C_A that subscribe to A's services SC_A is a composite variable of service characteristics: quality of object mediated (voice, images etc.), mediation capacity and accessibility.

Many European telecommunication providers charge customers per call in addition to a fixed subscription fee. A particular customer's willingness to pay for subscription reflects both the value of being able to receive calls and the value of calling less the variable charges incurred for making calls.

Interconnecting the services of A and B increases the value of

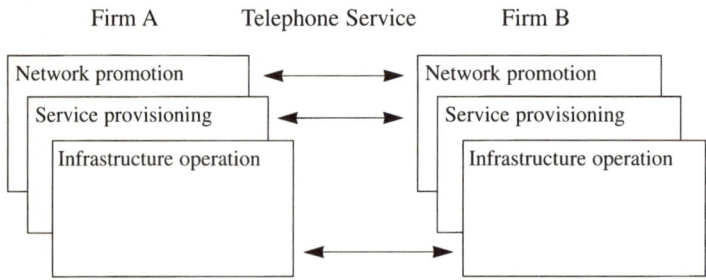

Figure 14.2 Horizontal co-production, co-operating and competing networks

subscription to either firm's services. With interconnect, the value for one particular customer of subscription to the services of firm A is a function of the combined subscriber sets of firms A and B and services characteristics that are compatible and interoperable between A and B. Thus,

$$V_{Ai} = f(S_A \cup S_B, SC_{AB})$$

Where: S_B denotes the subset of C_B that subscribes to the services of firm B SC_{AB} denotes compatible and interoperable services of firms A and B.

The value of each subscription is enhanced by interconnection. Firms A and B can cover their costs of interconnecting by charging their respective subscribers. In a Five Forces analysis (Porter 1980), A and B can be considered as both suppliers and customers of each other for interconnects. If S_A is larger than S_B, then the value of the interconnect is higher for B than for A because of network externalities. Firm A could thus be expected to look for ways of exploiting its bargaining power.

European liberalisation changes the simple industry model in which co-producing firms act solely as suppliers and customers of each other. In the liberalised telecommunication market, firms that co-produce through parallel interconnections (Brennan 1997),[5] also compete for the same customers. The customers of each firm still benefit from the increased value of subscription that the interconnection provides, but the relative value of the two services is equalised. Simplified, a customer facing a choice between firm A and firm B, assuming equal subscription prices, is concerned with the ratio V_A/V_B. An interconnect agreement that seamlessly integrates the services of A and B, in which the price of inter-firm connections equals intra-firm connections, makes $V_A/V_B = 1$. The above interconnect agreement eliminates the possibilities of any real differentiation between the firms, and the firms can only compete on cost. Mediators thus face a trade-off in parallel interconnect decisions: increasing service subscription value through interconnection with competitors reduces differentiation-based competitive advantages. This type of trade-off will, in principle, be present in all industries with positive network externalities. Mediation industries are unique in that competitors are also the main co-producers. Network externalities therefore effect both the distribution of value appropriation between co-producers and the rivalry between competitors.

In a number of mediation industries, firms that act as mediators between other mediators arise. In some cases the inter-intermediary is transparent, as when the end user buys all services from an integrated access provider. In other cases, the inter-intermediary is explicitly identified. British Mercury is an example of an early long-distance service

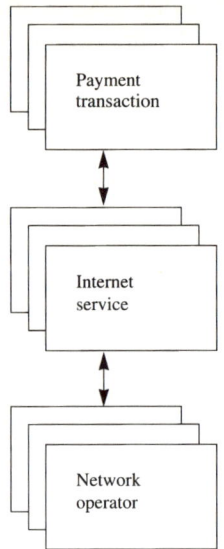

Figure 14.3 Vertical co-production

provider in Europe, and the US has had general long-distance operators since deregulation in 1984.

The presence of inter-intermediaries both carries traffic and communicates prices on inter-network communication. As an example, Least Cost Routing (LCR) operators provide low-cost international connection. They are forcing the prices of inter-country calling in Europe down toward transmission costs plus national interconnect, by using national interconnect arrangements to terminate calls.

Vertical co-production

Mediators also co-produce value in a layered structure in which the network services of one mediator serve as a platform for a higher-level service. Multiple mediators serve the same customer, but at different levels. This is depicted in Figure 14.3.

Consider as an example the case of electronic payments over the Internet (see Figure 14.3). Currently, the telecommunication network serves as the platform for the Internet service, which in turn serves as a platform for the electronic payment service. The customer typically subscribes to all three and they are used concurrently to produce the desired service, i.e. electronic payment. There are firms offering services for profit at all three levels. All the firms are mediators and mediate the transaction jointly, but at different levels in the value system.

The banks mediate payments by credibly exchanging transactions between accounts, the Internet service providers mediate standardised packets between IP-addresses, and the telecommunication operators mediate bit streams between phone numbers, so that, together, the firms co-produce the payment transfer service in a layered business system. In the simplest case, with only one firm at each level, the firms supply the same customer with different components of the service. The firms have a strong impact on the value of each other's respective services, but they are not, in a conventional sense, suppliers or customers of each other. There is, however, one exception. The Internet Service Provider (ISP) must subscribe to the telecommunication service although the ISP may never originate traffic, and thus pays little. Similarly, the bank subscribes to the Internet service. Each firm pays its lower level only a fraction of the value created in the co-production of their respective services. It is the common customer of all three networks that typically pays each contributor separately. In fact, the value creation may run counter to the nominal flow of economic transactions between two firms M and N. Nevertheless, a telecommunication network has little value unless there are customers who need to exchange information. A higher-level service such as the Internet increases the value via the increased need, and thus raises the willingness to pay for traditional telephone subscription, as has been seen in most European countries. As such, the Internet provider could be considered as much of a supplier to the telecommunication operator as the reverse. The layered nature of co-production in mediation also renders the traditional concepts of supplier and customer relationships insufficient for describing and analysing relationships between mediators.

The layered co-production can be described in the following manner: two firms, M and N, co-produce a layered service when both firms mediate between the same customers and the mediation service of M requires that the customers of M also subscribe to the services of N, $S_M \subset S_N$.

$$V_{Mi} = g(S_M \subset S_N, SC_M, SC_N)$$

The value for one particular customer of subscription to the services of firm M is a function of firm M's subscriber base and the characteristics of M's services. However, use of M's services over N is constrained by subscriptions to N, $S_M \subset S_N$. The value of M's services also depends on the characteristics of N's services, which are a necessary complement of M's service. In a number of actual and potential co-production cases, the services may also be provided independently. The co-produced service can be provided to the common customers of firms M and N, i.e. to the customers in $S_M \cap S_N$. For example, the Internet is not the main carrier of bank transactions, but Internet banking may be available to customers of both a bank and an Internet service provider. When M offers similar services over multiple lower-level networks, the relationship between M's services should be treated as horizontal interconnects discussed above. For example, if electronic payment transfer is only possible between customers who have explicitly subscribed to this service, then there is no interconnect and the value of this service is lower than if customers can use the service for all their transactions. Another example is provided by interconnects between regular mail, electronic mail and fax. Such interconnects increase the value of each of the services, and the networks over which the services are made available.

Conversely, the value for a particular subscriber to the services of N depends on what N can be used for, broadly defined, the functionality of N's services. M's services represent potential uses for N's service and hence strongly impact on the value that a particular customer could gain from subscribing to N's services. Thus, there is a reciprocal dependency between the services of M and N.

To summarise, N's services provide a network over which M's services can be provided. Enhancements to, and extensions of, N's services increase the quality and coverage of M's services. M's services provide applications for N's services. Enhancements to and extensions of M's services increase the value of N's services. There are thus strong incentives for M and N to co-operate because their collective efforts greatly enhance the value of their respective services. The unresolved issue is, however, how M and N will share the value generated. There is potentially high asset specificity (Williamson 1979) associated with either firms investment in their services, although less for N than for M, and both firms are highly dependent on the quality of the services of the other. However, there are limited direct transactions between M and N that can be used as a mechanism for distribution of the co-produced value.

The bargaining power afforded by a producer over a supplier in the traditional Five Forces model is in part contingent on exclusive access to the customer. This may lead to a willingness of distributors to develop a market for a product with the knowledge that exclusive access to the customer base offers a source of investment protection. In layered co-production between mediators, customer sets have to overlap. Across-layer vertical integration is thus greatly simplified relative to the traditional supplier–producer structure of manufacturing industries. An implication is that we should expect unstable co-productive relationships and thus reluctance toward committing resources, even if the combined Net Present Value (NPV) of investments is positive. The ease of vertical integration creates a game in which the value from resource commitments may quickly be redistributed between the layers. Mergers and joint ventures may be perceived as the only way to secure investment protection.

Unique properties of service innovation in mediation industries

Value is embedded in multi-level, multi-point exchanges between customers in mediation industries, and service innovations mirror this structure. We propose to categorise innovations as horizontal, single point functional and vertical. In addition, technological hardware and software innovations may enable innovations in the mediation service, which are important as they enable the other types of innovations that we describe below. However, technological innovations are increasingly achieved by equipment suppliers rather than by the mediators. The discussion below, therefore, focuses on the concept of innovation in mediation rather than innovation in mediation equipment technology.

Horizontal innovations

Horizontal innovations change: either the object mediated, the means by which the object is mediated, or the entities between which the object is mediated. A completely new mediation service changes all three aspects. The rollout of a cellular phone network is an example of such an innovation even though it initially appears mainly to change the way voice calls are mediated; on closer scrutiny, it also affects between whom calls are mediated. The mobile phone is a personal instrument with personal contracts replacing household phone lines. Also, although the object change at present appears minor, the quality of voice transmission is changed, and in several European countries there is an early diffusion of text messaging.

If calls could only be made to other cell phone owners, the value of the first cell phones would be low due to strong network externalities, but because the object, voice calls, remained basically the same as for regular telephony, it was possible to interconnect the two services and overcome the externality issue. The key to the initial value of the innovation was thus to be found in the interconnection to a juxtaposed network. Managing the value of a new mediation service entails the management of juxtaposed networks that increase connectivity through virtual extensions of the services and the firm (Domowitz 1995).

Single point functionality innovations are those where the value of the innovation does not depend on adoption of the innovation by more than one customer. Potential horizontal innovations may appear as single point innovations by interconnection with partially compatible networks and thus be easier to diffuse. The full potential of horizontal innovations may subsequently be realised as the network of subscribers increases beyond critical mass. At that point, full cost or functionality advantages may be realised within the new network.

For example, cell phones may initially provide easy access to the general phone network, but at a relatively high cost. However, in a fully developed contract set, like those found in Norway, Sweden and Finland, potential cost benefits in voice traffic may be passed on to consumers in competition with traditional PSTN. Similarly, ISDN is currently diffused mainly as a faster access to the Internet. When critical mass of ISDN subscription is reached, the potential value of point-to-point ISDN services will increase.

Vertical innovations

A vertical innovation implies the development or adaptation of sub- and super-networks relative to an existing mediation service. A sub- and super-network diffusion may itself constitute a horizontal innovation, but to the existing network it represents a vertical innovation.

Super-networks, defined as mediation services provided over an underlying mediation service, add functionality to the underlying network. Super-network innovations require either mutual adaptation between different level mediators or co-ordination around standards that define the relationship between layers. At the technical level, the ISO/OSI (Tannenbaum 1981) model provides such a standard, subject to specific implementation. There is also a need for standards at the commercial service mediation layer to reduce the need for transaction specific investments by the potential participants in a layered mediation economy.

An example of a vertical innovation is telephone banking using personal card reader telephones and digital services in the switching system. Such an innovation both increases the functionality of the phone service subscription and the functionality of the banking service. The innovation also requires investments both by the telephone operator and by the bank.

How will the investments made, by either higher- or lower-level mediators, be protected in the market under a free competition regime? As mediators, both the bank and the telecommunication firm face similar challenges. Should the new functionality in the telecommunication network be available exclusively for the operator that installed the terminals, or the bank, or should it be made available for use by all other telecommunication firms and banks at non-discriminatory rates?

Sub-network development shares the properties of super-network development but the vantage points of the actors are reversed. Seen from an existing mediation level a sub-network increases the availability of the service. A service provider who can offer fixed line, cellular or cable-TV-based services has a broader reach, and thus higher service functionality, than one that is limited to a single service platform.

Regulating competition and co-operation in telecommunication and related mediation industries – pursuing the missing links?

We have argued earlier for a horizontal and vertical co-production industry structure in mediation industries.[6] While there are strong externalities in both the horizontal dimension and in the vertical dimension, although of different kinds, both require strong co-operation between firms in the maximization of value. Firms may only be willing, however, to invest in diffusing new innovation services if they are allowed to protect their investment. On the other hand, too much freedom to protect investments may lead to monopolies because the network externalities could make it difficult to establish new firms when incumbents have a high market share.

Horizontal links – connecting to competition

In the horizontal dimension there are positive demand side externalities that require high up-front investments, which in the Value Network model is called network promotion and contract management. In addition, there are high infrastructure investments to establish a valuable and viable network. Likewise, the value for subscribers is further enhanced when firms representing additional customer networks join the network; however, allowing firms without customer networks to join at marginal cost may create free-rider problems.[7] A regulatory regime that demands symmetrical interconnect charges cannot solve this problem, as can be illustrated by a simple example with an incumbent firm A and a new entrant B. Firm A has invested heavily in developing the network in an initial situation where the service had low value and has deferred cash flow until the network becomes valuable by giving away terminal equipment and charging below cost subscription fees. B is a new operator, with no customers, who wants to join. Without interconnect, B is faced with A's initial problem. B has no valuable service until a critical mass of customers can be developed. If a low interconnect charge is imposed on A then B will sell A's services without A's investments in the contract set. If A chooses a high interconnect charge (above marginal cost) then B has a strong incentive to under-price customers with heavy traffic termination such that A will pay B for terminating calls. Customers of firm A pay for service and for service opportunity, i.e. capacity of the network. With the wrong interconnect incentives, B may engage in activities that puts pressure on A's network in a way that reduces overall value to A's customers, while only gaining a marginally higher income on interconnect.

Networks may, due to positive externalities, converge toward monopolies and thus some regulation preventing this is required. On the other hand, a regulatory regime that rewards free-riders on incumbents initial network promotion and capacity investments may stifle further invest-ments due to uncertain cost recovery. Thus, there may be a need for regulatory practices that accomplish the equivalent of patent protection and copyright for the initial capital intensive network promotion activities, to ensure competitive mediation industries.

Vertical links – getting a slice of the action

Layered services exhibit strong mutual complementarity. For example, Internet services increase the value of regular phone services, whereas improvements in the telephone system, such as upgrading from PSTN to ISDN, improve the value of Internet service. The complementarity represents a second and vertical form of externality. Whilst the value of the complementary services is driven by positive network externalities, the value of one service layer also drives the value of other layers. Establishing a super-ordinate layer requires mutual adaptation or strong open standards.

New service layers can create both monopoly rent and free-rider situations. First, the monopoly situation is reviewed. A network provides its customers with both access opportunity and services. In the network operation, costs are mostly fixed at a given capacity level. Where there is variable service pricing, prices generally reflect a usage pattern that covers the total cost of network operation. Increased use of the network may thus lead to lower service prices, not necessarily due to greater efficiency but to a greater transaction volume over which fixed costs can be spread. Consider, for example, a firm that offers services in fully automated telephony system with capacity to carry average phone calls of 2 hours per day. However, households in the area only call an average of 30 minutes per day. There is a variable fee on calling that covers total costs and provides the phone company with a reasonable profit. Therefore, if households doubled their average daily calling, prices could be halved. By these means, capacity utilisation is improved, but the change does not actually represent an improvement of the efficiency of the phone system. Rather, the customer is making use of a latent resource already paid for. Several European operators charge voice call rates for Internet traffic, and may thus in the short run collect monopoly rents because the tariffs are based on average voice traffic in a system with mostly fixed costs.

Consider the reverse situation in which the free-rider problem becomes apparent. The incumbent phone company had decided on only fixed fees for the subscription and no variable charges, based on the assumption that on the average calling will not exceed 2 hours per household. With the introduction of a higher-level service like the Internet, the average connect time may exceed the 2 hour capacity and further investments are needed to recover costs. The higher-level layer may become a free-rider on the lower level, which may not be able to fully recover the costs of the increased capacity demand. This has been a real concern of the Regional Bell Operating Companies (RBOC) in the US with the explosive growth of the Internet.

The above examples illustrate how layers mutually affect cost and value. The inter-layer relationships may become unstable once new layers have been established by the assistance of a sub- or super-layer. Since all layers share the same customers, one layer may gradually replace activities in super- and subordinate networks. For example, the Internet currently runs over the phone system but soon the phone system could be running over the Internet.

Thus, a challenge shared by both firms and regulatory bodies is the promotion of efficient broad service coverage and high network functionality through sub- and super-networks innovations, respectively.

Conclusions

There are a number of unresolved dilemmas hidden in the unique properties of mediators that complicate regulating the industry. Value is created and captured by the contract set of the network, whereas infrastructure costs may dominate determination of interconnect terms. Networks may provide increasing returns to scale, but there is also high cost and high risk associated with establishing new mediation services. Deregulation, designed to promote free competition, may in fact create barriers to innovation, despite intentions to the contrary. Both juxtaposed and overlaid networks have reciprocal value relationships from co-production. Firms make *ex ante* co-operative investment decisions with difficult to control *ex post* value appropriation. This may lead to mergers as the preferred way of protecting joint investments.

Networks have unstable, competitive, co-productive relationships, both horizontally and vertically. There is a potential tension between opening converged monopolies and offering investment protection for the creation of new networks. In the current liberalisation effort there has been a strong drive toward opening up the networks of the established telephone operators. The development of new innovative networks may require that firms be allowed to protect investments made in diffusing new contract sets.

Notes

1 This chapter is based on research conducted jointly with my colleague Charles B. Stabell. He contributed valuable input to an earlier version on this manuscript. The research reported is partially funded by Telenor. Discussions with a number of Telenor executives, managers and researchers have been helpful in developing our understanding of the value system in telecommunications.
2 This section is adapted from Stabell and Fjeldstad (1998) with the kind

permission of John Wiley & Sons Ltd. For more examples from other mediators, and a thorough discussion of value configuration analysis, the reader is referred to that article.

3 A short form for 'firms that can be modelled as value networks'.

4 Called vertical industry structure in manufacturing.

5 For an analysis of the competitive game in parallel interconnections see Brennan (1997).

6 SECT (96) 2378 'Group 2 involves sectors such as air transport, telecommunications services and TV broadcasting services; these are areas in which the regulatory framework has restricted or even forbidden market access through the award of special and exclusive rights and where regulation of companies' behaviour is designed to balance "market failures" or to promote the "general good".'

7 This may not seem like a problem in the case of voice telephony as one could argue that the contracts set investments were made by public monopolies and thus should be considered a free resource. The free-rider problem discussed here may however limit the development of new networks.

15 Conclusion

Global liberalisation and national adaptations

Kjell A. Eliassen and Marit Sjøvaag

In this book we have analysed the liberalisation process of the tele-communications sector. Our main focus has been on the EU, and in order to broaden the picture of the process in a sector that is increasingly global in nature, we have included studies of the Czech Republic, Israel and Thailand. We have described the process from its early stages in the UK (and the US) in the late 1970s, through the establishment of a unified EU regulatory regime in the decade 1987 to 1997, to a full opening of all segments from 1 January 1998. In addition, we have tried to explain both the rationale behind the establishment of this unified regime and to account for variations in the ability and willingness to implement and practise this regime correctly within the different countries. Finally, we have shown how this development is linked both to the technological development and the emerging new business logic of the new 'infocom' sector.

We find it useful at this stage to summarise the main findings concerning the general pattern of regulatory reform in Europe, both in the telecommunications sector and in related sectors.

The logic of a common European telecommunications sector

One can discuss – as many scholars have – to what extent the European Commission has been the main driving force behind the liberalisation process in the telecommunications sector. The presence of one main 'inventor' and 'initiator' of policy would make it easier to accept a certain uniformity and coherence of the 'ideology' on which the policy was built. We do not wholly subscribe to this view, as we find it somewhat superfluous and lacking in detail.

It is, however, vain to deny that the organisation has been influential in the process. As is shown in Chapter 2, the functional strategy at the European level was to break the sector into segments and liberalise them one at the time. Starting with customer premises equipment, other segments followed and this incremental strategy eventually led to the full opening of the sector. We do not believe, however, that this would not have happened without political consent among the main principals of the sector, including national policy-makers.

Basic agreement on the fact that 'something needed to be done' was a necessary condition for the events that both led up to and followed the Commission's Green Paper of 1987, 'the milestone of European tele-communications liberalisation'. The declared goal for the current policy is to establish a competitive market while at the same time ensuring that certain social aspects such as universal service are guaranteed. It is obviously too early to evaluate the resulting policy framework at this stage, nonetheless one has to conclude that the development over the last decade has been startling.

Realising that the state has taken on a new role in relation to its activity *vis-à-vis* the market, we asked how this has been done in this particular case. Theoretical considerations of the problems of regulation (Chapter 3) point to the questions of distribution of social goods, legitimate state intervention, and design problems: in sum, the question of control, both by the state of the economic actors, and by the general public of the state officials, lies at the heart of this discussion.

It is argued (Chapter 4) that the EU Member States have adopted different approaches to regulatory reform at both domestic and EU level, resulting in a series of models of agency-based regulation. The EU model permits a considerable degree of variation and discretion at Member State level, and is based on mutual adjustment and adaptation. These Member State differences are explained in terms of their approaches to regulatory reform, which warrant analysis of the rationale of regulation and reform, and in turn prompts the typology/taxonomy of telecommunications regulation in the EU. The European regime (EU and Member States) is described as 'policy syncretism', the result of interaction between several systems rather than a teleological process of integration.

The convergence of technologies poses a new set of difficulties upon policy-makers in the field of telecommunications. Chapter 5 discusses the regulation of content both in the multimedia sector, including traditional broadcasting, and in the new communication and information services. The chapter shows how it is important, in the view of the European Union, to harmonise legislation at EU level because differences between Member States can generate disproportionate barriers to the free move-ment of audio-visual and information services within the Union. However, it is difficult to claim that a regulatory framework exists at EU level as of today. The chapter also shows how the extent to which the EU can intervene is limited both geographically, the multimedia sector being inherently global in nature, and culturally, as the Member States are eager to preserve and promote their cultural sovereignty.

The media sector imposes a different range of challenges to the policy-makers, for two main reasons. First, telecommunications regulation has up to now mostly been a technical issue, with the exception of the question of universal service obligations. Second, media and culture have traditionally been handled at a *national* (and often even sub-national) level, while the telecommunication sector is a transfrontier service. It therefore seems unlikely that an 'optimal' regulatory framework of the global communication world will come into being in the near future. The new communication world is still in its infancy, and regulation will probably be an issue-by-issue process.

How are these different pieces of EU regulation implemented at the national (and in some countries sub-national) level? Is this liberalisation process really taking place in the Member States?

European liberalisation: too good to be (completely) true

Within the framework of the European Union we have investigated in this book the implementation of EU regulations within three different tele-communications regimes. The first one, Britain (Chapter 6), was the early mover in Europe, licensing a second operator more than a decade before the opening of the telecommunications markets in other countries. The second and the third cases in the book, Germany (Chapter 7) and France (Chapter 8), have placed themselves more or less in the mainstream of the process of liberalisation in Europe, as the two chapters show. Germany, however, has vigorously been implementing EU regulation, even if it started off somewhat slowly. This becomes more pronounced when compared to France, where one has seen a relatively restrictive policy from the ART on the issue of licensing.

A comparative analysis of the situation in these three European countries leads us to believe that there is a link between the speed by which the markets are opened and the extent to which the incumbent operator preserves its market dominance. The degree of competition varies between different segments of the market, with the fixed-line voice telephony segment being the most prone to dominance. Based on existing evidence, it seems that the chances of the incumbent organisation retaining a dominant position is greater in countries where the liberalisation measures have been introduced slowly. The reason for this might be that the old monopolist has been given time to adjust to the new regime. Equally, countries where the incumbent operator has been fighting the introduction of new measures seem to move towards greater competition at a faster pace. This, however, is dependant on the behaviour of the regulator. A regulator might not be able to stop the introduction of competition that is threatening the national operator, but it has significant powers to delay the process and shape its outcome.

Britain was the first country to liberalise and privatise well ahead of the regulatory development at the EU level. As Chapter 6 shows, the regulatory reform did not in any way mean a decrease of state intervention in the sector. Rather, both the government and the new independent regulator, Oftel, together with other principal actors, were active in building a new legislative framework regulating the activities of privately owned suppliers. Since the early 1980s the process has been characterised by the legacy from the privatisation of BT, where behavioural regulation was centred on that company. Moreover, the form, speed and extent of the liberalisation process were to a large extent determined by the decisions of a regulator wishing to ensure effective competition. Oftel's powers, its rapidly growing expertise and the weakness of general competition law in Britain, facilitated the development of sector-specific rules, which further strengthened the role of Oftel. Regarding the incumbent operator, it is estimated that BT will have over 60 per cent of the market at the turn of the century, i.e. after fifteen years of 'competition'. This underpins our argument that an operator will be able to retain its strong position when given time to adjust to the new market regime.

Although Germany was no driving force in the 1980s, it is argued (Chapter 7) that relevant German advocates of liberalisation – including the Federal Ministry of Economic Affairs and, to some extent, the Ministry of Posts and Telecommunications – tried to initiate reforms both at national and European level. Germany was one of the countries which viewed the liberalisation process as part of an effort to make Germany more competitive in a market economy. The real effects of the liberalisation process is, however, still difficult to assess. Recently, a significant degree of liberalisation has been achieved, but the dominant position of Deutsche Telekom is still a reality. Deutsche Telekom was allowed time to prepare for competition, as licences were granted for network operation from 1996 while voice telephony remained under monopoly provision until 1 January 1998. Although the number of licensees has increased significantly from 88 in January 1996 to 269 in February 1998, it is estimated that the incumbent will hold between 80 and 90 per cent of the market share for some time in the future. It is interesting to note, however, that this does not seem to be solely in the voice telephony market, where Deutsche Telekom had a monopoly until 1998, but also in other segments such as advanced services and VANS, due to the already digitised network the company owns.

The French development has been one of the great surprises to observers of regulatory reform in European telecommunications. The French were implementing new regulations through legislative changes in 1996, and the regulator was in operation from 1 January 1997. As has been discussed in Chapter 8, however, the crucial point in the implementation of this new regime seems to be licensing practices. The ART has been reluctant to give out new operating licences, and has also showed 'interventionist tendencies' under the auspices of universal service obligations. By rendering the licensing process cumbersome, the possibilities that large organisations will invest in France in order to create hubs decreases. There are signs, however, that the procedures are improving, and that the ART is exercising its authority to a greater extent in favour of new entrants, even though it is not yet possible for them to obtain access to the unbundled elements of France Télécom's local loop.

In this volume we have analysed telecommunications policy within three of the biggest EU countries, three countries with a (rather) successful liberalisation and privatisation process. This is, to some extent, in contrast to developments in the southern part of Europe. Some of these countries, like Greece and Spain, have been given extended time to comply with the EU regulations. Others, like Italy, have had enormous difficulties in setting up and making function a new regulatory framework. In protestant northern Europe all countries have been very successful in complying with the EU rules and regulations. The main pattern of complying with the EU regulation is shown in Figure 15.1.

Before going into a more comprehensive attempt to explain these differences we could perhaps learn something about the mechanisms at work by taking a closer look at the Italian situation. Italy was relatively late in introducing competition to the telecommunications market, and has spent the last year or so trying to 'catch up'. Solid progress has been made in implementing a number of European Union directives but several key issues still need to be resolved before this activity is completed and genuine competition becomes a reality. A key piece of the regulatory framework that is still to be implemented is the functioning of an effective independent regulatory authority. An independent regulator is crucial to the implementation of the new regulatory framework, and a lack of such makes introduction of competition very difficult. Effective regulation of the incumbent operator, Telecom Italia, is deficient in another key respect: while its competitors all operate under new licences, Telecom Italia continues to operate under the old monopoly regulations.

Several other important issues still remain to be resolved, such as interconnection to Telecom Italia's network, separation of accounts for its business activities and number portability. In spite of these difficulties, several new actors have entered the Italian telecommunications market. Licences for fixed-line telephony have been awarded, as well as three mobile licences. But why do we see these difficulties in the Italian case, and how can we explain this slow pace of regulatory reform?

Some of the main reasons are to be found in the functioning of the political system itself. Italy has a long tradition of a strong state presence and active intervention in economic processes. There is a lack of 'market culture'; governments and people are used to considering certain sectors, particularly public utilities, as unconditionally state owned. Therefore, there exists a certain difficulty in adapting to the new environment of competition, liberalisation, multiplicity of actors etc. The new regime that is being globally established is still regarded with suspicion, and one could

Figure 15.1 Liberalisation checklist

	Liberalisation of public networks and voice services	Published interconnect conditions[1]	Costs-based interconnect tariffs (EU Benchmark)[2]	Effective accounting separation	Cost-based USO contributions[3]	Independent NRA[4]
Austria	★	●	◆	◆	★	◆
Belgium	★	●	◆	◆	◆	●
Denmark	★	●	★	●	★	★
Finland	★	●	●	●	★	●
France	★	●	★	●	◆	★
Germany	★	◆	●	●	★	★
Greece – derog. 1.1.2001		●	◆	◆	?	●
Ireland – derog. 1.1.1998		●	◆	◆	?	●
Italy	★	●	◆	◆	◆	★
Luxembourg – derog. 1.1.1998		◆	◆	◆	★	◆
Netherlands	★	●	◆	◆	?	●
Portugal – derog. 1.1.2000		◆	◆	◆	★	★
Spain – derog. 1.1.1998		●	◆	◆	?	★
Sweden	★	●	★	●	?	★
Switzerland	★	●	◆	●	★	★
UK	★	★	★	★	★	★

★ Implemented   ● Partially implemented   ◆ Not implemented

[1] However, most offers do not include the full range of interconnect services but only basic voice services.
[2] Managed by the NRA and enabling non-discriminatory carrier selection codes.
[3] Competitors' contributions to universal service to be waived or based on genuine costs.
[4] Independent from the government with sufficient powers and resources.

Figure 15.1 Liberalisation checklist

even say that Italy is still trying to delay the 'conquering' of its national environment. However, the process of change is going in the 'right' direction.

Some preliminary explanations of the national variations

How can we explain these national variations? One important aspect covered in the book is the interrelationship between the rather uniform processes of liberalisation and privatisation at the EU level and, to a large extent, also at the global level, and the interesting national variations in the implementation processes in each and every country within Europe. It seems important to search for explanations of the interrelationship between global, regional and national processes of liberalisation and privatisation.

As the changes in the telecommunications sector show, the emergence of regulatory regimes in Europe takes various paths and methods: '[W]hile nations may be engaged in a single game, the players have different ideas of what the game is and how to win' (S. Vogel 1997: 181). Diversity in policy outcomes, despite common policy challenges, is usually attributed to differences in institutions. Thus the way between 'agora' and 'acropolis' is not a straightforward, trouble-free path, but a diversity of actors and veto-points have to be taken into consideration. Beyond differences in the policy environment which lead to demands for regulatory action, divergences in policy outcomes can be attributed to two dimensions, political and administrative, which affect decision-making during the process of regulatory reform and the further development of the regulatory regime. Thus rather than allowing for the pre-eminence of one actor in the process, analysis has to accommodate multiple principals, a number of issue dimensions and the extent of transaction costs caused by distinct decision-making rules.

Let us first look at the political dimension. The United Kingdom has been called the 'heaven of self-regulation' (Baggott 1989: 438), one reason being the UK's constitutional inheritance of a non-codified constitution. Traditional national perceptions of the relationship between the public and the private sphere are crucial to the design of a regulatory framework (see Hancher and Moran 1989: 271–99). Different backgrounds in, for example, Anglo-American or Roman law matter, as well as the national tradition in policy-making with differences between, for example, the supposed British 'laissez-faire' state, French statism and German associational policy-making.

The nature of the government, whether coalition or majoritarian, as well as the nature of the state, whether unitary or federal, will also be important for the regulatory outcome. Coalition governments are always more likely to require detailed compromises to embrace their more diverse electoral constituencies. The participation of sub-national governments in regulatory affairs will add a further, at least spatial, dimension. We see this clearly in the current difficulties with the regulation of convergent industries, where culture other than the telecommunications sector has traditionally been the responsibility of lower-level governments (with some notable exceptions, especially France). Uncertainty about future policy has to be reduced and certain 'pay-offs' have to be guaranteed to the participating actors. The more participants that are involved and have to give their consent in the initial decision-making process, the more detailed will be the rules guiding the initial regulatory and organisational regime in the reformed sector.

For example, in the case of British utility privatisation the main demand was to privatise the enterprises within the lifetime of one parliament, as the doctrine of 'parliamentary sovereignty' means that a parliament cannot bind a future legislature. Therefore, the aim of policy-makers is to make the policy organisationally irreversible. In contrast, in cases of coalition governments within a federal state, which, because of constitutional rules, are required to find extra-large parliamentary majorities to pass the necessary legislation, far more detailed initial legislation at the early stages of organisational reform will be seen as irreversibility has to be achieved by agreement and consent. Steven Vogel (1997) has highlighted the importance of 'regulatory competition' between states: regulatory regimes are designed in order to support domestic industry.

But if the national authorities are continuously trying to support domestic industry, how can we explain the shift in practice observed in the case of France? With the abolition of 'royal suppliers' to the telecommunications sector in the 1980s, the (re-)privatisation of Alcatel and the introduction of competition in the CPE segment, a new trend entered the way of doing business in the French telecommunications industry. We believe the answer must comprise two different elements. First, no sector policy is completely isolated from the total political picture. The financial situation deteriorated from the 1970s onwards, and it became increasingly intolerable to keep big industrial companies (such as Alcatel, and later also the incumbent telecommunications operators) under state ownership, because the need for investments to maintain the necessary level of research and development was bigger than the state could handle.[1] Second, the perception of the 'home market' has changed. From being in direct competition with the Germans, the British and the Americans, the French increasingly saw themselves as being in the same situation as other Europeans, the main threats being the US and Japan. One might even go as far as to argue that what France has attempted to do within the framework of the EU is not qualitatively different from what they did within their national borders prior to the 1980s.

Further crucial actors are trade unions and business groups. Whereas trade unions have potential veto power to block policy reforms (see, for example, the French and, to a lesser extent, the German cases in telecommunications), the role of business groups in general will be ambivalent due to a trade off between the threat to their members' existence from emerging international competition and lower costs due to liberalised services and the end of cross-subsidisation in favour of domestic users. The role of large business customers (such as the financial service industry in the UK) and of domestic producers (such as Siemens in the German case, see Cawson *et al.* 1990) has been crucial.

Of particular importance in the context of the 'capture' literature on regulation is the role and position of the national operator. Factors such as the economic and technological position and the need for investment affect the calculations of decision-makers. Thus in the British case, the potential impact of necessary investments in British Telecommunications on the Public Sector Borrowing Requirement (PSBR) was one of the key motivations for change. The French operator, in contrast, had by the 1980s developed into one of the most competitive undertakings. By 1996, however, public finances were in dire straits and strengthened the argument for privatisation of France Télécom.

Of similar importance is the relationship between the status and interest of the management of the operator and the political decision-makers. This relationship will lead to a 'regulatory bargain' which to some extent determines the extent of organisational change in the 'privatised' era and the extent of competition (Veljanovski 1991). Thus a possible fragmentation of British Telecom was successfully vetoed by the managers of the enterprise. In the Norwegian case, however, the reality was diametrically opposite. The lack of willingness on the part of the politicians to introduce competition in the home market, coupled with a realisation of the future competition, led the top management to split the former 'dinosaur' Telenor into several smaller units that competed amongst themselves. The rationale behind this process was that real-life experience of competition was the only possible way for the employees to understand the need for a change in behaviour. The extent of the management's scope of influence on these macro-issues of privatisation will depend on the willingness of political actors to grant management access to the policy-making process.

Another important dimension is the variations in administrative traditions across Europe. National diversity also originates at the design stage as policy-makers (usually civil servants) hardly ever design something from a blank sheet. Policy-makers adapt, 'draw lessons' and 'read across' from other experiences (Rose 1993; Olsen and Peters 1996). Once it has been clarified what the political objectives of regulatory reform are, two main sources of learning can be identified.

Learning from internal sources

Issues on competition, public services and the relationship between political control and economic liberty of the operator have often been discussed in the past. Nevertheless, evidence suggests that organisations draw less on the written historical record but rather on the individual short-term memory of its members. Thus policy-makers look at the experience of regulation in other policy sectors which are regarded as similar or which have undergone similar regulatory change. In the UK, for example, lessons from previous utility privatisation were applied to the drawing up of later regulatory regimes.

Learning from external sources

Learning from other countries or other sub-national states which have dealt with the same policy problems before, provides decision-makers with the advantage of the 'second mover'. This allows policy-makers to learn and imitate organisational design but also to obtain first indications of the weaknesses and strengths of that regime.

Membership in supranational organisations is said to lead to 'fusion' processes in that the political and economic dynamics of the supranational level become part of the organisational logic on the national policy-making level (Wessels and Rometsch 1996). In the telecommunications sector, the European Union has become a major player, with the Commission aiming to liberalise the sector in an 'incrementalist' fashion, especially following the 1987 Green Paper (see Thatcher 1996, 1997; Fuchs 1994). Thus, in the particular case of telecommunications, the regulatory scope for Member States to pursue national industrial policies has been ended. Although regulatory directives from the EU provide Member States with some discretion, they represent challenges to the domestic policy agenda and provide at least a rhetorical support for regulatory change at the national level. The extent to which supranational institutions are able to shape regulatory reform depends on national willingness to reform as well as common institutional starting points (see Schmidt 1997a).

Which source of learning will be most important will partly depend on the institutional legacy of the individual sector. Of crucial importance is the reference point according to which regulatory reforms are designed. Thus, in cases where actors are mainly interested in the sector in itself, solutions are sought from experiences in other countries. In cases where policy-making is mainly oriented towards the policy output only, i.e. 'privatisation', policy solutions are sought from other 'privatisation' experiences. The background of the relevant actors not only matters in the way policy is being 'learned', but also as to which 'ideas' are selected to guide the policy process and institutional choice. Ideas not only matter in setting the general political direction of regulatory reform but also in the regulatory detail.

Learning and imitation processes are mediated by the overall administrative landscape, as some states do not have a tradition of independent bodies exercising public tasks. Thus in the British case, Oftel was designed on the lines of the Office of Fair Trading, while in Germany the regulatory authority followed the organisational provisions of German administrative law and was modelled as an autonomous body (Bundesoberbehörde) subordinate to the Economics Ministry.

So far we have described the national variations in the implementation of telecommunications liberalisation and privatisation in the EU member countries and discussed how these variations could be explained according to both political and administrative differences among the countries in question. One of our tasks in this book has been to describe and to analyse some telecommunications developments outside the EU framework. We have thus considered a prospective member country (the Czeck Republic), a relatively free-market (liberal) country (Israel) and one Asian country new to the process of telecommunications liberalisation and privatisation (Thailand).

The WTO and liberalisation outside the European Union

The development of the new regulatory regimes within the European Union has taken place within an international process of similar characteristics. The wave of liberalisation has embraced the global domain, mainly through the WTO. For countries outside the EU, the GATS agreement has spurred regulatory reforms aimed at the mutual opening up of markets, especially within the basic telecommunications services. It is clear, however, that the diversity of both political and administrative traditions are much greater in this context, and hence national variations in the resulting regulatory regimes should be expected to be greater.

Any classification of systems on a global scale is bound to be very general. There might be greater diversity between countries within the same geographical region than between two countries from separate regions. However, it is customary to group countries in such regions, and this can be defended through their (more often than not) similar experiences in the past. The Central and Eastern European Countries, for example, might not be a homogenous group, but at least they share the experience of a totalitarian regime since the Second World War. The Asian countries, on the other hand, are said to have a 'basic logic' of informal networks, and work ethics somewhat different from the European one.

There are several problems connected to this type of grouping of countries. An in-depth analysis has to take account of national traditions in each and every country, and talking about 'Asia' as opposed to

'Europe' leads to over-simplification and lack of detail. We therefore propose that the cases from outside the EU (the Czech Republic, Israel and Thailand) are seen as three attempts to highlight further characteristics of the global reform process, and not in any way as exhaustive for the situation in any of the regions.

Regarding the situation in the CEECs, one major reason for the rapid regulatory reform has been their wish to enter the European Union as soon as possible. In order to achieve this, adapting to the regulatory regime of the EU is paramount. In addition, privatisation was seen as a means of attracting the substantial financial resources needed to develop the telecommunications sector.

As shown in Chapter 9, financial resources were not the only decisive reason for the Czech Republic opting for a strategic partner solution. Equally necessary was the connection to global alliances, and a strengthening of the competitiveness of SPT Telecom in the face of increased competition within the framework of liberalisation of the European telecommunication market. Chapter 9 shows the limited liberalisation of the Czech telecommunications market. However, even this simplified and limited approach has brought about striking peculiarities. The Czech government has selected the least attractive and also the least developed regions for privatisation, and also added several other restrictions. Nevertheless, a number of private firms competed for entering this market. This seems almost to be too good to be true. But if this gives profits after 2–3 years of massive investment, it shows us what enormous potential lies in the Czech market as a whole. It can, however, be argued that the firms are building a foothold in the Czech market, which would explain their rather relaxed attitude towards the expected profitability and returns on investment. The expectation of future profit would ease the pain of underwriting even significant losses, especially since the experience would provide them with insider knowledge and a position which could give them an advantage after the year 2000 when the Czech telecommunication market is expected to be fully liberalised.

As a contrast to the development in Central and Eastern Europe, telecommunications liberalisation, and in some instances privatisation, in Asia is not orchestrated by the development of a comprehensive common general regulatory plan for the future, even if the processes of regulatory reform in Asia were to be based on the new WTO agreement.

Of the two telecommunications systems outside Europe that we have considered in this voulme, Israel has by far the most liberal regulatory regime but, on the other hand, the privatisation process seems to be more advanced in Thailand. In Israel we have witnessed a very rapid liberalisation process. The most important telecommunications markets are already competitive, in particular the cellular and international communications markets, and in 1999 competition will also be introduced for the two remaining segments. Even radio and TV will be liberalised.

As stated in Chapter 10, the Israeli process was 'liberalisation from above' because of the critical role played by state officials in the establishment of the new competitive regime. Thus, 'the scope and the depth of the state's involvement in the enforcement of competition in the Israeli telecommunications market leads to the interpretation of this market's liberalisation as "regulated competition" . . . The future of the liberalisation processes in the converged areas depends therefore much on the role and functioning and of a new regulatory authority to be created.'

Thailand started, as shown in Chapter 11, with a process of partial privatisation in order to solve the problem of rapidly creating many new telephone lines. The telephone concessions to private sector companies were based on the Build-Transfer-Operate (BTO) principle, and the state monopoly was in this way not fundamentally changed. In 1991/1992, TelecomAsia, in Bangkok, and TT&T in the rest of the country, obtained licences to build and operate lines for a fixed number of years before having to return them to the state. There are plans both to continue this scheme and to implement a more realistic privatisation of the two state telecommunications companies. A gradual liberalisation process has also been under way for mobile communications. Further liberalisation and privatisation depends, however, both on the political will to carry out these processes and the putting in place of the necessary regulations and institutions. The chapter describes and analyses some of the problems involved in these developments. Future liberalisation strategies will also have to take into account the new global regulatory regime established by the WTO.

From telecom technology to information services: the agenda for the future

Looking ahead, what will be the great challenges for the regulation of the telecommunications sector in the future? The most immediate factor that comes to mind is the development of new technologies and the challenges this present to regulators, especially the convergence of tele-communications with other sectors such as broadcasting and multimedia. As discussed in Chapter 12, future systems will be characterised by four factors. First, broadband communications, which make it possible to transfer large enough quantities of data to have one-to-one transfer of real-time moving pictures (video) and sound and making them interactive. Second, mobility, so that these systems can be accessed from virtually anywhere on the globe. Third, wireless communication, making all services accessible through a handset. Fourth, multimedia and Internet technologies, constituting the major networks and protocols in the 'Information Super Highway'.

Regulating according to technology has always been difficult. As the speed of technological development increases, the task of regulating becomes ever more complex. Furthermore, as we have already discussed, the national arena becomes increasingly less appropriate as the level at which regulation is upheld.

In addition to the changing technological environment, business logic is also fundamentally changing in the telecommunications sector. Mobile services grow at an amazing pace (Chapter 13) and, the rapid speed of development and diversification necessitates a combination of economies of scale and differentiation. The consequence will be an upsurge of new niche markets, which will be functionally rather than geographically defined.

How to deal with the problems arising from the transition from administration of state bureaux to the regulation of private enterprise is also not self-evident. Within the telecommunications industry value creation will lie as much in the establishment of and participation in networks, as in the delivery of the communications services themselves (Chapter 14). There is a tension between the opening up of the old monopolised industry and offering investment protection for the creation of new networks, and we might see a situation where it becomes paramount to allow firms to protect investments when the new contract sets themselves are poorly defined.

In the future, value creation in the (converged) telecommunications sector will be linked increasingly to intangible assets. This area of the economy is one where national governments have shown surprisingly little will to act to date. Indeed, discussion on the harmonisation of regulations for intellectual property rights (as an example of intangible assets) has only to a very limited extent led to tangible results.

With new information technologies and telecommunications developments, large, international firms transfer knowledge across national borders. Intranet and Internet solutions provide instantaneous access to information on a global scale, and value is created within systems that today are outside the scope of most government's supervision. Since there is no agreed-upon formulae for valuing such intangible assets, a large portion of these firms' assets are not included in their value base. This has enormous consequences for the taxation of such enterprises. The related issues of intellectual property rights and electronic commerce, both a consequence of the convergence between telecommunications technologies and the multimedia industry, are things that the regulators at all levels have to take seriously in the near future.

Some final comments

The variety of national solutions to the challenge of telecommunications regulation is striking. We have in this volume seen how the implementation of these new policies varies according to national political and administrative traditions, even in a situation where the technological (and to a large extent financial) challenges are similar.

What will be the future of European telecommunications regulation? Three issues that we have focused on in this volume will, in particular, determine future developments. First, in the very near future, we will witness technological developments which will rapidly change a number of the established concepts in this field and make the logic of certain aspects of regulation irrelevant. One example is the current definition of mobile communications as a basis for regulation, which will become redundant with the change from fixed to mobile communications as users demand total flexibility between fixed, mobile and even satellite telephony. This process, which lies strictly within the telecommunications sector, including the development of new services, will change so rapidly that a regular update of the regulatory regimes is needed in order to uphold free competition within the telecommunication market defined either nationally or at the regional level.

The second point is the consequences arising from the continued internationalisation and globalisation of the industry itself. This will both change the effectiveness of the national regulation and further increase the need for regional and global regulatory regimes. The companies themselves prefer a unified system and as few regulatory institutions as possible. This question is further complicated by the relationship between sector-specific regulation and general competition regulation. When the former monopolies lose their dominant position in the market and com- petition increases, the need for sector-specific regulation can be questioned. The same type of logic exists also at the EU between DG XIII and DG IV. Our assumption is, however, that because of the large number of actors at all levels of policy-making, and the multitude of interests involved, the present complicated picture of multi-level and multi-institutional regulation will persist for the foreseeable future.

This issue is also linked to the third theme which recurs in various chapters in this book, namely the convergence process. The speed of the technological merger of telecommunications, media and information technology, and the huge volume of business and high profitability involved, would, under any circumstances, have challenged the political regime. The same holds true for the changing issues involved in the regulation debate concerning not only frequencies and concessions but also content and ownership. This development highlights, as we have shown, extremely complicated and important issues for our society.

At the same time, however, the dispersal of regulatory authority between several administrative units and levels further complicates the development of a new regulatory regime. Regulation of content and ownership will constitute the major battleground for efforts on European regulation in the future, and actors that are new to the telecommunications field, e.g. authors, publishers and universities, will play an important role.

These three issues create many challenges for future research. It is interesting to study the persistence of national diversity in order to identify factors that influence decision-making at the national level, both to increase our understanding, and to predict better practices for future policy-making. This book has in many ways been based on such a 'backward-looking' method. However, it is also important to understand the technological, economic and political situation at present and its potential for development. Only in that way can scholars, policy-makers and technicians approach the optimal use of this new and potent technology.

Note

1 Moreover, the increasingly global nature of the telecommunications industry hampered the possibility of state-owned companies building alliances, as other actors were reluctant to move into partnership with public firms.

Bibliography

Akerlof, G.A. (1970) 'The market for "lemons": Qualitative uncertainty and the market mechanism', in *Quarterly Journal of Economics*, vol. 84, pp. 488–500.

Anglo-American Committee of Inquiry (1946) *A survey of Palestine. Prepared in December 1945 and January 1946 for the information of the Anglo-American committee of inquiry,* Jerusalem: The Government Printer.

Antonelli, C. (1992) 'The Economic Theory of Information Networks' in Antonelli, C. (ed.) *The Economics of Information Network,* Amsterdam: Elsevier Publishers, pp. 5–27.

Antonelli, C. (1997) 'A regulatory regime for innovation in the communications industries' in *Telecommunications Policy*, vol. 21, no. 1, pp. 35–45.

Arlandis, Jaques (1993) 'Trading Telecommunications' in *Telecommunications Policy*, vol. 17, April, pp. 171–85.

Armstrong, M., Cowen, S. and Vickers, J. (1994) *Regulatory Reform. Regulation of Economic Activity,* Cambridge: MIT Press.

Arnon, A. and Preschtman, H. (1992) *The Privatisation of Natural Monopolies*, Discussion Papers, no. 14/92, Jerusalem: Research Department, Bank of Israel.

ART (1997) *Rapport Public d'Activité 1997*, Autorité de Régulation des Télécommunications, Paris.

Baggott, R. (1989) 'Regulatory Reform in Britain: The Changing Face of Self-Regulation', in *Public Administration*, vol. 68, no. 4, pp. 435–54.

Baldwin, R, and McCrudden, C. (1987) *Regulation and Public Law*, London: Weidenfeld & Nicolson.

Baldwin, R. (1996) 'Regulatory legitimacy in the European context: the British Health and Safety Executive', in Majone, G. (ed.), *Regulating Europe*, London: Routledge.

Bank of Israel (1995) *Annual Report*, Jerusalem: The Government Printing House.

Barke, R.P. and Riker, W.H. (1982) 'A Political Theory of Regulation with some Observations on Railway Abandonments', in *Public Choice*, vol. 39, pp. 73–106.

Barney, J.B. (1991) 'Firm Resources and Sustained Competitive Advantage', in *Journal of Business*, pp. 99–120.

Barry, B. (1995) *Democracy and Power*, Oxford Clarendon Press.

Bauer, Johannes M. (1994) 'The Emergence of Global Networks in Telecommunications: Transcending National Regulation and Market Constraints', in *Journal of Economic Issues*, vol. 28, no. 2, pp. 391–402.

Baumol, W.J. (1977) 'On the proper cost test for natural monopoly in a multi-product industry', in *American Economic Review*, vol. 67, pp. 809–822.

Becker, G. (1983) 'A Theory of Competition among Pressure Groups for Political Influence', in *Quarterly Journal of Economics*, vol. 98, no. 3, pp. 371–400.

Beesley, M. (1981) *Liberalisation of the use of British Telecommunications network*, London: HMSO.

Bell, A. (1995) 'Recent Development in Interconnection Arrangements in UK Telecommunications'. Paper presented at Interconnection Pricing Workshop, Milan.

Bell, A. (1997) 'Governance in the regulation of Telecommunications: the Case of the UK'. Paper presented to Telecommunications Workshop, November 1997, European University Institute, Florence.

Bental, B. and Spiegel, M. (1995) 'Network Competition, Product Quality, and Market Coverage in the presence of network externalities', in *The Journal of Industrial Economics*, vol. 43, no. 2, pp. 197–386.

Berg, G. (1996) 'The GSM Evolution Towards UMTS', in *Telecommunications International*, vol. 30, no. 10, pp. 35–8, 125.

Bernstein, M. (1955) *Regulation of Business by Independent Commissions*, Princeton: Princeton University Press.

Bezeq (1995) *Annual Statistics: 1994*, Jerusalem.

Birkinshaw, P., Harden, I. and Lewis, N. (1990) *Government by moonlight – The hybrid parts of the state*, London: Unwin Hyman.

Black, J. (1997) 'Constitutionalising Self-Regulation', in *Modern Law Review*, vol. 59, no. 1, pp. 24–55.

Blackman, Colin R. (1998) 'Convergence between telecommunications and other media. How should regulation adapt?', *Telecommunications Policy*, vol. 22, no. 3, pp. 160–70.

Blackman, Colin R. and Denmead, Michael (1998) *1998 – A New Era for EU Telecoms Regulation*, Briefing Report Series, Cambridge: Analysys Publications.

Blair, T. (1998) 'The Third Way', speech to the French National Assembly, 24 March 1998.

Blodgett, M. (1997) 'Upbeat on Unplugged', *Computerworld*, vol. 31, no. 22, p. 4.

Borthwick, R. and Stehmann, O. (1994) 'A strategy towards infrastructure competition in the European Union' in *Telecommunications Policy*, vol. 18, no. 8, pp. 616–28.

Brennan, T.J. (1997) 'Industry Parallel interconnection agreements', *Information Economics and Policy*, vol. 9, pp. 133–149.

Bridgeman, J. (1996) 'The relationship between EU Competition Law and National Competition Law on the Eve of Maastricht II'. Paper presented to the International Bar Association 26th Biennial Conference, October 1996.

Broadman, H.G. and Balassa, C. (1993) 'Liberalizing International Trade in Telecommunications Services' in *The Columbia Journal of World Business*, Winter 1993.

Bruce, Robert R. and Cunard, Jeffrey P. (1996) 'Restructuring the Telecommunications Sector in Asia: An Overview of Approaches and Options', in Wellenius, Björn and Stern, Peter A. (eds) *Implementing Reforms in the*

Telecommunications Sector, The World Bank Regional and Sectoral Studies, Avebury, Aldershot.

BT (1998) 'Liberalisation in Europe – mid-year progress report' in *Choice.com.*, Issue no. 3, June 1998.

Burton, J. (1997), 'The Competitive Order or Ordered Competition?: The 'UK Model' of Utility Regulation in Theory and Practice', in *Public Administration*, vol. 75, pp. 157–88.

Cadwalader, D. (1997) 'ITU-T Secretary-General, Pekka Tarjanne: Paging – pioneering services easy to liberalize, deregulate and handle', in *In the Air*, December 1997.

Carsberg, B. (1986) 'What are fair prices for BT's services', *Oftel News,* no. 5, December 1986.

Carsberg, B. (1989) 'Injecting competition into telecommunications' in C. Veljanovski (ed.) *Privatisation and Competition*, London: IEA.

Carsberg, B. (1991) 'Office of Telecommunications: Competition and the Duopoly Review' in Veljanovski, C. (ed.), *Regulators and the Market*, London: IEA.

Cave, M. (1994) 'Competition in Telecommunications: Lessons from the British Experience', in *Communications & Strategies*, no. 13, (1st quarter 1994), pp. 61–78.

Cawson, A., Holmes, P., Webber, D., Morgan, K. and Stevens, A. (1990) *Hostile Brothers*, Oxford: Clarendon Press.

CEC, Commission Directive 96/2/EC (1996) amending Directive 90/388/EEC with regard to mobile and personal communications, OJ no. 20, 26 January 1996, 59 p.

CEC, *EU Action Plan: Satellite communications in the Information Society,* Brussels, 5 March 1997, 17 p. (COM(97) 91 final).

CEC: 88/301/EEC, Commission Directive on competition on the Markets in telecommunications terminal equipment.

CEC: 90/388/EEC, Directive on Competition on the Markets for Telecommunications Services.

CEC: *Strategy and Policy Orientations with Regard to the Further Development of Mobile and Wireless Communications (UMTS)*, Brussels 15 October 1997, 16 p. (COM(97) 513 final).

Cellular Telecommunications Industry Association Web site (1998), http://www. wow-com.com/consumer.

Clements, Bernard (1998) 'The impact of convergence on regulatory policy in Europe', *Telecommunications Policy*, vol. 22, no. 3, pp. 197–205.

CMEU (1996) 'Conclusions of June 20 Energy Council', *EU Council of Ministers Conclusions*, 8081/96.

Communications Ministry (1992) R*eport of the Committee for the Examination of the General Licence of Bezeq and the Policy Document*, Jerusalem (Maoz Committee).

Communications Ministry and Ministry of Finance (1991) *Report of the Committee for the Examination of the Telecommunications Sector and Its Change*, Jerusalem (The first Boaz Committee).

Communications Ministry and Ministry of Finance (1993) *Report of the Committee for the Examination of Bezeq's Tariffs*, Jerusalem (Shorer Report).

Communications Ministry and Ministry of Finance (1996a) *Final Report of the*

Public Committee for the Examination of Licensing and Regulation in Tele-communications, Jerusalem (The second Boaz Committee).

Communications Ministry and Ministry of Finance (1996b) *Report of the Inter-ministerial Committee for Re-examination of Policy and Competition in the Telecommunications Sector*, Jerusalem (Wax-Brodet-Leon Report).

Computer Science and Telecommunications Board (National Research Council) (1994) *Realizing the Information Future*, Washington, D.C.: National Academy Press.

Coopers & Lybrand Consortium (1994) *The TOT Restructuring and Privatisation Study, Phase III Report on Evaluation of Restructuring and Privatisation Strategies, vol. I: Main Report*, September 1994.

Cullen International SA (1997) *Regulatory Observatory*, Draft Report on the Czech Republic, Brussels.

Czech Republic (1992) 'Telecommunications Act of the Czech Republic No. 150/1992', Prague.

Czech Telecommunication Office (1994) 'Tariff Policy as a Tool of Regulation in Telecommunications'. Draft of internal paper, Praha.

Dang-Nguyen, G. (1988) 'Telecommunications in France' in Foreman-Peck J. and Müller P. (eds) *European Telecommunications Organisations*, Baden-Baden: Nomos.

Dang-Nguyen, G., Schneider, V. and Werle, R. (1993) 'Networks in European Policy-Making: Europeification of Telecommunications Policy', in Andersen, S.S. and Eliassen, K.A. (eds) *Making Policy in Europe: The Europeification of National Policy-making*, London: Sage.

Day, F. and Trang, H.N. (1997) *Regulation of Wireless Communications*, Rockville MD: Government Institutes.

Demsetz, H. (1968) 'Why regulate utilities?', *Journal of Law and Economics*, vol. 11, no. 1 pp. 55–65.

Department of Trade and Industry (1991) *Competition and Choice: Telecommunications Policy for the 1990s*, Cmnd. 1461 London: HMSO.

Department of Trade and Industry (1997) *A prohibition approach to anti-competitive agreements and abuse of a dominant position: draft Bill*, London: DTI.

Derthick, M. and Quirk, P.J. (1985) *The Politics of Deregulation*, Washington: Brookings Institution.

Dery, D. and Sharon E. (1994) *Bureaucracy and Democracy in Budgetary Reform*, Tel Aviv: The Israeli Institute for Democracy.

Detecon (1994) 'Study on the Possibilities for Tendering GSM Services in the Czech Republic', Prague.

Domowitz, I. (1995) 'Electronic Derivatives Exchanges: Implicit Mergers, Network Externalities and Standardization', in *The Quarterly Review of Economics and Finance*, vol. 35, no. 2, pp. 163–75.

Doron, G. (1979) 'Administrative regulation of an industry: the cigarette case', *Public Administration Review*, 39: 163–70.

Dowding, K. (1991) *Rational Choice and Political Power*, Aldershot: Edward Elgar.

Dowding, K. (1996) *Power*, Minneapolis: University of Minnesota Press.

Doyle, C. (1992) 'Telecommunications services' in *Europe in 1996: Economic Analysis and Forecasts*, ERECO, pp. 471–82.

Doyle, C. (1993) 'The economics of mobile telephony in East and Central Europe: the case of the Czech Republic.' *Telecommunications Policy*, vol. 17, no. 5.

Doyle, C., Hrubý, Z. and Müller, J. (1993) 'Czech telecommunications and transition: How fast and what form should deregulation take?' Occasional paper, Department of Applied Economics, University of Cambridge.

DPTE (Ministère Délégué à la poste, aux télécommunications et à l'éspace) (1996) 'Rapport du groupe d'expertise économique sur l'interconnexion et le financement du service universel dans le secteur des télécommunications', Paris.

Duch, R. (1991) *Privatizing the Economy*. Ann Arbour: University of Michigan Press.

Dunleavy, P. and O'Leary, B. (1987) *Theories of the State: The Politics of Liberal Democracy*, London: Macmillan.

Dunleavy, P.J. (1991) *Bureaucracy, Democracy and Public Choice*, Hemel Hempstead: Harvester Wheatsheaf.

Dyson, K. and Humphreys, P. (1986) 'The Politics of the Communications Revolution in Western Europe' in *West European Politics,* vol. 10.

Economides, N. (1996), 'The Economics of Networks', in *International Journal of Industrial Organization*, vol. 14, no. 6, pp. 673–99.

EIU (The Economist Intelligence Unit) (1995) *Telecoms regulation in Europe*, Research Report.

Ekonom 21/1995 and 48/1995, Prague.

Emmett, A. (1997) 'The wider, the better', *America's Network*, 1 February 1997, pp. 32–4.

Erbenova, M. and Hrubý, Z. (1995) 'Tariffs and Regulation in Telecommunication: The Case of the Czech Republic'. Paper at the ACE telecommunication work- shop, Cambridge 1995.

European Bank for Reconstruction and Development (1992) *Annual Report 1991*, London.

European Commission (1987) 'Towards a Dynamic European Economy – Green Paper on the Development of the Common Market for Telecommunications Services and Equipment', COM(87) 290, 30 June.

Fiorina, M.P. (1982) 'Legislative Choice of Regulatory Forms: Legal Process or Administrative Process', *Public Choice*, vol. 39, no. 1, pp. 33–66.

Forestieri, G. (1993) 'Economies of Scale and Scope in the Financial Services Industry: A Review of Recent Literature', in *Financial Conglomerates*, OECD, Paris, pp. 63–124.

Forrester, Norall and Sutton for the European Commission (1996), T*he Institutional Framework for the Regulation of Telecommunications and the Application of EC Competition Rules*, Luxembourg, Office for Official Publications of the European Communities.

Foster, C.D. (1992) P*rivatization, Public Ownership and the Regulation of Monopoly*, Oxford: Blackwells.

Fredebul-Krein, Markus and Freytag, Andreas (1997) 'Telecommunications and WTO discipline. An assessment of the WTO agreement on telecommunication services', in *Telecommunications Policy*, vol. 21, no. 6, pp. 477–91.

Frydman, R., Rapaczynski, A., Earle, J.S. *et al.* (1993) T*he Privatization Process in Central Europe, volume I*, Central European University Press, Praha.

Fuchs, G. (1994) 'Policy-making in a system of multi-level governance – the Commission of the European Community and the restructuring of the tele-communications sector' in *Journal of European Public Policy*, vol. 1, no. 2, pp. 177–94.

Gandal, N. (1994) 'The Development of Cable Television in Israel', *Tele-communications Policy*, vol. 18, pp. 342–7.

Garfinkel, Lawrence (1994) 'The transition to competition in telecommunications services', in *Telecommunications Policy*, vol. 18, no. 6, pp. 427–31.

Genschel, P. and Plümper, T. (1997) 'Regulatory Competition and International Cooperation', *Journal of European Public Policy*, vol. 4, no. 4, pp. 626–42.

George, S. (1985) *Politics and Policy in the European Community*, Oxford: Clarendon Press.

Gerschenkron, A. (1962) *Economic Backwardness in Historical Perspective: Essays*, Cambridge, MA: Harvard University Press.

Gillies, D. and R. Marshall (1997) *Telecommunications Law*, London: Butterworths.

Goldman Sachs (1994) 'UK Research, Vodafone Group, plc'.

Goldman Sachs (1995) 'Germany Research, German Cellular Preview'.

Gong, J. and Srinagesh, P. (1997) 'The Economics of Layered Networks', in McKnight, L.W. and Bailey, J.P. (eds): *Internet Economics*, Cambridge, MA: The MIT Press, pp. 63–75.

Gorel, A. (1997) *The False Charge*, Tel Aviv: Alfa Communications.

Graham, C. (1994) 'Self-Regulation', in Richardson, G. and Genn, H. (eds) *Administrative Law and Government Action*, Oxford: Oxford University Press.

Graham, C. and Prosser, T. (1987) 'Privatising nationalised industries' in *The Modern Law Review*, January 1987.

Grupp, H. and Schnöring, T. (1992) 'Research and development in tele-communications' in *Telecommunications Policy*, vol. 16, no. 1, pp. 46–66.

Haas, E.B. (1958) *The Uniting of Europe*, London: Stevens & Sons.

Hall, P.A. (1992) 'The Movement from Keynsianism to Monetarism: Institutional Analysis and British Economic Policy in the 1970s', in Steinmo, S., Thelen, K. and Longstreth, F. (eds) *Structuring Politics: Historical Institutionalism in Comparative Analysis*, Cambridge: Cambridge University Press.

Hall, P.A. (1986) *Governing the Economy*, Cambridge: Polity Press.

Hämäläinen, J. (1996) 'Design of GSM High Speed Data Services', PhD Thesis, Tampere University of Technology.

Hancher, L. and Moran, M. (1989) 'Organizing Regulatory Space' in Hancher, L. and Moran, M. (eds), *Capitalism, Culture and Regulation*, Oxford: Oxford University Press.

Hausman, J. and Tardiff, T. (1996) *Valuation and Regulation of New Services in Telecommunications*, MIT Course 15020, course material.

Hay, D.A. and Morris, D. J. (1991) *Industrial Economics and Organization: Theory and Evidence*, Oxford: Oxford University Press.

Helm, D. (1995) 'British Utility Regulation: Theory, Practice, and Reform', *Oxford Review of Economic Policy*, vol. 10, no. 3, pp. 17–39.

Hernes, Gudmund (1978) *Forhandlingøkonomi og blandingsadministrasjon*, En publikasjon av Maktutredningen, Bergen, Oslo, Tromsø: Universitetsforlaget.

Hesoun, F. (1994) *Liberalisation, Regulation and Telecommunication Market in the Czech Republic*. Praha: Mimeo.

Hills, J. (1986) *Deregulating Telecoms: competition and control in the United States, Japan and Britain*, London: Pinter publishers.

Hirshleifer, J. (1976) 'A Comment', *Journal of Law & Economics*, vol. 19, pp. 241–4.

Hix, S. (1994) 'The Study of the European Community: The Challenge to Comparative Politics', *West European Politics*, vol. 17, no. 1, pp. 1–29.

Honda, J., Nakagawa, I. and Yamazaki, A. (1995) 'Unbundling the Local Network: The Three-Layered Model as a New Telecommunications Industry Structure', *Information Infrastructure and Policy*, vol. 4, pp. 343–64.

Hood, C. (1994) *Explaining Economic Policy Reversals*, Buckingham: Open University Press.

Hood, C. (1996) 'Control Over Bureaucracy: Cultural Theory and Institutional Variety', *Journal of Public Policy*, vol. 15, no. 3, pp. 207–30.

Hood, C. and Scott, C. (1996) 'Bureaucratic Regulation and New Public Management in the UK: Mirror-Image Developments', *Bureaucratic Gamekeeping Discussion Paper No. 2*, London: London School of Economics.

Hood, C., James, O., Jones, G., Scott, C. and Travers, T. (forthcoming) *Regulation Inside Government: Waste Watchers, Quality Police and Sleazebusters*, Oxford: Oxford University Press.

Hooper, G., and Sicher, A. (1996) 'Advanced TDMA digital AMPS mobile data and messaging capabilities', Proc. of COM'96. *First Annual Conference on Emerging Technologies and Applications in Communications (Cat. 96TB100035)*, pp. 162–5. Los Alamitos: IEEE Comput. Soc. Press.

Horn, M. (1995) *The Political Economy of Public Administration*, Cambridge: Cambridge University Press.

Horowitz, D. and Lissak, M. (1989) *Trouble in Utopia: The Overburdened Polity of Israel*, Albany: State University of New York Press.

Hospodarske noviny, various issues 1994 and 1995, Prague.

Hruby, Z. (1992) *Telecommunications Investment and Tariff Policy in the CSFR*. OECD Working Paper, Paris.

Hruby, Z. (1994) 'Regulation and Tariff Policies in the Energy and Telecommunications Sectors: The Case of the Czech Republic'. Paper presented to the conference Regulation of Utilities in Economies in Transition, London Business School.

Hruby, Z. (1995) 'Mobile Telecommunications in the Czech Republic' in Schenk, K.E., Mueller, J. and Schnöering, T. (eds), *Mobile Telecommunications: Emerging European Markets*, Boston and London: Artech House.

Hruby, Z. (1997) 'Towards Limited Competition and Streamlining Regulation' in Schenk, K. E., Kruse, J. and Mueller, J. (eds) *Telecommunications Take-Off in Transition Countries*, Aldershot: Avebury.

Hruby, Z., and Seda, R. (1995) 'Czech telecommunications: Financing of network expansion and the choice of strategic partner', Paper presented at Utilities regulation network workshop, Berlin.

Hu, R. *et al.* (1996) 'Commercialization of PACS in the South-East Asia', *ICCT'96. 1996 International Conference on Communication Technology Proceedings (Cat. No.96TH8118)*, vol. 11, no. 2, pp. 849–52, Beijing 5–7 May.

Hunt, A. (1997) 'Regulation of Telecommunications: the Developing EU

Regulatory Framework and its Impact on the United Kingdom', in *European Public Law*, vol. 3, no. 1, pp. 93–115.

Hunt, S. and Shuttleworth, G. (1996) *Competition and Choice in Electricity*, New York: John Wiley & Sons.

Hurrell, A. and Menon, A. (1996) 'Politics Like Any Other? Comparative Politics, International Relations and the Study of the EU', in *West European Politics* vol. 19, no. 2, pp. 386–402.

Ishii, K. (1996) 'PHS: revolutionizing personal communication in Japan', in *Telecommunications Policy*, vol. 20, no. 7, pp. 497–506.

Katz, M. and Shapiro, C. (1992), 'Product Introduction with Network Externalities', in *The Journal of Industrial Economics*, March, vol. 40, no. 1, pp. 55–83.

Katz, M. and Shapiro, C. (1985) 'Network Externalities, Competition, and Compatibility', in *American Economic Review*, vol. 75, pp. 424–40.

Katz, Y. (1992) *The Development of Cable TV in Israel*, PhD Dissertation, Loughborough University of Technology.

Keating, M. (1995) 'A Comment on Robert Leonardi, Cohesion in the European Community: Illusion or Reality', in *West European Politics*, vol. 18, no. 2, pp. 408–12.

Keeler, T. (1984) 'Theories of Regulation and the Deregulation Movement', in *Public Choice*, vol. 44, no. 1, pp 103–45.

Kelly, T. (1990) 'Telecommunications in the Rebirth of Eastern Europe', in *The OECD Observer*, vol. 167, pp. 19–22, Paris.

Kelly, T. (1991) 'Telecommunications and Markets in Eastern and Central Europe', presentation at the Third Economist Telecommunications Conference, London.

Kelman, S. (1992) 'Adversary and Cooperationist Institutions for Conflict Resolution in Public Policy-Making', in *Journal of Policy Analysis and Management*, vol. 11, no. 2, pp. 178–206.

Keren, M. (1995) *Professionals against Populism*, Albany: State University of New York Press.

Kesavapany, K. (1996) 'An Overview of Recent Developments in the WTO' in Yue, Chia Siow and Tan, Joseph L.H. (eds) *ASEAN in the WTO – challenges and responses*, Singapore: Stamford Press.

Kiessling, T. and Blondeel Y. (1998) 'The EU Regulatory Framework in Telecommunications – A Critical Analysis' unpublished article, Brussels.

Knieps, G. (1997a) 'Market Entry in the Presence of a "Dominant" Network Operator in Telecommunications', Discussion Papers No. 34, Institut für Verkehrswissenschaft und Regionalpolitik, Universität Freiburg.

Knieps, G. (1997b) 'Ansätze für eine "schlanke" Regulierungsbehörde für Post und Telekommunikation in Deutschland', Discussion Papers No. 38, Institut für Verkehrswissenschaft und Regionalpolitik, Universität Freiburg.

Kolko, G. (1965) *Railroads and Regulation 1877–1916*, Cambridge: Harvard University Press.

Kramer, Richard A. (1992) 'Divisions in European Telecommunications: EC Authority and the Illusion of Competition' in *Communications & Strategies*, No. 7.

Krasner, S.D. (1991) 'Global Communications and National Power. Life on the Pareto Frontier', in *World Politics* vol. 43, pp. 336–66.

Kubasik, J. (1995) 'Mobile telecommunications in Poland', in Schenk, K.-E., Mueller, J. and Schnöering, T. (eds): *Mobile Telecommunications: Emerging European Markets*, London: Artech House.

Lasserre, Bruno (1992) 'A perspective from a national regulator' in *Telecommunications Policy*, vol. 16, December, pp. 705-11.

Lawson, N. (1992) *The View from No. 11*, Bantam Press, London.

Leite, F. *et al.* (1997) 'Regulatory Considerations Related to IMT-2000', in *IEEE Personal Communications*, vol. 4, no 4, pp. 14–19.

Leonardi, R. (1993) 'Cohesion in the European Community: Illusion or Reality', in *West European Politics*, vol. 16, no. 4, pp. 492–517.

Leonardi, R. (1995a) *Convergence, Cohesion and Integration in the European Union*, London, Macmillan.

Leonardi, R. (1995b) 'A Response to Michael Keating', in *West European Politics*, vol. 18, no. 2, pp. 413–17.

Levi-Faur, D. (forthcoming, 1998) 'The Developmental State: Israel, South Korea and Taiwan Compared', *Studies in Comparative International Development*.

Levine, M.E. and Forrence, J.L. (1990) 'Regulatory Capture, Public Interest, and the Public Agenda: Towards a Synthesis', in *Journal of Law, Economics, and Organistion*, vol. 6 (special issue), pp. 167–98.

Levy, David A.L. (1997) 'Regulating Digital Broadcasting in Europe: The Limits of Policy Convergence', in *West European Politics*, vol. 20, no. 4, pp. 24–42.

Lijphart, A. (1975) *The Politics of Accommodation: Pluralism and Democracy in the Netherlands*, Berkeley: University of California Press, 2nd ed.

Lijphart, A. (1977) *Democracy in Plural Societies: A Comparative Exploration*, New Haven: Yale University Press.

Lindberg, L. (1963) *The Political Dynamics of European Integration*, Stanford, Stanford University Press.

Lindblom, C. (1959), 'The Science of Muddling Through', in *Public Administration Review*, vol. 19, no. 2, pp. 79–88.

Lindblom, C. (1970), 'Still Muddling, not Yet Through', vol. 39, pp. 517–26.

Lipsey, R., and Lancaster, K. (1956) 'The General Theory of Second Best', in *Review of Economic Studies*, vol. 24, pp. 11-32.

Loughlin, M. and Scott, C. (1997) 'The Regulatory State', in P. Dunleavy, A. Gamble, I. Holliday and G. Peele (eds) *Developments in British Politics 5*, Basingstoke: Macmillan.

Lütz, S. (1996) 'The Revival of the Nation State? Stock Exchange Regulation in an Era of Internationalized Financial Markets'; *MPIfG-discussion paper 96/9*, Köln: MPIfG.

Macey, J.R. (1992) 'Organizational Design and Political Control of Administrative Agencies', in *Journal of Law, Economics and Organisation*, vol. 8, no. 1, pp. 93–110.

Macmillan, J. (1994) 'Selling Spectrum Rights', in *Journal of Economic Perspectives*, vol. 8, no. 3, pp. 145-62.

McClelland, S. (1996) 'Towards the world's largest market', in *Telecommunications (International Edition)*, vol. 30, no. 10, pp. S1–S34.

McCubbins, M.D., Noll, R.G. and Weingast, B.R. (1987) 'Administrative Procedures as Instruments of Political Control', in *Journal of Law, Economics and Organisation*, vol. 3, no. 2, pp. 243–77.

McGowan, F. (1998) 'EU Industrial Policy', in El-Agraa, A. *The European Union: History, Institutions Economics and Policies*, 5th edition, London: Prentice Hall Europe.

Madani, K. (1996) 'Future technologies for wireless personal communications', in *Microwave Engineering Europe*, May 1996, pp. 36–8, 40, 42, 44–5.

Majone, G. (1994) 'Paradoxes of privatization and deregulation', in *Journal of European Public Policy*, vol. 1, no. 1, pp. 53–69.

Majone, G. (1994) 'The rise of the regulatory state in Europe', *West European Politics*, vol. 17, no. 3, pp. 77–101.

Majone, G. (1996) *Regulating Europe*, London: Routledge.

Majone, G. (1996a), 'The European Commission as a Regulator', in Majone, G. (ed.), *Regulating Europe*, London: Routledge.

Majone, G. (1996b) 'Regulation and its Modes', in Majone, G. (ed.), *Regulating Europe,* London: Routledge.

Majone, G. (1997a) 'The new European agencies: regulation by information', in *Journal of European Public Policy*, vol. 4, no. 2, pp. 262–75.

Majone, G. (1997b) 'From the Positive to the Regulatory State: Causes and Consequences of Changes in the Mode of Governance', in *Journal of Public Policy*, vol. 17, no. 2, pp. 139–67.

Majone, G. (ed.) (1989) *Deregulation or Re-regulation*, London: Pinter Publishers.

Mansell, R. (1992) 'The West Looks East: Reformulating Telecommunication Strategies', in *Innovation,* vol. 5, pp. 67–86.

Mansell, R. (1993) T*he New Telecommunications. A Political Economy of Network Evolution*, London: Sage.

March, J.G. and Olsen, J.P. (1989) *Rediscovering Institutions: The Organizational Basis of Politics*, New York: The Free Press.

Marshall, J.F. and Bansal, V.K. (1992) *Financial Engineering*, New York Institute of Finance.

Mayntz, R. (1983) 'The Conditions of Effective Public Policy: a New Challenge for Policy Analysis', in *Policy and Politics*, vol. 11, no. 2, pp. 123–43.

Mayntz, R. and Scharpf, F.W. (1995) 'Steuerung und Selbstorganisation in staatsnahen Sektoren' in Mayntz, R. and Scharpf, F.W. (eds.) *Gesellschaftliche Selbstregelung und politische Steuerung*, Frankfurt/M: Campus.

Melody, William H. (1998) T*elecom Reform. Principles, Policies and Regulatory Practices.* Lyngby: Den private ingeniørfond, Technical University.

Meyers, J. (1997) 'Cellular revisited', in *Telephony*, March 3, pp. 28–32.

Ministry of Economy of the Czech Republic (1994) *Main Principles of the State Telecommunication Policy*, Prague.

Ministry of Economy of the Czech Republic (1995) *Information Memorandum for GSM Tender*, Prague.

Monopolkommission (1996) *Wettbewerbspolitik in Zeiten des Umbruchs,* Hauptgutachten 1994/95, Baden-Baden: Nomos.

Moon, J., Richardson, J.J. and Smart, P. (1986) 'The privatisation of British Telecom: a case study of the extended process of legislation',in *European Journal of Political Research*, vol. 14, pp. 339–55.

Moravcsik, A. (1991) 'Negotiating the Single European Act: national Interests and Conventional Statescraft in the European Community', in *International Organization*, vol. 45, pp. 19–56.

Mueller, D. (1989) *Public Choice II*, Cambridge: Cambridge University Press.

NERA (1997) 'Issues Associated with the Creation of a European Regulatory Authority for Telecommunications', A Report by NERA and Denton Hall for the European Commission DGXIII March 1997.

Niskanen, W. (1973) *Bureaucracy: Servant or Master*, London, Institute for Economic Affairs.

Noam E. (1992) *Telecommunications in Europe*, Oxford and New York: Oxford University Press.

Noam, E.M. (1994) 'Beyond Liberalization II: The Impending Doom of Common Carriage', in *Telecommunications Policy* vol. 18, pp. 435–52.

Noerpel, A.R. (1996) 'Personal Access Communications System: An Alternative Technology for PCS', in *IEEE Communications Magazine*, vol. 34, no 10, pp. 138–50.

Noll, R.G. (1987) 'Economic Perspectives on the Politics of Regulation', in R. Schmalensee and R.D. Willig (eds) *Handbook of Industrial Organisation*, Amsterdam: Elsevier Science Publishers.

Nourouzi, A. (1997) 'The World in Your Pocket', in *Telecom International*, vol. 1, no. 3, pp. 13–15.

Nulty, Timothy E. (1996)'Challenges and Issues in Central and Eastern European Telecommunications' in Wellenius, Björn and Stern, Peter A. (eds) *Implementing Reforms in the Telecommunications Sector, The World Bank Regional and Sectoral Studies*, Aldershot: Avebury.

OECD (1992) 'Mobile and PSTN Communications Services: Competition or Complementarity?' Draft Report of the Working Party on Telecommunication and Information Services Policies, Paris: OECD.

OECD (1997) Report on Regulatory Reform, Paris: OECD.

OED (1993) *The Oxford English Dictionary*, Oxford, Clarendon Press.

Oftel (1985) *Determination of terms and Conditions for the Purposes of an Agreement on the Interconnection of the BT System and the Mercury Communications Ltd System*, London: Oftel.

Oftel (1988) *The Regulation of British Telecom's Prices. A Consultative Document,* Oftel: London.

Oftel (1991a) *Licence Modification Proposals to Implement Duropoly review Conclusions*, London: Oftel.

Oftel (1991b) *Modifications to the Conditions of the Licences of British telecommunications plc and Mercury Communications Ltd*, London: Oftel.

Oftel (1993) *Interconnection and Accounting Separation*, London: Oftel.

Oftel (1994a) *Interconnection and Accounting Separation: The Next Steps*, London: Oftel.

Oftel (1994b) *A Framework for Effective Competition*, London: Oftel.

Oftel (1995a) *Effective Competition: Framework for Action*, London: Oftel.

Oftel (1995b) *Universal Telecommunications Services*, London: Oftel.

Oftel (1995c) *Pricing of Telecommunications Services from 1997. Oftel's Proposals for Price Control and Fair Trading.* London: Oftel.

Oftel (1996) *Pricing of Telecommunications Services from 1997. Oftel's Proposals for Price Control and Fair Trading*, London: Oftel.

Oftel (1997a) *Network Charges from 1997*, July, London: Oftel.

Oftel (1997b) *Network Charges from 1997. Consultative document*, May, London: Oftel.

Oftel (1997c) *Guidelines on the operation of Network Charges, October,* London: Oftel.

Oftel (1997d) *Submission by the DGT to the DTI Review of Utility regulation,* London: Oftel.

Oftel (1997e) *Proposed arrangements for Universal Service in the UK from 1997,* London: Oftel.

Oftel (1997f) *Universal Telecommunication Services. Consultative Document,* February, London: Oftel.

Oftel (1997g) *Universal Service. Statement,* July, London: Oftel.

Oftel (1997h) *Dealing With Anti-Competitive Behaviour in Telecoms,* London: Oftel.

Oftel Annual Reports, various issues, London: Oftel.

Oftel Market Information Updates, various issues.

Ogus, A. (1994) *Regulation – Legal Form and Economic Theory,* Oxford: Oxford University Press.

Ogus, A. (1995) 'Rethinking Self-Regulation', in *Oxford Journal of Legal Studies,* vol. 15, no. 1, pp. 97–107.

Olsen, J.P. and Peters, B.G. (eds) (1996) *Lessons from Experience: experiential learning in administrative reforms in eight democracies,* Oslo: Scandinavian University Press.

Olson, M. (1965) *The Logic of Collective Action: Public Goods and the Theory of Groups,* Cambridge, Mass.: Harvard University Press.

Olson, M. (1982) *The Rise and Decline of Nations,* New Haven: Yale University Press.

Page, A.C. (1986) 'Self-Regulation: The Constitutional Dimension', in *Modern Law Review,* vol. 49, no. 2, pp. 141–67.

PDP (1985) *The Penguin Dictionary of Psychology,* Harmondsworth: Penguin.

Pelkmans, Jaques and Young, David (1998) *Telecoms 98.* Brussels: Centre for European Policy Studies.

Peltzman, S. (1976) 'Toward a More General Theory of Regulation', in *Journal of Law and Economics,* vol. 19, no. 3, pp. 211–40.

Peltzman, S. (1989) 'The Economic theory of regulation after a devade of de-regulation', in *Brookings Papers on Economic Activity* (Microeconomics), pp. 1–41.

Pitt, D. (1990) 'An essentially contestable organisation: BT and the privatisation debate' in J.J. Richardson (ed.), *Privatisation and deregulation in Canada and Britain,* Aldershot: Dartmouth.

Porter, M. (1980) *Competitive Strategy. Techniques for Analyzing Industries and Competitors,* New York: Free Press.

Porter, M. (1985) *Competitive Advantage. Creating and Sustaining Superior Performance,* New York: Free Press.

Posner, R. (1974) 'Taxation by Regulation', in *Bell Journal of Economics and Management Science,* vol. 5, no. 3, pp. 335–58.

Power, M. (1994) *The Audit Explosion,* London: Demos.

Prapinmongkolkarn, Prasit (1997) 'Financing the Infrastructure Development Project – A Case Study of Thailand's Experiences', paper presented at the Interregional Workshop on Development Project Financing, ESCAP, Bangkok 25–7 June.

Prosser, T. (1994), 'Regulation, Markets and Legitimacy', in J. Jowell and D. Oliver (eds), *The Changing Constitution*, Oxford, Clarendon Press.

Prosser, T. (1997) *Law and the Regulators*, Oxford: Clarendon Press.

Rappaport, T.S. (1996) *Wireless Communications, Principles and Practice*, Upper Saddle River NJ: Prentice Hall.

Richardson, J. (1996) 'Policy Making in the EU: Interests Ideas and Garbage Cans of Primeval Soup', in J. Richardson (ed.) *European Union: Power and Policy-Making*, London: Routledge.

Riley, A.J. (1997) 'The European Cartel Office: A Guardian without Weapons?', in *The European Competition Law Review*, vol. 17, no. 1, pp. 3–16.

Rose, R. (1993) *Lesson-Drawing in Public Policy*, New Jersey: Chatham House.

Rubsamen, Valerie (1989) 'Deregulation and the State in Comparative Perspective. The Case of Telecommunications' in *Comparative Politics*, October, p. 105.

Sandholz, W. (1993) 'Institutions and Collective Action: The New Telecommunications in Western Europe', in *World Politics*, vol. 45, pp. 242–70.

Sappington, D. and Weiseman, D. (1996) *Designing Incentive Regulation for the Telecommunications Industry*, Cambridge, MA: MIT Press.

Saunders, Robert J., Warford, Jeremy J. and Wellenius, Björn (1994) 'Telecommunications and Economic Development', 2nd ed., A World Bank Publication, Baltimore and London: The Johns Hopkins University Press.

Sauter, W. (1997) *Competition Law and Industrial Policy in the EU*, Oxford: Clarendon Press.

Scharpf, F.W. (1989) 'Decision Rules, Decision-Styles and Policy Choices', in *Journal of Theoretical Politics*, vol. 1, no. 2, pp. 149–76.

Scharpf, F.W. (1996) 'Negative and Positive Integration in the Political Economy of European Welfare States'; in Marks, G., Scharpf, F.W., Schmitter, P.C. and W. Streeck (eds), *Governance in the European Union*, London: Sage.

Schaub, A. (1996), 'Competition Policy in the Telecoms Sector', in *Competition Policy Newsletter*, vol. 1, no. 2 (Brussels, DG IV), pp. 1–7.

Scherer, Joachim and Bartsch, Torsten (1998) 'Telecommunications law and policy in the European Union', in Scherer, J. (ed.), *Telecommunications Laws in Europe*, 4th edition, London: Butterworths.

Schmidt, S.K. (1991) 'Taking the Long Road to Liberalization' in *Telecommunications Policy* vol. 15, pp. 209–22.

Schmidt, S.K. (1996) 'Privatizing the Federal Postal and Telecommunications Services', in Benz, A. and Goetz, K.H. (eds), *A New German Public Sector? Reform, Adaptation and Stability*, Aldershot: Dartmouth: pp. 45–70.

Schmidt, S.K. (1997a) 'Sterile Debates and Dubious Generalisations: European Integration Theory Tested by Telecommunications and Electricity', in *Journal of Public Policy* vol. 16, no. 3, pp. 233–71.

Schmidt, S.K. (1997b) 'Behind the Council Agenda: The Commission's Impact on Decisions', *MPIfG Discussion Paper 97/4*, Köln: MPIfG.

Schmidt, S.K. and Werle, R. (1998) *Coordinating Technology. Studies in the International Standardization of Telecommunications*, Cambridge, MA, London: The MIT Press.

Schneider, V. (1992) 'Organized Interests in the European Telecommunications Sector', in Greenwood, J. Grote, J.R. and Ronit, K. (eds), *Organized Interests and the European Community*, London: Sage.

Schneider, V. and Werle, R. (1990) 'International Regime or Corporate Actor? The European Community in Telecommunications Policy', in Dyson, K. and Humphreys, P. (eds), *The Political Economy of Communications. International and European Dimensions.* London: Routledge, pp. 77–106.

Schneider, V. and Werle, R. (1991) 'Policy Networks in the German Telecommunications Domain', in Marin, B. and Mayntz, R. (eds), *Policy Networks – Empirical Evidence and Theoretical Considerations*, Frankfurt a.M.: Campus: 97–136.

Schneider, V., Dang–Nguyen, G. and Werle, R. (1994) 'Corporate Actor Networks in European Policy-Making: Harmonizing Telecommunications Policy', in *Journal of Common Market Studies* vol. 32, pp. 473–98.

Scholz, J.T. (1991) 'Cooperative Regulatory Enforcement and the Politics of Administrative Effectiveness', in *American Political Science Review*, vol. 85, no. 1, pp. 115–36.

Schuler, B.W. and Meyer, L. (1998) 'Recent Events in the German Telecommunication Regulation – Political and Industrial Implications'. Report 1/98, Sandvika, Norway: Centre for European and Asian Studies at the Norwegian School of Management.

Schwartz, E. (1993) 'Politics as Usual: The History of European Community Merger Control', *Yale Journal of International Law*, vol. 18, pp. 607–2.

Scott, C. and Audéod, O. (eds) (1996) *The Future of EC Telecommunications Law*, Cologne: Bundesanzeiger.

Scott, C., Hall, C. and Hood, C. (1997) 'Regulatory Space and Institutional Reform: The Case of Telecommunications', *CRI Review*, London: Centre for the Study of Regulated Industries.

SEC (96) 2378 Commission Staff Working Paper, 'The 1996 Single Market Review Background Information for the Report to the Council and European Parliament'.

Selznick, P. (1985) 'Focusing organisational research on regulation', in R.G. Noll (ed.) *Regulatory Policy and the Social Sciences*, Berkeley: University of California Press.

Shankerman, M. (1996) 'Symmetric Regulation for Competitive Tele-communications', in *Information Economics and Policy* vol. 8, pp. 3–23.

Shepsle, K.A. (1992) 'Bureaucratic Drift, Coalitional Drift, and Time Consistency: A Comment of Macey', in *The Journal of Law, Economics and Organisation*, vol. 8, no. 1, pp. 111–25.

SPT Telecom (1994) 'Rozvoj telekomunikacni site SPT Telecom, a.s.' [Development of the Telecommunications Network of SPT Telecom], Prague.

SPT Telecom (1994) 'Prvni Telekomunikacni Projekt: Strategie urychleni' [The First Telecommunications Project: Strategy of Acceleration], Prague.

SPT Telecom (1994) *Prvni Telekomunikacni Projekt: Strategie urychleni* [The First Telecommunications Project: Strategy of Acceleration], Prague.

SPT Telecom (1994) *Rozvoj telekomunikacni site SPT Telecom, a.s.* [Development of the Telecommunications Network of SPT Telecom], Prague.

SPT Telecom, a.s. (1995) 'Prospekt ke kotaci na Burze cennych papiru Praha, a.s.' [SPT Telecom, joint-stock company: Prospectus to quotation on the Prague Stock Exchange], Prague.

Stabell, C.B. and Fjeldstad, Ø.D. (1998) 'Configuring Value For Competitive

Advantage: On Chains, Shops and Networks', in *Strategic Management Journal*, vol. 19, pp. 413–37.

Stadnik, D. (1996) 'Partner pro druhou licenci GSM', in *Telekomunikace*, Praha, 4/1996.

Stern, J.P. (1995) *The Russian Natural Gas 'Bubble': Consequences for European Gas Markets*, London, The Royal Institute of International Affairs.

Stevers, E. (1989) 'Telecommunications Regulation in the European Community: The Commission of the European Communities as a Regulatory Actor', *EUI Working Papers*, 98: 421.

Stigler, G. (1971) 'The theory of economic regulation', in *Bell Journal of Economic and Management Science*, vol. 2, no. 1, pp. 3–21.

Stiglitz, Joseph, E. (1997) *Economics*, 2nd ed., New York: W.W. Norton & Company.

Stoffaës, Christian (1995) *Services Publics. Question d'Avenir*, Paris: Editions Odile Jacob.

Strategis Group (1997): *World Cellular and PCS Markets: 1997*.

Streeck, W. and Schmitter, P.C. (1985) 'Community, market, state – and associations', in *European Sociological Review*, vol. 1, no. 2, pp. 119–38.

Stuart, J. (1996) 'Teledesic Network and Space Infrastructure Architecture and Design Features', *IEEE 2nd International Conference of Engineering of Complex Computer Systems*, Montreal, 21–25 October, pp. 147–50.

Sturm, R. and Wilks, S. (1997) 'Competition policy and the regulation of the electricity supply industry in Britain and Germany', *Anglo-German Foundation for the Study of Industrial Society*.

Swann, D. (1988) *The Retreat of the State: Deregulation and Privatisation in the UK and the US*, Brighton: Wheatsheaf.

Tanenbaum, A. (1981) *Computer Networks*. Englewood Cliffs, N.J.: Prentice Hall.

Taylor, P. (1989). 'The New Dynamics of EC Integration in the 1980s', in Lodge, J. (ed.), *The European Community and the Challenge of the Future*, London, Pinter Publishers.

Taylor, P. (1991) 'The European Community and the State: Assumptions, Theories and Propositions', in *Review of International Studies*, vol. 17, no. 2, pp. 109–25.

Telecommunication Office (1994) 'Tariff Policy as a Tool of Regulation in Telecommunications'. Draft of internal paper, Praha.

Teubner, G. (1987) 'Juridification', in G. Teubner (ed.) *Juridification of Social Spheres*, Berlin: de Gruyter; pp. 3–48.

Thailand Development Research Institute (1993) 'Future Direction of the Communications Authority of Thailand', September 1993.

Thatcher, M. (1994) 'Regulatory reform in Britain and France: organizational structure and the extension of competition', in *Journal of European Public Policy*, vol. 1, no. 3, pp. 441–64.

Thatcher, M. (1996) 'High Technology' in Kassim, H. and Menon, A. (eds) *The European Union and National Industrial Policy*, London: Routledge.

Thatcher, M. (1997) 'The Development of European Regulatory Frameworks: The Expansion of European Community Policy-Making in Telecommunications' in Stravridis, E., Mossialos, E., Morgan, R. and Machin, H. (eds) *New Challenges to the European Union: Policies and Policy-Making*, pp. 297–328.

Thatcher, M. (1998) 'Institutions, Regulation and Change: New Regulatory

Agencies in the British Privatised Industries', in *West European Politics*, vol. 21, no. 1, pp. 120–47.

Thatcher, Margaret (1993) *The Downing Street Years*, London, Harper Collins.

Thelen, K. and Steinmo, S. (1992), 'Historical Institutionalism in Comparative Politics', in Steinmo, S., Thelen, K. and Longstreth, F. (eds) *Structuring Politics: Historical Institutionalism in Comparative Analysis*, Cambridge, Cambridge University Press.

Thomas, E. (1997) 'Competitive Threat', in *Infrastructure Finance*, May, pp. 37–8, 40.

Thompson, J.D. (1967) *Organizations in Action*. New York: McGraw-Hill.

Thorein, T. (1997) 'Liberalisierung und Re-Regulierung im Politikfeld Tele-kommunikation. Eine wissenszentrierte Policy-Analyse des bundesdeutschen Telekommunikationsgesetzes', in *Rundfunk und Fernsehen* vol. 45, pp. 285–306.

Tivey, L. (1982) 'Nationalised Industries as Organised Industries', in *Public Administration*, vol. 60, pp. 42–55.

Toffler, A. (1990) *Power Shift: Knowledge, Wealth and Violence at the Edge of the 21st Century*, New York: Bantam.

Tranholm-Mikkelsen, J. (1992) 'Neo-functionalism: Obstinate or Obsolete? A Reappraisal in the Light of the New Dynamism of the EC', in *Millennium*, vol. 20, no. 1, pp. 1–22.

Turner, Colin (1997) *Trans-European Telecommunication Networks. The challenges for industrial policy*, London: Routledge.

Ungerer, H. (1988) Telecommunications in Europe, Luxemburg: Office for Official Publications of the European Communities.

Ungerer, Herbert (1992) 'European policies and regulation' in *Telecommunications Policy*, vol. 16, December, pp. 712–16.

Van Miert, K. (1994) Speech at the Royal Institute for Foreign Affairs, London, 28 November 1994 (RAPID summary, ref: IP/94/1104).

Veljanovski, C. (1991) 'The Regulation Game', in C. Veljanovski (ed.), *Regulators and the Market*, London: IEA.

Verhoest, P. (1995) 'Regionalism and telecommunications infrastructure competition' in *Telecommunications Policy*, vol. 19, no. 8, pp. 637–45.

Vialle, P. (1998) *Stratégies des opérateurs de télécoms*. Paris: Editions Hermes.

Vickers, J. and Yarrow, G. (1988) *Privatization: An Economic Analysis*, Cambridge: MIT Press.

Vogel, D. (1995) *Trading Up – Consumer and Environmental Regulation in a Global Economy*, Cambridge: Harvard University Press.

Vogel, S. (1997) 'International Games with National Rules: How Regulation Shapes Competition in "Global" Markets', in *Journal of Public Policy*, vol. 17, no. 2, pp. 169–93.

Vogel, S.K. (1996) *Freer Markets, More Rules. Regulatory Reform in Advanced Industrialised Countries*, Ithica and London: Cornell University Press.

Wade, J. (1995) 'Dynamics of organizational communities and technological bandwagons: An empirical investigation of community evolution in the micro-processor market', in *Strategic Management Journal*, 16ss, pp. 111–33.

Walker, Dawson (1996) 'International accounting rates. A perspective', in *Telecommunications Policy*, vol. 20, no. 4, pp. 239–42.

Waverman, L. and Esen, S. (1997) 'European Telecommunications Markets on the Verge of Full Liberalization', in *Journal of Economic Perspectives*, vol. 11, no. 4, pp. 113–26.

Waxe, S. (1995) *National Telecommunications Authority*, An internal document of the Israeli Communications Ministry by the Director-General.

Weber, M. (1972/orig. 1922) *Wirtschaft und Gesellschaft*, Tübingen: Mohr.

Wellenius, Björn (1996)'Telecommunications Restructuring in Latin America: An Overview' in Wellenius, Björn and Stern, Peter A. (eds) *Implementing Reforms in the Telecommunications Sector*, The World Bank Regional and Sectoral Studies, Aldershot: Avebury.

Werle, R. (1990) *Telekommunikation in der Bundesrepublik: Expansion, Differenzierung, Transformation*, Frankfurt/M.: Campus.

Werle, R (1995) 'Staat und Standards' in Mayntz, R. and Scharpf, F.W. (eds) *Gesellschaftliche Selbstregelung und politische Steuerung*, Frankfurt/M: Campus.

Werle, R. (1996) 'Verbände im Politikfeld Multimedia – Akteure, Rollen, Aufgaben', in H. Kubicek *et al.* (eds), Jahrbuch *Telekommunikation und Gesellschaft 4, Öffnung der Telekommunikation: Neue Spieler – Neue Regeln*, Heidelberg: R.v.Decker's, pp. 201–16.

Wessells, W. and Rometsch, D. (eds) (1996) *The European Union and member states: towards an institutional fusion?*, Manchester: Manchester University Press.

Wieck, R. (1997) 'Der zukünftige Wettbewerbsrahmen auf liberalisierten Tele-kommunikationsmärkten', in Deutsche Verkehrswissenschaftliche Gesellschaft e.V, DVWG (ed.), *Wettbewerbspolitik in deregulierten Verkehrsmärkten. Interventionismus oder Laissez Faire?*, Bergisch Gladbach: DVWG: 94–104. Schriftenreihe der Deutschen Verkehrswissenschaftlichen Gesellschaft e.V., Reihe B 199.

WIK/EAC (1994) 'Network interconnection in the domain of ONP', Study for DG XIII of the European Commission.

Wilks, S. (1992) 'The Metamorphosis of European Competition Policy', *RUSEL Working Paper No. 9*.

Wilks, S. (1996a) 'Regulatory Compliance and Capitalist Diversity in Europe', in *Journal of European Public Policy*, vol. 3, no. 4, pp. 536–59.

Wilks, S. (1996b) 'The Prolonged Reform of United Kingdom Competition Policy', in Doern, G.B. and Wilks, S. (eds) *Comparative Competition Policy: National Institutions in a Global Market*, Oxford: Clarendon Press.

Wilks, S. (1997) 'The Amoral Corporation and British Utility Regulation', in *New Political Economy*, vol. 2, no. 2, pp. 279–97.

Williams, R.J. (1976) 'Politics and the ecology of regulation', in *Public Administration*, vol. 54, no. 2, pp. 319–31.

Williamson, O.E. (1979) 'Transaction Cost Economics: The Governance of Contractual Relations', in *Journal of Law and Economics*, vol. 22, pp. 233–61.

Willman, P. (1994) 'Negotiating structural and technological change in the tele-communications services of the United Kingdom', in Bolton, B. (ed.), *Telecommunications Services: Negotiating structural and technological change*, Geneva: ILO.

Wilson, G. (1989) 'Social Regulation and explanations for regulatory failure', in *Political Studies*, vol. 32, no. 2, pp. 203–25.

Wilson, J.Q. (1980) 'The Politics of Regulation', in Wilson, J.Q. (ed.) *The Politics of Regulation*, New York: Basic Books, pp. 357–94.

Witte, E. (ed.) (1988) *Restructuring of the Telecommunications System: Report of the Government Commission for Telecommunications*. Heidelberg: R.v. Decker's.

Wolf, C.R. (1988) *Markets or Governments: Choosing Between Imperfect Alternatives*, Cambridge: MIT Press.

Worthy, John and Kariyawasam, Rohan (1998) 'A pan-European telecommunications regulator?', in *Telecommunications Policy*, vol. 22, no. 1, pp. 1–7.

Wright, V. (1993) 'Public Administration, Regulation, Deregulation and Re-regulation' in K.J. Eliassen and J. Kooiman (eds) *Managing Public Organizations* London: Sage.

Wu-Jhy C. *et al.* (1996) 'Personal Access Communication System in Taiwan', in *International Conference on Communication Technology Proceedings (Cat. No. 96TH8118)*, vol. 2, pp. 845–8, Beijing 5–7 May.

Index